A LIGHT *in the* DARKNESS

ALSO BY JAVIER SUARÉZ-PAJARES

Concierto de Aranjuez: Storia del capolavoro di Joaquín Rodrigo
(with Leopoldo Neri)

A. T. Huerta: Life and Works (with Robert Coldwell)

El guitarrista almeriense Julián Arcas (1832–1882): Una biografía documental (with Eusebio Rioja)

Iconography: Joaquín Rodrigo: Images of a Life Fulfilled

Iconography: Manuel de Falla: The Image of a Musician

ALSO BY WALTER AARON CLARK

Joaquín Rodrigo: A Research and Information Guide

Los Romeros: Royal Family of the Spanish Guitar

Isaac Albéniz: A Research and Information Guide

Federico Moreno Torroba: A Musical Life in Three Acts
(with William Krause)

Enrique Granados: Poet of the Piano

Isaac Albéniz: Portrait of a Romantic

A
LIGHT
in the
DARKNESS

The Music
and Life of
JOAQUÍN RODRIGO

Javier Suárez-Pajares · Walter Aaron Clark

Foreword by Julian Lloyd Webber

Translation and editing by Nelson Orringer

W. W. NORTON & COMPANY
Independent Publishers Since 1923

For information about permission to reproduce selections from this book,
write to Permissions, W. W. Norton & Company, Inc., 500 Fifth Avenue,
New York, NY 10110

For information about special discounts for bulk purchases,
please contact W. W. Norton Special Sales at specialsales@wwnorton.com
or 800-233-4830

Manufacturing by Lake Book Manufacturing
Book design by Buckley Design
Production manager: Lauren Abbate

ISBN 978-1-324-00445-5

W. W. Norton & Company, Inc.
500 Fifth Avenue, New York, N.Y. 10110
www.wwnorton.com

W. W. Norton & Company Ltd.
15 Carlisle Street, London W1D 3BS

1 2 3 4 5 6 7 8 9 0

Our book is dedicated to all those who
love and perform Rodrigo's music.

"*La música nos une en la distancia*"

("Music unites us from afar")

—Joaquín Rodrigo

CONTENTS

ILLUSTRATIONS

MUSICAL EXAMPLES

FOREWORD

I N SEPTEMBER 1979 I wrote a letter to Joaquín Rodrigo to ask if he would consider composing a cello concerto for me. I was 28 years old and Maestro Rodrigo was nearly eighty. My letter was written more in hope than expectation, for I had yet to play in Spain and I had no idea whether the revered composer had even heard of me. Along with my letter, and hoping that it might whet his appetite, I decided to enclose a recent recording I had made of Debussy's *Cello Sonata* with the comment, "I feel the style of cello writing used by Debussy has never been fully developed."

There were two reasons behind my request to Rodrigo—by far the more important being that I liked a great deal of his music! The other was slightly more complex. As a solo cellist I was acutely aware that—despite many fine new compositions for cello and orchestra—only the Shostakovich First Concerto, written in 1959, had become standard repertoire, and I felt that Joaquín Rodrigo might compose another.

In truth I did not expect a reply to my letter, which I put to the back of my mind while continuing to immerse myself in a busy concert schedule. As the weeks went by I had almost forgotten my audacious request, when what was soon to become a familiar-looking manila envelope arrived through my postbox. It was from Rodrigo himself, and my heart skipped a beat as I read: "Your musicality and brilliant technique have impressed me. Of course, I would like to compose for you a work for cello and orchestra." Letters went back and forth, and it was finally arranged that I would stay with the Rodrigos in Madrid the following April.

During my visit I played Joaquín and his charming, indispensable wife, Victoria, vast quantities of cello music, often by composers (usually British!) who were quite unknown to both of them. Once Joaquín had declared himself pleased with what he had heard, we proceeded to enjoy an extremely convivial lunch during which Joaquín announced that he was going to dedicate his new concerto to me. It was then that I encountered the maestro's uncompromising side for the first time; emboldened by copious amounts of Rioja, I wondered out loud if he might perhaps consider giving his new work a British flavor—a sort of Concierto de Londres? As I spoke very little Spanish and Joaquín spoke very little English, I relayed my question through Victoria and sat back awaiting his reaction. Slowly, an incredulous expression dawned on his face: "¡No! ¡No!" he choked, "¡Es imposible! ¡Es imposible!" And I immediately retreated to the safety of a discussion on whether the first movement should have a *tarantella* or *bolero* rhythm.

Of course, my question had been naïve, for Joaquín Rodrigo was a Spaniard to his core. (Much later, I dared to suggest that parts of *Concierto como un divertimento* were extremely difficult—to the extent that it might even discourage cellists from playing it. My comment was met by a dismissive "¡Es fácil!") The English composer Edward Elgar once said, "You pay nothing for wearing your own nose." Rodrigo, remaining proudly in the line of Albéniz, Turina, and Falla, certainly wore "his own nose," never once deviating from his roots or his musical style.

My overriding memory of Joaquin Rodrigo is of a man of great kindness and generosity of spirit who radiated a profound sense of inner peace. He certainly had no truck with any sympathy for his obvious disability. One of the most revealing letters I received from the Rodrigos came from Victoria in November 1984: "It is said that Joaquin lost his sight at the age of 3, which is wrong. When I met Joaquín in Paris in 1928 he could see the light and the colours. He lost his sight after 45 years, by an abcess in one eye. This is very important, and for that reason he must not be called 'the blind composer' as his activity has been that of a normal person."

I played Rodrigo's *Concierto como un divertimento* all over the world with some of the world's finest orchestras and conductors. Whether in London, Sydney, or Berlin, reaction to the new concerto followed a similar pattern. Either the new concerto was welcomed for its freshness and immediacy (reviewers often remarked that they could hardly believe it was the work of a composer who was nearly eighty) or it was disparaged for not being "contemporary enough." Audience reaction was invariably positive—with the last movement having to be encored at its premiere. The considerable originality of the *Adagio nostalgico* slow movement usually passed by without notice; accompanied by flute, clarinet, celeste, and divided strings, it opens with a delicate tracery of sound over which the cello spins a beautiful, haunting melody—the "Castilian popular song" was how Joaquín described it to me.

The phenomenal success of Rodrigo's *Concierto de Aranjuez* has served as a distraction from the many merits of his other music. Joaquín Rodrigo is a famous composer whose music remains largely unknown; there is a treasure trove waiting to be discovered.

Julian Lloyd Webber
March 2022

A LIGHT *in the* DARKNESS

Chapter 1

Ah, la maledizione!

The Fall into Darkness,
Being Born for Music
(1901–1920)

Sagunto (1901–6): Riot and Sickness

On 31 December 1906, in the city of Sagunto, about twenty miles north of Valencia on the Mediterranean coast, an angry mob protested against excise duties levied on basic goods. People of different ages, social origins, and political ideas came united against a long-disputed tax. At the end of each year, the state government auctioned off this tax to the highest bidder, which largely financed the administration and public services, thus assuring income without having to pay the management fees that the collector ultimately passed on to the taxpayers. The immediate demand was that the city council should take charge of the tax collection without involving any intermediary, as had been the continuous practice in Sagunto up to 1906. This legal formula had been applied in some municipalities to alleviate fiscal pressure, making it more progressive in accordance with the levels of income and allowing for more exemptions. But the general

1

demand was that the tax be abolished. This protest was a manifestation of waxing republicanism, which would soon transform Spain in dramatic ways.

There had been widespread disenchantment with the Liberal Party, whose peaceful alternation in power with the Conservative Party, the so-called Turno Pacífico, characterized the political dynamics of the Restoration (1874–1931). The Liberals, despite their promises, had not done away with the excise duty. This unleashed widespread revolts, and one of the bloodiest took place in Sagunto. There, on the first day of 1907, the people gathered in front of the town hall until the Civil Guard opened fire, leaving two dead and at least eight gravely wounded. Panic spread in the community, and the Central Government made the civil governor of Valencia go to Sagunto to quash the revolt, as he did with uncompromising efficiency.[1]

Besides exemplifying social conflict in Spain at the start of the twentieth century, Sagunto was a city with great symbolic value, noted for its heroic resistance to the armies of Hannibal, but also as the site of the uprising of General Martínez Campos, the coup d'état that ended the First Spanish Republic (1868–74) and restored the Bourbon monarchy. The feeble monarchy and its regime of alternating parties rightly feared revolution in Sagunto. The local taxpayers resented not only the levy but also the established system of political patronage, or bossism.

Protesters had gathered on the last night of the year at the Teatro Principal in Sagunto and headed to the home of the local political boss, who had made off with the collected excise taxes in 1906 and now sought to do the same in 1907. The law safeguarded him, and the people could merely let him know their disgruntlement, as they did outside his home, threatening him and throwing stones.[2] This boss was not in the least intimidated, and he scolded the protesters, who dispersed.[3] But that night, he spirited his family to safety out of Sagunto, returning the following day to appear at the town hall and administer taxation for the year to come.

The political boss was one Vicente Rodrigo Peirats (1857–1940), strict, landholding, conservative, and surely among those

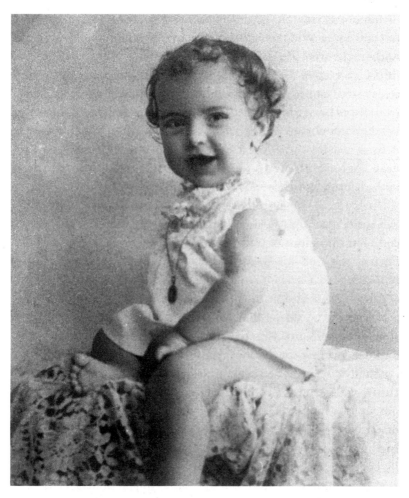

Rodrigo shortly before losing his sight, ca. 1902

who had supported the uprising of Martínez Campos. United in
a second marriage with Juana Vidre Ribelles, Vicente Rodrigo
was the father of a large family whose youngest child was
named Joaquín. Joaquín had just turned five, and a short time
earlier had gone blind. It is not difficult to imagine his bewilderment in the face of the insults and threats in front of his
house, the uproar of his siblings, the rock-throwing, and the
escape by night.

However, leaving Sagunto behind and moving to a residence in the city of Valencia was not the first pivotal event in his life. Rather, the first was the sickness that would eventually deprive him of his sight. The various accounts of Joaquín's life usually stress that, as he himself told it, he lost his eyesight at age three from diphtheria, contracted during a local epidemic in Sagunto. While no doubt he was a victim of the diphtheria bacillus, there is little reason to believe that there was an epidemic anywhere near Sagunto at the time he was afflicted. But if a diphtheria outbreak did not cause Joaquín's blindness, what did?

Everything suggests that the condition suffered by Rodrigo was an ocular diphtheria of a conjunctival type, a sickness then common in regions of northern Germany, where it was described during the mid-nineteenth century, but quite rare in Spain. According to García Mansilla, "the prognosis is quite serious because it is a condition that almost always affects the cornea and frequently causes blindness."[4]

We do not know exactly when Rodrigo suffered the sickness, but the process probably lasted several weeks and produced much discomfort. "I recall," he said, "the tantrums I would throw when they were healing me. The local anesthestics were not up-to-date, and therefore I would react to the evil tricks of the doctors like a fool, and I would bitterly scold them."[5] In the first phase of the sickness, it was a matter of removing by cauterization the false membranes generated in the eye, as would be done for a case of a purulent conjunctivitis. Expressly discouraged for the treatment of diphtheric conjunctivitis, the chemical cauterization undoubtedly increased the damage. Rodrigo's memory of those difficult times harmonizes with the observations that Wecker makes about the application of cauterization: "Children put up roadblocks in a thousand ways, against the application of the caustic agent. [. . .] cauterizations are very painful for children."[6] Once the diphtheric character of the suffering was diagnosed, therapy was to be applied with injections of Roux serum so that the infection would subside; however, in Joaquin's case, irreversible damage to the cornea had already been done.

Though Rodrigo would remain blind, even up to the age of 45 he retained the capacity to distinguish light from darkness and perceive massive objects at a distance of three feet; thus, he could see the presence of an obstacle in his way. Moreover, he could vaguely intuit colors. The famous ophthalmologist José Antonio Barraquer (1852–1924) treated his condition while Rodrigo was still a child, and finally operated on him in Barcelona, but without the hoped-for results. Much later, in the 1940s, Dr. Ramón Castroviejo (1904–1987), one of the most eminent ophthalmologists of his time, told Rodrigo that perhaps it would be possible to operate on him in his clinic in the United States. This plan was not carried out, and the composer lost the minimal visual capacities he had earlier possessed.[7]

Being blind affected every aspect of Rodrigo's life and brought him closer to music through an acute aural sense. Nonetheless, he preferred to link his musical inclinations to the coincidence of having been born on 22 November 1901, on the feast day of Saint Cecilia, patron saint of musicians. Crucial in those first years of his existence was the escape of his entire family from Sagunto to Quartell, his mother's home town, on 31 December 1906, and from there to Valencia, where they finally settled. The Rodrigos were unknown there and could insinuate themselves into society more discreetly.

Valencia: Politics and History

In the first decade of the twentieth century, the Valencian population was almost 230,000, making it the third most populous city in Spain, after Madrid and Barcelona. From the political point of view, while conservative bossism dominated in Sagunto and much of Spain, in Valencia prevailed the revolutionary, anticlerical republicanism promoted by writer Vicente Blasco Ibáñez (1867–1928), one of the first literary points of reference for the young Joaquín. "Blasquism" (referring to that author's ideology) governed the city from 1901 to 1923, with elements of a cultural populism rooted in Valencian society. That Valencia, critical and combative, was a breach in monarchical, conservative Spain. Culture formed a central part of Blasco Ibáñez's program for social renovation, as we may gather from the motto published by Félix Azzati in the newspaper founded by that writer: "Every rebellion is within culture. With weapons, a crime is committed; with an idea, a nation is built."[8]

But beyond this reality of the city in which Joaquín Rodrigo was to be professionally trained, Valencia had a long and rich musical history going back to the sixteenth century. A significant milestone at the Valencian court of the viceroys Ferdinand of Aragón and Germana de Foix was the compilation of the *Cancionero del Duque de Calabria* (Songbook of the Duke of Calabria, later known as the *Upsala Songbook*), which was eventually printed in Venice in 1556. Twenty years earlier, Luis de Milán published *El Maestro*, the first printed compendium of music for a guitar-like instrument called the vihuela. This collection is one of the jewels of Renaissance instrumental music. In this same century, the Cathedral of Valencia was among the most powerful archiepiscopal sees of Spain. Its music chapel became one of the leading such institutions in Spain. At this magnificent cathedral, one of the great musicians of the early Spanish Baroque, Juan Bautista Comes (1582–1643), was trained under maestros like Ginés Pérez (1548–1600) and Ambrosio Cotes (ca. 1550–1603), who led the Valencian chapel during the final years of the sixteenth century. Comes is celebrated for his sumptuous polychoral sacred music. It was during that period that the Royal Seminary School of Corpus Christi was founded, and it would become a major center for Valencian music.

Antonio Teodoro Ortells (1647–1706) was trained at the Corpus Christi chapel, becoming one of the most important Spanish musicians of his age. Juan Bautista Cabanilles (1644–1712), a contemporary of Ortells, was among the brightest luminaries of the Spanish organ in the Baroque and renowned for his highly inventive free-style tientos. He was the central figure in a brilliant tradition of Valencian organists, extending up to the time of Pascual Pérez Gascón (1802–1864) and beyond to the brothers Francisco and Segundo Antich into the twentieth century.

In the eighteenth and nineteenth centuries, two musical celebrities, Vicente Martín y Soler (1754–1806) and José Melchor

Gomis (1791–1836), trained at the Cathedral of Valencia, and later broadened their horizons throughout Europe. Martín y Soler's opera *Una cosa rara* eclipsed Mozart's *Le nozze di Figaro* at its Viennese premiere in 1786, and the composer then took up residence in St. Petersburg to direct and compose at the Italian opera theater founded there by Catherine the Great.

However, a crisis of diminishing resources throughout the cathedral-based musical system in Spain during the 1800s disrupted the teaching and exercise of the music profession. In Valencia, this crisis led to the establishment of a system of music training based on new institutions such as private schools and cultural associations like the Liceo Valenciano (Lyceum of Valencia) and the Sociedad Económica de Amigos del País (Economic Society of Friends of the Country) which, in the mid-nineteenth century, established a school of song directed by the organist Pérez Gascón. These developments led directly to the founding in 1879 of the Conservatory of Music of Valencia by Salvador Giner Vidal (1870–1911), among others. Giner, a student of Pérez Gascón, directed the Conservatory from 1894 to 1909 and was the central figure in the evolution of the Valencia Philharmonic at the turn of the twentieth century.

Three important representatives of Valencian music would emerge from composition classes given by Giner at the Conservatory of Valencia during Joaquín Rodrigo's years of training: Vicente Lleó (1870–1922), José Serrano (1873–1941), and Manuel Penella (1880–1939), all of them composers of successful zarzuelas (operettas). At the beginning of the twentieth century, these composers, well-established in popular music-theatrical entertainments, reflected the impact of political populism in music. To the degree that Blasquism gradually became more moderate, it would encourage elitist interest in the canonical repertoire of classical music, which Rodrigo would take up, casting aside the crowd-pleasing zarzuela.

Spanish republicanism had a basic interest in the improvement of education, and Blasco Ibáñez's political group collaborated in this regard with the so-called Republican Union, a consortium over which presided a political intellectual, Nicolás

Salmerón (1838–1908), alongside Francisco Giner de los Ríos (1839–1915), the great renovator of Spanish pedagogy. Both were adherents of Krausismo, "the philosophy of Karl Christian Friedrich Krause, an idealism based on the recognition of God and His manifestation in this world. Krausism endeavored to build in the world the ideal place where both men and women would achieve their full potential."[9] The most important advantage that republican Valencia offered to young Joaquín at the start of the new century was access to this kind of progressive schooling.

The Valencia School for Deaf-Mutes and the Blind

Inaugurated in the academic year 1887–88, Valencia's School for Deaf-Mutes and the Blind (Colegio de Sordo-mudos y Ciegos) was a healthcare institution directed by the Sisters of the Third Order of Saint Francis of Assisi. Brígida Alonso, a blind woman

School for Deaf-Mutes and the Blind, Valencia

educated at the National School for Deaf-Mutes and the Blind of Madrid, had entered their convent the year before.

She had maintained her own school for the blind in Valencia; when she entered the Franciscan convent, she immediately took on the mission of educating the deaf there as well.[10] She sent a group of nuns to learn the teaching methods used at the Madrid National School, a progressive model for this kind of pedagogy. "The sisters returned from Madrid provided with a certificate that accredited them in Spain as capable of teaching deaf and blind students, and with this document [they decided to] inaugurate the School without wasting time, in October 1887."[11]

This private initiative, supported by public institutions, had spread throughout different Spanish provinces in the mid-nineteenth century. But the Valencia School was set apart by its distinctive interest in music training. It had everywhere been common practice to impart elements of music theory and somewhat more advanced instrumental studies—in piano, organ, violin, and plucked stringed instruments, especially, guitar and bandurria (a lute-like instrument)—and to teach blind children to tune pianos. This enabled students to develop basic musical activities. However, in Valencia it was decided to teach them the principles of musical composition, deemed the loftiest musical activity. The history of the School published in 1893 relates that, besides the normal teaching of music, "in view of the very high interest that musical art holds for the blind, an upper class of composition has been established under the direction of the intelligent professor Don Francisco Antich, and another class for stringed instruments, entrusted to the well-known guitarist Don Francisco Rocamora."[12]

Thus Rodrigo and his schoolmates enjoyed the advantages of a school that (1) guided blind students toward the highest level in the music curriculum; (2) provided a dedicated and exceptional faculty, among whom Francisco Antich stood out; and (3) was committed to the development of improved didactic systems. All this led to a phenomenon without parallel elsewhere in the world: the School produced not only Rodrigo but also two additional blind composers who occupy prominent places in

Spanish music of the twentieth century: Francisco Cuesta (1889–1921) and Rafael Rodríguez Albert (1902–1979).

In reading and writing music, Joaquín relied on a variety of Braille developed in the mid-nineteenth century by Gabriel Abreu (1834–1881), a blind musician educated in the National School of Deaf-Mutes and the Blind in Madrid, and later professor at that institution. It is a system based on Braille but modified and broadened, offering 256 combinations as opposed to the merely 63 of the original Braille. This system was the most widespread in Spain until well into the twentieth century. However, though the system of musical writing that the blind were learning at the Valencia School was Abreu, Braille was used by them for reading and writing literary texts.

The School had personnel who were very committed to their work, and many professors had blind assistants for their classes. Their system produced outstanding results: nowhere else was there to be such a high concentration of blind composers in so specific a time and place.[13] Both for its advanced methods and impressive results, and despite a scarcity of resources, the School for Deaf-Mutes and Blind of Valencia gained national fame.

Rodrigo probably entered the School in the academic year 1910–11, at a propitious time. After occupying several properties that were far from adequate, the School had finally found a suitable home in the Plaza de la Bocha. In that school year, Rodrigo likely would have barely begun his musical studies. In a performance put on by the students after examinations to demonstrate in public their notable progress and the effectiveness of the education they were receiving, Rodrigo merely participated by reciting a poem, though it is possible that he sang in the mixed chorus of blind students.[14] But by the end of his third year of classes (1912–13), he appeared in the press as one of the students who participated in the ceremony of awarding prizes for the school year. On 22 June 1913, he sang the serenade *Non ti destare* by Antonio López Almagro (1839–1904) and was enthusiastically applauded. In June 1916–17, he appeared with his schoolmate Emilio Chust playing a duet from *Les Huguenots* arranged for piano and harmonium.[15] Finally, in April 1920, the

First Communion, 1910

tenth and final year of his education at the Valencia School, he performed in a celebration for the Mother Superior of the school. The *Diario de Valencia* informs us that "the blind students Joaquín Rodrigo and Vicente Ballester [. . .] put on display their vast studies of music, the first on violin and the second on piano."[16]

Rodrigo's decade at the Valencia School was the maximum allowable time for studies there, according to the regulations of the National School of Madrid, which established the pedagogical model for all other such institutions. Rodrigo lived in a buoyant period of the Valencian institution, and he benefited from a program of studies that not only enabled him to read and write in the several systems of writing for the blind but also gave him a basic education in religion, morality, hygiene, citizenship, grammar, arithmetic, history, and geography. At the same time, he supplemented general learning with comprehensive training in solfège, harmony, and counterpoint and fugue. In applied music, Rodrigo took classes in song, violin, and piano. The education was geared toward composition, and in a later interview, Rodrigo was likely alluding to works composed in this period:

— What was the first thing you composed?
— Well, it was a "little mazurka." Maybe afterwards it
   was a little waltz and a tiny song . . .
— Have you titled them?
— No. I did not arrive at names. But everything at that
   time had women's names. They could have been called
   "Conchita" or "Margarita."[17]

Rodrigo made the acquaintance at school of the person who would become his most valued mentor at this stage of his development, Francisco Antich (1860–1926), and through Antich, Eduardo López-Chavarri (1871–1970), who shortly afterwards was to become the first supporter of his works.

Teachers and Points of Reference

Antich was a worthy representative of the great tradition of Valencian cathedral organists and among the most respected musicians in Valencia during this epoch. He had been educated as an organist in one of the initial cohorts of students at the Conservatory of Valencia, and his life was practically circumscribed by the limits of the city. Nevertheless, he stayed abreast of the latest developments in music north of the Pyrenees, in particular, the music of César Franck. Antich formed part of the original faculty of the School at the end of the nineteenth century, and he was eventually hired to teach the most advanced courses and

students. In his accounts of his training, Rodrigo never emphasized the education he received at the school, but rather spoke
of Antich as a private teacher. Antich was an albino, and his
visual capacities were limited. Therefore, beyond his bonhommie
and erudition, he had a particular sensitivity and was capable of
developing the most appropriate strategies for teaching a blind
youth like Rodrigo.

Antich likely gave Rodrigo the basic technical knowledge
needed to approach composition, but the one who guided him
to the musical avant-garde of his time had to be López-Chavarri.
Composer, pianist, orchestra leader, musicologist, and professor of history and aesthetics of music at the Conservatory of
Valencia and one of the authorities of Spanish music criticism,
López-Chavarri would exert an enormous influence on the initial
development of Joaquín Rodrigo's career.

Rodrigo met López-Chavarri in January 1915 at an exhibition
of paintings in the Círculo de Bellas Artes de Valencia (Circle
of Fine Arts of Valencia), where López-Chavarri gave a lecture
on "Music and Painting," an event graced by the young sister-
and-brother piano duo of Amparo and José Iturbi. José interpreted *Pictures at an Exhibition* by Mussorgsky, earlier discussed
by López-Chavarri; afterwards, he and Amparo interpreted the
Suite No. 2, Op. 23 ("Silhouettes") by Anton Arensky, as well as
an arrangement that the siblings had made of *Acuarelas valenci-
anas* (1910) by López-Chavarri.[18]

López-Chavarri harbored the dream of Valencia's entrance
onto the map of contemporary Spanish music, then dominated
by non-Valencians Enrique Granados, Manuel de Falla, and Joaquín Turina. Though all three composed musical theater, none
excelled in zarzuela, and their reputations rested on their concert
music. López-Chavarri had pinned his hopes on Francisco Cuesta,
the blind youth also educated at the Valencia School. Cuesta's
progress was promising, as shown by his *Cuadros de antaño*, a
suite written for the Orquesta de Cámara de Valencia (Chamber
Orchestra of Valencia) and premiered by it on 24 March 1916. The
enthusiasm of the cultural elite for Cuesta's suite was so great
that they gave a banquet in his honor and seated him at the side

of the great Valencian painter who became another point of reference for Joaquín Rodrigo: Joaquín Sorolla (1863–1923).[19]

The clue for knowing when that first meeting between López-Chavarri and Rodrigo took place comes from Rodrigo himself, when he remarked that they used to meet at the home of pianist Leopoldo Querol every Sunday for musical sessions.[20] Curiously, Rodrigo did not include among his recollections that the evening presenting the exhibition of visual art, the concert by the Iturbis, and the lecture by López-Chavarri ended in a *tertulia*, a conversation led no doubt by Francisco Cuesta, who was then invited by the Iturbis and others present to sit at the piano and render his most recent compositions, "which were much acclaimed and justly applauded."[21] Aside from those memories Rodrigo wanted to convey and those he did not, he was no doubt impressed by the musical heights to which a blind youth from a good family could aspire, as exemplified by Cuesta. Cuesta and Rodrigo shared a prosperous bourgeois background, a pronounced predilection for modern music, and a fundamental attraction to opera. Cuesta said that Bizet's *Carmen* impelled him to be a musician.[22] Rodrigo was to say much later that Verdi's *Rigoletto* provided him a similar conversion experience: "I was not a precocious child, but after hearing a harpsichord concert and the opera *Rigoletto*, I felt such emotion that I knew I was going to devote myself entirely to [music]. Immediately I began to study piano and violin, as well as composition."[23]

Music and literature interested him in these years. He had an assistant for the blind, an employee of his father named Rafael Ibáñez, who kept him company and constantly read to him— from, among other works, the novels of Blasco Ibáñez. Besides the stylized Valencianism of López-Chavarri's work, Russian music would be an early and powerful influence on the musical sensibility of Rodrigo. His calling for music solidified in March 1916, when he became a member of the Valencian Philharmonic Society, founded in 1911 and playing a crucial role in the development of musical life in Valencia during the first half of the twentieth century.[24]

We know that Rodrigo took a special interest in orchestration at this time and studied the *Traité general d'instrumentation* (1863) by François-Auguste Gevaert (1828–1908).[25] That book was not available in Braille, but a blind man who was making a living by playing piano in the dives of Valencia approached López-Chavarri, asking him to dictate a summary of the treatise. The blind man took careful notes and then sold them to Rodrigo. This was an unusual but nonetheless effective means of learning the material.[26] Gevaert's treatise was a standard reference work; in fact, it was the basis of Russian orchestral music that then served as an alternative to Germanic post-Romantic symphonism. Nevertheless, what Rodrigo was always to remember was not this book but rather a recital by harpsichordist Wanda Landowska.

When Landowska first visited Valencia, Rodrigo had hardly begun his education at the Valencia School. She made her first appearance in Valencia at the Teatro Principal on 20 January 1911, after a notable advertising campaign that included the public exhibition of her harpsichord.[27] Taking advantage of Landowska's successful debut, the Teatro Principal engaged her for two more concerts, on 3 and 5 May 1912, during her next tour of Spain. Yet, the Valencian public exhibited little enthusiasm for the refined art of the harpsichordist, and the second concert was not well attended.[28] Rodrigo might have attended these early recitals, but it was not until her next appearance before the Valencian public, in 1920, that Rodrigo's education and sensibilities were sufficient to appreciate her art.

In that year, Landowska visited Valencia on two occasions. During the first, she gave concerts at the Teatro Principal on January 19, 21, and 23, all supported by the city's cultural upper crust but greeted with indifference by the Philharmonic public at large.[29] On her second visit, she gave three concerts organized by the Philharmonic Society, on December 17–19, by which time Rodrigo was already affiliated with that organization. It was the first of these performances that genuinely impressed him. In it, Landowska played "Le Coucou" of the *Premier Livre de pièces de clavecin* by Louis-Claude Daquin and the *Toccata con lo Scherzo del Cucco* by Bernardo Pasquini.[30] This may well have provided the impetus or inspiration for his subsequent use of the cuckoo's song in a wide variety of works, as a kind of musical signature.

The End of the Beginning

Spain's neutrality during the First World War had spurred a cycle of economic prosperity resulting from foreign demand for its raw materials and manufactured goods; however, by 1919, this era was approaching its end. The prosperous times had increased the social divisions between rich and poor in an apparently unsustainable way, and political instability soon returned. True, Rodrigo experienced all of this on the side of those enjoying the most favor, and he had much for which to be grateful: elementary studies at the School, compositional tools received from Antich, the notes of Gevaert's treatise, the quiet example of Cuesta, López-Chavarri's barely noticed but necessary presence, and finally, the decisive stimulus of Wanda Landowska's subtle art. But things would not always go his way, and Rodrigo was on a musical road that was far from straight but rather replete with twists and turns. The reality of being blind, which he had assumed already in childhood was his normal state, began to weigh more heavily upon him. Well might he have sympathized in silence with the tragic antihero of Verdi's *Rigoletto*, who cried out, "*Ah, la maledizione!*"—Ah, the curse!

Chapter 2

"Music! . . . Music!"

In the Avant-Garde
(1921–1927)

Valencia in May 1921

"'Music! Music!' cried the populace," until a noisy band formed by the peasants "altered the peace of the entire little plaza" with its first mazurka.[1] In *Arroz y tartana* (1919), Valencian novelist Vicente Blasco Ibáñez illustrated the introduction of music into the social fabric of rural Valencia with bands and mazurkas, though in the Valencian capital, opera was the preferred entertainment and cultural showcase of the upwardly mobile bourgeoisie. Rodrigo experienced those two worlds juxtaposed by the novelist. He fondly recalled the rehearsals of the local band during his early childhood in Sagunto, and his first composition was a mazurka. Once in Valencia, he loved the opera performances that he attended with his mother and sisters. This exposure in his formative years was the womb in which his musical sensibilities gestated.

Giner and López-Chavarri were the founding members of a hoped-for school of composers from the Levante (the east coast of Spain), whose first fruits would transcend mere regional boundaries in the person of Francisco Cuesta, Giner's student at the Conservatory. He was a protégé highly esteemed by López-Chavarri and his circle as the most promising figure of Valencian music. There was no doubting the high expectations that this musician was summoned to meet. Unfortunately, Cuesta died at dawn on May 23 of bronchopneumonia, just three days short of his thirty-second birthday.

The desolation caused in local cultural circles by this passing was extraordinary. Cuesta's tragic demise was like ice water hurled on the city's hopes at the moment when all most strongly believed in the possibility of a Valencian—and universal—music. Cuesta had aimed to bring about the dream of López-Chavarri: to achieve a music both modern and Valencian at the same time. His premature death frustrated that hope, and his memory quickly faded into oblivion, only prolonged by the writer Pedro Gómez-Ferrer, by the constant retelling of the history of Valencian music by López-Chavarri, and only rarely in the repertoire of pianist Leopoldo Querol, Cuesta's fellow student. López-Chavarri and Querol, moreover, would very soon discover a new stimulus in their project to place Valencia securely within the mainstream historical narrative of European music. The savior of their dreams would take the form of yet another young blind man, twelve years younger than Cuesta.

Beyond the Catalogue: Pre-Joaquín de Ante-Rodrigo

Rodrigo's first departure from Spain took him as far away as Germany, though the only documentary evidence we retain of this trip is a postcard that Rodrigo sent to Antich: "Dear Maestro. I find myself in Wiesbaden, where I am healing, where they have given me hope. This town is one of the musical centers of Germany and also one of the most beautiful. Joaquín Rodrigo. [PS] I haven't forgotten about the assignment you gave me."[2] He had taken with him a musical assignment from his teacher. The nature of the assignment is unknown, but in Germany he would find time to immerse himself in the currents of contemporary music. His stay in Germany lasted over three months: "There I listened to much music, and I thought seriously about being a musician."[3]

With his family in the 1920s

In the early 1920s Rodrigo audited classes in music history given by López-Chavarri at the Valencia Conservatory. Rodrigo told an anecdote about the end of his attendance at the Conservatory, when there appeared in López-Chavarri's class the "stiff and stern Don Amancio Amorós [. . .]. When he asked me in which class I was enrolled, and after I answered him that I was only an auditor, he politely said to me, 'Here we don't want auditors, only students who are enrolled, even though they may not have any auditory faculties.'"[4] Rodrigo was summarily dismissed as an auditor.

We may wonder why Rodrigo did not officially matriculate at the Conservatory if Cuesta had in fact undertaken official studies there. Understandably, since Amorós's main mission as director of the Conservatory was to solve its serious financial problems, it made his blood boil to see a middle-class youth like Rodrigo, who rode around in a chauffeured American car, receive lessons for free. Consequently, he cited and enforced regulations, adding the sardonic comment about preferring students who paid, although they lacked auditory faculties, over freeloading auditors. What Amorós could never have imagined is that his institution, later transformed into the Conservatorio Superior de Música, would one day be named after the young auditor he had expelled!

In order to find a way forward, Rodrigo took careful note of what Cuesta had done, of the hopes that he had aroused, and of the void that he had left in the realm of Valencian music. And he would have to pay heed to López-Chavarri's ardent summons to aspiring Valencian musicians: "They would doubtlessly know how to bring about something serious, lofty, worthy of the delicate memory that Cuesta leaves among us."[5] The path was clearly marked, but Rodrigo ought to have been very attentive to the seriousness and loftiness of purpose to which López-Chavarri alluded, because what the majority of local music lovers appreciated about Cuesta was the modernity of his Valencian style, and that modernity was unmistakably concentrated in the harmonic treatment of folkloric musical material.

Nonetheless, López-Chavarri encouraged transcending the regional style by entering the international realm through neoclassicism. As much as he wanted to label Cuesta as a partisan of Valencian music, he had already perceived neoclassical tendencies in a crucial work in his oeuvre, the *Cuadros de antaño* (Paintings of Days Gone By). López-Chavarri referred to this work as a "suite in the old style."[6] In it, one critic singled out "the delicious harmonic language—quite modern—which in later works would lend value to his style."[7]

What followed was Rodrigo's first compositional step worthy of notice. It is a piece that was never included in his catalogue, but one that always had a special place in his memory, reflecting not only the example of *Cuadros de antaño* but also the impact on him of Wanda Landowska's harpsichord artistry. That work is the *Homenaje a un viejo clavicordio*. Though this is the most important of Rodrigo's early creations, and one about which we will shortly have more to say, it is not his first preserved work. Bearing an earlier date are a *Vals* for piano dedicated "To my best [female] friend" in May 1921; a *Melodía*, "Ensayo para voz de soprano y piano sobre la poesía Soliloquio de Carrasquilla Mallarino" (Essay for Soprano Voice and Piano on the Poem *Soliloquio* [Soliloquy] by Carrasquilla Mallarino), dated 20 April 1922; and a set of composition exercises from August 1922. We do not know what tender love inspired Rodrigo's simple little waltz in C♯ minor. Copied in ink with a graphic naïveté proper to an amateur barely familiar with musical notation, full of signs related to the interpretation and, in addition, with the fingering for the right hand of a chromatic descending scale, its initial impulse perhaps originated years earlier, because the date 1921 seems superimposed on a previous 1919.

The waltz's thirty-nine measures, amusing but impersonal, bear no resemblance to the panache of the *Melodía*, in which the great songwriter that Rodrigo was to become first stands revealed. Already on display here is his exquisite sensitivity in setting questioning phrases to music, a sensitivity that would characterize his later songs, several of which we consider to be among the finest in the Spanish repertoire, for instance, *Cántico de la esposa* (1934) on the *Spiritual Canticle* of Saint John of the Cross: "Where did you go hiding, / Beloved, and you left me just to moan?" or the refrain of *Pastorcito santo* (1952) by Lope de Vega: "Where are you going, for it is cold / so early in the morning?" The excellent lyrics of this *Melodía*, by the Colombian poet Eduardo Carrasquilla Mallarino (1887–1956), constitute a relentless interrogation of the sort that so appealed to Rodrigo:

What are the winds saying
In the mountain range
To the panoramas
Of the distance?
What is the naïve moon
Of ice saying

To the lake that copies
The quietness of the sky?
Eclogue, rhapsody,
Ballad? No, nothing.
The ear does not understand
That song.
Respond to yourself
Heart.

How did Rodrigo write this music, and who was transcribing it into conventional notation in ink? The *Melodía* needed a complex notational design, one that probably demanded an original in raised writing. We do not know whether such an original survives among the barely explored Braille manuscripts in the Archivo de la Fundación Victoria y Joaquín Rodrigo, or even if one existed. But we may safely assume that the assistant in either case was Rafael Ibáñez. Besides accompanying Rodrigo and reading to him the literature that he craved and devoured, Rafael learned how to copy music. The scores of the *Vals* and *Melodía* are copies by the same hand (copyist A). However, as far as the music is concerned, a great evolution has clearly taken place, from the clumsy insecurity of the *Vals* to the almost professional assuredness of the *Melodía*.

In 1923 Rodrigo dated a set of pieces that he left out of his official catalogue, alongside others that demarcate the beginning of his output. Among the first, one sonata stands out, with a movement in A major featuring a slow introduction. It seems to be a formative compositional exercise in a Romantic style. Both the score of the sonata, dated February 1923, and the score of the *Fuga a cuatro partes para piano* (Fugue in Four Parts for Piano), dated 1922, are signed by Rodrigo; in addition, there is a titled but unsigned piece in a fugue-like style—probably for organ— dated 14 August 1922. All of these are written by the same hand, but different from the preceding manuscripts, rendered in a more professional calligraphic style (copyist B). These were clearly exercises assigned and supervised by Francisco Antich. The same can be said of an *Ave María* from 1923 for female voice and an ensemble of two each of oboes, flutes, clarinets, and bassoons. The copyist was definitely not the teacher. Nevertheless, it is possible to discern Antich's hand on the unsigned copy of the *Fuga a cuatro partes para piano*, dated 22 August 1922, and of the *Homenaje a un viejo clavicordio*.

While these pieces illustrate Rodrigo's competence in replicating the traditional forms of academic composition, the ensuing works we survey reveal the development of his own voice, already apparent in his *Melodía* of 1922. Especially noteworthy is the *Lied para piano*, dated 5 March 1923, and the *Preludio No. 1* for piano, dated May 21 of the same year.

These two works were clearly copied by Rodrigo's amanuensis during this period (copyist B). Of particular interest is the *Lied*, whose style hews closer to the French *mélodie* than to the German *Lied*. It exhibits a dynamic structure in which a climax is achieved through incremental thickening of the texture, increasing of the tempo, and generating of harmonic tension between G minor and C major. The Prelude draws on the sonorities of French pianistic Impressionism, using whole tones suggestive of Debussy's *Voiles*. It also displays harmonic anomalies of a notational character: the score displays a key signature of six sharps, normally indicating F♯ major, but its harmonic structure corresponds to a Mixolydian mode (i.e., a major scale with a lowered seventh degree) on C♯. In other words, Rodrigo uses the key signature corresponding to the modality, and he does it precisely a month after having concluded the *Ave Maria* in B Dorian (a minor scale with a raised sixth degree), but written in the customary fashion, without any alteration in the key signature. Rodrigo was among the first composers in Spain, if not the very first, to write the key signature in this way. (Appendix 1 provides a table listing the manuscript sources of Rodrigo's early works, both published and unpublished.)

The ingenious name coined by poet and music lover Gerardo Diego to refer to his first poems was Pre-Gerardo Ante-Diego; indeed, he later applied a similar appelation to the fledgling compositions of Manuel de Falla: Pre-Manuel de Ante-Falla. We take the liberty of doing something similar with the incipient musical essays by Rodrigo, referring to them as Pre-Joaquín de Ante-Rodrigo. These early pieces of Rodrigo—like the first books of poems of Gerardo Diego—shed considerable light on what was going to be his distinctive path as a creative artist. They clarify his interests, illustrate his desire to acquire solid compositional technique, make visible the first sparks of his genius, and clearly point toward Opus 1 in his catalogue. For in 1923, the main copyist of this repertoire wrote out, at the composer's dictation, three pieces for violin and piano: *La enamorada junto al pequeño surtidor*, dated 31 March 1923, *Pequeña ronda alborotada*, dated 9 June 1923, and *Canción en la noche*, dated August 18. Although the latter's delicately Andalusian character places *Canción en la noche* on the margins of uncatalogued works at this stage, the other two form (or were made into) Rodrigo's only composition with an opus number: *Dos esbozos*, Op. 1.

As the composer himself recognized, the *Dos esbozos* (Two Sketches, "La enamorada junto al pequeño surtidor" and "Pequeña ronda alborotada") are evocations of the El Parterre gardens in Valencia, static vignettes in which Rodrigo begins to contemplate his irretrievable childhood from a distance and with a certain nostalgia. "La enamorada junto al pequeño surtidor" is a direct reference to the small fountain in the Valencian gardens, making this one in a long and time-honored line of "jeux d'eau" pieces. The violin sings the emotive melody of the loved one. The steady stream of refreshing water gurgling from the fountain symbolizes the vivifying presence of the beloved, as well as the desire to create new life in the context of a loving union. The perpetual flow of water in the verdant surroundings of the garden expresses a very human longing for perpetuate life. As the composer himself put it, "Everything I sensed in those gardens—fountains, jasmine—was expressed in this piece."[8]

Yet, the first movement arrests our attention precisely because of its subdued nature. There is no flamboyant pianistic display or violin virtuosity to simulate some fountain in the style of Bernini, though clearly there was ample precedent in the piano repertoire for a *jeux d'eau*, of the kind that Liszt and Ravel created. What stands out here is Rodrigo's distinctive voice, his

Musical ex. 2.1: *Dos esbozos*, Op. 1, Main theme of "La enamorada junto al pequeño surtidor," mm. 1–10

refusal to resort to musical clichés. Instead, the accompaniment features a gently repeating pattern both rhythmically and harmonically, with downward gestures in both hands. The score is marked *sempre piano*, and the violin is muted (*sordino*). The upward motion we expect from the fountain's waters appears in the soloist's opening gesture of an upward-leaping fourth, which is then repeated. Burbling triplet figures round out this opening statement before its subsequent reiterations (musical ex. 2.1).

Rodrigo seeks to capture here not so much an outward display of aquatechnics as the inward state of being that arises from them. The fountain serves as a symbol for the young girl's inner effusion of amorous feelings. At first this is nothing more than a quiet murmuring in her consciousness, but a series of modulations, increasing chromaticism, and the ascending register convey a gradual intensification of her passion, culminating in a high E_5 at m. 53, marked *Più animato*. Accordingly, at m. 56 the piano accompaniment changes from eighth notes to sixteenths, as an animated rhythmic analog to the violin's lyric ascent. The downward-cascading arpeggios undergo a metrical metamorphosis at m. 69 as the piano shifts to 2/4 time, though the violin remains in 6/8. This abrupt "modulation" in the meter of the accompaniment and the ensuing polymetrical effect dissipate as suddenly as they appeared, at m. 72, with the return of 6/8, though now with falling triplets driving toward the cadence as the girl's inner state returns to a sort of meditative calm, reposing on an E_4 for three whole measures, in the mellow radiance of joyous reflection.

This is no Roman or Parisian fountain but rather a Spanish one, though Rodrigo's musical depiction of provenance is nothing if not subtle. A listener could be excused for feeling the

occasional droplet of Spanish fountain water on her skin in certain modal colorings of a Phrygian sort, at mm. 35–43 or mm.
63–67, or the triplet figurations at the ends of phrases. But these
are at most faint allusions, not direct references of any nationalistic sort. In the final analysis, the significance of this "sketch"
is not what it tells us about a hypothetical young girl. Just as the
fountain symbolizes her, so she symbolizes the composer. It is his
inner life of which we catch a glimpse here.

The second piece, "Pequeña ronda," or "Little Round," is an
energetic study in the manner of nineteenth-century composers like Grieg or even Granados, but the harmonies are strictly
twentieth century and recall Bartók or Kodaly.[9] American listeners might initially be reminded of a Copland-style hoedown.
The ostinato rhythm is the generating factor here, and a pedal D
unites the entire piece.

Antonio Gallego feels that there is "a problem" in the structure of Dos esbozos because of an imbalance in the durations
of the two pieces, the second barely a minute and the first over
four.[10] But we might see the "Pequeña ronda" instead as a sort of
framing device, bringing the previous meditation to an extro-
verted and rousing conclusion. Given its folklike reliance on
drones and verbatim repetition of ideas, four minutes of such a
conclusion might well have worn out its exuberant welcome, and
thus the proportions strike us as appropriate. This is, after all, a
sketch, and it could have served as the basis for a more extended
work. But then it would not have been a sketch any longer, much
less pequeña! Pre-Joaquín de Ante-Rodrigo naturally gives way
to a first Joaquín Rodrigo, who at the end of 1923 resolutely commences his catalogue with a series of works that mark him as
the new promise for Valencian music, though a promise of a kind
rather different from what might have been expected.

The Curtain Goes Up . . . and "Now Rodericus is disinfecting the piano"

Until Dos esbozos, everything had gone as foreseen, but between
July and October 1923—a politcally fraught period in Spain
after the coup d'état in September of General Miguel Primo

de Rivera—Rodrigo sought to enter the National Music Contest of 1923–24, which was announced in May.[11] He composed the *Suite para piano*, a work very distant from the *Homenaje a un viejo clavicordio*, not only in its pithy title (the name of the genre, nothing more) but also in the treatment of the musical material, clearly oriented toward the European avant-garde at the same time that it moves far away from characteristically Valencian music.

Rodrigo's *Suite para piano* (1923) was an auspicious and somewhat surprising debut from the 22-year-old composer. The work is clearly inspired by the French dance suites of the Baroque period, especially those by Couperin and Rameau, and it consists of a Preludio (dedicated to Leopoldo Querol), Siciliana (dedicated to Óscar Esplá), Bourrée (dedicated to Ernesto Halffter), Minué (dedicated to Adolfo Salazar), and Rigodón (dedicated to Amparo Iturbi). Yet, this is no mere exercise in epigonism, much less "frigid academicism," in the words of Antonio Iglesias,[12] for not only are these numbers thoroughly modern but they also already bear the stamp of Rodrigo's distinctive musical personality, as well as a non-Spanish character that might perplex those familiar only with his more popular works. Despite their antiquarianism, they are highly experimental and thoroughly au courant, even avant-garde, in the context of their time.

This was not, of course, his first venture into musical archaism. In the previous year he had penned his first formal composition, *Homenaje a un viejo clavicordio*, a collection of Baroque-style dances. The three movements are entitled "Sarabanda," "Pavana," and "Giga." In one of the preserved manuscripts of the "Pavana," however, the title "Gavota" appears scraped off. The "Sarabanda" is dated Valencia, 23 November 1922, and the "Giga," December of the same year. These juvenilia remained unpublished, but it was one he did not forget; in fact, he later recorded the three pieces for Spanish National Radio, and he remarked to Antonio Iglesias that "perhaps one day I will decide to publish them."[13] Perhaps, but in the end, not.

A simple analogy will help us to understand the significance of the *Homenaje*. If you walk through a comprehensive art museum like the Prado, you are likely to see aspiring painters absorbed in the exercise of copying one of the Old Masters on display. They do not pretend to be creating an original work of art; rather, they are imitating a painting in order to acquire the craft, the technique, to be able to do something original. In similar fashion, these were clearly studies in imitation of earlier forms and procedures, conventional in their harmony, voice leading, and general style. And as Gallego points out, they are not only imitations of early musical genres but of ones with a Spanish pedigree.[14] This excursion into the past may well have been inspired by Wanda Landowska's harpsichord recital in Valencia that year. In any event, their collective subtitle, "Fragmentos de una suite," suggests something of their tentative nature, that he was dangling one foot in the pool before taking the plunge. In the *Suite para piano*, plunge he did, into the deep end, head first.

To be sure, there was nothing novel about a twentieth-century composer writing a suite of pieces inspired by Baroque models. Graham Wade pointed to obvious prototypes, such as Debussy's *Pour le piano* (Prélude, Sarabande, Toccata) of 1901, and the *Suite bergamasque* (Prélude, Menuet, Clair de lune, Passepied) of 1905. Another obvious analog is Ravel's *Le Tombeau de Couperin* (Prélude, Fugue, Forlane, Rigaudon, Menuet, Toccata) of 1917.[15] By Rodrigo's own admission, these composers served as models for him in his early compositional career.

All of the dances in Rodrigo's *Suite para piano* are represented in these prototypes. The rigaudon is one of the less frequently encountered numbers in such suites and further leads one to suspect that Ravel's *Tombeau* exerted some influence on the Spanish composer. We might also cite Isaac Albéniz's three *Suites anciennes*, composed in the mid-1880s, nearly a decade before he moved to Paris. We have no evidence of Rodrigo's familiarity with this music, but it shows that this practice antedated neoclassicism and was not limited to France.

Both Albéniz and his esteemed contemporary Enrique Granados were avid performers of Domenico Scarlatti's keyboard works, which in turn exerted influence on their respective masterworks, *Iberia* and *Goyescas*. However, Rodrigo's *Suite* exudes nothing of

the sort of late-Romantic nationalist pathos typical of those collections. There is no intimation in this *Suite* of Spanish dances,
though the occasional resort to hemiola rhythms may suggest as
much. We would do well to recall that certain clichés of Spanish
folklore, such as the alternation of 6/8 and 3/4 and the use of
"Phrygian" cadences (iv^6–V), were typical of Baroque music in
general and did not have a Spanish origin.

Neither Albéniz nor Granados lived long enough to drink
from the well of neoclassicism that Stravinsky made available and from which Falla refreshed his own style in the 1920s.
Rodrigo was a late bloomer as a composer. But this *Suite* reveals
a level of maturity and sophistication that belies its early loca-
tion in the composer's catalogue. It is thoroughly up to date in its
resort to both Impressionist and neoclassical techniques, while
retaining something that is idiosyncratically Rodrigo.

Indeed, the essential ingredients of his style are already on
view in this collection. Chief among these are not only his penchant for historicism, for recreating forms from the pre-1800
era, but also his adherence to tonality, a creed from which he
would stray only much later in his career, and then in response
to the dictates of his subject matter, as we shall see. True, mor-
dant dissonances, especially bitonality, are abundant, but these
provide surface color and never threaten for very long an under-
lying sense of key throughout the entire *Suite*. Moreover, he does
not renounce a sense of beat or recognizable metrical patterns.
Again, there may be passages of metrical ambiguity, but they are
the rhythmical equivalent of his harmonic colorism. Rhythmic
complexities do not obliterate a sense of pulse any more than his
astringent dissonance eliminates a sense of tonality.

In short, he was of a predominantly "French" musical disposition, with a preference for the formal clarity of simple part
forms (mostly binary) without resort to complex polyphonic textures or extended development. Thus, his pieces are of modest
length, though he exhibited a gift for stringing together short,
evocative pieces into larger musical utterances. This final point
raises a caveat, which is this: Rodrigo's movements are by no
means isolated vignettes resulting from a lack of compositional

technique. Because his colorful musical language commands our attention from the outset, we may be seduced by surface detail in harmony and rhythm and remain unaware of the way in which he unites his thematic inspirations motivically, giving his works a coherence that one might describe as "economical" or even "organic." There is a first-rate musical intellect at work behind the beguiling sounds that emerge from his fertile imagination.

The *Suite para piano* opens with a Preludio. Historically, the purpose of such a number was to give the instrumentalist an opportunity to exercise the fingers, to display dexterity untethered by the requirements of a dance. Preludes exhibit no set form and feature instead an improvisatory quality emphasizing scales and arpeggios in a free-flowing rhythm unrelated to any particular choreography. The digital pyrotechnics of this particular prelude conform to that model and make a striking impression. But there are some significant departures from the norm.

We immediately notice the jarring dissonance created by the juxtaposition of two tonal centers, a half step apart: E minor and E♭ minor. In the very first measure, Rodrigo throws down the gauntlet and makes his presence known, especially insofar as the stridency of the dissonance is heightened by the conspicuous technical acumen needed to render it. Here is the sort of "disinfecting the keyboard" for which he would become famous, or infamous, in Valencian musical circles. This may not be as startling to us now as it was to audiences in 1923, but there was an element of the *enfant terrible* here, producing a "shock of the new." Rodrigo's use of bitonality betrays a predilection for major and minor seconds in his harmonic language, especially in his employment of symmetrical scales, that is, whole-tone, octatonic, and chromatic. For instance, the arpeggiated patterns in mm. 19–25 are built from whole-tone scales. Seconds lie well on the hand, especially if you're blind, and suggest a tactile approach to composing at the keyboard. Thus, as Dena Kay Jones points out, "The minor and major 2nd relationship between the two hands is a common stylistic element in many piano works of the composer."[16]

We might easily overlook another important detail, the melody floating above the cacophony below. This presents a simple motive that will return throughout the *Suite*, thus uniting the disparate movements in a way that was not at all typical of Baroque dance suites, in which the various movements were closed forms connected to one another by little more than key and general affect. Each movement is also cyclic, in that the motive is heard in various guises at both the beginning and end of the dance. What further intrigues the analyst is that this motive in its simplest, most direct form is withheld until the penultimate movement, the Minué. What we are hearing are essentially variations on a theme before the theme itself (musical exx. 2.2a-f).

Musical ex. 2.2a: Germinal motive from *Suite para piano*

Musical ex. 2.2b: Germinal motive from *Suite para piano*, Preludio, mm. 1–5

Musical ex. 2.2c: Germinal motive from *Suite para piano*, Siciliana, m. 1

Musical ex. 2.2d: Germinal motive from *Suite para piano*, Bourrée, m. 1

Musical ex. 2.2e: Motive from *Suite para piano*, Minué, m. 1

Musical ex. 2.2f: Germinal motive from *Suite para piano*,
Rigodón, mm. 5–6

However, Rodrigo's experimentalism is not confined to pitch organization, whether horizontal or vertical. As Jones points out, "the placement of bar lines and downbeats is aurally ambiguous."[17] In regards to form, however, the procedure is conventional, as the ABAB-coda layout of the Preludio is consistent with instrumental dances of the French Baroque.

As its name implies, the siciliana originated in Italy. Its distinguishing characteristic is rhythmic, the use of dotted rhythms in 6/8 meter. The binary form Rodrigo deploys, AABB, is also standard, and the alternating key centers of E minor and G major are conventional. The "idée fixe" of this *Suite* appears at the outset here in retrograde, using the siciliana rhythm. Rodrigo does not tarry in developing this material, and as Jones observes, the melody line in m. 3 is "simply a rearrangement and transposition of the principal musical idea."[18] Further thematic integration is already achieved in m. 2, with a melody derived from the "top melodic fragment" of the Preludio's B section.[19]

The agogic use of ornamentation emphasizes main beats, especially clusters of grace notes in the B section. In addition to quartal harmonies, simultaneous and consecutive seconds and sevenths supply nonharmonic color, especially the cross relations in mm. 10–11. These might remind some listeners of the blues scale, and the influence of American jazz is not inconceivable, given the French predilection for that art form and Rodrigo's predilection for all things French. Jones is quick to point out that "Rodrigo does not employ the flat third or seventh scale degrees in this manner in any other piano work."[20] One other intrusion here may be of the avian kind, as Iglesias finds an evocation of Rodrigo's beloved cuckoo bird in the descending fourths in mm. 1 and 12.[21] This will become the composer's intervallic calling card in many later works. This movement is, in the opinion of Gallego, the "most traditional" of the suite, and presages the *Siciliana* for cello and piano of 1929, as well as the slow movement of the *Concierto de estío* for violin and orchestra of 1943.[22]

The bourrée was traditionally a fast dance in 4/4 meter. Rodrigo's version adheres to that design and additionally features more development of the *Suite* motive, now in inversion. He goes through a series of relative and parallel tonal centers, E major, C♯ minor, and C♯ major, and the harmonic language eschews bitonality in favor of a modal quality. The overall structure is a kind of AAB bar form. But we are clearly in the twentieth century here, not the seventeenth, and cluster chords created by seconds in the left hand in mm. 11–15 provide a stark reminder of that.

By this point in the *Suite*, we may need a bit of a rest, and the triple-meter Minué obliges by its disarming, even refreshing, simplicity. Comprising a total of thirty-two measures, it is divided into A and B sections, each sixteen measures long. The first is in E minor, and the second in the parallel major. The accompaniment throughout is sparse. The *Suite* motive appears here in its original and simplest, most direct form. As Jones observes, the closing harmonies create a sensation that is "open-ended,

ambiguous, and unsettled,"[23] preparing us for the final movement, in which Rodrigo is once again up to his old tricks.

Rodrigo has saved his best for last. This is the longest and
most complex number in the *Suite*, and in addition to its astringent dissonances, it requires hazardous leaps in the left hand
of more than three octaves, a reminder of Rodrigo's notorious
tendency to "take no prisoners" in matters of technique. However, the formal layout could not be simpler, AB-coda, with both
sections in B minor. The *Suite* motive appears in transposition
right at the start and is stretched out over thirteen measures.
Clusters of seconds in the right hand soon add some harmonic
spice, while whole-tone harmonies appear at the climax of the
A section, which concludes with a lengthy development. The B
section restates some of the A material before heading off in a
new direction, reaching a dramatic coda at m. 89, which recapit-
ulates thematic material heard earlier. Bitonal clashes between
D♯ minor and E minor persist to the final measure, in which E
minor emerges triumphant.

As Jones points out, this ingenious work embraces many of
the elements that constitute Rodrigo's musical personality at
this time, and later.[24] These include Impressionism, nationalism,
neoclassicism, satire, and maybe even jazz. There is a persistent
love of jarring dissonance and a penchant for motivic development. He also "repeats a lot of the same musical material within
the same movement."[25] In sum, the *Suite para piano* was a noteworthy and a promising debut for an emerging talent.

During this early period, the young composer frequented the
circle closest to López-Chavarri, in the company of pianist Leopoldo Querol, a very significant figure at the outset of Rodrigo's
career. In addition to being a concert performer and champion
of the new Valencian music, Querol possessed a humanistic background rarely encountered among virtuosos of that epoch. In 1927
he was awarded the title of Doctor of Philosophy and Letters from
the University of Madrid.[26] López-Chavarri later recalled that he
first became acquainted with Rodrigo's music at Querol's home,
where the pianist hosted a "pleasant conversation group, listening to music ceaselessly and acquiring knowledge of all kinds of

music, ancient and extremely modern. One day he brought to the gathering some brief impressions for piano, already original, full of personality."[27]

Rodrigo also remembered those Sunday visits to Querol's house:

> I recall that the musical sessions invariably began
> with a Haydn symphony, played four-handed (with
> Chavarri always playing the lower parts). I then was
> suffering from the measles of dissonance. Hardly did
> the symphony end, when I hurled myself onto the piano
> and shook out a series of minor seconds and dissonant
> chords; Chavarri would always say to me, "Now Rodericus
> is disinfecting the piano." During spring and summer,
> we would go every afternoon to the beach at Las Arenas
> and there, in that friendly pavilion overlooking the
> sea, but since vanished, Chavarri and Enrique Gomá,

Pavilion over the Sea, Las Arenas beach (Valencia)

the exquisite musician and very fine critic, would read
me biographies, essays of musical analysis, treatises of
harmony and composition, etc. I owe much in my musical
education to these two great friends.[28]

That Pabellón del Mar en la Playa de Las Arenas (Pavilion over
the Sea on the Beach of the Sands), Grand Casino, and Restaurant,
inaugurated in 1922, was the meeting place of all Valencian artists
and of those who passed through that region during the tourist
seasons of spring and summer. It was very popular with musicians,
especially the indispensable López-Chavarri, who did not fail to
mention in his Las Provincias columns recollections of social circles and conversations at Las Arenas, while in the esteemed company of Leopoldo Querol and Amparo Iturbi, who played there on
more than one occasion. As Rodrigo was to recollect years later,
"Never will I forget those summer evenings when we would meet
on the beach of Las Arenas. We would speak about music, and the
conversation groups would change into true classes. [. . .] I found
friendship and support; I found, above all, comprehension."[29]

Without this musical Valencia, its get-togethers, readings of
Gomá and López-Chavarri, the members' attentive kindness,
and the constructive criticism aroused by the barbarous outbursts of Rodericus on the piano, Rodrigo would not have been
able to satisfy his greedy appetite for the latest musical novel-
ties. Neither would he have dared to disrupt the complacency of
the local music-loving establishment, so pleased to contemplate
its rich history and to dream of projecting its identity into the
future, with some creations reflecting recent trends in European
music. Even then, in a piano recital given by Querol at the Teatro
Principal of Valencia, in January 1923, the music of the Valencian
"modern school" that he presented was the Andalusianist Ley-
enda del castillo moro by López-Chavarri, some works of Cuesta,
and some dances by Manuel Palau,[30] another youthful promise of Valencian music educated at the Valencia Conservatory,
where he entered as a professor as early as 1919. He was a good
friend of Rodrigo's, hailing like him from a well-to-do family and
attracted to avant-garde music.

With Manuel Palau and Rafael Guzmán

Several of the works written by Rodrigo in these years were dedicated to his closest friends within the Las Arenas circle. To Palau he dedicated a *Canción y danza* composed between February and April 1925, which is possibly the most outstanding and personal contribution of Rodrigo's to stylized Valencian music. Its freely improvisational character is heightened by rhythmic independence between the right and left hands, which offer a mixture of various irregular groupings. Its dramatic structure resembles that of the *Lied* but is somewhat more expansive in its buildup to, and dissolution of, an agitated climax. This is all done within a very static modal system (B Mixolydian), with a theme derived from "La enamorada junto al pequeño surtidor" of *Dos esbozos*. The work skillfully dissolves any line demarcating a song from a dance. Thus, *Canción y danza* reveals a young Rodrigo striving to master a thoroughly modern musical language, unwilling to lash himself to the mast of traditional Valencian tastes.

For the critics López-Chavarri and Enrique Gomá, Rodrigo wrote a *Bagatelle*, dated September 1926. The composer himself

later recalled taking this work to one of his composition lessons with Paul Dukas in Paris, proudly presenting it as the fruit
of a single day's labor. "What a pitiful day!" was the maestro's
laconic reply. This was a very severe judgment for a graceful
work, Scarlattian in its texture, dynamics, repetitions of short
motifs, and imitative exchanges between melody and accompaniment in the main theme. This was one of the few piano works
by Rodrigo that the Valencian public could hear in concert, when
Leopoldo Querol debuted it on 23 May 1927 at the Teatro Principal. For this occasion, a brief explanatory note was published:
"Born from a purely formal suggestion, this little work, with its
light gracefulness, aspires to be a smile with which its author
expresses gratitude for the constant attentiveness in the past
summer shown him by his dear friends Eduardo López-Chavarri
and Enrique Gomá."[31]

   To Querol, Rodrigo dedicated the bitonal "cutting remark" of
the Preludio from the *Suite para piano*, with the clash of the second minor between the arpeggios of G♭ major in the left hand
and G major of the right hand, finally resolved at the end—more
theoretically than actually—in their relative minors. If we consider that the French composer Darius Milhaud published in
Feburary 1923 his crucial article "Polytonalité et Atonalité" in *La
Revue Musicale*, which López-Chavarri surely received at once,[32]
we can understand to what extent in 1920s Valencia the music
experts were up-to-date not only in music theory but also in its
practice through composition. Yet, as far as we know, when his
career as a concert performer took off, Querol did not play the
Suite para piano, although he did perform the Prelude of the *Suite
en ut* (1920) by Francis Poulenc at the Teatro Principal in Valencia
at a concert of the Philharmonic Society. The Prelude had been
premiered by Ricardo Viñes,[33] to whom the catalogue of the composer's work also ascribes the premiere of Rodrigo's *Suite para
piano* in Paris in 1928. Nor has it been documented that Querol
played the *Rondoletto*, an undated work from that early period
and possibly copied by that very pianist. On its cover appears
the dedication, "To you, Don Leopoldo Querol" as a Christmas
greeting signed by "A jongleur." He did not, in those years, even

play another piece that Rodrigo had dedicated to him in the style of the *Rondoletto*. This work, originally titled the "Égloga a la Mozart" in the first handwritten list that survives of the composer's works,[34] would metamorphose into the best-known and most widely performed piano work written by Rodrigo—his *Pastoral* for piano (1926). This is the first work to introduce the song of the cuckoo as Rodrigo's characteristic musical signature.

These first pieces by Rodrigo for piano took a long time to reach the public. The graceful *Rondoletto* was likely delayed due to its lack of ambitions beyond being a clever present for a friend, while the *Suite para piano* required time because of its astringent "disinfections" of the keyboard, which likely struck the general public as some sort of practical joke unworthy of serious consideration. Nonetheless, Rodrigo affirmed that the *Suite para piano* encapsulated all his concerns and intentions, "which later have done no more than mature in a calm fashion."[35]

Another piano piece, *Berceuse d'automne* (1923), also found a place in his early catalogue. Rodrigo always held this piece in affectionate regard, and in the opinion of his first biographer, Federico Sopeña, it remained one of his most inspired efforts.[36] It features a simple modal melody based on a G-major scale with lowered fifth and sixth degrees (an intervallic palindrome). This is accompanied by an ostinato of two chords juxtaposing the mode's structural fifth (G–D) with another perfect fifth a half step lower (F♯ to C♯, with a B♮ as added fourth), thus creating a polytonal effect.

However, the *Berceuse d'automne* seems positively delicate in comparison with another work that emerged from Querol's soirées in 1926: the *Preludio al gallo mañanero* (Prelude to the Morning Rooster), whose first manuscript was written in ink by López-Chavarri. The playfully descriptive title of this piece is something for which we should be grateful, for absent that we would have few tools with which to pry loose any meaning behind its positively astringent dissonances and helter-skelter rhythms. Here is the locus classicus of Rodrigo's keyboard-disinfecting manner, one that unites his inveterate archaism with post-Lisztian virtuosity and even nascent atonality. The

Preludio to his earlier *Suite para piano* was clearly a harbinger of this stand-alone *Preludio*, but we are several degrees of magnitude beyond that now.

It merits repetition that Rodrigo is not experimenting for the sake of experimentation, to push the envelope of the musical language he inherited simply because it was there to be pushed. Rather, the end dictates the means here. Unlike a great deal of music in the twentieth century, this piece is not *about* the way it was composed. It was composed in a certain way because it was *about* something beyond the music itself.

Despite the ear-searing dissonances and wild rhythmic eccentricities of this piece, especially its manic alternation of meters, from 9/8 to 6/8, 3/8, 2/4, 3/4, and 5/8, it is yet another instance of Rodrigo's penchant for archaisms. By his own admission, his principal inspiration was the harpsichord pieces of the eighteenth century that imitated bird songs, such as Couperin's evocation of the lark and nightingale, or Rameau's of the hen. And he shared Daquin's fondness for the cuckoo's distinctive call. But here he has chosen a rooster, and he makes clear that his depiction is neither poetic in the manner of Couperin, nor "overly soft, overly poetic" like programmatic pieces of the Impressionist type, though one occasionally discerns here certain Impressionistic traits in the use of symmetrical scales (chromatic, octatonic, and whole tone) as well as the piano writing. Though this piece reminds Rodrigo scholar Consuelo Martín Colinet of Debussy's *Doctor Gradus ad Parnassum*, another ironic evocation of the French *clavecinistes*, Rodrigo's bird song is "a more biting work, singing exactly like a rooster in the morning."[37] In fact, we have here not only a rooster but also a hen, whose songs provide the principal thematic ingredients of the piece (musical ex. 2.3a–b). A brief literary snippet of uncertain derivation appears at the outset of the work, emphasizing the centrality of the hen to this "story," such as it may be: "And Mother Hen had said to her chicks: Do not wander off, or the old, ugly, and bad fox will eat you!" (*Y la clueca dijo a sus polluelos: no os alejéis mucho ¡que el zorro viejo, feo y malo os comerá!*)

Rodrigo also seeks to capture a spirit of humor he perceived in the French keyboard music that provided his inspiration. But there is nothing sarcastic in his sense of humor. He is simply having fun, and that is what we are to have as well. Nonetheless, this is a cleverly conceived vignette and merits serious scrutiny. The *gallo* is portrayed using close intervals with accents on the highest pitch in the melody, a comical barnyard squawk. A subsequent descending interval mimics the actual sound of a rooster in his domain. Strident *acciacaturas* and syncopated rhythms suggest his comical antics. This rhythmic agitation is reflected in the harmonic tumult, as Rodrigo reverts to his beloved bitonality already on display in the Preludio of the *Suite para piano*. Contrasting key signatures bear immediate witness to this dissonant procedure: the right hand has one sharp, and the left, six sharps! This bitonal ambience prevails throughout the piece, and the vignette concludes with a G-major triad in the right hand against the left hand's F#-major chord. Thus, neither key ever gains the upper hand, resulting in the effective absence of a tonal center. He also reprieves the texture of the earlier Preludio, with an interlocking pattern between right and left hands in which the left is a sixteenth note after the right.

This separation of the hands by a half beat is the rhythmic equivalent of the half-step separation of the tonal centers, G major in the right and F# major in the left (or later E minor juxtaposed with D# minor). His predilection for symmetrical scales, something inherited from the Impressionists, appears in rapid passages featuring the octatonic scale, in which half and whole steps alternate. If one had to reduce Rodrigo's harmonic procedures to a single interval at this point in his career, it would be the second, major or minor. This preference has its basis not only in the evolution of harmony in Western music, from the fifths of the Classical period to thirds in the Romantic and to seconds in the twentieth century, but it may also reflect the fact that for the blind composer, executing lines that were a second apart and thus kept the hands close together was simply more natural. From a strictly performative standpoint, "The seconds are easier to feel on the piano, as Rodrigo would not be able to see the keys. The topography of white key versus black key may have been an easier way for him to feel the keyboard."[38]

Musical ex. 2.3a: *Preludio al gallo mañanero,*
Rooster theme, mm. 13–19

Musical ex. 2.3b: *Preludio al gallo mañanero,* Hen theme, mm. 56–57

There is a typically neoclassical tendency toward organicism and economy in Rodrigo's use of melodic materials. There is nothing very lyrical or expansive in such an approach, but there are descriptive thematic ideas that he skillfully develops. After the rooster has had his boisterous say, the *gallina*, or hen, makes her debut. Her "leitmotiv" is not quite as strident as the rooster's, but it is nonetheless vivacious. As a secondary character in this drama, her time in the spotlight is less, and the dominant avian soon reasserts himself. Though these two themes dominate the work, its formal layout is susceptible to a variety of interpretations. Martín Colinet posits three possibilities: a sonata form, but with B before A in the recapitulation; da capo form, ABA; or an arch form, ABCBA, plus development and a coda.[39] Jones prefers an ABA'CB'D-coda scheme.[40]

In any case, a coda highlights the rooster's exclamation, climaxing on a triumphant cock-a-doodle-doo, indicated by the composer as "Papa gallo, lanza su terrible quiquiriquí." This "reveille" may have been intended as a musical metaphor for an army barracks in a period of assertive militarism. For it was in September 1925 that a victorious landing in Alhucemas finally brought an end to the ruinous Moroccan War. Be that as it may, a concussive clash of chords, G major in the right hand against F♯ major in the left, brings these birdbrained high jinks to a clucking conclusion.

Jones perceives another bird in this barnyard, and that is Rodrigo's beloved cuckoo, whose distinctive descending-third call gradually emerges in mm. 130–142.[41] Though musical depictions of the morning rooster and the hen dominate the scene, with the apparent intrusion of a cuckoo, the composer himself asserted that "various other animals also receive mention, some of them quite rare, without the author knowing exactly what they are (ornithologists have studied them but have not yet ascertained their identities)."[42]

Rodrigo described this piece using the adjective *punzante*, biting or stinging.[43] This is the effect that his persistent use of the major/minor seconds has, in both its harmonic, bitonal sense and also its appearance in note clusters, cross relations, and symmetrical scales. All of these modernistic gestures might leave one wondering if there is any musical suggestion here of the birds' nationality, assuming that they are Spanish. Various commentators, principally Jones, perceive a possible hint of the *tarantas* rhythm in the rooster's theme, while the hen's rhythm suggests a similarity to the *seguidilla*.[44] Martín Colinet expanded on these possibilities by proposing not only the *tarantas* and *seguidillas* as feasible sources of inspiration but also the *guajiras* and *tanguillo*.[45] The composer himself had nothing to say on that subject. The folkloric connection is very subtle, if present at all. The 6/8 meter and use of hemiola are common to many Spanish songs and dances, but not exclusive to them. The same must be said of Phrygian cadences, which could also suggest a Baroque gigue. This aspect of the score may well resemble a sort of Rorschach test, in which we will see what we expect to see. This piece, with its undeniably neoclassical imprimatur, represents Rodrigo's flight from both Andalusian and Impressionist styles.

The Orchestral Debut: *Juglares* (1923–24)

But before works as modern, strong, and full of character as *Suite para piano, Berceuse d'automne,* and *Preludio al gallo mañanero* inaugurated his catalogue and gave such brilliant material form to his concerns, aims, and affects, Rodrigo had presented himself before Valencian music lovers with an initial dose of modernity. This was a "symphonic essay" (a *scherzo,* as López-Chavarri would christen it, to make it more palatable) entitled *Juglares,* a word that refers to wandering minstrels and entertainers during the Middle Ages. The best one-word translation in English is actually the French equivalent, *jongleurs.* He orchestrated it, with noticeable changes from a piano piece excluded from the catalogue titled *Juglares: Impresiones de una farándula que pasó* (Jongleurs: Impressions of a Troupe of Entertainers That Passed By). An undated manuscript of the piano piece survives, signed by "Sanchis," a professional copyist who inscribed in ink some of Rodrigo's compositions from this period. The orchestral version, entitled *Juglares: Ensayo sinfónico* (Jongleurs: Symphonic Essay), debuted Sunday evening, 20 July 1924, in the municipal gardens of the Viveros, where the recently formed Orquesta Valenciana (Valencian Orchestra) performed it under the baton of José Manuel Izquierdo, an outstanding local violinist who had trained with the Orquesta Filarmónica (Philharmonic Orchestra) of Madrid.[46] Both Gomá, for his column in the *Diario de Valencia,* and López-Chavarri, for his in *Las Provincias,* carefully reflected on Rodrigo's public debut. As Gomá wrote,

> On the program appeared [. . .] *Juglares,* by Rodrigo, the
> young composer (blind, to be sure, like the unfortunate
> Francisco Cuesta), who with kindly sincerity professes
> his taste for sharp harmonic neologisms and for musical

expressions in the latest fashion, which this is not the time to judge, but which reveal from the start that its author carries a watch "set at European time." It will be necessary to take into account the future production of young Rodrigo, whose sensitivity does not seem to be absent.[47]

After raising the possibility that—quite apart from what had been heard in concert—Rodrigo was perhaps a sensitive person, the critic passed to the next paragraph to judge with complete satisfaction two works by Francisco Cuesta, *Danza valenciana* and *Orientales*, interpreted in the same concert, without sparing praise for Cuesta: "a creator who evinced that he was one of the most talented musicians that Valencia has produced."[48] Despite the fact that Rodrigo always counted Gomá among his dearest friends, the column devoted to this public premiere leaves no doubt about the critic's thinking or about his preferences.

After Gomá's critique, the daily newspaper *El Pueblo* referred to *Juglares* as an "attempt at orchestral composing with a view to ultramodernism."[49] That very day López-Chavarri published an article wholly devoted to Rodrigo:

A youth [. . .] who with his music *truly* displays himself brilliantly. [. . .] Rodrigo, distinguished spirit, eager to hold a good position in the avant-garde, premiered last Sunday an original *scherzo* titled *Juglares*: the humor, the indiscipline, the disorderly joy under which there appears a throbbing of melancholy, perhaps of pain, was ably expressed musically by Rodrigo with singular success. It was music, to be sure, like the pages of our admired Carlos Esplá; perhaps also those of Max and Alex Fischer [. . .], but always youthful, restless, searching. His harmonic audacities, his *blurrings*, are products of youthful energy; more than acts of daring, these often turn out to be innocent mischief-making.[50]

While Gomá took a distant stance toward the debut of *Juglares* and aligned himself with his reactionary reading public,

López-Chavarri defended the work without reservations, situating it within well-informed aesthetic coordinates and trying to justify, understand, and even make it comprehensible. Since friends like Gomá displayed so many misgivings, it is easy to imagine how the conservative members—indeed, the majority—of Valencian music lovers most likely received *Juglares*. These things usually leave no historical trace, but some years later, when López-Chavarri communicated to his readers Rodrigo's successes in Paris, he did not fail to recall how, in these first moments of his career, "stupidity and ill will so strongly came out to greet him, now in the form of ignorant critiques, now in the form of know-it-all advice, now in the mockery of practical people."[51]

With *Juglares*, Rodrigo came onstage—he showed himself to the audience—as a jongleur of the people, and it is very possible that as this work was gestating in his imagination, he had in mind a small article by the eminent republican politician Álvaro de Albornoz, published in *El Pueblo* in March 1924, in which he portrayed the jongleur as follows:

> He was a rogue whose job was the humble one of
> producing laughter. In feudal residences, in courts, in the
> public square, he played his farce or made his pirouettes.
> The leap, the funny face, the pun were the devices of
> his agility and his ingenuity. He showed up at weddings
> and christenings, he insinuated himself into public
> celebrations as well as into private parties. These lowly
> jongleurs were the buffoons of the people.[52]

This bittersweet reading of Rodrigo redeems the character of the jongleur from any baseness and presents, on the one hand, the festivity of the people and, on the other, the inner life of the entertainer.

In *Juglares*, Rodrigo once again uses music as a means of describing an exterior world that he can only imagine and not actually see. Yet, his "vision" is always remarkably evocative and convincing, and no more so than in this unpretentious work of some five minutes in duration. It was composed in 1923, the same year as *Dos esbozos* and *Suite para piano*, and premiered the following year in its orchestral version; he also made a reduction for piano four hands, an arrangement neglected among his manuscripts until it was resurrected years later by the piano duo of Miguel Zanetti and Fernando Turina, who revised and recorded it.

This work first reveals to us, unlike its contemporaries from that year or the subsequent four-hand version, Rodrigo's nascent legerdemain as an orchestrator, influenced by his idol Ravel. The young Spaniard deploys a colorful orchestral palette to paint this scene, and the ensuing prominence of percussion, double reeds, and trumpets evokes musical sounds that would accompany juggling and other crowd-pleasing capers in a medieval setting, out of doors where the racket they produced was guaranteed to attract an audience.

The work's structure is correspondingly direct and unambiguous, in ABA form with an allegro A section and a contrastingly lyrical and slow B section. The piece begins with an "announcement" in the snare drums, followed by muted horns over *tremolando* strings, and then a festively jaunty melody in the clarinet (musical ex. 2.4), soon shared with the flute and oboe. At points there are strangely dissonant *tutti* interjections that suddenly roll in like fog off the Valencian coast.

If the piece had an enigmatic title like Prelude, for instance, would the music suggest to us jongleurs or some other outdoor entertainment? Probably not. The highly introspective middle section is itself an enigma in this context and forms yet another example of Rodrigo using extramusical associations as a means for revealing his interior life, one of placid yet at times disquieting introspection. Far from ending with the anticipated bang, the music dissipates into nothing, as if it had never been.

Nonetheless, as the composer himself indicated in his subtitle, "Symphonic Essay," *Juglares* was hardly more than a rehearsal of what was to come. Moreover, even though it lacks a fanfare finale, it was a work that Rodrigo very probably conceived for

Musical ex. 2.4: *Juglares*, mm. 13–20

performance outdoors, as the Valencian Orchestra in the Munici-pal Gardens would once more put it on their program during the following concert season.[53] The very cursory notice in *Diario de Valencia* of a performance on 18 July 1925 hints that the public could not digest this music, given the social ambience in which those concerts took place: "The stay in the Gardens turned out to be pleasant, with friendly, more or less audible music [. . .] and in the presence of so many pretty girls."[54] The following year, Manuel Palau penned the following observations about its third summer performance: "*Juglares,* by Rodrigo, is the work

Honorary mention in the National Music Prize of 1925

with which the treasured composer came to light over a year ago. Melodic ideas of a supreme aristocracy, *up-to-date* harmonization, and a formal concision that seems distinctive in Joaquín Rodrigo's production strengthen *Juglares* to situate its author in an eminent place among our young composers."[55]

However, *Juglares* was already to a great degree passé, because Rodrigo had pushed his career forward with his second orchestral composition, *Cinco piezas infantiles*, with which he had presented himself at the National Music Contest of 1924–25 and won an honorable mention from the jury.

When Trains Collide: López-Chavarri versus Adolfo Salazar

On 10 July 1924, the *Gaceta de Madrid* published a Royal Decree convoking the National Contest of Music for the the term 1924–25. Open to musicians from Spain, Portugal, South America, and the Philippines, on this occasion it proposed two themes: either a work for orchestra with a prize of 4,000 pesetas, or a collection of songs with piano or orchestral accompaniment with a prize of 2,000 pesetas. Scores would be judged by a very distinguished jury: conductor Bartolomé Pérez Casas, chair; composer Óscar Esplá, secretary; Manuel de Falla, Adolfo Salazar, and Facundo de la Viña, spokesmen. Judging from the deliberations of the jury, from which Falla withdrew at the last minute,[56] the entries were numerous. It was decided to award the prize for symphonic composition to the *Sinfonietta* of Ernesto Halffter, with an honorable mention to *En un barco fenicio* by Jesús Guridi; *Dos impresiones sinfónicas* by Julián Bautista; *Preludio y romanza* by Julio Gómez; and *Cinco piezas infantiles* by Joaquín Rodrigo.

Although the jury was unanimous in its decisions, the large number of honorable mentions was clearly meant to signal that its selections had not been easy to make. It must also have struggled to maintain a degree of independence within the small world of Spanish symphonic composers, all of whom knew one another. Indeed, the succeeding announcement of the National Prize for Music specified that the names of those constituting the jury would be kept secret until its final decisions became public.[57] The awarding of this prize also makes it clear that within the ranks of the younger composers, those from Madrid—Ernesto Halffter and Julián Bautista—and those from the Levante—Rodrigo and

Rodríguez Albert—had the greatest muscle. In reality, those from Madrid had shown their strength and their influence from the first competition for those prizes (1922–23). But the appearance of Rodrigo and Rodríguez Albert in the contest of 1924–25 did not pass unnoticed by a critic so attentive and involved in the development of the Spanish musical avant-garde as Adolfo Salazar. After celebrating as outspokenly as possible the success of his pupil, Ernesto Halffter, he devoted one of his influential columns in the daily *El Sol* to revealing the perplexity that the Valencian musician aroused in him.

Salazar's article is central to understanding the Spanish musical avant-garde of the 1920s and the reception of Rodrigo's work in that context. He situates the young musical renovators in the main sectors of bourgeois and industrial power of those years—Madrid, Catalonia, the Basque Country, and the Levante—thereby omitting an Andalusia that was backwards in socioeconomic terms. It turns out to be very meaningful that, of these regions, the first that attracted his attention after Madrid was the Levante. This surely resulted from his experience on the jury of the First National Prize of Music, 1924–25, through which he became familiar with the music of Rodríguez Albert as well as of young Rodrigo, whose photograph appeared in *El Sol*:

> I have no reason to hide among my notes—as a
> spokesman of that jury—that the terms of greatest
> praise and the most favorable opinions mostly refer
> to musicians of whom I had never heard until then.
> One of them, Joaquín Rodrigo, signed a curious score:
> *Cinco piezas infantiles*. It was curious for an assortment
> of details that I would not be able to define except in
> technical language and adding a strange thing to the
> delicious terms in which that work was conceived: a
> spirit full of youth and freshness, a naïveté of procedures
> both original and denoting influences of the finest taste,
> a clarity and spiritual joy full of attractiveness.[58]

Further on, Salazar indicates his surprise after making Rodrigo's acquaintance and realizing that he was blind:

> For musicians who well know that "reading" a modern
> score is as indispensable as listening to it, let them
> imagine the effort of imagination, enthusiasm, and
> hope of this poor blind boy, who, for I don't know what
> admirable gifts of guesswork, comes to "realize," to
> "learn" the most complex and subtle modern scores.
> Especially let this be taken into account when one lives,
> as does Rodrigo, in a province that, though cultivated,
> cannot gain exposure to all the ideas and modern music
> that a person might desire.[59]

This review was anything but favorable to Rodrigo: "poor blind boy," cornered into a provincial periphery where cultural innovations would never arrive; his *Cinco piezas infantiles* were a "rare thing," "curious," "a denoter of influences," and not ingenious but rather ingenuous in procedure. Further, Salazar wrote something more unnecessary and more unnecessarily ambiguous regarding Rodrigo: "He went off to Germany, and there continued the expansion of his musical spirit, while wise doctors tortured him physically . . . , without the least result." Without the least result of what? The tortures or the expansion of his musical spirit? The comma after the ellipsis implies the latter. Eduardo López-Chavarri, a critic himself and a reader who readily perceived Salazar's innuendo, immediately sallied forth to rebut him with an article published in *Las Provincias*, in which he contested the centralist vision of Salazar and his obsession with the latest fad:

> I greatly mistrust that aesthetics that only applauds
> what is new because it is "the newest thing," because
> it is what is "worn now . . . ," a bourgeois, feminine
> criterion that makes us ask, Are we in the life of Art
> or in the home of a modest dressmaker? Narrowness,
> narrowness of horizons characterizes an aesthetics that

cannot transcend, however much it might want to, the
implacable limits that the barren plain surrounding
Madrid imposes! [. . .] Let us deplore the error with
respect to *backwards* provincialism (always the criterion
of the little dressmaker!), and let us say that, precisely
because of the sea, we [Valencians] are closer to all places
than the center [Madrid] can be![60]

The Valencian critic does not fail to contribute to the most
common criticism leveled against Salazar: that of doing everything in his power to favor Ernesto Halffter, as opposed to the
other musicians of his generation, especially Rodrigo, who was
not yet 25 years of age. The critic condemned them all to play
a subordinate role in the face of the absolute leadership of a
Halffter who was prematurely celebrated, snobbish, and finally, a
wastrel. In this fashion, López-Chavarri established his inclusive
vision of the Levantine musical tradition and rejected the views
of Salazar, who had already decided that, after Falla, the great
Spanish musician was Ernesto Halffter:

God forbid that I should make predictions; God forbid me
from trying to arouse the vanity of the young artist by
praising him only because he writes works in the modern
style; how, then, would a true musical temperament
write them? It is necessary to praise Rodrigo, the same
as Palau was praised, the same as the unfortunate Paco
[Francisco] Cuesta was praised; for all of them carry in
their souls the authentic gift of music.[61]

Salazar did not respond. He would add López-Chavarri's
name to the list of his adversaries, and he remained intransi-
gent. But this incident displayed his bewilderment in the face
of a work that perhaps might put in jeopardy the National Prize
awarded to Halffter's *Sinfonietta*. At that time, Rodrigo periodi-
cally traveled to Madrid, and everything seems to indicate that,
in his passion for avant-garde music, he tried to approach Salazar and Halffter, because he dedicated to them, respectively, the

Minué and Bourrée of his *Suite para piano*. The critic published his chronicle devoted to Rodrigo in which, speaking of his works, he said that he had written several "little pieces" for piano, among them a *Prelude* and a series of three little works: *Siciliana*, *Bourrée*, and *Minueto*, "which is almost the one I prefer for its soft fragrance that smacks of Fauré and Ravel, its sweet inflexion, and its distinguished fabrication, products of a fine, select soul."[62] Although Salazar never helped the aspiring composer in any way or offered him any constructive criticism, instead simply brushing him aside, Rodrigo never regretted his dedication of this piece to Salazar.

The premiere of the *Cinco piezas infantiles* was delayed until 16 February 1927, when the Orquesta Sinfónica de Valencia, conducted by José Manuel Izquierdo, finally presented them at the Teatro Principal. According to the composer's program notes for this auspicious occasion,

> These very short five pieces have no pre-established program. They are fleeting suggestions without importance, in which a healthy humor joins a merry confidence. No. 1, "They are boys passing by." This is a brief rondo with an alert, mischievous air, in which is heard trumpet calls and drum rolls; No. 2, "After a story." A vaguely nostalgic page, in which there remain distant echoes of fairies and enchanted princes; No. 3, "Mazurka." Simply a mazurka, in which children beautifully dance. No. 4, "Prayer." This is the naïve prayer of a child before bed; No. 5, "Final clamor." The children, now almost grown, become excited, play, are frisky, and have fun. It is a joy to watch them. Siegfried's Dragon wants to frighten them but to no avail. Even face to face with him, they would no doubt begin to play soccer.[63]

Rodrigo sometimes arranged his own works for different media. Even as he was writing for the piano, he clearly had other sonorities in mind, particularly those of the orchestra. Even when he composed for the guitar, he saw the potential for creating an arrangement for orchestra or keyboard. In the case of his *Cinco piezas infantiles*, though he conceived the work for orchestra, he soon made a version for two pianos.

Composing a set of short musical vignettes inspired by childhood also had abundant precedent. Schumann's *Kinderszenen* for piano served as the prototype for Enrique Granados's *Cuentos de juventud*; Rodrigo was no doubt familiar with both works, and now, in his relative infancy as a composer, he set out to contribute to this time-honored genre. In the manner of an eighteenth-century suite, the general alternation of tempos is fast-slow-fast-slow-fast, providing a satisfying symmetry.

Rodrigo's distinctive style is already evident in these early compositions. No matter what we may say about the various influences operating on his development, his works can never be accused of mere imitation. Moreover, his programmatic works are most remarkable not for what they convey about the things he is describing but rather for the window they provide into his own musical personality, which will remain consistent throughout his career. This personality combines in equal measure a penchant for humor, at times cutting and even boisterous, with a deeply introspective tendency, an intimate interiority at once emotionally placid and intense.

As Wade points out, the orchestral version of these pieces reveals "brilliant handling of orchestral colour," and a gift for orchestration thus manifests early in his catalogue.[64] This gift is especially useful in the first movement, which evokes the sounds of children at play, amusing themselves with toy soldiers, which in turn require martial noises of a percussive kind. The principal melody is similarly noisy and has a kind of "nyah-nyah" quality, characterized as it is by both short motivic outbursts and elemental, downbeat-heavy rhythms. The thematic ideas in this movement often exhibit an infantile character in their narrow range and simple, quarter-note-dominated rhythms. Iglesias finds this true in a theme that emerges in the second section (mm. 57–85;

Musical ex. **2.5:** *Cinco piezas infantiles*,
"Son chicos que pasan," mm. 57–62

musical ex. 2.5), as it reminded him of a "canción de corro infan-
til," or a sort of "ring around the rosey" song.[65] This has led Wade
and others to perceive the influence of Stravinsky's *Petrushka*
ballet, with a similar sort of repetition of simple, narrow-range
motives.[66] However, Rodrigo's *Cinco piezas infantiles* reveal the
influence of Ravel's 1922 orchestration of Mussorgsky's *Pictures
at an Exhibition*, which not only served as a model for his instrumentation but also provided actual melodic material. "Son chicos
que pasan" is remarkably similar to "Tuileries" by Mussorgsky,
whose rendering of the racket of children playing in the prome-
nade of a park corresponds to Rodrigo's piece.

"Después de un cuento" suggests the calm following the
storm, a calm brought on by the reading of a story and subsequent thoughtful repose. The very first measures feature Rodrigo's signature "cuckoo" motive of a descending third, though
this cuckoo is in a relaxed state and sings its song softly and in
long notes. The motive will recur throughout the movement. The
harp adds magical color in this scene, woven into a texture of
gently tremolando strings and overarching melodies enfolding
the peaceful activity.

But this mood cannot last for long, and it is soon supplanted by
a "Mazurka" depicting a conflict between a boy doll and a girl doll,
the first preferring a duple-meter march rhythm, which is incompatible with the triple-meter rhythm of the Polish mazurka. The
strident back-and-forth between rhythms and themes has a comical effect, spiced with Rodrigo's disinfectant harmonies. There was
a similar sort of inter-gender confrontation between the rooster
and hen in *Preludio al gallo mañanero*. The piece is laid out in a very
symmetrical part form, ABACA-coda. All of this commotion can
mean only one thing, though, and that is that bedtime has arrived.

Marked "slowly with simplicity," "Plegaria" reminds one of Jesus's assertion that children are the stuff of which heaven is made (Matthew 19:14). Yet, there is a vein of melancholy in this music, a vein never far from the colorful, at times riotous, surface of Rodrigo's art. The wistful sound of the clarinet introduces a melody remarkable for its shortwinded simplicity and flat melodic contour, the result of note repetition, which strongly suggests the verbal repetitions characteristic of many prayers. The ABA layout of the movement further adds to its affective directness.

However, the collection ends with a bang and not a whimper, with the "Gritería final." In a cyclic gesture, Rodrigo reprises the march theme from the third movement to suggest the irrepressible impulse to misbehave common among children. Indeed, the word *gritería* comes from the Spanish *gritar*, "to shout," and the Real Academia Española defines it as "a confusion of high and out-of-tune voices." When Rodrigo was not praying, he was shouting. One suspects that at times he could do both simultaneously. Energetic rhythms evoke juvenile playground antics, while the dissonant clash of many voices fills the air. The formal plan of ABACA-coda suggests great variety and elaboration, but instead the music is as condensed as it is impressive.

From a programmatic standpoint, these disparate scenes are united only by their focus on childhood. But they are not an otherwise scattershot assortment of subjects but are in fact tied together by a cleverly overarching tonal design. True, the movements exhibit different tonalities, but with the exception of "Plegaria," all of them revolve around F♯ in varied ways. The first piece is in D major, though it is without a key signature and features an important section in D Dorian. However, it begins and ends with a very dissonant juxtaposition of F♯ and F♮. The second piece starts from the interval of the descending major third, which characterized so decisively the first piece, and unfolds in F♯ Mixolydian, with the corresponding key signature of five sharps. The Mazurka is in D major, thoroughly saturated with dissonances, but it concludes with a stubborn repetition of F♯. "Plegaria" acts as an interlude outside this tonal scheme. "Gritería final" is a conclusion in F♯ minor, and its last chord repeats the minor-second clash with which the first piece began and ended.

The critical reception of these insouciant vignettes reflected the tensions that much new music generated among the public and the critics of Valencia. Hence, Bernardo Morales Sanmartín, under the pseudonym of "Fidelio," hastened to confess his distaste: "We would be insincere and would not agree with the spirit of our musical chronicles in which we have condemned the imitation of ultramodernist musicians, if we did not say that we are sincerely sorry to find ourselves face to face with a new case of foreign influences on our young musicians."[67] It is scarcely conceivable to us now, in the wake of the postwar avant-garde, that these charming little pieces could have ruffled any critical feathers, especially considering that 1927 was the year in which Schoenberg's String Quartet No. 3, Op. 30, was composed, as well as Webern's String Trio, Op. 20. This was only a year after Berg's *Lyric Suite* saw the light of day. Rodrigo's music was by no means atonal, much less serial.

Somewhat more favorable was the critique published in *El Pueblo* by Salvador Ariño, a prudent, well-informed man, who made knowing reference to the meeting of the International Society of Contemporary Music that had taken place in Zurich in June 1926. Still, he had conservative tastes in music and saw fit to deride the final piece by labeling it "Gritería infernal" ("Infernal clamor") instead of "Gritería final" ("Final clamor"):

Avant-garde music, as is said nowadays, did not convince everyone, naturally. The author of this chronicle, frankly, did not find the work as a whole unpleasant, especially when he expected a copy of what was the last Meeting of Modern Music in Zurich: a piece lasting the length of a yawn, with four chords and lacking any melodic idea. No, in the blind man Rodrigo there is a certain emotion ("Son chicos que pasan," "Mazurka")[. . .]. The "Infernal clamor" seemed to us piecemeal, perhaps reconcilable for technicians, but not at all attainable for the masses.[68]

From the debut of *Juglares* in 1924 to the premiere of the *Cinco piezas infantiles* three years later, Rodrigo firmly maintained his status as a *provocateur* and *enfant terrible* of Valencian music, both in public and in more private circles. Yet this was not a pose but rather an inborn orientation that Palau tried to present positively when, with respect to the final debut, he wrote, "I don't say that there are no modern composers who cease to complicate their writing to *épater les bourgeois* (allow me the Gallicism). But I sincerely appreciate present-day music and know Rodrigo well enough not to doubt his sincerity, always present when he composes."[69]

Finally, the critic of *Las Provincias*—surely López-Chavarri, although this time the column appears unsigned—once again showed his unswerving enthusiam for Rodrigo's music by underscoring "the exquisite sensitivity of its author" and his "very felicitous instinct to handle the timbres of the orchestra." He remarked that "although the reading of the work in the score makes the hair stand on end for its strange harmonies," once it is heard, "everything vanishes and there arises a very luminous work, one of an artist."[70]

What is certain is that, despite his detractors, Rodrigo felt obliged to salute from the proscenium while he received an effusive ovation from the public.

Falla in Valencia, 1925

For Valencia's music lovers, a rapprochement with the avant-garde was facilitated by Manuel de Falla's visit to the city in early 1925 for the Spanish debut of the staged version of his neoclassical puppet opera *El retablo de maese Pedro* (Master Peter's Puppet Show), performed by the Orquesta Bética de Cámara (Seville Chamber Orchestra) under the baton of Ernesto Halffter. First they presented the concert version at the Teatro Principal on February 2, and two days later the Valencian press hailed "the premiere in Spain of the full representation of the *Retablo*, that is to say, with puppets and with all the breadth that the author conceived for such an exceedingly beautiful score of music."[71] Nobody remained indifferent to this musical event. Some understood it more and some less, but no one questioned the authority of Falla or his neoclassical style.

For Joaquín Rodrigo, acquaintance with the *Retablo* had a greater impact even than *Rigoletto* years before, not to mention harpsichordist Wanda Landowska and pianist Ricardo Viñes. It was a new milestone in his memory, and he said so in writing:

> That premiere was an event in my life. I still recall and will always recall the intense emotion I felt when listening to that music, so new, so original, so embedded in our history, and opening a new and broad road to Spanish music. The Orquesta Bética, that amenable orchestra founded by Falla, debuted it under the direction of Ernesto Halffter, still very young. For this reason, Falla spent some days in Valencia. Nevertheless, I did not meet Don Manuel on that occasion; my timidity hindered me, although it was justified, and I was sorry about it time and again, since without it, perhaps, I would have gone to Granada to work with him.[72]

Rodrigo's discovery of the *Retablo* coincided with his creation of the first art song that he included in his catalogue, *Cantiga: Muy graciosa es la doncella*, on a poem by the pre-Renaissance poet Gil Vicente (ca. 1465–1536). This song inaugurates not only a profusion of inspired vocal works from his pen but also introduces a style trait that will characterize his works in this genre, the almost complete disappearance of the piano at certain moments. As a result, the accompaniment is thrown into relief, achieving extraordinary efficacy in characterizing the three individuals who appear in the strophes of the ditty: the knight, the sailor, and the shepherd. In particular, Rodrigo very effectively represents the sea with a limping rhythm that recalls that of "La Carpe" from *Le Bestiaire* (1919) of Francis Poulenc, which Rodrigo could have heard among the musical illustrations of Prunière's lectures at the Valencia Conservatory.[73]

One comment that Rodrigo made about Falla's puppet opera could perfectly apply to this song of his, so close in its inception to *El retablo de maese Pedro*: "The musical style, in its sobriety, consists of a mixture of archaism and novelty that Spanish music had never known, and this work paved the way for composers to continue."[74]

Cantiga: Muy graciosa es la doncella was first composed as a stand-alone work and only later incorporated into a group of songs entitled *Canciones de dos épocas*. Gil Vicente was a dramatist and poet of Portuguese birth who wrote forty-four plays in both Portuguese and Spanish, or some combination of the two.[75] "Muy graciosa es la doncella" was a *villancico* (at that time a theatrical song) from his Spanish-language drama *Auto da Sibila Casandra* (ca. 1513?). Rodrigo, ever the devotee of fine literature, especially drama, exhibited very refined taste in choosing this particular text to modify for use in this composition.

Like the songs *Romance de la infantina de Francia* (1928) and *Serranilla* (1928), this setting features a female protagonist. It has a popular air about it and harkens back to the troubadour songs of the Middle Ages in its blending of the rustic and the divine.[76] In fact, the focus of the song's attention is on the Virgin Mary herself, and this theme, as well as Rodrigo's title, are reminiscent of the thirteenth-century *Cantigas de Santa María*, compiled during the reign of Castilian king Alfonso X, "The Wise." Those monophonic medieval songs were melodious meditations on the virtues of the Virgin and the marvelous miracles she performs on behalf of those who appeal to her. Rodrigo's inveterate historicism is once again on display, influenced by the teachings of musicologist and composer Felipe Pedrell (1841–1922), the patriarch of Spanish musical nationalism who promoted Spain's great legacy of literature and music as the proper wellspring from which Spanish composers should draw inspiration.

Rodrigo was not the only creative artist to have found these verses attractive. In 1835, the American poet Henry Wadsworth Longfellow rendered his own translation, perhaps the first in English and an eloquent tribute to Gil Vicente:

She is a maid of artless grace,
Gentle in form, and fair of face.

Tell me, thou ancient mariner,
    That sailest on the sea,
If ship, or sail, or evening star
    Be half as fair as she!

Tell me, thou gallant cavalier,
    Whose shining arms I see,
If steed, or sword, or battlefield
    Be half so fair as she!

Tell me, thou swain, that guard'st thy flock
    Beneath the shadowy tree,
If flock, or vale, or mountain-ridge
    Be half so fair as she![77]

The short little poem ranges over a very wide area, embracing such far-flung themes as warfare, oceans, mountains, and valleys. Where in this wide world could one hope to find any thing, place, activity, or person as enchantingly beautiful as the fair Virgin herself? Yet, as seductive as the composer found this text and its message, he took conspicuous liberties with the poem by rearranging its stanzas. The poem itself is laid out in a refrain form, and after the initial couplet, each of the succeeding three strophes ends with the *estribillo* "es tan bella." Rodrigo adheres to a varied-strophic design in setting this poem but utilizes only the first line of the opening couplet, "Muy graciosa es la doncella," discarding the second line, "¡cómo es bella y hermosa!" This opening line then serves as the refrain, instead of "es tan bella."

It is not at all clear why he suppresses the second line of the opening *estribillo*, especially because the succeeding refrain, "es tan bella," is derived from and a direct reference to it. It is not indispensable to the meaning, but in the opinion of Gallego, the "religious connotation" of the poem is lost, as the "graceful maiden so beautiful and precious" is Mary herself after giving birth to the baby Jesus.[78] Perhaps Rodrigo had some other maiden in mind? Not content to limit himself to this modification in the poem, Rodrigo alters the arrangement of the strophes

TABLE 3.1 *Cantiga: Muy graciosa es la doncella*

Original version by Gil Vicente	Rodrigo's adaptation	Modern English translation of Rodrigo's adaptation
Muy graciosa es la doncella ¡cómo es bella y hermosa! Digas tú, el marinero que en las naves vivías, si la nave o la vela o la estrella es tan bella.	Muy graciosa es la doncella. Digas tú, el caballero que las armas vestías si el caballo o las armas o la Guerra es tan bella.	Very graceful is the maiden. Tell me, knight, You who are adorned with weapons, If the horse or the weapons Or the war is so beautiful.
Digas tú, el caballero que las armas vestías, si el caballo o las armas o la Guerra es tan bella.	Muy graciosa es la doncella Digas tú, el marinero que en las naves vivías, si la nave o la vela o la estrella es tan bella.	Very graceful is the maiden Tell me, sailor, You who live in ships, If the ship or the candle or the star is so beautiful.
Digas tú, el pastorcico que el ganadico guardas si el Ganado o los valles o la sierra es tan bella.	Muy graciosa es la doncella Digas tú, el pastorcico que el ganadico guardas si el ganado o los valles o la sierra es tan bella.	Very graceful is the maiden Tell me, shepherd, You who guard the flock, If the flock or the valleys Or the mountain is so beautiful.
	Muy graciosa es la doncella	Very graceful is the maiden

themselves, so that the sequence is knight-sailor-shepherd and not sailor-knight-shepherd. It could well be that he modifies the music for each strophe in order to convey its meaning, and he wanted the song to end with the "shepherd" because that subject called for the least dramatic setting, allowing the piece to end as quietly as it began. There is thus a symmetrical affective arch, extending from the unassuming beginning to the pastoral calm of the concluding measures (see table 3.1).

Rodrigo's musical language is concise yet rich in detail. The opening half couplet cum refrain is a vocal incipit without the piano—the sort of monophonic invocation typical of the original *cantigas*. The ensuing piano part is notable for its sparseness, with brief chordal interjections between lines of the strophe. His antiquarian penchant extends to the harmonic language, which is modal, starting in C♯ Aeolian as a sort of "dominant" preparation for F♯ Aeolian. The alternation of modes between ritornello and strophe will continue throughout, until the final F♯-minor chord. In this way, Rodrigo synthesizes the past and the present, by blending archaic modality with very modern harmonic procedures and subtle shifts in meter and rhythm.[79]

What most intrigues here is the formal design. Rodrigo utilizes a varied-strophic layout in which the melody remains the same but the accompaniment changes to meet the descriptive requirements of each strophe. The knight's setting is appropriately solemn and austere. Nonharmonic tones and nonfunctional

Musical ex. 2.6a: *Cantiga, "Muy graciosa es la doncella,"* Knight variation of main melody, mm. 9–14

Musical ex. 2.6b: *Cantiga, "Muy graciosa es la doncella,"*
Sailor variation of main melody, mm. 30–36

Musical ex. 2.6c: *Cantiga, "Muy graciosa es la doncella,"*
Shepherd variation of main melody, mm. 47–50

harmonies provide the musical interest to hold our attention. The sailor's strophe exhibits rhythmic nuances suggestive of a barcarole. The pedal notes and ostinatos of the shepherd's strophe create a pastoral mood. The piece concludes with a final unadorned iteration of its opening, invoking the graceful maiden (musical exx. 2.6a–c). The restrained and subtle pathos of this song, its unobtrusive poignance, impart to it the sort of graceful beauty that the text ascribes to the Virgin herself. It remains among his finest vocal confections.

Cantiga: Muy graciosa es la doncella initiated a group of important pieces completed in the ensuing years and forming a kind of miniature play, with the *Serranilla* of 1928, on a poem by the Marquis of Santillana, Íñigo López de Mendoza, and the *Romance de la Infantina de Francia*, also composed before 1928. On one occasion, these were grouped by Rodrigo into the *Tres canciones sobre textos castellanos*. Federico Sopeña had already suggested the possibility of such a play,[80] and Antonio Gallego found support for this idea in the existence, within the first incarnation of Rodrigo's works, of a *Pavana para la Infantina del Romance*.[81] Two copies of this piece have surfaced among the uncatalogued drafts in the Archivo de la Fundación Victoria y Joaquín Rodrigo. One of them is full of blots but bears the handwritten signature of Rodrigo, assisted by the hand of Eduardo López-Chavarri. The *Pavana* contains only seventeen measures and exhibits a sort of incidental quality. It may not have been intended by its creator as a fully autonomous work but instead as part of the *Romance de la Infantina de Francia*.

Finally, in this same style we include the *Zarabanda lejana* for solo guitar of 1926, though it is definitely a stand-alone work. Among his best-loved creations, it has traditionally been regarded as his first composition for that instrument and, like his first songs, a masterful initiation of the most celebrated and renowned aspect of his output, music for the guitar. So pleased was he with this composition that he soon thereafter set about crafting a transcription of it for piano, and later an arrangement for orchestra, to which he added a second piece, *Villancico*. We will have more to say about this pivotal work in the succeeding chapter.

However, Rodrigo did not start his guitar catalogue in such a successful way. In fact, there was a previous and failed attempt to contribute to the instrument's repertoire, one that has remained in obscurity until now. This returns us to the musical circle of the Pavilion over the Sea on the Beach of Las Arenas in Valencia, and an increasingly strong connection with Manuel de Falla.

The Alhambra, Falla, and the Guitar

The first work that Falla brought forth after fulfilling his dream of relocating near the Alhambra in Granada was the *Homenaje a Debussy* for guitar. Though dated Granada, summer of 1920, it was actually composed during the final weeks of his residence in Madrid. The modern consensus is that this composition marks the beginning of a new period in the history of the guitar, its entry into the universe of the musical avant-garde. Falla's integrity and vision in presenting these seventy measures of very original guitar music assured him a place among the most important composers in his musical environment. These included Paul Dukas, Erik Satie, Albert Roussel, Florent Schmitt, Maurice Ravel, Béla Bartók, Igor Stravinsky, Gian Francesco Malipiero, and Eugene Goossens. All would contribute pieces to a landmark issue of *La Revue Musicale* dedicated to Claude Debussy.

Falla's homage to Debussy soon had a major impact. In a concert on 17 December 1923, at Madrid's Teatro de la Comedia of Madrid, celebrated guitar virtuoso Andrés Segovia debuted an entire set of new works for his instrument. In addition to the *Homenaje*, these included the *Sonatina* of Federico Moreno Torroba; *Sevillana*, Op. 29, of Joaquín Turina; *Romancillo* of Adolfo Salazar; and *Peacock Pie* of Ernesto Halffter, the young talent who represented what would later be referred to as the Generation of 1927. Andrés Segovia's importance in this new epoch of the guitar is obvious, but in fact the guitarist who debuted the *Homenaje a Debussy* and prepared its publication in collaboration with Falla was not Segovia but rather Miguel Llobet, a leading student of Francisco Tárrega (1852–1909) and Segovia's main competitor during the initial years of his concert career.[82]

López-Chavarri was keenly aware of this rebirth of the guitar repertory and participated very early in it by writing in 1922 a sonata dedicated to Llobet, who performed it during his tour through Austria and Germany in 1924. Andrés Segovia first concertized in Valencia in 1915, though he would not reappear there until 1920 and 1921.[83] Between 1923 and 1924, López-Chavarri composed a *Bolero* dedicated to Segovia, and in autumn 1924 he received a rather encouraging letter from the guitarist.[84]

During the years in which López-Chavarri began his outstanding catalogue of music for guitar, in collaboration with both Miguel Llobet and Andrés Segovia, Rodrigo was simply one more point of light within the constellation of Valencian musicians that revolved around López-Chavarri. Thus, Rodrigo must have been well aware of his mentor's progress in breaking a new path for young composers. The reality was that new music composed for the guitar would gain exposure in concerts both at home and abroad, and that it would be published. This was a compelling incentive, one to which Rodrigo was not indifferent.

However, in all likelihood it was not those considerations that encouraged Rodrigo to write for the guitar. Other stimuli were needed, and they came in 1925. The first was doubtlessly Falla's stay in Valencia and the idea that Rodrigo surely harbored of going off to study with him in his secluded residence at the foot of the Alhambra—had he dared propose it to him. The second was the return to Valencia of Josefina Robledo, a well-known and highly regarded pupil of Tárrega.

After having spent more than a decade in South America, based in Buenos Aires but touring throughout Uruguay, Paraguay, and Brazil, this teacher and guitarist made her way back to Valencia.[85] That was where she had debuted as a wunderkind in 1907,[86] giving three concerts at the Teatro Eslava, on April 26 and May 3 and 11. Afterwards, she played in a concert organized by the Mercantile Atheneum in its Gothic Salon on May 20, where López-Chavarri introduced her. In fact, the guitar scene in Valencia was dominated by outstanding teachers rather than by eminent performers of the caliber of Llobet and Segovia. Josefina Robledo did much to amend that state of affairs, and soon she was moving in López-Chavarri's circle.

Rodrigo dedicated his *Preludio al atardecer* (Prelude to the Sunset) to Josefina Robledo, but at some point deliberately scratched out the dedication. It would come as no surprise if the guitarist rejected Rodrigo's style of composition, since there are no fingerings on the manuscript. Moreover, the composer himself abandoned it as a piece for guitar and used it instead as the inspiration for a longer and more elaborate work for orchestra, the *Preludio para un poema a La Alhambra*. In reality, the *Preludio al atardecer*, in its original version for guitar, already bore the subtitle that indicated the source of its inspiration: "In the evening sighs a guitar, there . . . almost in the Alhambra." There, almost in the Alhambra, where Falla settled and signed his *Homenaje a Debussy*. Not only does the main theme of Rodrigo's *Preludio* derive directly from the quote of "La soirée dans Grenade" from Debussy's *Estampes* that Falla reveals at the end of his tribute to the French maestro, but on the surface of his sonority is the harmonic structure of the open strings of the guitar, as in the *Homenaje a Debussy*, although transposed: the first chord (E♭, A♭, D♭, F) has the intervalic structure of the central strings of the guitar (A–D–G–B) and can be played on those strings with a capotasto on the sixth fret. Later on, that chord is completed with the B♭ (E♭, A♭, D♭, F, B♭), which calls for the incorporation of the highest open string (E), and is transposed to the seventh fret from which is made a *glissando* to the fourth fret (D♭, G, C, E♭, A♭). In this last chord it is necessary to stop the G on the fifth fret, which, however, does not present any problem.

Yet, the most important factor in the *Preludio al atardecer* is the form in which Rodrigo's work reinterprets the harmonic ambience of Falla's piece. Written in a variant of Phrygian mode on E with a key signature of A minor, the *Homenaje a Debussy* persistently cadences on E, not A. Rodrigo presents a broader harmonic palette. At crucial moments there appear B-major and D-major triads, as well as some prominent chords in E major played with right-hand strumming (*rasgueado*), but he manages to double Falla's effect of a lack of a tonic by using the same Andalusian mode in C, with a key signature of F minor. In this sense, it is a tribute to Falla's *Homenaje a Debussy* and to its composer. We also find Rodrigo's characteristic saturation of dissonances, demonstrating that his "disinfecting" was not confined to the keyboard or to the orchestra but was applicable to the fingerboard of the guitar as well. Rodrigo's work is a marvel. The Andalusianism is handled in a fashion that transcends mere cliché. Of all the works inspired by Falla's *Homenaje a Debussy*, this is the only one that permits comparison with the piece by the Andalusian maestro and the first that displays a complete assimilation of what Falla initiated in that miniature masterpiece.

Not only is the *Preludio al atardecer* remarkable in its inherent musical value, but its idiomatic use of the guitar's technical resources is equally astonishing if we take into account that no guitarist assisted Rodrigo in its composition. We readily perceive this in the rolled chords on E major, one of the positions that guitarists learn in the first days of studying the instrument. Rodrigo writes them with five pitches but without utilizing the fourth string for the duplication of the E. These strokes on E major, or on E major with an added sixth, in accordance with the way they are written, are proof that no guitarist guided Rodrigo. The ensuing measures present a collage of flamenco sounds, rapid-fire bits of *falseta*-type *picados* (scales) and strident *rasgueado*-style strumming, but always of a short-winded nature that seems to lack overall direction. Yet, for all its evocations of flamenco guitar, it is not exactly idiomatic for the instrument and poses severe challenges to any guitarist steeped in the traditional techniques and musical language of the instrument. This may be why it remained sunk in obscurity.

All of that notwithstanding, it is amazing how accurately Rodrigo is able to visualize in his mind the instrument's fretboard. There is only one five-measure passage creating a textural climax (in conjunction with an alternation of 3/4 and 6/8) that needs some fancy fingering in order to be playable. The rest is perfectly practicable in a surprising way for a composer who had never played a guitar but perfectly assimilated not only its mechanics but some of its most essential resources: artificial harmonics by themselves or mixed with chords made with natural sounds, *glissandi* of notes by themselves or of complete chords, strumming, and a rare technique in which a scale played with the left hand without plucking is then played immediately afterwards an octave lower with both hands.

Preludio al atardecer is a remarkable gem that has unjustly remained in obscurity for nearly a century. Though composed in the same year as the celebrated *Zarabanda lejana*, the two pieces could hardly be more different. Whereas the "Distant Sarabande" is a wistful evocation of long-ago courtly dances, this work evokes both Falla's *Homenaje* and popular guitar, though in a strangely disjointed and abstracted way that might remind one of a Cubist painting by Picasso. Then again, by 1926 Rodrigo had lost most of his vision and was himself living a "prelude to evening" that would plunge his world into total darkness. Perhaps Picasso's Cubist paintings are not the best visual analog after all. The Blue Period's *The Old Guitarist* might better convey the emotional barometer of these measures.

Yet, as disturbingly introspective as this piece occasionally becomes, Rodrigo's inveterate whimsy is never far away. There is an unmistakable evocation of his beloved cuckoo here, already in mm. 1–2, in the descending major third from E♮ to C♮ as part of a descending C-major triad (musical ex. 2.7). This motif will recur throughout the piece in various guises.

Still, apropos of its title, the piece ends darkly on a widely spaced chord consisting of G♭, A♭, and C, this last note played as an artificial harmonic. The concluding five measures present a simple melody played in harmonics, D♭, E♭, F, G, E♮, D, against nonharmonic tones below, concluding with C in the treble and A♭/G♭ down below, the outer notes thus forming a tritone and conveying the ambiguity of nighttime.

Preludio al atardecer, Rodrigo's first tribute to Falla and his first composition for guitar, remained forgotten as if it had been

Musical ex. 2.7: *Preludio al atardecer*, mm. 1–2

an error, when in reality it had been a great accomplishment. But this did not discourage the composer—save his fit of temper in so energetically erasing his dedication—and fortunately he returned to the guitar with a piece of a very different character: *Zarabanda lejana*, inspired by one of the most relevant episodes in the history of Valencian music. Like the *Preludio al atardecer*, the *Zarabanda lejana* had an evocative subtitle: "To the vihuela of Luis Milán," a Valencian courtier at the beginning of the sixteenth century whose *El Maestro* (1536) was a pedagogical compendium of various types of works for the vihuela, particularly six "Pavanas," still popular with guitarists today. Though the vihuela was smaller than the modern guitar, sported six sets (courses) of double strings (though the highest was usually a single string), was tuned like a guitar except with its major third between the middle courses (thus, E–A–D–F♯–B–E rather than E–A–D–G–B–E), its music can readily be adapted to the modern guitar.

Milán's book includes fantasies, songs, and pavanes, but no sarabandes, a form belonging more to the Baroque guitar than to the Renaissance vihuela. But Rodrigo simply intended with his subtitle to link his work with the musical history of Valencia and to adhere to the aesthetics of neoclassism, which he had already explored in some of his first works. In this sense the *Zarabanda lejana* might seem reminiscent of the "Sarabanda" from the *Homenaje a un viejo clavicordio*. But such a facile comparison overlooks all the maturity attained by Rodrigo in the first five years of his career as a composer. Interestingly, the opening motive, with its repeated chords ornamented with on-the-downbeat grace notes, is reminiscent of the first measures of his "Sarabanda" from the *Homenaje* of four years earlier. Though the *Zarabanda lejana* may well have evolved from its eponymous predecessor, it represents a dramatic departure in its expressive harmonies and haunting melodic grace.

Considerable confusion regarding the dedication to Milán has persisted in the literature on Rodrigo's eloquent *Zarabanda*. However, we must dispense with the notion that there is any connection between Milán, his vihuela, and the zarabanda.

The dignified court sarabande that we know from the Baroque era, and on which Rodrigo's is clearly modeled, did not exist in Milán's time. The first permanent manifestation of the zarabanda in print comes to us from Italy, not Spain, written for the Baroque guitar in guitar tablature, not the vihuela in the unique system of tablature utilized by Milán.[87] Whether Rodrigo fully appreciated these historical realities is unknown to us, but it hardly matters. Despite the dedication he lovingly but somewhat misleadingly placed on the score, his *Zarabanda lejana* is musical art of a very high order.

Although we do not have an exact date for the composition of *Zarabanda lejana*, Rodrigo refers to it as having been composed in 1926. He likely wrote it practically at the same time as the *Preludio al atardecer*. That is the year of its publication by Unión Musical Española, which had an office in Valencia. Therefore, it was probably the first work published by Rodrigo, and one of the first contributions to the renascence of the guitar's repertoire. In 1926, López-Chavarri also published his *Siete piezas* (Seven Pieces) with Schott, though immediately afterwards, Andrés Segovia took charge of Schott's guitar collection. Also in 1925–26, guitar virtuoso Regino Sainz de la Maza (1896–1981) began to release his compositions and transcriptions through the Unión Musical Española, although he did not begin to publish original guitar music by the young non-guitarist composers of the Generation of 1927 until some years later.[88]

Indeed, it was in the 1920s that the modern guitar repertoire began to take shape, as Segovia urged compatriot composers, especially Falla, Moreno Torroba, and Turina, to compose works for him. Torroba's *Suite castellana* was followed by the *Sonatina* in 1923, still an evergreen favorite with guitarists.[89] Though Torroba would go on to write dozens of works for the instrument, Falla's sole contribution to the repertoire was his *Homenaje a Debussy*. Not to be outdone and also at Segovia's urging, Turina would soon follow with his *Sevillana*, Op. 29 (1923), *Fandanguillo*, Op. 36 (1925), and *Ráfaga*, Op. 53 (1929).

The significance of all these efforts is that the composers were not themselves guitarists, though Falla apparently had some rudimentary facility on the instrument.[90] Segovia knew well enough that, other than transcriptions, the guitar's repertoire up to that time comprised almost solely works by guitarist-composers, from the sixteenth century onward. He was determined to widen the instrument's appeal to non-guitarist composers, without abandoning its historic identity as a Spanish instrument and the enduring popularity of works with a Spanish flavor. Encouraging Torroba, Falla, and Turina was the logical thing to do. Rodrigo now joined their ranks.

Rodrigo's pioneering effort is a nod in the direction of the man whose compositions represent the beginning of the guitar's repertoire. And yet, as Graham Wade points out, the *Zarabanda lejana* lies more comfortably on the piano than on the guitar.[91] Chord changes that are relatively easy to execute on the keyboard in a smooth, legato fashion are awkward on the fingerboard without the sorts of rhythmic hiccups for which guitarists are sometime criticized. The piece thus sounds more natural when rendered on the piano, for which Rodrigo soon published an arrangement, though technically accomplished guitarists can supervene these difficulties in a convincing way. And the sound of plucked strings is more consistent with the general affect Rodrigo strives to express.

The piece is marked *andante quasi adagio*, that is, "walking pace, almost slow." It opens with a three-bar introduction consisting of the repetition of a single note, utilizing a hypnotic rhythm that will inform the entire work (musical ex. 2.8). The dynamic level is *piano*, though a crescendo-decrescendo in the third measure creates a sense of anticipation leading to the main theme. The combination of these initial elements creates a beguiling serenity here, an introspective sense of mystery that draws us in through subtlety, not force. This effect is reinforced by the metrical ambiguity. Though notated in the 3/4 time typical of the sarabande, the alternation in mm. 1–2 of a quarter note with two eighth notes, followed by two quarter notes, creates the sensation of duple meter, a sort of premonition of the 2/4 measures that are interspersed throughout. Yet, when those two-bar passages appear, the rhythms are adjusted to create the

Musical ex. 2.8: *Zarabanda lejana*, mm. 1–8

sensation of 3/4 again. Rodrigo is playing a clever game with our expectations.

The traditional sarabande characteristically featured an emphasis on the second beat, and the initial evenness of three quarter notes belies that stress. Just beneath the surface, however, occasionally clashing dissonances and expressive harmonic changes evince an intensity of emotion that contrasts with the piece's otherwise placid affect. The pungent cross-relations convey a plangent mood only relieved by cadential patterns that resolve in predictable ways.

The formal design of the work also departs from the historical sarabande's straightforward binary form. To be sure, there are A and B sections, but their arrangement, AABAB, reflects the departure from traditional practice that we observed in the rhythm.[92] Rodrigo's intent here is to *suggest* the sarabande, not *recreate* it. In fact, as Graham Wade has pointed out, "this piece has closer affinities to Ravel's re-creation of the spirit of the antique dance in *Pavane pour une Infante défunte* (1899)."[93] Though the cadential patterns have a delicately archaic aspect, this is tonal music with a very clear structure. The A setion is in unambiguous D major, while the B section commences in D minor and then migrates to F major, via C and B♭, before ending in D major. Its modulatory quality gives it the feeling of a development.

In what sense is this sarabande "distant"? The intimacy of

the guitar and the subdued dynamics the composer calls for create the sense of hearing this music at some distance in space.
But the sarabande is also distant from us in time, in the same
sense that Milán and his music are. Rodrigo's historicism is
clearly not concerned with authenticity but rather with allusion,
in a symbolic sense. His Zarabanda is a metaphor for an irretrievable past, not an attempt to restore it. This is apparent in
the innovative rhythmic and harmonic procedures that mark
this as a work of the twentieth century, not the sixteenth or
seventeenth. It is thus removed in a stylistic sense from earlier
prototypes. Yet, despite rhythmic and harmonic anomalies, the
melancholy solemnity of this piece dissolves into reassuringly
plagal cadences, that is, from G major to D major chords, or IV–
I, that exude a faint air of sanctity. This is finally not a worldly
antique dance but rather a modern testament to faith, a belief
that, as Robert Browning put it, "God's in his heaven [and] all's
right with the world!" This is a zarabanda distant not only in
time, space, sound, and style but also in spirit.

The composer very clearly explained the position of the Zarabanda lejana in the context of his works at the beginning of
the 1920s:

> As a curious anecdote, I will add that, then concerned
> by certain harmonic problems of the moment and
> concentrating on the hunt for possible neologisms
> derived from them, I did not give any attention to this
> little work, which emerged from my mind with a brief
> tug, nor did I show any interest in it. How strange! I
> did not feel that kind of revelation (so often a passing
> thing) that one feels before every new work, and when
> one critic (may God bless him) said that I had composed
> a small masterpiece, I felt astonishment, and I attributed
> it to good friendship, not totally up-to-date, of the critic
> in question.
>
> Very soon, it reached the hands of the not very
> numerous, [indeed] rather scarce guitarists of that time,
> among them, the indisputable authority Llobet, whom I

did not know. One day I received a letter; it was from the great guitarist. The letter was aflame with praises and confirmed the opinion of the critic. It ended by saying, "You intuit the guitar and should keep on writing for it. In it I predict great successes for you."[94]

Although this letter mentioned by Rodrigo has not been preserved, it appears that the *Zarabanda lejana* circulated widely, thanks to the printed edition. In fact, a copy of it survives among Llobet's scores, now in the Museu de la Música of Barcelona. Nonetheless, it must have seemed to guitarists a rather modern work, and they took a long time to play it in public, despite the fact that, as the composer himself recognized, it has a much less avant-garde character than what he had been composing all along, especially in his piano music.

A review published by Alfredo Romea in the prestigious *Revista Musical Catalana* reflects what most guitarists of the time probably thought of this piece:

It is of modern confection and contains really curious sonorities evocative of the works—quite commendable in their time—of the famous vihuela player. This is one of the most original pieces and the newest, perhaps the most meritorious of its age. It is true that from the instrumental point of view, the chords of Mr. Rodrigo's work for guitar offer some difficulty to perform, more than once unattainable if one wants to take care to make the phrases unified in what concerns their color or sound quality. But this small deficiency, if we take the liberty to observe it, does not really diminish the considerable value of the *Zarabanda lejana* as a whole. [. . .] Let it be seen, thus, as a commendable work.[95]

The guitarist responsible for the premiere of this composition was Regino Sainz de la Maza, in 1929. Later, another of Tárrega's main students, Emilio Pujol, who was to develop an important friendship with Rodrigo, republished the *Zarabanda lejana* in 1934 within the collection Bibliothèque de Musique Ancienne et Moderne pour Guitare, which he edited for the French publishing firm Max Eschig. This French edition, with fingerings added by Pujol and without the dedication to José Balaguer, introduces important changes to the first edition, as well as some details—harmonics and *portamenti*—that clearly reflected Pujol's preferences as a guitarist. This was the version that eventually gained widespread currency, especially after 1954, when Segovia added it to his repertoire and recorded it (LP, Brunswick AXTL 1069).

Lauded by Llobet, edited and revised by Pujol, debuted by Sainz de la Maza, and recorded by Segovia, the *Zarabanda lejana* helped Rodrigo regain his balance after an initial stumble with the *Preludio al atardecer*, and it officially began his catalogue of guitar music. However, though this was a major step forward in his career, it represented something of a step backward relative to the modernist mania that so strongly characterized his first works. Now he would make room in his output for reflection; indeed, after the creative effervescence of these early years, there was a marked attenuation in his productivity in 1927, one that would persist for the next five years.

Antonio Iglesias refers to a lost *Gran marcha politónica* for piano duet composed in 1927.[96] However, we have been able to locate under the same title a work for piano four hands dated 1926 in the Special Collection Eduardo López-Chavarri held at the Biblioteca Valenciana "Nicolau Primitiu." In his notes to *Tres viejos aires de danza*, the composer himself dates to 1927 the version for piano of the "Minué" that appears in his handwritten list of works from that year. But we have yet to find this piano version. What is preserved is a piano work that Rodrigo left out of the catalogue: *Jardin après la pluie*, a parody of Debussy's title *Jardin sous la pluie*, a work that, like the *Preludio al atardecer* and the *Zarabanda lejana*, has an explanatory subtitle: "Prelude following the somewhat forgotten manner of the old Impressionist era."

In a 1949 lecture, Rodrigo summed up his view of the history of music during this initial phase of his creative career. What interests us here is that, instead of assuming the neutral position of the historian, he presents a narrative based on personal experience:

> The Great War happens and when the horrible nightmare is over, the young musicians want nothing to do with that Debussyan softness, with that perennial nostalgia, with that misty and supremely aristocratic Parisian spleen. The epoch of the -isms begins: of cubism, of Dadaism, of surrealism. The *arrivistes* think that, following Stravinsky's example, they can be lackadaisical and write whatever emerges from the cookie cutter. There arises the era of the ugliness of the eternal pedals of incoherent harmonies and the cultivation of extravagance. But musical art only emerges the victor for all of that. This is what the tradition-bound don't understand: musical art gets richer in the postwar decade than in the whole eighteenth century and a good part of the nineteenth. Everything is assayed, knocked out of orbit, the instrumental zone is dislocated, harmony, the laws of counterpoint are overturned, the harmonic system of Rameau topples over, keys and modes get mixed. Through doors opened as wide as possible enters an army of bad and ugly manners, crudeness, but with them also enter health and life in abundance.[97]

After the polytonal fevers of his first major works, which had attracted the attention of his musician friends but only the indifference of performers (and in some cases rejection by conservative critics and audiences), at the end of the initial period of his career, Rodrigo moderated the novelty of his musical language and wrote less strident works, like the *Pastoral* and *Zarabanda lejana*. But he was just beginning his creative journey, and he would soon leave Valencia behind. Ahead of him lay Paris.

Chapter 3

Long Live Paris!

(1927–1931)

Autumn in Paris

Rodrigo always recounted that his father opposed his move to Paris. Don Vicente Rodrigo had never been interested in music and doubted it could be a means for his son to make a living. But that was not a pressing need. The young musician lived well, did what he liked when he felt like it, and was under no obligation whatsoever. He imagined himself as a great composer, he liked to provoke conservative audiences with his works, and among his friends he had achieved a certain recognition as an *enfant terrible* of Valencian music. His brothers and sisters had moved out on their own, and the domestic commotion of his childhood had by now abated. His mother spoiled him, and a large staff of servants doted on him. Moreover, he had an attendant, Rafael Ibáñez, who was employed full-time by his father not only to go with him wherever necessary but also to read to him whatever he requested.

Ibáñez, ten years older than Rodrigo, was for many years his shadow, the guarantee of his independence, his secretary, and, when necessary, even his advisor and confidant. He also learned to read music and to write down in conventional notation the compositions that Rodrigo composed in Braille using his slate and stylus. And he helped satisfy Rodrigo's voracious literary appetite by reading to him writings that were not available in Braille. Having at his side someone as trustworthy, devoted, discreet, and diligent as Ibáñez was a stroke of good fortune, as well as a comfort that he owed to the good economic situation of the family.

But between those daily luxuries that he could allow himself while living with his parents and the actual financing of his Parisian adventure, there was a gap that he was able to close thanks to a confluence of factors. In the first place, Don Vicente, already turning seventy years of age and recently grieving the death of his firstborn,[1] was ever more distant and unaware of family life. In the second place, there were very favorable economic conditions, especially the weakness of the French franc in relation to the Spanish peseta.[2] Lastly, Rodrigo's friend, the pianist Leopoldo Querol, played the role of his scout.

Querol and Rodrigo had formed a close friendship. Querol never hesitated to single out the composer among young Valencian musicians as "the one far ahead of the rest."[3] For his part, Rodrigo showed up dutifully in Madrid, early in the spring of 1927, to attend the defense and celebration of the pianist's doctoral thesis. According to Querol himself, the success of his thesis had made way for an "issue of university policy as far as the orientation to be imposed on a master's of History, to make room in it for a Chair of History of Music."[4] That chair took twenty-five years to create, and the first to occupy it would be Joaquín Rodrigo.

In September 1927, after having successfully completed his doctorate, Querol won a three-month fellowship to study piano in France from October to December.[5] The pianist sent a letter from Paris to López-Chavarri, asking him to give Rodrigo his regards and telling him that he would write him soon "to send him the list of expenses."[6] It is clear that Rodrigo wanted to know how much money he would need to live in Paris.[7]

The encouragement and recommendations of López-Chavarri

and any practical information that Querol furnished suggest the urgency Rodrigo felt to get out of Valencia; thus, he and Rafael Ibáñez appeared in Paris in mid-November of 1927. They knew nothing for certain, neither where to stay nor what to do, but they were very lucky. After spending a week with Querol, they contacted the violinist Abelardo Mus, a longtime Paris resident and the 1926 winner of First Prize for Violin (with gold medal) from the Paris École Supérieure de Musique et de Déclamation. Mus directed them to the home of Valencian decorator and illustrator Francisco Povo. Povo had achieved fame at the beginning of the 1920s as a painter of fans and an illustrator of the covers of novels published by Blasco Ibáñez in his publishing house Prometeo; he revalidated his success in 1926 with a monographic exhibition in the French capital.[8] Well connected within musical and cultural circles, Povo was also an old acquaintance of Rodrigo's mother, and generously hastened to welcome the new arrivals in his home at 53 Rue du Château d'Eau, where they settled at once. Rodrigo's enthusiasm overflowed at the start of the first letter he sent to López-Chavarri from Paris, dated 30 November 1927:

> Long live Paris, long live Paris, long live Paris . . . ! Here
> we are trotting through the streets, going down to the
> subways, climbing onto the streetcars, getting on the
> buses, taking taxis (though seldom), in short, we have
> turned into true Parisians. Except they don't understand
> us, we don't understand them, we don't know which bus
> to take, we don't know the streets, we don't know how
> to get to the theaters—in short, true Parisians. [. . .] I am
> in my glory. [. . .] I feel simply at home, since Povo lives
> alone with his wife and with a young maid—Spanish,
> too. [. . .] We use the whole house, and I work in the living
> room, where the central stove is and the piano facing
> Strasbourg Boulevard. [. . .] Do you understand now my
> cries of "Long live Paris"?[9]

Once the basic issues of food and lodging were so quickly and satisfactorily addressed, Rodrigo faced the academic part of his stay with the same aplomb. His hope was to study with Maurice Ravel, but since this leading French composer no longer taught classes, he had to seek an alternative. The month of November, with the concert season in full swing, was a time of frenetic musical activity in Paris. The Théâtre de la Opéra-Comique was then replaying *Ariane et Barbe-bleue* (Ariane and Bluebeard) and Rodrigo, who attended one of the performances, remained absolutely fascinated with the work.

After the *Rigoletto* of his childhood and the more recent impact of Falla's *El retablo de maese Pedro* on his sensibilities, *Ariane et Barbe-bleue* was the work that made the greatest impression on Rodrigo at this decisive moment in his career. Years later, he was to write some very perceptive lines on Dukas's opera:

> It is like a compromise between the ideals of a Wagner
> and of a Debussy; the heroine, "Ariana," harbors his
> ideal [Dukas's] as a man and a musician: the tenacious,
> ceaseless search for truth, justice in sweetness and
> firmness; the eloquence with which she expresses herself,
> so sober, so musical, is a bridge stretched toward a future
> of lyricism, whose possibilities and consequences have
> not been exploited and can illumine the difficult road of
> present-day opera.[10]

Rodrigo then made the consequential decision to study with Dukas, whose relationship at the start of the century with Albéniz and Falla would situate him in the historical lineage of Spanish music during the early twentieth century. To approach Dukas, Rodrigo counted on the help of an old friend of López-Chavarri, a central figure in the French Hispanism of the period: Henri Collet, who gave him a letter with which the Valencian musician introduced himself at the home of the maestro:

> What emotion I felt on approaching his house, there
> in Passy, not far from the Bois de Boulogne! I recall
> that, when I asked "Madame Janitress" for the maestro,
> a rather short man, with a great umbrella (he never

went anywhere without it) and enveloped in a dense
beard, came out of the doorway and answered, "It's me."
With great embarrassment, I explained my aims in my
minimal French; I seemed to understand that he was
saying to me to come up and spend a moment with
him. [. . .] At that moment, I came to know his French,
a French that it took me months to understand, tucked
into his beard and by way of an opaque, almost hoarse
voice. I seemed to understand that he told me to go to
see him at the École Normale de Musique (Normal School
of Music), and that I bring him a few of my works; I did.[11]

Dukas had joined the École Normale de Musique during the
1926–27 school year, where he took charge of composition classes.
Although the trimester had begun in October 1927, enrollment
was always open, and Rodrigo was admitted in November. In
the second part of the first letter that he sent to López-Chavarri
from Paris, he relates his introduction into the school and the
effect of his music, so disconcerting for the students as it was
pleasing to the maestro:

[Dukas] has received me in the École Normale before his
students and saw some of my works that I did not play
very well. If you promise not to tell anyone, I will tell you
I was very successful. The students, who seemed to me did
not invent gunpowder [i.e., were not rocket scientists], were
frightened by that uninterrupted series of punches and
pellets. Maestro Dukas (and I will never forget this) said to
me, "If my advice deserves some credence from you, don't
give up music, you will do something very interesting,"
he said, "I see no need for you to redo your studies.
Nonetheless, if you wish, we can work on the orchestra,
since I am apprised of how difficult it is for you."[12]

Besides the possibility of getting into some specialized course
in composition, open to students of any nationality and to those
not needing credit for official degrees—after paying a high

enrollment fee—what Paris offered a young musician was a level of high culture without compare.[13] And everything was affordable thanks to the favorable exchange rate.

Thus, in the first seven weeks of residing in Paris, Rodrigo voraciously attended concerts of all kinds: operas, ballets, symphonic concerts, and chamber recitals, all of them "as innumerable as the stars of the sky and the sands of the sea."[14] He also attended a Schoenberg festival in which the Viennese composer himself directed *Pierrot lunaire*, played by the Colonne Concert Orchestra with Marya Freund as soloist and presenting in German Schoenberg's original version of this work.[15]

On December 1, in the Church of the Madeleine, Rodrigo was able to hear the Bach B-Minor Mass, and on the date of Beethoven's birth, December 16, he took in the Ninth Symphony, "complete, complete, thank God," as Rodrigo exclaimed in a letter to López-Chavarri.[16] Further, on November 26 he would attend a program of the Concerts-Pasdeloup at the Théâtre Mogador, consisting of *King David* by Honegger (directed by him and with Jean Cocteau as narrator), *The Song of Madness* by Jacques Ibert, and *Suite in F* by Albert Roussel. Ever on the go, the next day he savored Franck's *Les béatitudes* at the Trocadero by Les Concerts Lamoureux, with 200 performers under the direction of Paul Paray. Nor did he pass up a gala at the Paris Opéra on December 27, at which the Ballets Russes of Sergei Diaghilev staged Prokofiev's *The Dance of Steel*, Henri Sauguet's *The Cat*, and Stravinsky's *Firebird*. "What do you think about the list?" Rodrigo asked López-Chavarri.[17] (Appendix 2 presents a distillation of reports in various newspapers, especially *Le Figaro*, *Le Gaulois*, *Comoedia*, and *Le Ménestrel*, to summarize his impressively avid concert attendance.)

Further, Rodrigo's Levantine musical circle, formed by Mus, the Iturbi siblings, Querol, and his teacher Ricardo Viñes, provided the basis for an active and stimulating social life. Conversing with people who were from different cultures but who shared his desire to create new music was a very effective means of enriching his education as a composer. Most important, he had found a great teacher, one who was going to change his life in every respect.

In the composition class of Paul Dukas, École Normale de Musique, 1927–28.
In the first row, seated in the center, Paul Dukas; at his right, the school
director, August Mangeot and Alexandre Démétriade (?), and to his left,
Marguerite Alioth and Fernande Peyrot. In the second row, from left
to right, Rafael Ibáñez (Rodrigo's aide), José Rolón, Yvonne Desportes,
Manuel M. Ponce, Joaquín Rodrigo, Sonia Krein (?), and Gustave
Samazeuilh. In the upper row, from left to right, Romeo Alexandrescu,
Tudor Ciortea, Ljubomir Pipkov, and Alex Borski (?).

Dukas and the École Normale de Musique

Classes at the École Normale de Musique were held on Mondays
and Thursdays during the school year 1927–28, from 10 a.m. to
noon. Along with Rodrigo, seated around the piano in Dukas's
composition class was a very international assortment of distinguished aspirants, including Manuel Ponce and José Rolón
from Mexico. There were also students from Romania, France,
Bulgaria, Russia, Greece, Poland, Switzerland, Canada, and the
United States. This demographic gave rise to a veritable "tower

of Babel," according to Rodrigo.[18] The students of the most varied nationalities benefited from the laissez-faire environment of
a private institution, unlike the public Conservatoire, where the
enrollment of foreigners was very restricted. However, to enter
the Tower of Babel governed by Dukas and to be able to take
advantage of the famous maestro's teachings, it was necessary to
arrive with a solid technical foundation. Once inside, an inten-
sive labor began, along with a continuous exposure to piercing
irony and the maestro's trenchant analysis.

Ponce recounted in detail the dynamic of Dukas's classes,
while stressing, like all his students, the enthusiasm, rigorous
judgment, and ironic tone of his observations:

> His course was one of advanced composition and critical
> analysis of musical works. Seated in front of a piano,
> surrounded by his students, who formed a motley
> international group, he corrected and critiqued the most
> diverse works: a symphonic fragment, a piano piece, a
> sonata, a fugue, a quartet. [. . .] Sparing with his praise, a
> "that's not bad" emerging from his lips was worth more
> than a whole admiring article among those read everyday
> in the newspapers. [. . .] On occasion, he punctured his
> fine irony by pointing out the mistakes in the works
> he examined. At other times the commentary was full
> of delight or involved a deep thought or a wise piece of
> advice. [. . .] Dukas was not astonished by the avant-garde
> *ultraísta* compositions some of his students were in the
> habit of showing him. His spirit, full of understanding
> and able to do justice to the maximum, managed to
> discover with accurate vision the point at which the
> composer found the fortunate expression of an idea or
> the refinement of an exquisite harmony. What he did not
> tolerate was ignorance. He did not believe in geniuses
> who did not know counterpoint. "Everything should be
> known, everything should be studied," he repeated at
> every step. He showed no mercy toward Stravinskyists,
> who were incapable of artistically harmonizing a chorale.[19]

In his biographical sketch of Dukas, Rodrigo described the classes of the École Normale de Musique in a way that completely accords with the description of Ponce, though giving us some extra details:

> The classes, which took place twice a week and lasted two hours, were divided into two stages: the first hour was for correcting works; the second, which interested me more, was for analysis. At the piano, with me always by his side, he would read symphonic works, chamber music, operas, etc.; his judgment was rapid, accurate, original, showing great understanding; his erudition was very great, he knew practically all music, and his opinions were evenhanded.[20]

According to Ponce, Dukas's 1926–27 course concluded with a complete and thorough study of Beethoven's quartets, which coincided with the centennial of the composer's death. The systematic analysis of Beethoven's works in Dukas's classes and the systematic analysis of his music made a lasting impact on the young Spaniard. In the very first interview he ever gave, when asked who his favorite composer was, he categorically affirmed, "With no hesitation: Beethoven."[21]

In the École Normale de Musique, Bach and Mozart coexisted with Beethoven: Bach for the study of counterpoint and fugue as a step immediately prior to free composition; Mozart, as the maximum example of a musical creator—"Look," Dukas would say to his students, "It's nothing: three chords, a few notes, no complication, and yet, it is all music!"[22] Dukas would not teach opera, focusing instead on symphonic music and orchestration; and yet, Wagner, too, sat on the great throne of the musical Olympus. In a well-known photograph of Dukas's class in the École Normale de Musique at that time, which includes Joaquín Rodrigo, the scene prominently features an impressive bust of Wagner.

In short, a bedrock principle of Dukas's pedagogy, as well as of Nadia Boulanger's, was this: profound knowledge of the past is necessary to advance in the present. This separated them completely from the anti-academic autodidacticism so much in vogue during the 1920s among adherents of the musical avant-garde—"the *Stravinskyists* incapable of harmonizing a chorale" to whom Ponce so contemptuously referred.

In Search of One's Own Road to Follow: A Lesson of Dukas

The students of the composition class of the École Normale de Musique were mostly in their twenties, but talented older students were also present (as well as some younger), attracted by the fame and authority of the maestro. The French composer Gustave Samazeuilh and the famous pianist Marguerite Hasselmans, as well as José Rolón, were all around fifty. The letters Rolón addressed his daughter in Mexico sensitively inform her of Dukas's teachings, including one of his pieces of advice that proved most decisive for his education. He quoted the maestro in his own words:

> Let us do a careful review of the aesthetics and techniques, from the Greeks to our days. Boulanger will efficiently help you to analyze all tendencies, both past and present. And once you have revised all styles, all techniques, all tendencies, then forget them all and be yourself. This I call *l'ignorance acquise* [acquired ignorance].[23]

Rolón relied on Nadia Boulanger's classes to delve into these studies in Paris, but Rodrigo probably had a head start thanks to the local composer in Valencia, no less masterful in his limited domain, López-Chavarri. In the same way that Dukas's piece of advice always weighed on Rolón's mind, so it must have set Rodrigo on the difficult road to search for his own voice, or rather, for a voice different from the one he had developed until then. This search called into question the route he had traveled until that moment, while he was exploring the polytonality which, in the musically frenetic Paris of those years, was merely one of many trends (or –isms) that composed (or decomposed) the avant-garde. According to Rolón, "Everybody is going crazy with so many isms: atonalism, bitonalism, polytonalism, ultrachromaticism, dodecaphonism [. . .] all of them attract me, but should we listen to the chanting of so many sirens? I don't know."[24]

Yet, although at that time it probably was not easy to know which route to take, it was necessary to make the decisions that young composers were making. According to a Spanish adage, "Tell me with whom you walk, and I will tell you who you are" ("Dime con quién andas y te diré quién eres"). Ernesto Halffter, guided by Salazar and among the most important Spanish composers of his generation, was a typical case of the Stravinskyists to whom Ponce referred. They had never confronted the academic exercise of harmonizing a chorale, seeking instead to preserve the relative freshness and originality of their own musical languages (although Halffter had orchestrated one of Bach's chorales in 1928).[25] Roberto Gerhard, convinced of the futility of being self-taught, decided to travel to Vienna in 1924 for the tutelage of Schoenberg, and Rodrigo, like Dúo Vital, enrolled in Dukas's classes at the École Normale de Musique.

As much as Dukas wanted to remain open to the new musical trends that were of such interest to his students, his aesthetics were far removed from all those modern movements, which were closer to Ravel than to him, being ten years older. But everything was not a question of chronological proximity, as each individual's spiritual inclinations exercised great influence as well. Thus, to acquire an idea of the conservative aesthetic climate that prevailed in Rodrigo's Paris, it is worthwhile to consider a text by Henri Collet, twenty years younger than Dukas but nonetheless very critical of everything that departed from late-Romantic nationalism. His essay, titled "The Future of Spanish Music," appeared in the May 1928 issue of *Gaceta Musical*, a Spanish-language journal that Ponce had begun to publish in Paris along with the celebrated writer Alejo Carpentier, who served as "editor-in-chief."[26] After noting Spain's favorable economic situation resulting from its neutrality during World War I, which enabled Spanish musicians to travel abroad, Collet observed that Spain was *the* European nation that could "put

forth the most tenacious efforts in favor of art, and serenely
give us a new formula, since it did not experience the multiple
concerns of the belligerent countries," referring to the nationalist movements that had fueled the Great War. The idea was
not a bad one, nor was it offtrack, and in fact great things could
be expected from a younger generation of Spanish composers
that included Ernesto Halffter, Roberto Gerhard, Antonio José
Martínez Palacios, and Pablo Sorozábal, besides Joaquín Rodrigo.
Nonetheless, Collet cautioned about the dangers facing these
young people, by bringing to light the crudest realities of his
ideology. His toxic anti-Semitism is on revolting display in this
commentary, a prejudice Rodrigo would never share: "Unfortunately, a portion of them show the influence of Debussy and,
later, of the French Dadaism of those who are neither musicians
nor even Frenchmen, but rather Jews or Semites and therefore
only dilettantes of harmonic voluptuousness and sensuous shud-
ders." Finally, Collet recommended: "affirm now your Spanish
superiority and the need to gather around the flag of the homeland to resist the battering force of the anarchical Asiatic tides."[27]

Diverted by preparations for the trip to Paris, the move, the
quantity of concerts, social life, and doubts with respect to which
aesthetic direction to give his music, Rodrigo spent the year 1927
without having completed any new work. The year 1928 hardly
began any better. In a letter he sent to López-Chavarri at the
beginning of February, he confessed his lack of productivity: "I
am working very little, [. . .] and I find it hard to perform the tra-
peze act that alone will satisfy Don Paulito [Dukas]." Further on,
he tells of his progress:

> With Dukas up to now I have done orchestration. I have
> orchestrated a prelude, two small works for strings [. . .],
> a wind quintet, a slow dance for symphony orchestra,
> and various class assignments. All this has earned me
> some cuffs to my head, but I keep going on and on,
> writing trombones and trumpets in octaves and with the
> drum and the cymbals, so that it's not for nothing that I
> come from Valencia.[28]

To be fair, these are not such modest advances if we consider that he had accomplished this in less than three months, interrupted by Christmas and without ceasing to attend concerts almost every day. He had orchestrated his *Preludio al atardecer* for guitar. In its orchestral version, it would be retitled *Preludio para un poema a La Alhambra* (Prelude for a poem to the Alhambra, 1927) and considerably lengthened, by about 60 percent. It constitutes an exuberant exercise in instrumentation for large orchestra. The two "small works" were probably the version for chamber orchestra of the *Pastoral* (1926) for piano, dedicated to Leopoldo Querol, and the *Minuet* (1926), dedicated to the young Valencian architect Enrique Pecourt. The original version of this piece has not been found. These two pieces, along with a "Giga" composed specifically for orchestra in the summer of 1929 and dedicated to the physician Alberto Maraguat, in all likelihood formed the subsequent *Tres viejos aires de danza*, which we discuss further on. These clearly reveal the influence of Viennese classicism prior to Beethoven, especially Mozart, who was one of Dukas's "saints" for the diaphanous quality of his orchestration, his unfailing wit, evocations of the natural world, and for the profusion of contrapuntal elements more germane to the chamber music of the end of the 1700s than to the symphonic repertoire. The *Danzas* further reveal Rodrigo's passion for Haydn, especially in the trio of the "Minué" and its surprising modulations, like the unexpected motion from B♭ major to C minor in m. 20.

Among the orchestrations mentioned by Rodrigo, we have uncovered a work that has yet to appear in any catalogue, *Jardin automnel*, a symphonic version of *Jardin après la pluie* (1927) for piano, composed in 1927. The orchestral version consists of sixty measures and is scored for two flutes, piccolo, oboe, French horn, trumpets, percussion, harp, celeste, and strings. As was the case with his *Preludio para un poema a La Alhambra*, the copyist was Rafael Ibáñez. Among these assorted "homework assignments," one should include the *Danza* for chamber ensemble, an orchestration of the "Sarabanda" from his *Homenaje a un viejo clavicordio*.

In an interview for the journal *Ritmo* with cellist and conductor Bernardino Gálvez Bellido, Rodrigo stated that upon reaching the midpoint of his studies with Dukas, he found the maestro "a man of admirable eclecticism." He then added, "After he has suggested to the student the bases of a modern technique, [. . .] he lets him do what he wants. He encourages the beginner to act freely on his own, while expanding his own sensitivity. He does not allow anyone's influences to weigh excessively upon the individual's imaginings."[29]

Much later, in an interview with the composer Xavier Montsalvatge, and with the perspective that time gives, Rodrigo made a very meaningful statement recalling the years he studied with Dukas:

> There operated in me a curious phenomenon: I got tired
> of the latest French music, just as [Ernesto] Halffter
> had. I raised no new idols and kept those I had already
> enthroned in Valencia with the help of the player piano
> and records. I remained a devotee of Stravinsky (except
> for his *Œdipus rex*, which does not convince me). I
> became acquainted with the latest Schoenberg and
> Bartók, which greatly intrigued me. Hindemith with all
> his transcendence was revealed to me, and I continue to
> believe that he is the great figure of our time.[30]

We will return to the crisis in Rodrigo's relationship to the French musical avant-garde during this period, which took place at the same time as the crisis of the avant-garde itself. But we should take into account that a work like the *Preludio para un poema a La Alhambra*, orchestrated and developed under Dukas's guidance, reflects, for the first time in his catalogue, a vision of Spain with an exotic character that in Paris of the 1920s turned out to be perfectly recognizable and even familiar. While observing Dukas's interest in the *Preludio*, Rodrigo would learn another important lesson: Paris expected "Spanish" music from Spanish composers, or "Mexican" music from Mexicans. According to Rolón, "when I composed in Mexico, I made French music, and now that I am in France, I want to compose Mexican music."[31] This idea was always on Rodrigo's mind in these years.

Manuel de Falla in Paris: *Une heure de musique espagnole*

Midway through his first school year in the École Normale de Musique, Rodrigo was to find himself caught up in his orchestration assignments when a crucial event took place in his career. Manuel de Falla, who had just arrived in Paris at the end of February 1928, appeared at the École Normale de Musique on Thursday, March 1, about 11 a.m., to greet Dukas and to share with him the joyous reason bringing him to the French capital: he was to receive the title of Knight of the Legion of Honor, a distinction that Dukas had received in 1906, the year before Falla had begun to study with him. One detail of the importance that Dukas attached to this distinction is to be found in Ponce's biographical sketch of him, in which he emphasized the following characteristic of the maestro: "Alien to outer vanities, he allowed only one sign to betray his modesty: the rosette of the Legion of Honor that bloomed in the buttonhole of his lapel."[32]

As a reflection of the history that had taken place twenty-one years before, when Dukas introduced Falla, then his student, to his friend Isaac Albéniz, on this occasion the Frenchman officiated at the introduction of Rodrigo, his new outstanding student from Spain, to Falla, who had already heard about Rodrigo from the Parisian critic Robert Brussel. It was Brussel who advised Falla to visit Dukas at the École Normale de Musique: "There is something that would greatly please Dukas, I am sure, and it would be that you spend a moment tomorrow morning (around 11) at his class in the École Normale de Musique. Dukas will be happy to see you and to introduce you afterwards to your countryman Señor Rodrigo, that interesting blind young man I've spoken to you about."[33]

A few days after their meeting, Falla asked Rodrigo to take part in a concert on 14 March 1928 in Falla's honor, which Brussel was organizing with the French Association of Artistic

Expansion and Exchanges in the elegant salons of the centrally located Hotel of the Salomon de Rothschild Foundation. Rodrigo probably felt great alarm, because he was not a concert performer and was not used to performing formally in public. With his multiple diversions and various tasks in Paris, he had largely abandoned serious piano practice for several months. For that reason, he sought salvation from pianist Ricardo Viñes, who disappointed him with the news that he was already busy preparing the portion of the concert assigned to him: *Exaltación* by Joaquín Turina, a song and dance by Federico Mompou, *Polka del equilibrista* by Manuel Blancafort, Falla's "Romance del pescador" (Ballad of the Fisherman) from *El amor brujo*, and the "Miller's Dance" from *El sombrero de tres picos*. The Iturbis could not bail him out either, because they were not then in Paris.

Hence he had to gird his loins and prepare to do battle by performing for this solemn occasion two of his own pieces: one

Concert program in honor of Falla's appointment as knight of the Legion of Honor

mild, the *Zarabanda lejana*, which by contrast with the tenuous, very delicate glow of Falla's "Fisherman's Ballad," would shine even more; and the other, *Preludio al gallo mañanero*, a challenging piece of extraordinary bravura and strategically placed to close the first half of the program. In fact, this would be its premiere performance. Moreover, he was to accompany Alicia Felici in singing his *Cantiga: Muy graciosa es la doncella*, in what would be his debut as a composer of art songs.

Rodrigo reported to López-Chavarri that the notice of the concert reached him only two days before.[34] This may have been an exaggeration, as in subsequent accounts he reported conscientiously studying the works.[35] But time and again he would later admit to having played poorly—"the rooster ended up plucked, but crowed mightily."[36] And he always insisted he made a glutton of himself at the party that followed the concert: "they decorated the maestro, but I paid no attention. I was killing my fright by stuffing myself with candy at the side of two large girls."[37] But maybe he did not play as badly as he said, because some time afterwards, the organizer of the concert, Robert Brussel, published an account that provided much material for conversation:

> One of the greatest composers of our times was telling me on that occasion, "I have seen Albéniz, Falla, and Rodrigo arrive in Paris; I don't know if the third is, of the three, the most gifted. [. . .] Certainly much of the *Preludio al gallo mañanero* is still to be found in *Iberia* or *The Three-Cornered Hat*, but what beauty in the conception, what freshness of feeling, what delicacy in the design, what brilliance in color!"[38]

The composer to whom Brussel referred was probably Dukas. The idea of placing Rodrigo in the same front rank as Albéniz and Falla within the history of contemporary Spanish music now began to take hold in Paris. Capitalizing on the auspicious debut of the *Preludio al gallo mañanero*, *Le Monde Musical* published the work's first few pages with an introductory text stating that this excerpt would allow the reader "to glimpse the talent of this notable musician (a student of Paul Dukas at the École Normale de Musique), who would waste little time in taking his place alongside Albéniz and Falla, although in him the influence of his country's popular songs is less marked than in his distinguished countrymen."[39]

It would be difficult to imagine a more meaningful occasion for Rodrigo's Parisian debut than this concert in so lavish a place, as a tribute to Falla, with a program selected by the Andalusian maestro, given before the cream of French political culture, the Spanish embassy, and all of musical Paris. Indeed, a list of personalities, aristocrats, and people from the world of music took up more than thirty lines in the press notices, finally petering out with "etc., etc."[40] And his music was sandwiched between the *Harpsichord Concerto* and the *Siete canciones populares españolas* of Falla, which opened and closed the program, respectively. This was in addition to selections by Turina and Mompou, who in time would become two of his closest friends. Also represented on the program was Ernesto Halffter, his great rival, thus setting the stage for a rematch after they had faced off in the National Music Contest of 1925. On this occasion, we could say that they tied. Halffter served up his *Dos canciones* on texts by Rafael Alberti: "La corza blanca" of 1925 and "La niña que se va al mar" of 1926. Salazar appeared on the program with his *Canción de poeta* and most likely received news of what had happened at the Hôtel Rothschild. He dashed off an article for Ponce's *Gaceta Musical*, which bore a warning unmistakably aimed at Rodrigo:

Our regions possess musicians of great worth, who do
not lag far behind most foreigners for whom occupying
the middle of the road [. . .] helps them to circulate
more widely. But our communications abroad are scarce,
and even among us they are not excellent. Therefore,
it is necessary that we know each other before aiming
to be known beyond our borders. There are those
who impatiently prefer to be known in Paris before

they are known in Madrid itself. The result is a rather childish conceit. Those tender little musicians change into a passing Parisian flight of fancy instead of being a Spanish reality. It doesn't seem pertinent to cite cases.[41]

Ever obsessed with his battle against the succession Albéniz-Falla-Rodrigo that was emerging within the Parisian narrative of contemporary Spanish music, Salazar wrote a spiteful paragraph to Falla at the end of 1928, in which he mentioned Rodrigo for the first time in private, in very scornful terms:

Something that [Andrés] Segovia told me in the presence of Esplá has struck me as odd, on the subject of praising excessively and over my protest the little Valencian blind boy Rodrigo, who tells him that he is your student, etc. Segovia responded, "Paul Dukas told me that Rodrigo had gone to Paris with more technique than when Falla arrived," to which I answered that you [Falla] had gone with [the opera] La vida breve, which Dukas without a doubt forgot, and I added that merely for the sake of increasing their business, they [teachers of the École Normale de Musique like Dukas] are capable of saying anything. That mercantilism, whether Dukas's or of a Beethoven revival, whether of Debussy or of his wife "arranging" manuscripts, causes me anger and scorn. The French have won the war thanks to the United States, and with that they have lost their shame!![42]

Whether Salazar liked it or not—while stubbornly trying to exalt Ernesto Halffter as being unrivaled and at the zenith of his generation, and to offer the world a simplified, powerful reading of the history of Spanish music of the twentieth century—Rodrigo had debuted in Paris with considerable success. Falla had introduced him and had congratulated him on his Zarabanda lejana. Édouard Herriot, Minister of Public Instruction and Fine Arts, was charmed by the Preludio al gallo mañanero and approached to greet him. As our composer recalled the occasion, "I had the lofty honor of having Monsieur Herriot get up and shake my hand, which after the Spanish ambassador saw this—he had been sleeping during the whole concert—like a good self-respecting Spaniard, he arose willy-nilly and did the same to me as the minister."[43]

Aside from the lack of interest in music on the part of the Spanish ambassador (he was the conservative monarchist politician José María Quiñones de León), those early spring days in the French capital confirmed the Parisian passion for Spanish music in general and for Falla in particular, whom they had adopted as their own. Two days before the concert at the Hôtel Rothschild, entitled "Une heure de musique espagnole," thus evoking the title of Ravel's famous opera *L'Heure espagnole*, the Opéra-Comique added luster to his knighthood by presenting an evening of Falla's music. This opened on March 12 and featured *La vida breve*, *El amor brujo*, and *El retablo de maese Pedro*, which were repeated until the end of the month.[44] Taking advantage of the occasion, Vicente Escudero and Antonia "La Argentina" Mercé sang and danced in *El amor brujo* and then appeared afterwards by themselves doing Spanish dances.[45] Not to be outdone, the Salle Pleyel offered a Falla Festival on March 19, featuring the orchestra of Walther Straram, conducted by Falla himself. According to Rodrigo, "The loge is worth 100 francs, and there are no tickets left anymore; fortunately, they reserved me two orchestra chairs, naturally for free. [. . .] As you can see, things are progressing."[46]

And they were progressing, because Falla's push had been important. Rodrigo wisely took advantage to stay close to him during this season, as we can gather from his memoirs:

> The maestro [Falla] came down every day to a small
> café right beside the Opéra Comique; he arrived there
> before the rehearsal and after Mass; he ate very little for
> breakfast; and he took out of his pockets a quantity of
> vials full of pills, which he took with special devotion. He
> spoke little, with a soft voice, reposed and very low, but
> everything he said was interesting and personal. One of

those times he said to me, "Rodrigo, I am going to give
you a piece of advice to follow: never sell your works
to the editors. You never know. Keep a percentage for
yourself, even if small. I will introduce you to my editor."
And so he did.[47]

Falla could probably not have introduced him to his main
Parisian publisher, Max Eschig, who had died unexpectedly early
in September, leaving the firm in the hands of Eugène Cools as
general director and causing his business to go through some
moments of uncertainty as a result. Instead, he must have introduced Rodrigo to another important firm, with whom he had
worked some time previously: Rouart, Lerolle et Cie. And, in
fact, this timely introduction to the world of Parisian publishing enjoyed the strong support of both Falla and Dukas, from
whom the young composer received advice and recommendations for the publication of his first works. This was yet another
crucial step forward during his first academic year in Paris, and
it would soon result in a series of published scores, inaugurated
in July 1928 by the emblematic *Preludio al gallo mañanero* (plate
number 11647), followed by the *Suite para piano* (no. 11648), the
Bagatela (no. 11649), and *Cantiga: Muy graciosa es la doncella* (no.
11650). The *Bagatela* was announced as a recent publication in
the November issue of *Le Monde Musical*, while the other three
were announced in July. Notice of the publication of the *Dos
bocetos* appeared in December.

López-Chavarri spent a few days in Paris with Rodrigo in
April 1928, and upon his return to Valencia, he devoted to him a
long, very significant article on the front page of *Las Provincias*.
He clearly intended this as a riposte to Salazar's latest slur against
the young musician, which had appeared in the *Gaceta Musical*:

The successes of Joaquín Rodrigo have great
transcendence. His teacher, Dukas, shows great
contentment. His classmates applaud and "laud" him,
the *Gaceta Musical* [*Revue Musicale?*] invites him to their
meetings, Pruniéres, Collet, etc., give him affectionate

consideration [. . .] and all this due to his own value, without sponsors. For there are some musicians who powerfully support some student, thereby closing the way to those who enter without any other aid than their sincerity and their conviction. And despite everything, they win the day.[48]

The reference to the team formed by Salazar and Halffter cannot be clearer, but at the same time López-Chavarri took advantage of his article to give a very clear impression of how Rodrigo had settled perfectly in the French capital, mastered public transportation, and had served him as an effective guide:

If you ever thought that his glories went to the head of our fellow Valencian, you would not know him well. He continues to be the studious, modest boy, eager to learn, sentimental [. . .], and he continues to show that he is an incomparable guide, a tireless provider of facilities and solutions, from knowing where the best acoustics are in such and such a concert hall, to taking us for the best and cheapest café-au-lait.[49]

Rodrigo, who moved like a fish in the waters of Parisian culture, received a clipping of López-Chavarri's article sent to him by Óscar Esplá, and he rushed to write his thanks to that critic and to convey to him how he kept busy attending phenomenal concerts while preparing his return to Valencia:

You still have me excited about last night's version of *Don Giovanni* performed by those from Vienna. Really, if there is something perfect in the world, it is the version of Mozart that these people present. But up to what point is this perfection good? Won't it incapacitate us to hear Mozart again? I run away from this and fall into the version of the *Pastorale* given by Mengelberg, and now I realize that on Friday there is waiting for me the Philharmonic Orchestra of Berlin. Bruno Walter and Koussevitsky are waiting, baton on shoulder, and everywhere is announced the performance of Œdipus rex. What should I do? Pawn my overcoat?[50]

The decision he made must have been to pawn his overcoat, because he stayed in Paris at least until the end of May. Thus he must have had time to see not only Don Giovanni but also the complete season of the Vienna State Opera—Fidelio, Der Rosenkavalier, Tristan und Isolde; another cycle of Mozart's operas, under the direction of Bruno Walter; the concerts directed by Serge Koussevitzky at the Salle Pleyel, including the debut of a suite written by Honegger for Phaedra by Gabriele d'Annunzio; and the concerts of Willem Mengelberg with the Concertgebouw Orchestra of Amsterdam. Of course, he could not resist going to the Théâtre des Champs-Élysées to hear the concerts directed by Georges Georgescu, with José Iturbi as soloist on May 2. And with a little bit of luck, he would get to attend the debut of Stravinsky's Œdipus rex on May 30, a work that he never found convincing. Ultimately, this prolongation of his stay in Paris would also allow him to prepare his works for publication. We know from his correspondence with López-Chavarri that in those days of the spring of 1928 he was in communication with the editor, although actual publication was postponed until the beginning of the following season.

A Work That Evinced a Crisis: Berceuse de printemps (1928)

Before Rodrigo's important debut as a published composer, and in the middle of his ceaseless activity of attending concerts, on April 21 his music secured a place in the repertoire of a great concert pianist, Ricardo Viñes, who himself occupied a place of honor in the development of French avant-garde piano music at the start of the twentieth century. To Viñes, Rodrigo wisely dedicated his Preludio al gallo mañanero. In a recital of Spanish music, which included pieces by Emmanuel Chabrier, Erik Satie, Debussy, and Ravel, all with a Spanish flavor, Viñes premiered the Berceuse d'automne. Rodrigo had composed it in 1923 and would later dedicate it to Pierre-Octave Ferroud, a young composer whose premature death in an automobile accident truncated a promising career. The desolate character of the *Berceuse d'automne* surprised the influential Parisian critic Paul Le Flem, who stressed its "mélancolie obstinée et pesante" (stubborn, weighty melancholy).[51]

Clearly, the music that Rodrigo had written years before continued to unsettle the critics. In this case, the sad, leaden autumn represented in this early piece would prove surprising for its Central European color rather than a Valencian character. Rodrigo was perfectly aware of the difficulty of presenting the work by itself, and in fact, the only new composition he added to his catalogue at this time was a *Berceuse de printemps*, whose manuscript, copied by Ibáñez like that of the *Berceuse d'automne*, is dated "Paris 1928." We also find it in a collection of handwritten pieces titled "Hommage des élèves de la classe de Paul Dukas à Nadia Boulanger. Paris, mai 28" (Tribute of Students of the Class of Paul Dukas to Nadia Boulanger, Paris, May 28).[52] In fact, this piece is dedicated to Nadia Boulanger, assistant professor to Dukas at the École Normale de Musique, and completes the set of *Deux berceuses*, preceding the despondent autumn lullaby with a piece of naïve joy. It is structured as a round (five repetitions of two musical phrases), written with a very simple, diatonic lyricism and presented within a rich harmonic palette.

The *Berceuse de printemps* helps us to understand the reason for Rodrigo's creative silence during these months. It reflects his distance from polytonal procedures and from the music of a geographically neutral or international character that he had been cultivating. Rodrigo found himself at a crossroads in search of a new, more tonal style, one identifiable as Levantine, as he characterized it.[53] However, musical Valencianism or Levantinism are problematic concepts which have not been clearly defined. What is more interesting is the tonal planning of a work that turns out to be so simple in its formal and melodic parameters. As we have indicated, the piece consists of five rotations of a theme made up of two phrases (a and b): the first rotation is in the tonic, while the second moves from the tonic to the relative minor; the third then up a step; then moving from the subtonic to the dominant in the fourth rotation; and finally again in the tonic. The following scheme (table 3.2) shows this structure.

This organization, which is the key to this composition, shows a skillful handling of modulation, something on which Nadia Boulanger insisted very strongly in her classes. Evidence of this is at hand in José Rolón's account:

> There we met Schoenberg [the "we" being Rolón and
> Ponce, though probably Rodrigo, too], and we chatted
> for a long time with him about his atonal ideas. You
> cannot imagine with what a spirit of incredible modesty
> he himself confesses he is not free of uncertainties and
> contradictions. What a great fellow he is! Nadia comes
> over to us and lets Schoenberg know that I work with
> her in revising the modulations. Schoenberg raises his
> arms and almost screams, "Superb, Nadia, superb!"[54]

In the *Berceuse de printemps*—which surely pleased Boulanger—Rodrigo did not hesitate to insert within its stubbornly tonal and very diatonic structure a polytonal detail. In the

TABLE 3.2 *Berceuse de printemps,* harmonic and thematic process

1		2		3		4		5	
1–26	27–32	33–60	61–67–70	71–80	81–86	87–92	93–98	99–108	109–112
a	b cad	a	b cad	a	b	a^b	b	a	b cad
I	(vi)	I	vi^{+3}	ii	(vii)	VII	V	I___	
B	(g♯)	B	g♯$^{+3}$	Dorian C♯	(a♯)	A	F♯	B___	

second rotation of phrase b, the timely addition of a G♮ within the harmonic context of G♯ minor achieves a polytonal nuance. Nor does he dispense with modality when, in the third rotation, he presents the phrase as transposed a major second higher, but without changing the key signature into what would be a Dorian mode with a final of C♯ (i.e., C♯ minor with a raised sixth degree). The cadence of the first, second, and final rotations, as well as the juxtaposition of the phrases "a" and "b" (a^b in our scheme) in the fourth rotation, are details of compositional elegance and ingenuity in a work that only on its surface appears to be naïve.

The first period of Rodrigo's Parisian stay would culminate in a new premiere: the version for string orchestra of his *Zarabanda lejana*, which was presented 6 May 1928 in the brand-new auditorium of the École Normale de Musique as the finale of the concert of "Premières Auditions d'Oeuvres des Elèves de la Classe de Composition de M. Paul Dukas" (First Hearings of Works of the Students of the Composition Class of M. Paul Dukas).[55] Although a double quartet performed this debut, on June 9, in a concert of the International Society of Contemporary Music at the Grand Palais, the same work was interpreted with a full set of strings.[56] There is hardly any news of this second concert, which offered works by the Swiss Conrad Beck, the German Paul Hindemith, the Italian Vittorio Rieti, the Russian Vladimir Deshevov, and the Mexican Manuel Ponce. But, according to López-Chavarri, the *Zarabanda lejana* was encored.[57] A few days previously, on May 31, Leopoldo Querol played a program of Spanish music in the chamber auditorium of the Salle Pleyel, and on his program appeared the music of Rodrigo alongside that of López-Chavarri, Viñes, Halffter, Palau, Nin Castellanos, Turina, Falla, Albéniz, and Granados.[58] In his review in *Le Ménestrel*, Collet highlighted the *Danse ibérienne* of Joaquín Nin Castellanos,[59] but only thanks to the remarks of López-Chavarri in *Las Provincias* do we know that the work by Rodrigo that Querol played was the *Bagatela*, which had premiered some time before.[60] Two weeks before this concert, Collet had made a surprise announcement: "The blind composer Joaquín Rodrigo, Paul Dukas's student, returns to Valencia, his native city, to work on some important symphonic compositions."[61] This is surprising precisely because a leading weekly of the French musical press deemed Rodrigo's return to Valencia newsworthy, when Falla's departure at the beginning of April had gone unnoticed. Moreover, it sought to inform the reader that Rodrigo had an assignment for his vacation.

Classes had ended at the École Normale de Musique, and Dukas soon departed on a journey as commissioner for music education, to evaluate the pedagogy in the provinces. It is obvious that the net result of Rodrigo's first school year would have been excellent if, during the long six months he resided in Paris, he had composed some new works besides the *Berceuse de printemps*. Aware of that and surely goaded by Dukas, he left Paris promising to return with his folder full of major new symphonic compositions. We shall see what he did.

Valencia . . . with Ravel

Rodrigo's intention was to spend a few days in Madrid before returning to Valencia. We do not know whether he did, nor do we know the exact date of his return, although we assume that he remained in Paris to attend Querol's concert of 31 May 1928 and the premiere of *Zarabanda lejana* with string orchestra on June 9. He would then have reached Valencia with the season practically over, perhaps in time to attend the June 27 opening of the summer season of the Orquesta Sinfónica de Valencia (Valencia Symphony Orchestra), directed by José Manuel Izquierdo in the gardens of the Viveros Municipales (Municipal Nurseries); and to be present at the final concerts of the Philharmonic Society in the Teatro Principal, featuring the Orquesta Sinfónica de Madrid (Madrid Symphony Orchestra) with its chief director, Fernández Arbós, on June 28, 29, and 30.[62] But he especially longed to bathe in the warm waters of the Mediterranean, to sunbathe half naked, shocking the natives, to settle himself again into the discussion groups in the Pavilion of Las Arenas, spend all night in the July Fair of the city, enjoy his mother's care, and take ample time to savor the mountain air in the country home of Estivella (21 miles north of Valencia), where the family usually spent about a month when the weather in the capital got too hot. And in those idle pursuits he would pass the summer, awaiting the appearance of the music published in Paris. Perhaps he devoted time to correcting printed proofs with Ibáñez or his Valencian friends, because the editions began to come out perfectly clean in August.

The most remarkable event of those restful months in Valencia—both for Rodrigo and for the Valencia Philharmonic—was Maurice Ravel's brief trip to the city during a wide-ranging tour of Spanish provinces that included visits to Bilbao, San Sebastián, Pamplona, Zaragoza, Valencia, Málaga, Granada, Madrid, Oviedo, and Portuguese Porto.[63] Ravel reached Valencia on 16 November 1928 to attend the festival organized in his honor by the Philharmonic Society in the Teatro Principal the following day. There a program was presented in which Ravel

With Ravel in Valencia, 1928. From left to right, Luis Ayllón, Eduardo López-Chavarri, unidentified, Maurice Ravel, Claude Lévy, Madeleine Grey, José Manuel Izquierdo, Leopoldo Querol, Joaquín Rodrigo, Eduardo Ranch, Jacinto Ruiz Manzanares, and unidentified

himself performed his *Sonata No. 2* at the piano with violinist Claude Lévy, and accompanied singer Madeleine Grey in his *Mélodies hébraïques*; the Valencia Orquesta Sinfónica conducted by Izquierdo played *Ma mère l'Oye*, the orchestral version of *Alborada del gracioso*, and, to close the concert, *La valse*. But before this finale, Ravel came up to the platform to direct the three orchestral melodies, *Shéhérazade*, sung by Grey, and *Tzigane* with Lévy as soloist. The violin-piano version of this latter work, interpreted by its dedicatee, Jelly d'Arányi, had already been heard in Valencia.[64] Apparently the conservative Valencian audience received it with serious reservations, as did the majority of Spanish philharmonic societies of that period.

Indeed, only a small segment of the audience would likely have been able to understand the meaning, let alone the exotic humor, of *Tzigane*'s out-of-kilter, "barbaric" music, despite the valiant educational effort of a critic like Eduard Ranch in *La Correspondencia de Valencia*.[65] Precisely that daily informs us of what happened after the festival:

> [Ravel] has shown that he is tireless while chatting and endlessly strolling through our city until the wee hours of the night in the company of some of our young artists. The night of the concert, after it ended, he was presented with an intimate supper in the *Termas* [an elegant restaurant on the beach of Malvarrosa], attended by Miss Grey, the composers Mr. Chavarri and Rodrigo, the pianist Leopoldo Querol, and our music editor Ranch, finally joined by Mr. Gomá, the critic of the *Diario de Valencia*. The hours passed pleasantly, and Monsieur Ravel was constantly displaying considerable ingenuity. Thus, for instance, when told that more people had attended Saturday's concert than any other, and when informed that the exact number of those present had been two thousand minus three, Maurice Ravel, with a very expressive gesture, said, "What could those three persons have been doing? They must have been conspiring against me!"[66]

The conspirators were probably not few in number, and many of them were likely to have been found among the two thousand who attended the festival. Their spokesman could have been the critic of *El Mercantil Valenciano*, Bernardo Morales Sanmartín, alias "Fidelio," who abominated any novelty, to such a degree that Rodrigo—who never usually spoke so ill of anybody—once wrote to López-Chavarri that "*Fidelio* is a braying ass."[67] He was not always that bad, and, on this occasion, the critic limited himself to pointing out that the sonata for violin and piano, "in view of its very special character," generated "applause full of understanding and murmurs of impatience."[68] But his disgust was as apparent as that of Gomá, who, though he considered himself one of Rodrigo's friends, also represented the conservative sectors and could not help but excuse the audience's attitude in one of the best reviews we have of this musical event:

> The works already known to the audience or more
> accessible to them were listened to with pleasure, but—
> and this is not strange at all—the extremism of the
> Sonata for piano and violin, for instance, was received
> with a natural attitude of reserved courtesy. Maestro
> Ravel, with his usual friendliness, told us afterwards that
> more or less everywhere, the same thing happened.[69]

The fact is that even the violinist Claude Lévy recognized in a letter he sent to Brussel from Valencia that the sonata had been a disaster, "very debated and at times even a bit *put down*! It's true that even in Paris, it is not always received with rapture!"[70] In this respect, it is very noteworthy that the audience could more easily excuse the exoticism of *Tzigane*—surely finding its virtuosity amusing and acceptable—than the exoticism of the jazzy blues of the second movement of the magnificent Sonata No. 2.

While the Ravel Festival at the Teatro Principal was a tribute of the Valencia Philharmonic elite, the following day, on November 18, a function directed more to the masses took place in the Jardines del Real. The Municipal Band played works by Valencian composers, among whom were Salvador Giner, Eduardo López-Chavarri, Manuel Palau, Pedro Sosa, and Francisco Cuesta. As a finale, Ravel conducted an arrangement of La valse, prepared by band leader Luis Ayllón, and the Marseillaise, which most likely appealed to the French musician as well as to the numerous local partisans of the Republic there in full force. There was also a spectacle of Valencian folk dances, and speeches pronounced by the Marquis of Villagracia as delegate of the mayor, the president of the Philharmonic Society and, as representatives of the musical guild, Manuel Palau and Eduardo López-Chavarri, whose words were the only ones that Ravel heard (and understood) in French.

Although Rodrigo was conspicuously absent from the program of Valencian music interpreted by the Municipal Band—something very significant and repeated to a degree we shall soon see—that very day of November 18, in the Salle Gaveau in Paris, the siblings Encarnación and Abelardo Mus debuted his Dos esbozos, Op. 1, for violin and piano.[71]

Rodrigo missed the Paris premiere of Dos esbozos and was surely hurt by not appearing on the same program as the Valencian musicians, but he was well rewarded by the opportunity to meet Ravel personally:

> I shall never forget the impression that meeting Maurice Ravel caused me when he came to Valencia to offer a concert of his works in that Philharmonic Society, by which I was appointed to accompany him through the city and to serve as translator in the rehearsals. I will always remember his fine irony and his swift replies and observations. At the time, Ravel was orchestrating what would later be his famous Bolero, which he played on the piano [. . .]. A year later, I was witness to the greatest scandal I recall in Paris when Ravel premiered the orchestrated version of this work.[72]

The Bolero, in the stage version danced by Ida Rubinstein, debuted in Paris on 22 November 1928, Rodrigo's birthday. Ravel, still on tour through Spain, happened to be giving a concert at the French embassy in Madrid in the presence of the loftiest personalities of the Spanish aristocracy and of the diplomatic corps. Nonetheless, it is probable that, as Rodrigo pointed out, Ravel was then working on the orchestration of the concert version that Arturo Toscanini was to debut with the New York Philharmonic on 14 November 1929, with a success diametrically opposed to the scandal caused by the Parisian debut, to which Rodrigo referred, with Ravel in front of the Orchestre Lamoureux 11 January 1930 at the Salle Gaveau. The first long year of the life of Ravel's *Bolero* would play a central role in Rodrigo's life, because he came to this debut in the company of someone who, as of spring 1929, would always be at his side.

The School Year That Was Almost a Blank Slate, 1928–29

Rodrigo stopped in Barcelona on his way back to Paris in November 1928,[73] and there he agreed to collaborate as the Parisian correspondent for the leading publication *Revista Musical Catalana*. This position would allow him to exercise his pen and his judgment as a critic. During this academic year, he continued to stay at the home of the painter Povo, making things easier and relieving the expense that living in Paris imposed on his family.

The day after arriving, he went directly to the École Normale de Musique to resume his classes with Dukas. The good news was that he found there Jesús Arámbarri, with whom he formed a fast friendship and who thereafter would go with him to concerts. The bad news was that the long symphonic works he had promised to bring with him from Valencia had never made the journey from pen to paper, and he showed up with only two songs. He himself casually relates the scene with Dukas:

> Uncle Paulo [Dukas] very much liked [the two songs], and asked me, "What orchestral pieces have you brought?" *Pas d'orchestre* [Nothing orchestral]. "And what piano pieces?" *Pas de piano* [Nothing for piano]. He remained awhile in thought, his eyebrows knit, and afterwards

smilingly said, "Ah! It's true that in Valencia you have a pavilion overlooking the sea with your friend Chavarri and your friend Gomá, who have probably worked at least as hard as you."[74]

Rodrigo was aware that maybe he should have shown up with something more, but that was all he had brought that was new: two songs on classical texts that are to be found in the famous anthology of Marcelino Menéndez Pelayo, *Las cien mejores poesías líricas de la lengua castellana* (Madrid 1908), undoubtedly the source from which Rodrigo had taken these poems. The *Romance de la Infantina de Francia*, dated Valencia, August 1928, was composed on the anonymous "Romance de la hija del rey de Francia," and the *Serranilla* was based on a poem of Íñigo López de Mendoza, Marquis of Santillana. This was the first entry in the anthology of Menéndez Pelayo, and it is dated Valencia in November (although López-Chavarri mentioned its existence already in August).[75] These two works are nonetheless important for their relative length (52 eight-syllable verses in the ballad and 44 six-syllable verses in the *Serranilla*) and for their stature as two small scenes with a certain dramatic development, presenting action and a dialogue between two characters: the infanta and knight in the ballad, and the herdswoman and knight in the *Serranilla*.

They are also significant because, in comparison with the *Cantiga*, they once more show, like the *Berceuse de printemps*, an abandonment of the experimental harmonies that inform his first works, in favor now of a much more defined structure within the limits of traditional tonality. In this sense, these songs accept the principles of tonality and adorn it with modal or bitonal interpolations. For even within the tonality—B minor in the ballad and F♯ minor in the *Serranilla*—they are works with a tonal plan as subtle as that of the *Berceuse de printemps*. Hence, the *Serranilla* also consists of a series of rotations around a refrain in F♯ minor with a modal episode (B♭ Dorian) and another of polytonal color, like those of the *Berceuse*, while the *Romance de la Infantina de Francia* plays with the polarity between the Dorian mode and the minor key within the same key signature, beginning with Dorian on E and concluding in B minor (key signature of two sharps). Both songs reinterpret a use of melody with a pre-Baroque character, very syllabic in the case of the *Serranilla* and richly adorned in the case of the main theme of the *Romance*, and they reinforce their archaic style with parallel movements of the bass in hollow fifths and some softer arpeggios that suggest the accompaniment of a plucked-string instrument.

In musical terms, the school year yielded little more: the two new songs that Rodrigo had composed in Valencia were published by Rouart, Lerolle et Cie in June, with the texts translated into French by Henri Collet. But the truly important event for Rodrigo's career was the performance by Walther Straram and his orchestra of the *Cinco piezas infantiles* at the Théâtre des Champs-Élysées on 28 March 1929, in a concert directly broadcast by Radio Paris and presented as a premiere, although we recall that the work was actually premiered in Spain five years earlier. Straram placed these pieces between *Escales* (1922) by Jacques Ibert and Debussy's *La Mer*, and they were better received than they had been in Spain. Leading critics like Émile Vuillermoz in *Excelsior* (1 April 1929), Louis Aubert in *Paris-soir* (2 April 1929), and Paul Le Flem in *Comoedia* (6 April 1929) wrote glowing reviews of Rodrigo's music, and Robert Brussel devoted to him his whole column on the third page of *Le Figaro* (5 April 1929).[76] His success was very noteworthy, and Rodrigo hastened to communicate it to López-Chavarri:

On Thursday the debut of the *Cinco piezas infantiles* took place in the Theater of the Champs Elysées. The thing truly went well. The theater managers rushed to send me seats for the best box, and this alone will prove to you that we are far away from our shiny Philharmonic. Querol, Rafael, two more friends, and I sat in it. I was really bothered and a bit nervous. The theater was full of people, a great number of them Parisian critics, [. . .] not for me, naturally, but for Straram and his orchestra. And Paul Dukas, yes indeed, was there for my sake, and I was very grateful, for the maestro, feeling a bit under the weather, never goes out at night.[77]

In the same letter, Rodrigo enclosed newspaper clippings of the reviews by Vuillermoz and Aubert, "two gentlemen difficult to satisfy, and whom I do not know, and that's why their favorable judgments are even weirder." He also included a piece of news that sheds light on his lack of creative activity during this second year of studies in Paris: "If you add to all this [the good weather and the success of the *Cinco piezas infantiles*] a short skirt, one that is very short, naturally you will understand that I am delighted with Paris."[78] The hint contained in this letter was completed in the following one: "Spring has crystallized, has become symbolized, by a sweet girl who [. . .] adores music and casually wanders through flowering paths, her hair and her thoughts flying in the wind."[79]

That woman was Victoria Kamhi (1902–1987), a young Sephardic girl born in Istanbul, to a family of wealthy Jewish merchants who were involved in the pharmaceutical business. Her father was Turkish and her mother, Viennese. Kamhi, who besides French spoke German and the Sephardic dialect of Spanish called Ladino, had just earned her degree as a piano teacher after several years of study in the Conservatoire with the great maestro Lazare Lévy.[80] She had been captivated by the excerpt of the *Preludio al gallo mañanero* that appeared in print in *Le Monde Musical* on 31 July 1928. Alexandre Demetriade, a student auditing Dukas's classes, was a friend of hers and introduced her to Rodrigo at a party that Kamhi threw at her home, with the aim of meeting the composer of the excerpt that had so impressed her. In her memoirs, Kamhi said the following about her introduction to Rodrigo:

> A deep emotion invaded me when he shook my hand. I was able to babble a few words of welcome, and it seemed to me that my little voice, a bit childlike, amused him. A merry smile lit up his face, revealing a row of very white teeth. What most attracted my attention was his broad brow, framed by curls of light brown hair. Then I realized that he almost did not see me.[81]

They immediately began to go out together and attend concerts. From the orchestra level she saw the success of the

Victoria Kamhi

Cinco piezas infantiles with the composer in his box receiving the applause.[82] They took long walks while searching for the parks and shadows of the fabled *ville lumière*. And thus the end of Rodrigo's school year disappeared while he explored all the corners of the Bois de Boulogne with his companion, experiencing with her the hopeful awakening of what would be a great love, enjoying the ascent of his fame in the Parisian music world and attending concerts as a correspondent for the *Revista Musical Catalana*. On March 29 appeared his first article, and from then on, we can reconstruct with great precision the most important concerts he attended and the opinion he had of them. This series of articles, all in the Catalan language, reveal an acute critic and an elegant writer, with a well-formed taste and reliable information about what was current in music.

His final column of the season, appearing in the June issue, turned out to be especially informative. In the first place, he commented with very little enthusiasm on the May 29 presentation of the Ballets Espagnols and of Antonia Mercé ("La Argentina") at the Opéra-Comique. This featured a repeat performance of the *Sonatina* by Ernesto Halffter, which had already been programmed the previous season, and the debut of *Triana*, one of Fernández Arbós's orchestrations of Albéniz's *Iberia*. In the second place, he remarked on the premiere of the revised version of *Amériques* by Edgard Varèse, presented by conductor Gaston Poulet with his orchestra at the Salle Gaveau May 30. Rodrigo ironically pointed out that Varèse needed to double again his already enormous orchestra (120 musicians with 11 percussionists) because the hubbub it produced paled in comparison to that of the Strasbourg Boulevard that he crossed every day. Otherwise, he wrote that what he had been able to hear of the music amidst the whistles, shouts, and foot-stamping of the audience seemed to him monotonous, amorphous, and inarticulate, and that the means selected by the composer to transmit "the emotion of the stormy life of New York" appeared to be "excessively naïve and primitive."[83]

After this concert, in which he was also able to hear the symphonic poem *Amazonas* by Heitor Villa-Lobos, Rodrigo spent early June at the opening of the first Salon International de la Symphonie, a project to connect orchestra conductors with composers and thereby stimulate the creation and performance of symphonic works. This project had been organized at the École Normale de Musique through the initiative of its director, Auguste Mangeot. Though Alban Berg, Honegger, Prokofiev, Ravel, Roussel, and Stravinsky joined the initiative by registering their works, it was far from being a success.[84] Collet, always keeping watch over the musical presence of Spain in the international arena, observed that the only Spaniards represented in that event were Rodrigo, with *Juglares* and *Cinco piezas infantiles*; Conrado del Campo, with *Evocación medieval* (1924) and *Una kasida* (1927); and Manuel Blancafort, with *El matí de festa a Puig-graciós* (1929). Collet was surprised that Jaime Pahissa, Manuel Palau, and Bartolomé Pérez Casas, who were enrolled, had not presented any compositions.[85] The lack of young composers representing the Grupo de Madrid (Madrid Group) at this event is just one indicator of the differences separating composers in Madrid from those in Barcelona. Rodrigo, who had attempted to align himself with the Madrid group in the early 1920s, now had even closer relations with the Catalans.

Valencia, Paris, Valencia

Because Ibáñez had a medical emergency, they left Paris on 11 June 1929, without even staying long enough to hear the *Cinco piezas infantiles* performed in the auditorium of the École Normale de Musique that very day. Neither did they stop in Barcelona, as Rodrigo had hoped. Instead, they traveled directly to Valencia, arriving on June 12.[86] The situation there was different from the one they had left behind: Rodrigo's father had had to mortgage his properties and was heavily indebted to the banks. These setbacks put him at a great disadvantage when the Great Depression descended in the last quarter of 1929. It was even more unfortunate that the Rodrigo family's main source of income was the exportation of agricultural products, mainly oranges. For a time,

With his sister-in-law on the beach in Valencia

the situation was ameliorated by good harvests and remained merely worrisome. So, for a time, our composer could continue to lead his normal life.

However, Rodrigo's creative stagnation persisted, and on one occasion, in a despondent mood, he wrote to his beloved, "I do not feel in me the sacred fire, and it is possible that my career is now over."[87] But he generally would hide the lack of musical production behind a façade of poorly feigned laziness:

I go to bed late, at 2 a.m., and, of course, I also arise very late. I am almost ashamed to tell you at what time I arise: at 11 and even later (don't scold me; in Spain life lags way behind). I get up, head to the sea, and go bathing. Since Rafael does not because he is afraid of drowning (he is always so cautious), I bathe with my friends. If Victoria saw me, on the beach I would seem like a Yankee multimillionaire: one friend takes along a towel, another throws it on top of me, the closest one grabs my arm, the one farther away puts himself by my side. In short, it is delightful to be well served. Afterwards, we sunbathe while lying on the sand, scandalizing the fearful, prudish people. We eat lunch at 2:30, I read a short while, at 6:30 we go back to the beach. There, in a pleasant pavilion overlooking the sea, I have a peaceful discussion with a somewhat heterogeneous group, of which I am the spoiled child. We eat very late, almost at 10:00, and afterwards I take part in another conversation group [. . .]. And you will ask yourself, when does Joaquín make music? Alas! Alas! I also ask myself the same thing, Vicky dear, I also. Isn't it alright that my life isn't bad?[88]

With this essentially vacation-like lifestyle, the only thing he positively accomplished in the summer of 1929 was to prepare the score of *Preludio para un poema a La Alhambra* for Straram, so that he could program it during the following season. On August 24, he went with his parents to Estivella, where he could concentrate somewhat on composing. He attempted

to write two dances for piano and even had written down
the themes, but he got stuck and did not finish them: "My
dances don't advance, and I am very sad, my Muse forgets
me."[89] At least well into the month of September, he succeeded
in composing his "Giga" for orchestra, on which he would put
the finishing touches, along with the orchestrations of the
"Pastoral" and the "Minué," all together comprising his *Tres
viejos aires de danza*:

> I have written it with a rapidity and ease that astonishes
> even me. Clearly, since it is a question of a more or less
> faithful imitation of the eighteenth century, I have not
> taken care to seek original harmonies or sets of unforeseen
> sonorities. Nevertheless, I am naïvely enjoying myself by
> making the innocent turtledove sing, as well as the joking
> cuckoo and the toads, all great friends of mine.[90]

Tres viejos aires de danza is a work for a chamber orchestra.
The three movements, "Pastoral," "Minué," and "Giga," reveal
that Rodrigo's penchant for the archaic is once again to the fore,
but more in the manner of his *Homenaje al viejo clavicembalo* and
not the *Suite para piano*. That is to say that there is no attempt at
irony or satire here, and no consequent musical means of distanc-
ing us from the subject matter by the use of nonharmonic tones,
bitonality, or polymeters, the stock-in-trade of French necoclas-
sicists. Rather, as the title seems to suggest, this is a sort of evocation of musical antiquity more closely resembling Respighi's
Ancient Airs and Dances, the first two suites of which appeared in
1917 and 1923 and may well have served as a prototype. However,
those works were modern arrangements of actual Renaissance
and Baroque pieces, whereas these miniatures flowed directly
from Rodrigo's fertile imagination.

"Pastoral" exhibits the dotted rhythms that characterize that
genre, though in 3/4 rather than 6/8, and it deploys a serenely
graceful melody, first in the strings alone and then passed
among the oboe, clarinet, and finally the horns, while the flute
plays Rodrigo's cuckoo signature. The formal technique here is

basically a set of variations, in which the melody is repeated within a kaleidoscope of changing orchestral colors.

The "Minué" is at once spritely and graceful, laid out in the ternary form typical of the Baroque dance, i.e., ABA-coda. As was the case in the "Pastoral," the harmonies, though not strictly Baroque, are very traditional and evince little of Stravinsky or Ravel. There are a few measures in the trio with playful dissonances, but they never threaten to disrupt a resolutely tonal harmonic language.

The "Giga" is a perpetual-motion carousel featuring hunting horns and the sort of riotous good spirits for which Rodrigo is fondly remembered. There are moments of rollicking calls and trills in the horns and darkly comical dissonances. Rodrigo's growing confidence as an orchestrator is on display here in the effective contrasting of instrumental "choirs" of strings and winds. The form is unexpectedly convoluted and features a three-part exposition, or ABC, the B and C sections of which are each repeated before a reprise of the entire exposition. This is followed by extended development in a concluding D section, which is likewise repeated.

Taken as a set, these pieces are every bit as original as they are derivative, a trick that Rodrigo was especially good at performing. Indeed, the work does not deserve the underestimation that Rodrigo gave it in the letter quoted above, and when it debuted in Valencia on 24 January 1930, with the Orquesta Sinfónica conducted by José Manuel Izquierdo, the work pleasantly surprised the large conservative sectors of the Philharmonic Society's audience. Yet, in the program notes, the composer insisted on keeping his distance from any retrogressive orientation suggested by those works: "Three musical moments at the margin of my career, suggested by the desire to give a modest tribute to the dear old maestros."[91] The critic of the daily La Correspondencia de Valencia—surely Eduardo Ranch—stressed that "those who are scandalized by the modern inspiration of men like our Rodrigo learn that the same talent knows how to express old themes."[92]

From López-Chavarri's news item, one reads between the lines that the Orquesta Sinfónica did not prepare this work well enough.[93] This is surprising, since it was premiering music that was friendly and not too complicated, by a local composer (Rodrigo was a member of the Philharmonic Society of Valencia). But it is even more surprising that Rodrigo did not attend this premiere. Instead, he was in Paris attending the third school year with Dukas. It is also surprising that the Valencian press did not point out that this had been a debut.

Between so many surprises probably lies the lack of understanding between Rodrigo and Izquierdo, who perhaps was offended when the entire French press ostentatiously announced the interpretation of the *Cinco piezas infantiles* by Straram as a "first time" or "first hearing," when he had given the actual premiere in Valencia. Then again, this was not to be the final occasion for friction between Izquierdo and Rodrigo, because in the summer concerts of 1930 in the Jardines del Real, on August 2, as a finale of the July holiday, the Valencia Orquesta Sinfónica gave a concert of works by Valencian composers, including Salvador Giner, Ruperto Chapí, Leopoldo Magenti, Juan Vert, Francisco Cuesta, Rafael Guzmán, the orchestra leader José Manuel Izquierdo himself, Enrique Gomá, Eduardo López-Chavarri, Manuel Palau, and José Moreno Gans.[94] Rodrigo was in the audience, and it is clear that in a list like the preceding, his absence turned out to be very conspicuous. Wounded, he wrote to his lady love,

I have been left out, I don't know why. [. . .] This is nothing new for me because among the orchestra musicians and the numbskull of a conductor (let us call him that), I do not enjoy great sympathies, first because they do not like my music very much, and second because I don't call them geniuses. When I am asked about the orchestra, I tell the truth.[95]

In the letter to follow, now in a better humor, he went back over the same theme and made his dislike of Izquierdo apparent: "My friends have mocked me and pulled my leg because the other day my name did not appear among the Valencian composers whose works made up the concert I told you about. I was there, it was horrible. [. . .] The numbskull of a conductor came to me all remorseful to ask my forgiveness and to tell me that it was an oversight."[96]

Nevertheless, between the insult of Rodrigo's absence from the premiere of the *Tres viejos aires de danza* in January and the offense of Izquierdo's failure to put him on the program with the rest of the Valencian composers in August, there was a sort of rapprochement on 9 July 1930, when the Valencia Orquesta Sinfónica played for the second time the *Tres viejos aires de danza*, this time in the presence of the composer. The reconciliation was somewhat mitigated by the orchestra's deficient interpretation, as Rodrigo emphasized ("they couldn't have played worse"), but at last he could hear the effect of his orchestration and show his contentment as a result:

> It is the first time I am satisfied with the orchestration. I only have to reinforce the flute at a few points with the oboe at the lower octave, and in other passages the oboe with the bassoon also an octave lower. That's all. I will also eliminate some slurs to give the piece more variety, by using the strokes of the bow and thus giving it more freedom and grace.[97]

The care Rodrigo used with the notation of slurs and phrase marks shows us the importance he attached to the interpretation and his interest in controlling it to the degree he could: "The interpretation is everything for composers," he said on one occasion.[98] It made sense for him to be concerned about this matter because, after his recent entry into the publishing market, his music began to circulate among different interpreters (see Appendix 3).

Rodrigo returned to Valencia from Estivella in mid-September 1929 with the "Giga" finished and much work still to complete: he had to make a clean final copy of this new composition, since the *Tres viejos aires de danza* were going to premiere in Valencia in January, and he also had to score the orchestra for the *Preludio para un poema a La Alhambra* that Straram wanted to debut in his 1929–30 season. He finished the two tasks, and further-more, on November 5, one week before departing for Paris, he informed Victoria Kamhi, "Today I have finished the *Siciliana;* I think you'll like it."[99] Written for cello and piano, the *Siciliana* is the first piece of chamber music that Rodrigo composed after the early *Dos esbozos,* Op. 1. In addition, it is notable because it shows for the first time the cultivation of a "great form" in Rodrigo's catalogue. According to the composer, he had constructed it "in Lied sonata form."[100]

The *Siciliana* is in binary form (mm. 1–83; mm. 84–124), emphasized by the reappearance of the main theme in measure 84 and Picardy-third cadences (mm. 80 and 123) at the end of each of the two parts. Table 3.3 below shows the equivalencies of the measures of the exposition and the recapitulation.

While the work's form is interesting, once again what is most noteworthy about the *Siciliana* is its harmonic structure (table 3.4). Rodrigo's piece passes through all the twelve minor key areas. On the other hand, the persistent use of the natural minor (Aeolian) reinforces its modal character.

Rodrigo debuted his *Siciliana* in a concert of Dukas's students at the École Normale de Musique on 19 March 1930, with himself accompanying cellist Diran Alexanian, assistant of Pablo Casals in his chair of that school.[101] A few days later and in that very place,

TABLE 3.3 **Siciliana, equivalencies of the measures of exposition and recapitulation**

Exposition	Recapitulation
1–8	84–90
9–22	90–101
42–52	101–111
	112–114
53–54	115–116
	117–124

TABLE 3.4 *Siciliana,* harmonic and thematic process

bars	1–24	24–41 / 42–48	48–55	55–68	69–74	75	76	77–80–83 //
keys	e–b	f♯–c♯ / b–f♯	d–a	f–c	f–c	g♯	a♯	d♯–d♯+3 //
Thematic material	A-B	A-B	C-D	C-D	C-D	C-D	D	D	D
		P	S						
		i	v	iii/v	v/v				
	Exposition				Development				

bars	84–101	101–108	108–111	112	113	114	115–119	120–124
keys	e	e–b	g	d	f♯	b	e–b	b–e⁹/+3
Thematic material	A-B	C-D	C-D	D	D	D	D	C
	P	S						
	i	i	iii/i			v/i		
	Recapitulation							

the composer would have the opportunity to introduce himself to Casals in person. It was at a concert that took place in honor of the performer on 18 March 1930, when a group of more than fifty cellists conducted by him played his *Sardana.*[102] According to Rodrigo,

> When I congratulated him after the concert with the timidity that is natural in the presence of a famous artist, I personally experienced his proverbial affability and his exemplary simplicity. He asked after my works and my stylistic orientations, and when I told him that I passed every year through Barcelona, on the way to France, he invited me to visit him at his home. This was the beginning of a sincere friendship based on the admiration I had for the multiple facets of this singular artist.[103]

He once again spent the school year 1929–30 between concerts and courtship, but this time he at least succeeded in finishing an important composition: the *Villancico* for string orchestra, signed 19 April 1930. It is the first work that Rodrigo composed in Paris. Paired with the orchestral version of the *Zarabanda lejana*, it now formed the symphonic diptych *Zarabanda lejana y villancico*. Thus, in its complete form, the Orchestre Féminin (an all-female orchestra) of Jane Evrard premiered it in March 1931. According to the composer, they played it well, although "the Villancico has the heebie-jeebies," he said, stressing the virtuosic dimension of this music that would be a common component of future compositions.

The *Villancico* makes inventive use of *divisi* strings to fill out the texture. Now, to be sure, the title of this work is likely to cause as much confusion as that of the *Zarabanda lejana.* The villancico is remembered today as a vocal work of religious devotion that became popular in the seventeenth and eighteenth centuries, not only in Iberia but throughout the Spanish Americas, where it often featured lyrics in local languages or dialects of Indigenous and African populations and was popular at Christmas or Easter. Before its transformation into a vehicle for vernacular religious sentiment, it was popular as a song and dance of the theater, as, particularly, the villancicos of Juan del Encina. But as its name implies, before all that it was a song and dance associated with village-dwelling peasants, or *villanos*, the root of the word *villancico*. Though this is a purely instrumental evocation of the villancico, without voices or lyrics, it exhibits the rustic *joie de vivre* of those earliest varieties of the genre and which persisted in its later incarnations. At any rate, it is clear that both the *Zarabanda lejana* and *Villancico* were inspired by prototypes of the sixteenth and seventeenth centuries.

Rodrigo himself described its form as a simple kind of sonata-rondo.[104] Sonata-rondo form, typical of the Classical period, exhibits an ABACABA format in which the contrasting middle section consists of development rather than new material. Though the sonata-rondo format may have no relation to the villancico, the composer obviously felt himself unconstrained by such musicological minutiae. At all events, this paean to the distant past in a work for string orchestra, skillfully composed, may remind some readers of the *Fantasia on a Theme of Thomas Tallis* by Ralph Vaughan Williams.[105] Though the sources of inspiration for the two works are quite different, there is still a certain purity, even solemnity, in the overall sound that accords with their antiquarian intent. At all events, Rodrigo would revisit the villancico in the fourth section of his *Concierto madrigal* (1966) for two guitars and orchestra, a reassertion of the genre that will make for an interesting comparison.

The fourth school year in Paris, 1930–31, began with the problem of finding an apartment, because Povo was going to return to Spain. Another challenge was the increasing strength of the French franc between 1929 and 1933, practically doubling what its value had been against the Spanish peseta in 1927. More ominously, Rodrigo's complicated sentimental relationship with Victoria Kamhi was stagnating. For the first time, he returned to Valencia to spend the Christmas holiday, and there he composed a new piece for piano to celebrate Victoria Kamhi's saint's day (December 23), *Air de ballet sur le nom de une jeune fille*, a fine musical portrait of the mischievousness and sweet yearning of his beloved. The theme of this work, which emerges out of the letters of her name "Victoria Camhi" (in this period she wrote her surname with C instead of K), has thrown students of Rodrigo's piano music off track, as they have misunderstood the composer's system of musical signs for each note. In fact, what he used was an ingenious cryptogram with the Spanish alphabet (including the ñ).[106] The resulting key is the following matrix:

A	B	C	D	E	F	G
–	H	I	J	K	L	–
M	N	Ñ	O	P	Q	R
S	T	U	V	W	X	Y
–	–	–	Z	–	–	–

Cryptogram utilized by Rodrigo

Beginning of Air de ballet sur le nom de une jeune fille

On the way to Valencia, Rodrigo stopped in Barcelona and accepted Casals's invitation to visit him:

> When they passed my card to him, he came out almost
> running and we spent two hours together. [. . .] I began
> to get bored and didn't know what to say, but several
> times I wanted to leave, and he wouldn't let me. I gave
> him the *Siciliana*, I played it on the piano, and he told me
> he liked it very much but found it a little long. I think
> so too at times, but isn't it because we grow accustomed
> to short little things, *aux petites choses*? He promised
> me to play it, but I am not as close to Casals as I am to
> Conchita Supervía.[107]

Passing through the whole harmonic circle in so thematically compact a work may well have given way to the perception of excessive duration that Rodrigo confessed he shared
"at times" with Casals. The composer's intuition about the
promise of the cellist was accurate because, for one reason or
another, Casals would never play a work by Rodrigo. Nevertheless, in early 1931, Conchita Supervía joined a lengthening list
of his interpreters. The famous mezzo-soprano incorporated
Serranilla into her concert repertoire and recorded it on 24
February 1931 for the company Spanish Odeón (SO 6934–1),
with Alejandro Vilalta as pianist.

Rodrigo had himself made a recording of *Zarabanda lejana*, *Berceuse de printemps*, and the *Air de ballet* during a visit to a piano-roll factory in Barcelona on "a very curious electric piano that leaves recorded on paper the interpretation that you play with all the nuances, ritardandos and accelerandos," as he reported Victoria Kamhi.[108] These recordings, probably made in the Rotlles Victòria de La Garriga (Barcelona), belonging to the Blancafort family of musicians, have not been found. At all events, the *Serranilla* sung by Supervía is the first commercial phonograph registry that we have found of his music. It was a very dramatized interpretation, typical of the mezzo-soprano's recitals in which, like a ballerina, she changed her dress for every group of songs.

Though not a premiere, because the composer had already presented the work in public while accompanying María Josefa Regnard in the École Normale de Musique, Supervía's interpretation of the *Serranilla* had greater repercussions. Joaquín Nin-Culmell, one of whose songs the mezzo-soprano also sang, accompanied by him, discovered Rodrigo at this very concert:

I will never forget the letter I wrote him after having heard Conchita Supervía sing his *Serranilla* at the beginning of the 1930s. "Long live Don Quijote," I wrote him enthusiastically about his *ritorno* [return] to the past and his removal from Spanish commonplaces. "The Marquis of Santillana," he answered me, "Has nothing to do with Don Quijote." He was clearly as right as could be, but I think that my enthusiasm, though literarily mistaken, moved him for its naïveté. We became friends. We would walk through the Bois de Boulogne, and I never failed to attend the premieres by Ricardo Viñes of his piano works and the debut by Straram's Orchestra of one of his first orchestral works, *El poema de La Alhambra* [sic]. At the same time, as a pianist, I put his *Suite* on my program, as well as the adorable and fine evocation of Luis de Milán called *Zarabanda lejana*.[109]

Not only did Supervía develop a fondness for Rodrigo's music, but Viñes also had some of his pieces in his repertory. The guitarist Regino Sainz de la Maza—whose relationship with Rodrigo would acquire special importance in the years to follow—at last premiered the guitar original of the *Zarabanda lejana* in Buenos Aires at the end of 1929. He placed this work in his programs of new guitar music written in those years by composers who were not guitarists.[110] Nonetheless, what had the most impact was the momentum of his symphonic music in Spain following Straram's introduction of it there in 1929 and the debut of *Preludio para un poema a La Alhambra* by his orchestra on 1 May 1930, though conducted by Eugène Bigot, for Straram had fallen gravely ill.[111] As if there were some sort of competition to perform his music, Spanish orchestras put in their programs during the 1929–30 season all the orchestral works composed by Rodrigo until then. First, the Madrid Orquesta de Cámara (Chamber Orchestra) under the direction of Arturo Saco del Valle played the *Zarabanda lejana* (10 January 1930); then, a few days later, the Valencia Orquesta Sinfónica, under the baton of Izquierdo, debuted the *Tres viejos aires de danza* (24 January 1930). Not to be outdone, the two great symphony orchestras of Madrid, with their permanent conductors directing, afterwards played *Cinco piezas infantiles*: the Madrid Orquesta Sinfónica on April 2 and the Orquesta Filarmónica on June 13. In Barcelona a week later, the Orquestra Pau Casals, conducted by Joan Lamote de Grignón, interpreted the *Cinco piezas infantiles*. According to the composer, their performance was "better and with more energy" than Straram's, though perhaps a bit fast: "I feel the work a bit slower, since although the music loses thrust, it gains nonetheless in clarity and ease."[112] (Appendix 3 lists the main performances of Rodrigo's music from his debut in the tribute to Falla in 1928 to the end of the 1930–31 season.)

The critical reception of these works was uneven. It was very good in Barcelona, where Joan Salvat in *Revista Musical Catalana*, Joan Llongueras in *La Veu de Catalunya*, and Baltasar Samper in *La Publicitat* rushed to celebrate Rodrigo's successes. It was lukewarm in Paris, where the *Cinco piezas infantiles* had attracted more attention than the *Preludio para un poema a La Alhambra*: "a small page of a twilight tonality in which, without aiming for an intense expression, the young Spanish musician amuses himself by using all the orchestral resources of pitch hand in hand with the most fervent colorists of the Iberian Peninsula," according to Pierre-Octave Ferroud;[113] "a charming page. The author? Joaquín Rodrigo, a name to be retained in the memory, among Paul Dukas's best students," according to Florent Schmitt, who, regarding the premiere of *Zarabanda lejana and villancico* by the Orchestre Féminin, limited himself to saying that they were "fort poétiques" (very poetic) pages.[114]

It went worse in Madrid, where the composer could not help but recognize that "the criticism has been neither good nor bad. [. . .] I already knew that my works would not be liked in Madrid. The [*Cinco piezas*] *infantiles* have not, and neither will the suite the day that it is played nor the [*Preludio al*] *gallo mañanero*, nor the songs."[115] A critic like Ángel María Castell, who derided the "tonal aberrations" of the avant-garde (in general and without referring to Rodrigo), stated that the *Cinco piezas infantiles* were listened to with attention and courteously applauded.[116] But what hurt him most was a critique by Turina, stating that in *Juglares*, Rodrigo's personality was more visible than in these later works. Salazar, as was his custom, did not miss the opportunity to attack the competitor of his pupil Ernesto Halffter, who, in this period, was beginning already to exhibit a loss of stylistic focus:

> From the version that I had the occasion to see years ago
> of Joaquín Rodrigo's *Piezas infantiles* to the one that the
> Orquesta Sinfónica has offered us, there is a considerable
> difference. What was then a simple sketch is today an
> elaborate work, conscientiously made, perhaps too well
> made in the sense of an unneeded overload of elements
> that the spirit of the work, simple and spontaneous,
> does not require. It is a little of the danger that Paris
> represents for young composers like Rodrigo, too

confident, well meaning, and with generous talent. Paris
has passed and its procedures today have a provincial
taste. Perhaps all France and especially Paris are today an
immense province with affected modes. When Rodrigo
comes back to Spain, he is going to find a fresh new
country without the worries and small manias of little
schools of the boulevard. The benefit that Paris may have
offered him will be wholly revealed then.[117]

Salazar presents here his characteristically optimistic vision
for a new Spain. But this premonition did not conform to future
realities, for when Rodrigo finally returned to Spain, what he
encountered instead was a devastated country. The critic also
advanced the notion that the *Cinco piezas infantiles* had changed
much between the "simple sketch" presented to the National
Music Contest (in which he was a judge) and this version, which
by his lights had been excessively revised and refined. We have
as little faith in the prophetic gifts of Salazar as in his good ear
for judging Rodrigo's music, but we know nothing of Rodrigo's
re-elaboration of this work, nor was this his normal method of
working. He did indeed show it to Dukas and consulted with him
about some very real concerns, to which the maestro responded
by letter. For example, Dukas told him that he did not think it
necessary to exchange the horn for the clarinet at the beginning
of "Plegaria." But Rodrigo followed his own intuition and gave
the theme to the clarinet. In any case, these are only details of
orchestration that do not suggest any major changes at all.[118]
Salazar's critique rings hollow.

Columnist, Critic, and Composer in Crisis

In 1930 and 1931, Rodrigo continued on as the Parisian correspondent for the *Revista Musical Catalana*. Through these writings, we know that he experienced *in situ* the tenth anniversary
of Les Six (the Group of Six). He wrote, "Nobody will deny the
value of a Honegger, a Milhaud, a Poulenc; I know all too little music of the other three," pointing out that the ballet *Les
Fâcheux* (1924) of Georges Auric "does not lend itself to great

commentaries."[119] Concerning the opera *Le Roy d'Yvetot* (1930) of Jacques Ibert, he wrote, "Here is a work full of estimable quality that could have been a delightful little work, but whose excessive proportions and the musician's fear of not appearing up-to-date make some of his scenes annoying."[120] In his April column he referred to the *Sardana* (a Catalan dance) of Casals that he heard in the École Normale de Musique, and à propos, cited a letter from D'Indy to Casals with an interesting reference to polytonal procedures: according to D'Indy, Casals "had known how to use polytonality—quite an annoying resource at the present time—in a perfectly logical way in which I believe I have discerned the arrival (beginning with an anti-tonal bass) of the parade that ends up by settling into the tonal fullness of the popular festival."[121]

He also spoke of Conrad Beck, a composer "of some talent," whose piano concerto of 1930 "reflects an undeniable virtuosity in the writing not far away from Hindemith's, less implacable and more human."[122] In the same column he highlighted the tribute to D'Indy with the interpretation of the *Légende de Saint-Christophe*, Op. 67, which had not been heard in Paris since its premiere in 1920, and the 1 March 1930 debut of *Préludes pour piano* by Olivier Messiaen, a composer who had always interested him: "an extremely interesting work, a refined product of an artistic sensitivity, full of very new and curious harmonies, without being illogical or born of a whim."[123] Regarding the *Bolero* of Ravel, whose premiere in the orchestrated version he dutifully attended 11 January 1930, he described it as "ingenious, but nothing more."[124] After Easter vacation of 1930 came the symphonic apotheosis with the Vienna Philharmonic conducted by Clemens Krauss, afterwards the New York Philharmonic with Toscanini, and as a finale, the Berlin Philharmonic with Wilhelm Furtwängler, who conducted Hindemith's *Concerto for Orchestra*, Op. 38 (1925), a work that greatly impressed Rodrigo:

> whose first movement is truly breathtaking. Everything yields to the tumultuous, unbounded joy of this music, the apex of Hindemith's art. The most inexorable

fugato gives the reply and leaps from plane to plane,
from mass to mass with such speed and with a courage
such that its effect, especially in a performance
like Fürtwangler's, completely dazzles us. To this
incisive writing the percussion responds with merry,
provocative jazz rhythms.[125]

During the summer of 1930, Rodrigo published two critiques
of the performances of the Madrid Orquesta Sinfónica in Valencia in the daily *Las Provincias*, while López-Chavarri was on
vacation. No Spanish critic of Rodrigo's time, not even Adolfo
Salazar, had viewed the most recent developments of the avant-
garde from a cultural perch as lofty as Paris, and certainly not
with the intensity and diligence with which Rodrigo experienced
it between 1927 and 1931. On the other hand, his practically
obsessive attendance at concerts and his particular interest in
being up-to-date in music, without neglecting the canonical performances of opera, symphony, and chamber music, had shaped
his aesthetic sensibilities and preferences as he took in the best
orchestras, conductors, string quartets, soloists. Therefore, it is
not surprising that the columns Rodrigo published that summer
made it obvious how formulaic and hollow, how bitter and petu-
lantly paternalist toward the public López-Chavarri was. Because
of his lack of education and information, such parochialism was
inevitable. As a result, López-Chavarri could never have written
anything as fair and balanced as the following judgment about
Adventures in a Perambulator (1914), by the U.S. composer John
Alden Carpenter:

We owe a debt of gratitude toward maestro Arbós for
putting us in heartfelt relations with J. Carpenter,
contemporary American composer. They tell us that
his *Adventures in a Perambulator* is one of his first
works. And in this case we must unreservedly praise his
modesty and economy of expression in not abusing the
easy onomatopeia that is so tempting and available to his
work. We will also praise his sober, well-meditated style,

the delicacies of his orchestration: the work's finale and parts of the first act are without a doubt the best, as well as the evocation of a toy piano made with a fine touch. But once having completed our praise, we will affirm that the work lacks great significance, and it also lacks personality. It is a composition made of music neither brilliant nor bold nor up-to-date. Everything is well known and trite, and although I well understand that it is from familiar elements that new works are born, this is not the case with Carpenter. [. . .] It is too long and too serious.[126]

At the beginning of 1930, Rodrigo enrolled in the foreign section of the Society of Critics of Paris with the object of acquiring the prized *carte rouge*: the license that would allow him to enter all concerts for free without detriment to his personal finances, which had already begun to suffer. Therefore, he needed good recommendations, accreditation for having resided a certain amount of time in Paris, proof of writing in a music review—up to this point he met all the qualifications—and three articles published in a daily newspaper. López-Chavarri helped him with this final requirement by publishing for him some texts in *Las Provincias* to amplify what he had written in his columns for the *Revista Musical Catalana*. These allow us to comprehend in greater detail his experience of the *Symphony of Psalms* (1930) by Stravinsky, which seemed to him to contain "more truth and, therefore, more depth"[127] than *Œdipus rex*, a work he did not find compelling.

In 1931 he published only two columns in the *Revista Musical Catalana*. In the first, he noted the strong points and the shortcomings of *Iron Foundry* (1926–27) by Aleksandr Mosólov, "direct, precise, concentrated, and reduced to the strictly precise aesthetic dimensions. [. . .] I neither believe that this is the genial work awaited by the present times, nor did I consider it an absurd outgrowth of them." Yet he highlighted his interest in the operetta *Les aventures du roi Pausole* (1930), "Honegger's entrance into the field of musical *vaudeville*," which delighted him, establishing

considerable distance between his tastes and the preferences of
"elite" commentators like Salazar and López-Chavarri:

> A few numbers in a set, some *couplés*, some duets,
> a little romanza, naïvely and adorably sung off key,
> and . . . that is all. All, have we said? No, no, no, in no
> way at all. If that unfortunately were all, the work could
> not have garnered nearly 200 repeat performances. But
> fortunately Pierre Louÿs is there hand in hand with the
> [librettist Albert] Willemetz. This team produces as a
> result one of the most piquant works we have seen. Salt
> and mustard by the bushel.[128]

He did not mention how disconcerted he was upon listening to some fragments of *Wozzeck* (1925) by Alban Berg,
interpreted by the Paris Symphony Orchestra on March 29.
Nonetheless, he did communicate the following to López-
Chavarri: "Although I am not a partisan nor a friend of this
music, a bit amorphous, disjointed, vague and without light,
I cannot help but recognize that there is emotion, something
not as frequent as it seems."[129]

The final column for the *Revista Musical Catalana* was published December 1931. Rodrigo had just arrived for his new school
year in Paris and immediately began his pilgrimage through the
concerts, with practically the same compulsive urgency he had
shown in 1927. It is clear that the music to which other composers had access through sheet music Rodrigo himself actually
needed to hear, and what Paris offered him in these years could
hardly be obtained in any other way:

> Crisis! This is the word passed from mouth to mouth
> and the first word heard on arriving in Paris. Everyone
> repeats it, it seems to be the song in vogue, and yet this
> crisis is not precisely reflected in the musical world. Since
> arriving I have found myself immersed in a sea of music.
> Sometimes it is the deliquescent Impressionist waves
> that the names of Debussy and his school carry to us;

other times, the strong current that the genius of Bach
hurls with force; others, finally, the restless youthful
storms, sometimes true, but most of them superficial and
snobbish. In fact, few weeks have been as interesting as
the last two of this past month of November.[130]

Despite the capacity that he had developed for criticism, and
although this would be an activity to which he would devote
much time in the future, he confessed, "I have no love for the
business of being a critic. [. . .] I think the activity of the composer and that of the critic are incompatible for the good exercise of criticism."[131] But what was certain was that, as far as his
activity as a composer was concerned, he continued experiencing difficulties in composing new music. His two dances, stalled
already in the summer of 1929, remained incomplete a year later,
however much Cools, as the editor of Max Eschig, had offered
to publish them for him. He would not cease trying to compose
them, but the only composition for piano that he finished in 1931
was a *Serenade* dedicated to José Iturbi.

Why did Rodrigo find it so difficult to complete these two
dances? In the Max Eschig catalogue of piano music, Ernesto
Halffter had published in 1928 the piano version of two dances
that would later become the most popular numbers of his ballet
Sonatina (1928): "Dance of the Shepherdess" and "Dance of the
Gypsy Girl," debuted by José Cubiles in 1927.[132] It is not certain that
Rodrigo attended the debut of the ballet in Paris in June 1928. He
was present for the repeat performance in 1929, and in his *Revista
Musical Catalana* column, he singled out as the best numbers "a
sung ballad, the shepherdess's dance, and the Gypsy girl's dance."[133]
Transparent music of a Scarlattian neoclassicism and a pianism
without complexities, impeccable, felicitous, effective—nothing
one might claim for the essential grace of these pieces, especially
the "Dance of the Shepherdess," would be an overstatement.

However, from the standpoint of technique and aesthetics,
they were very far from the ground Rodrigo was exploring in his
piano works: complex, problematic, unwilling to do away with
counterpoint (studied and practiced), and always harmonically

sophisticated. It is very probable that waging this new battle with Halffter in the terrain of dance was the source of Rodrigo's difficulties in finding the tone for his own dances, which had to be distinctive. He did not find it; he did not write them.

However, as we have already pointed out, Rodrigo dated in 1931 a *Serenata* composed in Paris for the great pianist of the Valencian circle, José Iturbi. Although Iturbi hardly paid any attention to this work, if he even premiered it, the *Serenata* is an ambitious, ample piece with a tonal character. Without compromising his style, Rodrigo throttled back a bit on his harmonic innovations in order to make it acceptable to Iturbi, who had very conservative taste in repertoire.

We hasten to point out that the first measure of the main theme, which appears in m. 17, is a literal quote of the first measure of Halftter's "Dance of the Shepherdess" (musical ex. 3.1). Rodrigo reinterprets and redirects this initial motive to contrast it afterwards with a theme of stylized character, like Falla's "Gypsy" tunes. In other words, Rodrigo's *Serenata* set the shepherdess to dancing with the "Gypsy" in a clear reference to Halffter's work.

What is more, in an interview with Gálvez Bellido in 1931, Rodrigo said that what he was working on at that time was a ballet that could be either for La Argentina or for "any of these dance

Musical ex. 3.1a: Rodrigo's *Serenata*, mm. 17–18

Musical ex. 3.1b: Haffter's *Danza de la pastora*, mm. 1–4

companies that make their way over there."[134] Ballet had given Falla economic security and independence enough to fulfill his dream of retreating to Granada; Halffter, with over thirty repeat performances of the *Sonatina* after its Paris debut in 1928, had pocketed 10,000 francs in two months.[135] Rodrigo, on the other hand, celebrated the 100 francs he earned from author's rights in October 1929. And as for the recording rights of *Serranilla* by Supervía, he did not receive one cent for having sold the work to his editor, without heeding Falla's advice always to reserve something for himself.

In fact, Rodrigo had no economic problems. He was aware of the burden he was for the "broad shoulders" of his "poor father,"[136] but this man, although his fortune was quite compromised, never stopped financing the life of his youngest son in Paris. Thus, Rodrigo lacked the means to make his own living, but neither did he have any real need to do so. That allowed total liberty whenever he created music—something positive— but it also negatively encouraged the cultivation of an apparent laziness that took him to the comfortable terrain of speculation instead of to the effort of activity. Hence, his ballet remained in his inkwell, and so did a big work for piano and orchestra of which he began to speak in the summer of 1930:

> I want to lay the foundations for an important work,
> something great for piano and orchestra, or orchestra
> alone. Which seems better to you? Not a concerto,
> but a free work. A very romantic nocturne by my
> Mediterranean Sea where the arches sigh and the horns
> throb, and flutes glide under the moon. And all will say
> when they hear it, "Caramba! Do you know that Rodrigo
> is likely in love?" This nocturne will uninterruptedly get
> linked to a dance about the mountain yonder. Brilliant,
> full of light and joy, rhythmic and painful, a bit rustic
> and a lot refined, what do you think? When I start
> thinking about all that, I get nervous and I can't sleep.[137]

In November he spoke to Gálvez Bellido about "a kind of concerto-like fantasy for piano and orchestra."[138] It may have been the same project, but it also went nowhere, and the problem with the dances for Max Eschig was resolved by giving Cools the *Air de ballet sur le nom d'une jeune fille* (M.E. 2803), the piano version of *Zarabanda lejana* (M.E. 2804), and the *Siciliana* (M.E. 2413) for cello and piano to publish . . . three "dances," in sum.

The year 1931 ended with the *Serenata* for piano as the only new composition. The creative crisis grew deeper thanks to the difficulty of orienting himself in the maelstrom of artistic trends that swirled in Paris, to which we must add Rodrigo's difficult romantic relationship with Victoria Kamhi, which had to be carried on in secret because of her father's strenuous opposition. And as if that were not enough, the political situation in Spain at this time became an all-absorbing theme. The famous phrase *Delenda est monarchia* (The monarchy must be destroyed) that renowned philosopher José Ortega y Gasset published in his daily *El Sol* (Madrid, 15 November 1930) became a reality when two days later, after the elections of 12 April 1931, the Second Republic was proclaimed.

Rodrigo's political position in this period is unmistakable. In the same way he had placed himself aesthetically against any conservatism, politically he opposed reactionary positions and admitted he was a republican and a leftist. As his social roots were among the educated, well-to-do bourgeois elite, he kept his distance from the violent populism that he found repugnant. But in a certain way he wished to excuse or diminish the importance of the popular revolts, and he allied himself with the new national pathway being followed:

My Spain is not the same, whether the reactionary elements want it or not, cavemen I call them. [. . .] Spain awakes from its lethargy of so many years, and these peoples, contemplative and impassioned at the same time, when they awaken and acquire awareness of their personality, are terrible and magnificent. This is the case of today's Spain. One can't imagine with what energy, what fire, what violence things are today argued and commented. Here everyone has become a republican, even the cat. Even my dad, who has always belonged to the conservative right.[139]

His posture even separated him from the Valencian circles he had frequented until then at the Pavilion of Las Arenas: "this year about the matter of the Republic they are very reactionary, and I don't like to talk to them. Especially the ladies are terrible. You already know that I belong to the left; for that reason, I can't agree with them. I don't like to socialize with anybody."[140] In fact, during the first years of the Second Republic, he even hardly corresponded with López-Chavarri.

Since there has been so much unsubstantiated speculation about Rodrigo's relationship with politics, or vice-versa, we should point out with respect to the following document that we perceive no dissimulation in these intimate, private manifestations of his ideology. Kamhi herself seems to have had an affinity for socialist ideas, but he explained as follows his vote in the constitutional elections of 28 June 1931:

> No, no, I have not voted for the socialists; I don't
> completely like their program. Also, and this is the first
> point, the socialist who presented his candidacy for
> Valencia was not very interesting. On the other hand,
> I never vote for parties nor for ideas, I vote for men.
> And they only interest me when they are good, honest,
> intelligent, and strong. I have voted for a radical socialist,
> for a leftist republican, for one in the center, and for two
> of the right. Of these, only one from the right has not
> won. Rafael has voted for the Catholics who have not
> been elected to office.[141]

And further on, even after insinuating that he would agree with the gradual expulsion of the clergy from Spain,[142] he said in a more casual tone, "I am a convinced partisan of democracy and a great liberal, but as an elite artist, at base, I am a lost aristocrat, and you are too, although you may say otherwise."[143] For the rest of his life, Spanish politics would remain a whirlwind of conflict and controversy until settling at last on a constitutional monarchy, one that would elevate Rodrigo himself to the ranks of the nobility in 1991. In any case, his statements in the future would be more circumspect, and his true ideology hardly discernible.

Chapter 4

Dark Times

Crisis and War
(1932–1938)

A Fateful Year, 1932

On 12 November 1931, Rodrigo returned to Paris after a long period of little productivity spent between Valencia and Estivella. His musical studies went by the boards while he concentrated on clarifying his relationship with Victoria Kamhi. In 1931 both had maintained a secret relationship because of her father's opposition. The indifference of his parents did not help at all. To remove themselves from the difficult situation, they seriously planned to marry. Neither one was especially religious, but to satisfy their families, they were willing to wed in accordance with Jewish and Catholic traditions. Family acceptance was important not only for social and emotional reasons, but also for economic ones: until they were able to support themselves, they would continue to depend on their parents to finance them.

When Rodrigo went back to Valencia for Christmas, he conveyed to his family his firm decision to get married, and with the consent of his father, he began to reckon with finances and nuptial arrangements. For her part, Victoria Kamhi devoted herself—with the overt aid of her sister and the more discreet help of her mother—to overcoming her father's dissatisfaction with this relationship. Finally, on 12 February 1932, the composer traveled to Paris in the company of Rafael Ibáñez. On February 17, he appeared at the luxurious residence of Isaac and Sofía Kamhi in the Rue de Passy to make a formal proposal for the hand of their daughter. He took a ring and an elegant bracelet as a proposal gift, along with a letter from his mother, in which she indicated her willingness to treat Victoria Kamhi as a daughter.

Everything was in vain. Isaac Kamhi flatly refused but with no explanation. It is obvious what considerations dissuaded a father of the 1930s from favoring the marriage of his daughter to a person of a nationality, culture, and religion different from the family's and dependent on them, both economically and physically, due to his impairment. There was no discussion, as Isaac Kamhi immediately left the house to attend to other affairs, giving his daughter no choice but to accept his decision in silence. Six years earlier, a refusal similar to this one had saved her from an undesirable marriage.[1] This time, however, the optimism and hope with which they had made their wedding plans were shattered by the single word with which Isaac Kamhi had stated his attitude: no! The following day, Rodrigo received by return mail in his hotel the bracelet and ring he had given. His beloved did not want to see him and pretended to be ill. Nor did they attempt to see each other thereafter, because they were aware that that would only worsen things. Rodrigo left Paris in utter dejection.

He sought solace during his return trip in a brief stay in Bilbao, where the local Orquesta Sinfónica, conducted by Jesús Arámbarri, performed the *Zarabanda lejana* and the *Tres viejos aires de danza*. As if nothing had happened, he wrote to Victoria Kamhi, "It's been a very pleasant week, and it has reminded me that I'm a musician, something I had been forgetting. [. . .] My pieces were very appreciated and quite well performed. You can't ask anything more of a provincial orchestra. [. . .]"[2] The fact of having finished only one composition in 1931—the *Serenata* for piano—did not speak well for the creativity of the composer, and the year 1932 was in no way more productive: only the thirty-seven measures of his *Cançoneta* for strings to that date.

All the catalogues of Rodrigo's oeuvre and the bibliographical sources date the *Cançoneta* to 1923, but this work does not appear in the list of initial compositions that he created until 1928, nor does its compositional style correspond at all to Rodrigo's of the early 1920s. Stylistically, it instead seems to belong to the early 1930s. The *Cançoneta* meets the aim of stripping the music of any dynamic thrust. It is a charmingly fainthearted piece, one that may very well reflect the composer's state of mind during a period of complex emotions.

Cançoneta means "little song," though the spelling is not Castilian but rather Valencian. Given the locality of its premiere, this is logical; however, this is a "song" for string orchestra, a brief lyric utterance whose mood is subdued, introverted, and melancholy. The muted strings, *pianissimo* dynamics, and generally low registers evince a nocturnal quality, the intimate interior space into which Rodrigo so often invites the listener. Occasional rays of luminous vitality penetrate the darkness in the form of *tremolando* strings, bird-like trills, and glistening harmonics, providing welcome contrast.

The overall formal design is traditional: rounded binary, that is, AABA-coda. The principal melody exhibits a pastoral rhythm, with dotted notes in 6/8 meter. Reinforcing this retrospective glance is an evocative use of tonal and modal harmonies. The basic harmonic movement is between the tonic, subdominant, and dominant, A, D, and E, thus structuring the work as a perfect cadence: I (mm. 1–11)—IV (mm. 11–14)—V (mm. 15–18)—I (mm. 19–37). But there are modal anomalies in the accompaniment that intensify its expressive effect. The A section (mm. 1–14, repeated) introduces notes from a D-minor scale over an A pedal, leading to the main melody in the first violin; immediately afterwards, the eight measures of the melody are harmonized in A Mixolydian (a major scale with a lowered seventh degree). The B section (mm. 15–18) presents a short-lived development in E Mixolydian, with cellos and violas taking the melodic lead before a restatement of the A section (mm. 19–27), in which the slightly abbreviated introduction ushers in a literal restatement of the main theme. Six measures of closure are linked by the echo of the final measures of the first violin, an echo produced by the second violins.

This meticulously organized work—at once sophisticated, emotionally direct, and unpretentious—reflects the maturity, self-assurance, and technique Rodrigo had acquired in Paris during his studies with Dukas. It is music in the essential sense that Rodrigo always valued, and according to his closest relatives, he was fond of humming it during the final years of his life. The composer himself recalled that in the 1930s he dictated the *Cançoneta* from his Braille manuscript to the orchestra conductor Enrique Jordá.[3] This manuscript has not survived, but Jordá corroborated the fact in a letter to Rodrigo.[4] Finally, the fact that the *Cançoneta* was not premiered until 11 December 1932, by the Orquesta de Cámara de Valencia, led by Francisco Gil, would recommend dating it to 1932, an otherwise sterile year for Rodrigo as a composer. Although the press nowhere indicated that it was a premiere, composer Luis Sánchez, critic for the Valencian daily paper *La Correspondencia de Valencia*, underscored the "delicious harmonies and strongly felt melodic line" of the *Cançoneta*, which "received affectionate applause."[5] In the daily *Las Provincias*, the critic did not put his byline on the column, but it was likely López-Chavarri who referred to the *Cançoneta* as "one of the most beautiful creations of the young maestro, whose orchestration is a felicitous find, enough to establish a musical reputation."[6]

During March through September 1932, there were occasional mutual scoldings, long periods without communication, outright breakups, and a state to which Rodrigo referred as "nervous depression," fed by readings of Giacomo Leopardi, "great poet of pain,"[7] with whose deformity and misfortune in love the composer empathized. However, when fall came, so did reconciliation. Victoria Kamhi ended her October 7 letter with the moving words, "Do you forgive me, Joaquín?" She thus regained the passion forged over the years. They once more concentrated their efforts on the best way to meet again. In those months she had matured a great deal and had achieved a stronger position in her family, after the economic crisis had put the family business in a real predicament. Poorer, but more secure, she conveyed to Rodrigo her decision to go off to Spain with her savings regardless of whether she had her father's permission, which she was not about to receive. She told him that she had made the decision "for many reasons":

> So as to see you and to find out if I can be happy in that land that for some is a paradise and for others a still medieval country, not very civilized and, consequently, unattractive to an intelligent, educated girl. I have often told you that I want to live like all women of the bourgeoisie, virtuous but a bit emancipated, in Paris, in Vienna, Amsterdam, Berlin, and London, I mean, in all the civilized parts of Europe. I think that this is also possible in Spain.[8]

This brief paragraph, written when she was reading *España* (1929) by Salvador de Madariaga and *La Barraca* (1898) by Blasco Ibáñez—two matchless texts for helping her understand the country into which she was about to descend—says much about the uniqueness of her personality. She considered herself an intellectual, and for her, culture was a diligent devotion and not merely the adornment of an "intelligent, educated" young woman. Her father had struggled to maintain a comfortable social position, and her mother, Sofia Arditti, aunt of Nobel-winner Elias Canetti, had Bulgarian roots and strong connections to Austria. Both obtained for their daughters, Victoria and Mathilde, an impeccable education in the French Lycée and the German College in Constantinople. Victoria focused on music; Mathilde, on painting.

Before settling in Paris, Victoria Kamhi spent time at a boarding school in Vienna. She came to speak fluent French, German, and Castilian, and in the months prior to her trip to Spain, she had held a job as social worker. Besides social work, history held much interest for her, as did literature, and she had considerable training as a pianist. She also felt attracted to the practice of painting. All this strongly united her to the composer, and when she arrived at the station at Barcelona, Joaquín and his older brother Francisco were eagerly waiting to drive her to Valencia. By a happy coincidence, the Chamber Orchestra of Alicante, conducted by José Juan Pérez, performed the *Tres viejos aires de danza* in the Atheneum of Alicante on 10 December 1932.[9]

The school year 1932–33 at the École Normale de Musique began unattended by Rodrigo, who wrote to Dukas to give him an opportune explanation. His teacher answered him very affectionately in November in a letter evincing the personal relationship that they had developed over the five previous school years: "I also often think about you, and I have missed you more than once when seeing the empty place beside the piano, [. . .] but I understand the financial reasons [. . .] full well that in these times of universal crisis have filled you with doubts about establishing yourself for a stay in Paris in uncomfortable conditions."[10] Shortly before then, Rodrigo had received a letter from his editor Jacques Lerolle with a tolerant but clear warning: "I see that you are following the example of your distinguished teacher Paul Dukas, who labors without producing anything definitive; for now I am not too worried because business is going very slowly and I have also had to cut costs."[11]

Things had begun to go better. The Christmas and New Year's season of 1932, with Victoria Kamhi at the Rodrigos' home, was celebrated with such lavishness that the young guest was dazzled: "It surprised me to see so much luxury, so much abundance, at the home of my future in-laws. [. . .] There were mountains of Christmas candies, marzipans, and other sweets, [. . .] plentiful banquets, paellas, and afternoon snacks, all accompanied by the deafening sound of tambourines and traditional drums."[12] They made the decision to get married in an exclusively civil ceremony under the laws of the Second Spanish Republic, which only recognized civil marriages.[13] When Rodrigo conveyed to his fiancée the "small difficulties" they would have to face at the time of getting married, she forcefully answered,

Wedding, 19 January 1933

You speak to me of the "small difficulties" that we would
encounter without telling me what they might be. For my
part there are none at all, and I don't want to talk to you
about my family. I only want to tell you, dear Joaquín,
that I can't resolve to get married in the Church without
changing religion, and that would be a hypocrisy that I
would regret my whole life. [. . .] I hope you understand
that you can't change religion the way you would a shirt,
and if you love me, you will not insist on it.[14]

If not in his professional life, then at least in the realm of
the heart, 1932, after a disappointing start, had come to a satisfactory conclusion. But the present state of felicity would not
last long.

The "Failures" of 1933: Wedding and *Tocata*

On 19 January 1933, in a county court in downtown Valencia, Victoria Kamhi and Joaquín Rodrigo were united in marriage in a civil ceremony attended by no one in the bride's family, on the express orders of her father. Only the closest members of the Rodrigo family were present. In its society news, the daily paper *Las Provincias* warmly took note of the event by stressing that "the gifts of sensitivity and talent" of the bride "wondrously match the qualities of the young and distinguished Valencian maestro."[15] To their acquaintances, the bride and groom communicated the news of their union by means of a laconic printed note sent by mail. Although they were adults who were exercising their right to do exactly what they wanted the way they wanted, they had made a brazen show of independence in the eyes of the traditional Valencian bourgeoisie, and there was no lack of gossip about the fact. But it did not matter very much to the newlyweds because the following day, Francisco Rodrigo drove them to Madrid along with Rafael Ibáñez. They had decided to settle in the capital and use it as a launching pad for the works of Rodrigo, one more efficacious than Valencia.

However, what works would they launch? Placing already-debuted works in orchestral repertoires was a privilege reserved for a select few. Rodrigo could consider himself very fortunate because his compositions had circulated after their premieres. One outstanding example was his *Zarabanda lejana y villancico*, which appeared in the repertoire of the Orchestre Féminin of Jane Evrard during its tour of Spain in January and February 1933. The ensemble's ambitious itinerary included San Sebastián, Bilbao, Santander, Oviedo, Madrid, Valencia, Barcelona, and Girona. Rodrigo's work was a highlight of the private concert it gave in the salons of the French Institute of Madrid February 3;[16] another in the Teatro Principal of Valencia the day after;[17] and one more in the Palau de la Música Catalana in Barcelona on February 8.[18]

Several days after settling in the capital, the Rodrigos were able to attend the premiere of the *Preludio para un poema a la*

Alhambra, performed by the Orquesta Filarmónica under the baton of Pérez Casas 28 January 1933 at Madrid's Teatro Español. The work went unnoticed, and one critic did not even mention it;[19] however, Falla congratulated the composer on the premiere,[20] and Maestro Pérez Casas's interest in Rodrigo's music became evident once again, as well as his willingness to play all his works. Furthermore, Pérez Casas had responsibilities and influence in those years of the Second Republic, for which he would later have to pay dearly, especially for his adherence to the manifesto, "Spanish intellectuals for the complete victory of the people."[21] Pérez Casas attempted to aid Rodrigo in many ways, and not just by putting his works on the program. However, the most the composer achieved was being named interim music professor (without salary) at the recently reformed National School for the Blind, inaugurated in April 1933. Luis Antón, principal violinist of the Orquesta Filarmónica, would be named tenured professor of violin.[22] The posts of associate professors were filled in accordance with competitive public examinations. Although they were open to blind candidates, they required official titles, which Rodrigo lacked,[23] and this made it very difficult for him to be placed in posts like these in which he could have undertaken fruitful labor.

On March 5, there was a gathering of the most gifted musicians based in Madrid, and in their number was Rodrigo. They celebrated a banquet in honor of Leopoldo Querol in the National Hotel of Madrid. It was a tribute to the recent successes of that pianist with the Orquesta Filarmónica in the same cycle of concerts in which the *Preludio para un poema a la Alhambra* had debuted.[24] Victoria Kamhi sat down at the presidential table, beside Querol and his wife, with Maestros Fernández Arbós and Pérez Casas's wife.[25] This gave the Rodrigos an excellent chance to establish useful relations with the Madrid Philharmonic Society, and they may well have become acquainted there with Ángel Grande, who was in attendance at the banquet.

After some fruitful years in England, Grande had returned to Spain and, in the summer of 1932, founded a chamber orchestra in Madrid comprising about thirty musicians. In 1933 he announced a concert series for Sunday matinees in the salon-theatre of the Circle of Fine Arts, which was the sponsoring institution. In the first concert of this cycle, Grande arranged the Madrid debut of Rodrigo's *Cançoneta*, with the composer in the audience. This work attracted the attention of the critics, who flocked to these concerts to lend their support to the ever-risky initiative of organizing a new orchestra. Yet, the commentaries of the composer Juan José Mantecón in *La Voz* and of the poet Gerardo Diego in his column for *El Imparcial* with regard to Rodrigo's work were parsimonious and formulaic.[26] Nonetheless, according to the journalist Ángel María Castell, Rodrigo, "present in the audience, received the ostensible tribute of pleasure and applause."[27]

During the months they remained in Madrid, the Rodrigos were happy, took trips through the suburbs, and enjoyed leisurely strolls through the gardens of the palace in Aranjuez, something they would always remember. They attended concerts of the Madrid Symphony and Philharmonic Orchestras and made friends with the married couple guitarist Regino Sainz de la Maza and Josefina de la Serna. Sainz de la Maza was for the time being the only performer of the original guitar version of *Zarabanda lejana*. He was committed to the renovation of the guitar repertoire, and he coordinated a series of guitar editions for the publishing house Unión Musical Española, under the title of "Biblioteca de Música para Guitarra" (Library of Guitar Music), from mid-1933 onward. The close proximity of Sainz de la Maza motivated Rodrigo to dedicate a new guitar piece to him. The result of this was the *Tocata*, a prodigious piece of transcendent virtuosity but one that would soon be considered a failure.

At the beginning of April, with their savings depleted and the Rodrigo family on the edge of bankruptcy, the newlyweds, with Rafael Ibáñez still by their side, had to return to Valencia. Rodrigo's older brother informed them of the difficulties that the family business was facing; he himself had to leave his own house to settle with his wife and children in the house of his parents. The elegant, spacious apartment on the Calle de Sorní in Valencia, where they had celebrated the previous Christmas so lavishly, had unexpectedly changed into a crowded shelter with few resources. There they remained until summer, when the family, as was its custom, went off to Estivella. Victoria Kamhi had imagined it as an ancestral home in the country; instead, what she found upset her a great deal:

> a big old house, right on the highway, with a tiny yard whose main feature was an ample henhouse, full of hens and chickens. The place could not have been noisier, and the heat was truly asphyxiating. Joaquín and I would get up very early in order to escape from the house in search of a little peace and quiet. We would climb up the hillside and sit, either in a vineyard or under an olive tree, where we would stay for hours. The family meals were unavoidable, and we had to endure the clamor of the little nephews, as annoying to us as the flies and mosquitoes that pursued us day and night.[28]

In those uncomfortable surroundings Rodrigo composed a masterpiece, his *Tocata* for guitar, of which two manuscripts written in ink survive.[29] Rafael Ibáñez made both copies while spending the summer in Estivella, and he stayed there with the couple when the rest of the family went back to Valencia at the end of the summer.

A study of the *Tocata* manuscripts again reveals the extent to which the composer had perfectly organized in his head the fingerboard of the guitar and the theoretical possibilities of the instrument. But he had opted to write a bold new piece with a merciless succession of sixteenth notes at a dizzying speed (quarter note = 144). A *tour de force*, this was like the celebrated *Toccata*, Op. 7 (1836) of Robert Schumann, the *Toccata*, Op. 11 (1911) of Sergei Prokofiev, or the "Toccata" that ends Ravel's *Le Tombeau de Couperin* (1919). Sainz de la Maza began to write the fingering on his copy, and he appropriately changed the arrangement of the chord that Rodrigo had written in the accompaniment of measures 15–22—possible within the fingerboard and more sonorous, but demanding an impossible extension of the left hand—and upon reaching the first line of the second page, he stopped: Rodrigo had written music which neither he nor any guitarist of that period could tackle.

Some years later, in a letter to Sainz de la Maza, Rodrigo referred to the "enormous and monumental failure of the *Tocata*."[30] As we shall see further on, he reused the music in a very different context, but the guitar original stayed forgotten until Leopoldo Neri, while conducting research for his doctoral thesis on Sainz de la Maza, found the copy in the private collection of the guitarist's son, Gonzalo.[31] The *Tocata*, revised by Pepe Romero and published by Ediciones Joaquín Rodrigo (EJR 190202), was debuted by Marcin Dylla in the Auditorium of the Queen Sofía National Museum Art Center on 1 June 2006. Since then, it has become a virtuosic showpiece for guitarists of the twenty-first century, who have conquered the diabolical tempo prescribed by the composer.

One recalls that the toccata (from the Italian *toccare*, "to touch"; *tocata* in Spanish) originated during the late Renaissance but reached maturity in the early Baroque as a free-form instrumental work, usually for keyboard, whose chief purpose was to present a dazzling display of digital pyrotechnics through the employment of rapid scales, acrobatic arpeggios, and textural complexities. The earliest and most enduring examples of this genre flowed from the pen of Girolamo Frescobaldi (1583–1643), though the only toccata to make its way into the popular imagination is by J. S. Bach, from his Toccata and Fugue in D Minor, which Walt Disney immortalized in the 1940 animated feature *Fantasia*. Given how closely associated the toccata historically was with the keyboard repertoire, it is more than a little ironic that the pianist Joaquín Rodrigo composed his first essay in this genre for the guitar.

However, the *Tocata* is much more than a piece for a display of technical skill; it is a new wonder of Rodrigo's musical inspiration and compositional craft. It is cast in sonata-allegro form, with an exposition (mm. 1–65), development (mm. 66–167), recapitulation (mm. 168–231), and coda (mm. 231–292). The exposition and recapitulation rely on the secondary contrasting

thematic area (mm. 47–65 and mm. 210–231) with the customary tonal adjustment: the key of E minor prevails in the principal theme group, while the secondary group explores Dorian
modes on A and E. Nonetheless, this conventional harmonic
framework is laid out in great detail and with a tonal richness
unprecedented in the guitar repertoire.

Though he does not systematically utilize all of the minor
keys as he had in the *Siciliana* for cello and piano, Rodrigo's
Tocata is full of tonal inflections—some as remote as D♯ major
in m. 94. But these are never concretized or stabilized; instead,
they are fleeting references that reinforce the sensation of par-
oxysmal velocity. This frantic harmonic rhythm continues into
the secondary thematic area, where notes on the dominant pedal
disturbingly avoid any sensation of repose. The coda, with its traditional function of lengthening and reasserting the tonic key,
thereby acquires significance: first it reinforces the E-minor scale
(mm. 231–268), then F major (mm. 269–276), with the intrusion of a D♭ that hints at a digression to the Neopolitan-sixth
sonority in E minor; and it ends with an arpeggiated tonic chord
that includes an added second, after six furious poundings on
the subdominant.

In all of this is evident a humanity only tentatively embraced
by the work's brutal speed. The contrasting slow sections, calm,
reflective, and lyrical, provide welcome relief. The coda also reveals
Rodrigo's musical "signature": the song of the cuckoo, which can
be interpreted in this context as a tribute to the *Toccata con lo
scherzo del cucco* of Pasquini, which had so impressed him in his
youth when he heard Wanda Landowska play it. Rodrigo gives
this signature a structural meaning when he passes from the
minor third (G-E), the usual representation of the cuckoo's song,
to the major third (A-F), to end with a perfect fourth (B-F♯),
which makes way for the repeated chord. Several years afterwards, the composer would amuse himself in the Black Forest of
Germany by analyzing the song of the cuckoo birds there. His
wife recalls, "We used to have fun listening to their unique song,
that went from an interval of the major second in the young
cuckoo to the perfect fourth in the adult cuckoo."[32]

Their road to maturity may have been strewn with setbacks, but the Rodrigos still needed to undergo another test, possibly the harshest one yet. Fall in Estivella was a season of economic hardships, relieved only by a lottery prize that kept them a bit above the poverty line. With that money they could redeem the piano they had pawned to relieve the debts of the family.[33] It would be possible for them to consider at that time a trip to Madrid in mid-November to attend the performance of *Tres viejos aires de danza* by the Orquesta Clásica (Classical Orchestra) led by José María Franco and to see Stravinsky, who was planning to visit the Spanish capital at the same time. Rodrigo came as close as he could to receiving praise for his music from the pen of the critic Adolfo Salazar: "*Tres viejos aires de danza* may be as old as air, but they have smoothness and freshness due to the ableness and finesse unique to their author."[34] As far as Stravinsky was concerned, he traveled to Spain accompanied by the violinist Samuel Dushkin, who had debuted the Violin Concerto in D in Paris in October 1931. On 22 November 1933, in the Capitol Room of Madrid, Stravinsky conducted Dushkin and the Madrid Orquesta Sinfónica in the Madrid premiere of this concerto.[35] To understand some works that Rodrigo would write several years afterwards, it is important to know the Baroque recurrences so prominent in concerto-style pieces of Stravinsky, like the Violin Concerto or the *Capriccio for Piano and Orchestra*, premiered in December 1929 and played by Soulima in the Palau de la Música Catalana in Barcelona on November 16, during Stravinsky's Spanish tour.[36]

Rodrigo continued composing, and in the Parisian periodical *Le Monde Musical*, he stated that "In the first place, I have written a *Tocata* for guitar that my friend Sainz de la Maza will perform during his South American tour. At present I am harmonizing three Valencian folk tunes for mixed chorus, after which I want to finish up my three pieces for piano."[37] He completed only the first of the Valencian songs, which is also the first choral work in his catalogue. This is the traditional Valencian number *Jo tinc un burro* (I have a donkey), his entrée into the realm of folk song, and it remains one of his few works for chorus. More than a mere harmonization, this arrangement gives the original a great boost with humorous counterpoint, points of imitation, and a beautiful inflection from the main key of G major to B minor. In addition, like so much of Rodrigo's music, it is self-referential, playfully alluding to the laziness that kept him from composing for so long. Thus, the folksong— though not the version that the composer harmonized—ended with a *seguidilla*-style quatrain synthesizing the two preceding ones, which were those employed by Rodrigo: "En casa del dimoni / ten burro i rella, / i per por a cremar-me / no faig faena" (In the devil's abode / I have a donkey and a plow / but for fear of getting burnt, / I do no work). When the Orfeó Valencià (Valencian Chorus) presented the work in a concert at the Conservatory of Valencia on 20 January 1934, *Las Provincias* published a commentary surely written, though not signed, by López-Chavarri: "a very pleasant novelty: the delicious joke of Joaquín Rodrigo on a jocose theme, *Jo tinc un burro*, with a completely Levantine wit and grace."[38]

Rodrigo was certainly not in the mood for parties and jokes, because his mother-in-law, Sofia Arditti, had spent the Christmas holidays in Valencia with the aim of offering her daughter a way out of the difficult situation in which she was living and took her off to Paris with her. The relationship of Victoria Kamhi with the Rodrigo family had become unsustainable. The couple had run out of funds and did not anticipate any way of obtaining them. Hence, on 18 January 1934, the day before her first wedding anniversary, Victoria Kamhi said goodbye to her husband in the Valencia station and returned with her mother to the comfort of her Parisian home. She had no alternative, but this time they established no distance between themselves and did not let a day go by without writing to each other.

Hundreds of Kamhi's letters survive from this period of separation; unfortunately, the letters written by Rodrigo during this same period have not been found. In any case, this correspondence shows the maturity of their relationship and a single aim: to get back together as soon as possible. Not even a month of separation had elapsed when she wrote him,

*With his dog, Vartan, in Estivella during a period
of separation from Victoria (1934?)*

Do not think that I don't need you, but look, if I must
suffer like last summer, I prefer to be far away from you.
The pain put me in a bad humor, and the bad humor
leads me to quarrel, to be misunderstood, and to live
indifferent to everyone around me. We shouldn't be crazy
enough to come together again without knowing if we
can stay together, that is, if you yourself can support me.
Now I know very well that I can't trust your family, and
that is why I am a hundred times happier here with my
parents, because they truly love me and do everything
possible for my well-being. With them I feel protected,
and that is what a woman like me most appreciates.[39]

And a week later, she felt compelled to add the following:

> I am sadder than a toad [. . .] if you say that it was an
> act of heroism for me to go away to Valencia, you are
> right, but my going back with my mom to Paris has
> nothing heroic about it, since I did it because in your
> house I would've died of consumption, as everyone says,
> so whoever thinks that I left only to keep you from
> getting upset is very much mistaken. We are not such
> naïve asses.[40]

Contests of 1934: Composing to Earn a Living

One of the greatest of Spanish poets, Saint John of the Cross,
resorted to verse in order to express all his anguish in the face
of his divine beloved's absence. Using the first four strophes of
Spiritual Canticle by the great mystic, Rodrigo created his *Cántico de la esposa*, one of the masterpieces of Spanish art song
of the twentieth century and his favorite work. It was the first
piece that he composed after the departure of his wife. The first
two lines read, "¿Adónde te escondiste, / Amado, y me dejaste
con gemido?" (Wherever did you hide, / Beloved, and you left me
here to moan?). This is a statement of intentions with a piano
accompaniment that creates a pedal of the ninth chord on F♯ but
with so essential a manner of expression that it can be played
with a single finger. The second strophe animates the rhythm
and is the only one ending in B, though with a raised third. The
third strophe contains the climax: "Buscando mis amores, / iré
por esos montes y riberas; / ni cogeré las flores, / ni temeré las
fieras, / y pasaré los fuertes y fronteras" (While seeking for my
loves, / I'll go throughout these hillocks and these stream banks;
/ I will not pick the flowers, / nor will I fear wild beasts, / And I
will pass by forts and through frontiers), with a constant acceler-
ation and a crescendo that goes from the initial *pianissimo* to the
fortissimo on which is built a cadence on E major. There are no
longer any tonics. The final imperative query, "Tell me if through
you [my love] has passed!," ends on the dominant seventh on
which it began, thereby opening an eternal space for the reply.

On the one hand, the text is practically declaimed in a recitative style that contributes to dramatic intensification; on the other hand, its technical means are as simple as they are efficacious. These two factors combine with Rodrigo's personal situation, his resolve to reunite with his wife, to give the song an emotional weight and genuineness that are difficult to achieve.

Rodrigo, who had begun to take seriously earning a livelihood from composing, wrote his *Cántico de la esposa* as the beginning of a set of songs that he had the aim of entering in the National Music Contest announced for 15 February 1934. This announcement, made by the National Council of Music and Lyric Theaters, was somewhat clumsy, because the March 15 deadline indicated for handing in works was too soon. To make up for the imminence of the time limit, the theme was left wide open:

A collection of songs for voice and piano accompaniment. [. . .] The authors can choose freely in accordance with their personal tendencies and taste, the quality and style of the poems that they are to use, always and whenever these respond to the aesthetic dignity characteristic of the musical form well defined under the universal name of *Lied* in the different great European schools. Likewise the contestants remain free to fix the number of songs forming each collection.[41]

Unwilling to waste any opportunity to assert his worth as a composer, Rodrigo submitted the March 5 manuscript of *Cántico de la esposa* for soprano. Afterwards, he was to write for light soprano the piece *Estribillo* (Refrain) on a poem by Salvador Jacinto Polo de Medina, "Y yo muera de amor por Perinarda; / desde que nace el sol hasta que para" (And may I die of love for Perinarda / from sunrise till sunset), a brilliant song with a demanding vocal part. The song is undated, but Rodrigo must have written it immediately before the one he wrote for mezzo-soprano on the little lyric *Esta niña se lleva la flor* (This girl wins the flower) by Francisco de Trillo y Figueroa, which bears the date March 9. As the composer was to tell Conchita Supervía, he composed it with her voice in mind.[42] Two days later, he finished his *Sonnet* for soprano using a text by Juan Bautista de Mesa. When the deadline was upon him, he sent his *Cuatro canciones* to the offices of the National Council of Music and Lyric Theatres in the following order: 1. "Esta niña se lleva la flor," 2. "Soneto," 3. "Estribillo," and 4. "Cántico de la esposa." Aside from their individual qualities, they form a very coherent cycle around the theme of love and absence. His labor had been intense, and Victoria Kamhi worried about her husband's health: "I am glad to see that you are working with so much vigor. I am sure that the songs are very pretty and will be very successful. But don't tire yourself out, and don't go to bed so late, because you can fall sick or at least get weak and nervous and that shouldn't happen."[43]

On March 27, there was a meeting of the jury formed by Óscar Esplá, president of the National Council of Music and Lyric Theatres, and the council members Conrado del Campo, Bartolomé Pérez Casas, Salvador Bacarisse, and Adolfo Salazar. Twenty-seven works had been entered, and the jury could not agree on the choice of a winner. They decided to divide the 2,500-peseta prize among the five proposals that they judged the best. The problem was that the quantity of the prize money awarded to each of those five composers was given in accordance with the number of songs that formed their cycle. Hence, Rodrigo received only 250 pesetas for his *Four Songs*.[44] This proportional division generated a very obvious ranking for a prize that, in principle, should have been awarded on the basis of judging all entries equally. In any case, it was a very bad idea, one that showed not only haste but also a notable lack of tact and wisdom on the part of the jury.

With the political crisis that was taking place in the Republic, many cultural initiatives of its first years were now in dispute. In fact, the National Council of Music and Lyric Theaters signed the act of its demise when all its members resigned in July 1934.[45] A bit earlier, an editorial in the review *Musicografía* put on the table the issue of this contest: "Have prizes been awarded to compositions according to their weight? Thus says one of the 'favored,' we are told."[46] But the composer that we positively know said that this prize had been awarded "by weight" was Joaquín Rodrigo. He related it by letter first to Frank Marshall,[47] and the following day to Manuel de Falla: "I have composed a collection of songs that were awarded prizes in a famous contest by the defunct National Council. The contest was decided by weight, for though it is not a very artistic measurement, it is at least (you cannot deny me that) infallible."[48]

Given the speed with which Rodrigo composed the cycle of the *Cuatro canciones*, he was clearly in fine lyric fettle, and before the end of the year he completed two new songs. First he wrote the *Cançó del teuladí* (Sparrow Song) on a poem by Teodoro Llorente Olivares, patriarch of the Valencian *Renaixença* (cultural renaissance) as a poet, journalist, historian, politician, and founder of *Las Provincias*, who then hired López-Chavarri as a music critic. Rodrigo dedicated this song to López-Chavarri's wife, the soprano Carmen Andújar, who performed it accompanied by her husband in a concert broadcast by radio on 4 April 1934.[49]

He dated the other song in Estivella on 19 September 1934. It is a very romantic barcarole composed on a text in German that Victoria Kamhi had written at age fifteen, when she was studying in Vienna: *Schifferliedchen* (Little Boat Song). She had sent it to him in April, asking several times whether he had received it.[50] In May she insisted he set it along with three other poems that she was sending him: "You would do well to find a German to read you my verses with correct intonation," she added.[51]

Several days after the final judgment of the National Council of Music was made public, the Círculo de Bellas Artes (Circle of Fine Arts) of Valencia, in collaboration with the local Orquesta Sinfónica, announced a contest for the composition of a symphonic poem. It did not please Rodrigo very much to deal with a genre so alien to the music that interested him. That genre was very rooted in the Romantic tradition, against which progressive composers like Rodrigo rebelled. And the prize money was a modest 500 pesetas. Then too, Rodrigo's relations with the Orquesta Sinfónica and especially with its conductor, José Manuel Izquierdo—also president of the music section of the Círculo de Bellas Artes—were not at all good. But this was another opportunity for him to attract attention in Spain, and he wanted to take advantage of it. This time, the rules of the contest were set out in detail: the theme of the poem was free, "inspired by motifs of national folklore, preferably [. . .] folklore grounded on the Valencian region." The composition should not last beyond fifteen minutes, and the orchestral formation was to be that of the Valencia Orquesta Sinfónica. The prize was indivisible, and the originals would be submitted anonymously. The deadline for submissions was June 30, and only afterwards would the jury be named.[52]

As of the beginning of April, Rodrigo was in Estivella and had only a month and a half to select the plot and compose his symphonic poem. He wrote to Manuel Palau May 13 to ask him about this competition. Two days later Palau wrote him to tell him that he did not intend to participate or to form part of the jury. He wished Rodrigo luck and also sent him the lyrics to the song of the "Lirio azul" (Blue Lily),[53] and these were the ones Rodrigo chose for his symphonic poem. The work he had ahead of him was enormous, and he must have finished it under great stress. "I see that you are possessed by inspiration, and I'm very glad; what I don't want is for you to keep working hours at a time. That would be barbarous and would endanger your health," Kamhi wrote him July 16.[54] Less than a week later, she asked him, "When do you intend to finish the poem?"[55] Five days before the deadline for submission, she reminded him what he was obliged to do after completing it: "Afterwards, you must make the concerto [for piano], and you should orchestrate a song for María Cid, who has great projects in store."[56]

There are several versions of the legend of the blue lily. Perhaps the best known is that of Cecilia Bohr in her *Stories of Enchantment*, published in 1877 under the pseudonym Fernán Caballero. According to this version, of Valencian origin, the king would bequeath his crown to the one of his three sons who brought him the flower of the blue lily. The youngest son found it, but the others stole it from him, killing him and burying him in a dry streambed. There was born a reed with which a shepherd fashioned himself a flute. When he played it, the instrument said (always in the Valencian tongue), "Toca, toca, bon pastor / y no ennamenes / per la flor del lliri blau; / man mort en riu de arenes" (Play, play, good shepherd, / and don't remember me / for the sake of the flower of the blue lily, / they have killed me in the river of Arenes). The king heard this song and commanded the shepherd to take him to the place where he had found the reed. There, in the presence of his other two sons, who denied their evil deed, they found the youngest son alive. He was missing a finger, out of which had sprouted the telltale reed. The young son inherited the kingdom, and the king punished his brothers.

Rodrigo gave the legend a less familiar, more tragic nuance, indicating that he had "modified it a little bit by concentrating it and giving it its present form."[57] The sick king wants to see the flower of the blue lily before dying and offers his kingdom to the son who will bring it to him. The little one finds it. The other two, hidden in bushes by the river Arenes, assault him and kill him. The reeds, bulrushes, oleanders, plants, rocks of the banks, stars, and wind of the sierra then sing the following lament: "Passa, passa, bon germà, / passa, passa i no em nomenes, / que me han mort en riu d'Arenes, / per la flor del lliri blau," the lyrics sent by Palau to Rodrigo, who took from its final verse his title, *Per la flor del lliri blau.* The translation, made by the composer himself, is the following: "Move on, move on, good wayfarer, / And remember me never anew, / For they've slain me in the river Arenes / for the bloom of the lily of blue."

It was announced in print on July 5 that the jury would consist of Vicente Peyró, Eduardo López-Chavarri, and Jacinto Ruiz Manzanares, and that twelve works had been received.[58] The verdict was made public July 11, and Rodrigo's work was unanimously selected by the jury.[59] Victoria Kamhi celebrated the verdict by mail: "As you see, the little Gypsy prophetess once again was right by telling you that you would be famous. Bravo, Pico [her pet name for Rodrigo], and *en avant* [press onward], and this is the beginning. You will do many great things."[60] From her perspective, this was not the time for him to rest on his laurels. Several days before she had communicated to him something that Leopoldo Querol's wife had told her: "that you have Gil a bit miffed because he asked you for a work for his orchestra and you have not yet written it. Also, she said that you have spoken ill of Valencia and too well of France. Careful, Pico, for you don't want to make enemies. Tell him you will write something when you have more time."[61]

The Valencia Orquesta Sinfónica, conducted by Izquierdo, premiered *Per la flor del lliri blau* on July 26 in the municipal gardens, Viveros Municipales. Although this outdoor space was not the best place to appreciate the subtleties of Rodrigo's music, his success was conveniently publicized and explained by López-Chavarri in his column for those who had not listened to it well or had not been able to attend that event of artistic life in Valencia, as the critic described it:

> *Per la flor del lliri blau*, the ever-popular children's
> story, with its characteristic tune, serves as the basis
> of the [symphonic] poem; this tune is combined with
> another popular folktune, the song of the *Tres tambors*
> [Three Drums]. Rodrigo combines these two elements
> with patent mastery: he treats them in a masterful
> counterpoint; he dresses them with the adornments of
> a splendid instrumentation, and thus the folk legend
> achieves a musical and poetic meaning of the highest
> quality [. . .] from the royal pomp, to the wanderings
> of the princes, to the conquest of the flower by the
> young prince, to his tragic end, to the lament that
> flowers, waters, stones, and airs express in the face of
> the treachery. And the legend is created, its music raised
> to the heavens by Rodrigo's genius and ending like an
> apotheosis of pain and grandeur.[62]

López-Chavarri was delighted with his verdict, though he stressed that many of the other compositions submitted to the contest were also "deserving of a prize for their ideas, structures, and the felicitous way they were orchestrated."[63] Victoria once more congratulated her husband: "I already knew that you were a genius; what I didn't know is that people would realize it so soon. Bravo, dear little Pico, and forward march!"[64]

On July 31, the work was played again in the same place, where "it was heard with great interest and understood by the audience much better than the first time." At the premiere, Rodrigo was asked to come forward, but he must not have listened to those requests (as we may deduce from some ellipses that appear in López-Chavarri's column). But this time, he indeed rose from his chair to greet the public from there, and the audience "applauded truly effusively."[65] It was requested that the work be performed at the Teatro Principal, but the conductor Izquierdo waited until December 22;[66] previously, on 24 November 1934, Pérez Casas performed *Per la flor del lliri blau* in the Teatro Español of Madrid with the Orquesta Filarmónica in a concert broadcasted by Unión Radio.[67] The success was great, and the composer, who waved from the loge, at last had the opportunity to hear the sonorous effect of his composition in the best acoustical conditions.

Rodrigo had come to Madrid the day before, accompanied by the young pianist Gonzalo Soriano. The same day as the debut, he and Victoria Kamhi were reunited, after two months apart. Surely it was she who read him the favorable commentaries devoted to him by Madrid critics: Rodolfo Halffter said that the *Zarabanda lejana y villancico* was the "exquisite product of a refined musician";[68] José Subirá referred to the same work as "a new sign of a spirit as subtle as is the exquisite Valencian musician";[69] and Salazar, in his longest review devoted to the composer (though fairly unsubstantial and not at all congenial), said that the title of his symphonic poem was "a bit baroque," but he recognized the importance of the fanfare with which the work began and wrote that it was, without a doubt, "the best composition to have emerged from his pen."[70]

Perhaps Rodrigo would not have agreed that this had been his best work to date. He told Falla that it was "a poem in the old style, with a literary program that illustrates the adventures of the hero." What is more, after recognizing that it appealed to the audience, he wrote, "There is nothing like literature in music to impress the public. [. . .] If the same music had been written without a program, it would not have appealed. The good audience is that way."[71] On other occasions, he referred to the time pressure under which he had to write this symphonic poem. He must have related that to Dukas, who rushed to write him a letter full of good sense and affection. "Because I have known your capability for a long time!" Without even seeing the work, he gave Rodrigo a stupendous lesson that, without a doubt, he would appreciate for its intrinsic value:

> You tell me, dear friend, that that ballad about a folk
> theme was written hurriedly, that you had too little time
> to deliberate in your innermost heart about the selection
> of elements and that you have had to be satisfied with
> what you call "the first music that passed through your
> head." Maybe it was precisely that which had spurred
> your eloquence and allowed you to find the intonations
> that would never have emerged from reflection, which
> is a simple intellectual operation, good for analysis with
> the mind at rest, but never replacing the spontaneity of
> the creative instinct. [. . .] You will even prove that the
> audience realizes it at once![72]

Clearly Rodrigo understood that he had had to reduce the demands he made on himself if he was going to meet the pressing deadline. Despite the fact that the selection of his materials had not been as judicious as he would have desired, the result was very effective. Some years later, it would be Rodrigo himself who, in a letter to Gilbert Chase, would give some clues about the architecture of his symphonic poem: two great sections divided, in turn, into two parts each.[73]

The first section of this symphonic poem begins with a broad fanfare as an introduction; thereafter, as Rodrigo points out, "the work, properly speaking, begins." It is notable that *La Peri* (1911) of Dukas—a work sharing with *Per la flor del lliri blau* a plot related to the quest for and loss of a flower—begins with an initial movement that is a fanfare in a style similar to Rodrigo's. The second part of the first section presents the main theme, "a broad phrase," according to the composer, that the viola offers, accompanied by harps. It is an original melody by Rodrigo but at the same time clearly derived from the folksong of the blue lily ("Passa, passa, bon germá"). According to the composer, this melody plays the part of a rhapsodist who introduces the work he is going to narrate: "Wayfarer, stop! Listen to the song of the blue lily."[74] Afterwards, the English horn repeats the melody, deferring to the violas. A four-part harmonization of the melody is divided between violas and cellos. The intricate contrapuntal writing at this point harkens back to the Renaissance. The violins restate the melody in a tempo modifying the initial Adagio with a quicker passage, while echoes of the fanfare begin to sound ("Do you hear the king's bugles? They call the princes to the royal chamber.") At once, this melody yields to a development circulating between keys. In its violin tremolos and counterpoint there resides possibly the most obvious tribute of the composer to Romantic symphonic convention ("The king is dying of a strange malady, but before he passes, he would like to behold for one last time the blue lily flower"). The tempo continues to speed up, from andante to allegro. The harmonic movement also accelerates (E minor, A Dorian, F♯ minor, E minor, A minor, B minor, etc.), representing the three brothers riding on horseback in search of the flower. A stable point is reached in G♯ minor and concludes this first part of the work in C major.

The second part of the work, according to Rodrigo, is "the march of the young prince, composed on the bases of segments of the folksong *Els tres tambors* [The Three Drums]." Some broad, legato chords over A major (I–V–I), the main key of this first section of Part II, represent the sense of triumph and ecstasy in beholding the flower: "The youngest of the three princes rides merrily and energetically; he crosses valleys and mountains, rivers and streams, walking, walking, ever upward. Now the flower is his; in his hands, he looks at it ecstatic. He returns with joy." The main theme returns in C♯ minor, intoned by the oboe followed by the French horn and repeated at once by the strings in its main key of E minor. Rodrigo referred to this return as a "reexposition" representing the "return of the young prince." This sets up another development section in part two, in which are juxtaposed and fragmented materials that have appeared before within a harmonic scheme moving once more through E Dorian, G Dorian, B♭ minor, and F♯ minor, all concluding with a very strong drumroll of triangle and cymbals: "hidden in the thickets the fratricidal daggers await you. The infante is dead." The end of the work is built upon the folk melody "Pasa, pasa, bon germá," which all nature sings.

In the program, Rodrigo refers to nine elements of nature: "the reeds are crying, the bulrushes, the oleanders; the willows are crying, the American agave, and the old poplar; the stones of the stream, the evening stars, the wind of the sierra." The music consists in turn of nine repetitions of the folk theme in the Dorian mode ("a kind of lament," according to Rodrigo), with its tonic distributed into a series of fifths: contrabassoon (A), bass clarinet (E), English horn (B), bassoons (F♯), flutes (C♯), oboes with clarinets (A♭), French horns (E♭), violins (B♭), and trumpets with trombones (E) to conclude with the reminiscence of the initial fanfare. An acoustical representation is thereby established, containing elements of the natural landscape that deserve to be highlighted:

Reeds	Contrabassoons
Bulrushes	Bass clarinet
Oleanders	English horn
Willows	Bassoons
American agave	Flutes
Old popular	Oboes and clarinets
Stones	French horns
Evening stars	Violins
Wind from the sierra	Trumpets and trombones

On November 18, barely a week before the Philharmonic performed *Per la flor del lliri blau* in Madrid, the Orquesta Sinfónica, conducted by Arbós, had played *Zarabanda lejana y villancico*.[75] In this context, a new chapter unfolded in the competition between Halffter and Rodrigo for hegemony among Spanish symphonic composers of their generation. Before the presentation of

Rodrigo's symphonic poem, the Philharmonic interpreted a suite from the ballet *Sonatina* by Halffter, to which that public had given a lukewarm reception. Such a reaction later contrasted with the excitement aroused by *Per la flor del lliri blau*. Henri Collet, curiously aware of these issues, affirmed in his column for *Le Ménestrel*, "In Madrid, the Orquesta Sinfónica drew applause for the *Zarabanda lejana y villancico* by blind composer Joaquín Rodrigo. [. . .] *Per la flor del lliri blau*, also by Rodrigo, elicited the most heated applause."[76]

In 1934, Rodrigo took his place in the front rank of Spanish composers of his generation. Besides the success of his orchestral works, his chamber music and compositions for soloists also began to attract major performers: Sainz de la Maza kept assiduously playing the *Zarabanda lejana*, and he fervently hoped to receive a new work from Rodrigo . . . one that *he* could play. Conchita Supervía had already sung *Esta niña se lleva la flor* in a concert broadcast by radio from England on 7 December 1934, perhaps heard by the composer, who had written the song with that mezzo-soprano's voice in mind.[77] His piano music was programmed by pianists like the Greek Demetrios Haralambis, who played movements from the *Suite* in Madrid,[78] and like Querol, who somewhat later added the *Preludio al gallo mañanero* to his repertoire and played it along with Halffter's Sonata in D in a recital for the Philharmonic Society of Zaragoza.[79]

Querol, who had made an important commitment to the composers of his generation, offered to premiere their works for soloist and orchestra. Rodrigo for some time had been composing a piano concerto "divided into four movements," with the aim of having Querol play it for the first time with the Orquesta Sinfónica led by Fernández Arbós.[80] Already in the month of March 1934, Kamhi wrote after a visit from Querol's wife, "they are asking you please to begin the concerto but without telling anyone, not even your good friends."[81] A subsequent news item written by Collet gave more information about Rodrigo's planned piano concerto. He indicated that the idea was for Querol and Arbós to play it on a tour through Geneva, Turin, and Rome. His wife asked him countless times for this composition:

[Querol's wife] told me that Leopoldo was very successful, and that his admirers hope to hear him next year in a concert of new pieces by a young Spanish author. A work of yours would have more success here than Bacarisse's, since you are better known. Also, you can favor him by writing a special brilliant finale to show off his technique. If it is applauded here, it will be a triumph for you both. That's why your Pica [*feminized form of Kamhi's pet name for Rodrigo*] asks you please to take advantage of this period of inspiration and write, or better still, finish your concerto, dedicating it to Leopoldo.[82]

But he was pouring his inspiration into the symphonic poem and kept putting off the piano concerto, until he finally developed a mental block to it. Other compositions of which he spoke in letters to his wife never materialized either, like some variations for violin and piano that the violinist Juan Alós asked of him,[83] and a work for a trio formed by cellist Juan Ruiz Casaux with pianist Enrique Aroca and violinist Enrique Iniesta.[84] And furthermore, he did not always triumph in the contests of 1934. At the end of the year, after the cessation of the National Council of Music, the Secretariat of National Contests of the General Directory of Fine Arts issued an original and interesting call for a National Prize. Instead of giving a prize for an individual composition, it was proposed that a prize be awarded for the professional career of composers who could demonstrate their labor between January 1931 and November 1934 by means of setting forth all the symphonic works, chamber music, or piano pieces that they had debuted in public concerts during those years.

According to contest rules, "both the quantity of works premiered as well as their artistic quality" would be considered.[85] The prizes could not remain unawarded. The main problem was that a deadline of only ten days was allowed for presenting documents. As a result, the composers found it very difficult to establish their credentials in a satisfactory way. The jury met in Madrid on 20 December 1934 and unanimously decided "That the 5,000-peseta prize be awarded to Salvador Bacarisse."

Nevertheless, the jury mentioned Rodrigo: "lamentably finding it impossible to award some compensation for the work of contestants Joaquín Rodrigo and Gustavo Pittaluga, [the jury] proposes that each be awarded honorable mentions."[86]

Since the contest rules had not allowed for the possibility of giving honorable mentions, on this occasion nothing was awarded to Rodrigo. But what would he have been able to enter? At the most, two orchestral works, *Per la flor del lliri blau* and the *Zarabanda lejana y villancico,* which probably would have been rejected because the *Zarabanda* had premiered before 1931; no chamber work, because it seems that the songs did not enter in that category; and nothing for piano. Even so, the recognition of his merits was important because at this very same time he was undertaking a more important project.

Scholarship of the Academy of Fine Arts, 1935–36

On 13 November 1934, the Academy of Fine Arts agreed to arrange the annual competition for their "Count of Cartagena" Scholarships: four for painters, two for musicians, and one for architects.[87] The entrants, between twenty and forty years of age, would be required to have a project for broadening their studies abroad and to hand in their applications and the necessary paperwork before December 15. But in addition to the official requirements, these scholarships were dependent on the support and endorsements that each applicant could raise.

Rodrigo had been keeping an eye out for the contest for months and had already begun preparing his resources. In fact, after Victoria Kamhi found out about a conversation the Querol couple had with Esplá, Salazar, and Bacarisse in April 1934, she advised her husband, "You shouldn't pump yourself up nor put on an air of self-satisfaction and contentment when you go parading over there, because many envy you, and you can hurt your chances for the stipend."[88] In other words, Rodrigo had to hide his pride and put on a display of the financial hardships he was suffering. Thus, as soon as the contest was announced, he wrote to Falla from Valencia to request his aid while revealing to him how complicated his personal situation was:

I do not want to hide from you, dear friend and maestro, that as a consequence of the dreadful crisis through which Spanish agriculture is passing, the economic state of my family, which was grounded on it, is very precarious, and at the present time, obtaining one of those scholarships would be the only solution to the difficult, very difficult situation I am experiencing. Maestros Arbós and Pérez Casas [both members of the Academy of Fine Arts] know all these circumstances, and in view of the affection they profess for me, have promised to take advantage of all their influence and vote in favor of my candidacy.[89]

This unleashed a swift and effective exchange of letters in which it became very clear that Falla was supporting Rodrigo's candidacy. In the first place, he wrote to Álvaro Figueroa y Torres, Count of Romanones, head of the Academy of Fine Arts:

I have absolutely no knowledge about who the applicants are; I know of only one: Joaquín Rodrigo, whose incontestable merits enable me to avoid introducing him to you, since in Spain, and to an even greater extent abroad, his name counts among the loftiest of our new generation of musicians. [. . .] I trust in you, Mr. President, to publicize my fervent plea in favor of the candidacy of Mr. Rodrigo among all your colleagues of the Academy. I am driven to undertake this cause not only by the reasons set down needlessly because everyone knows them, but also by the economic reverses suffered by Joaquín Rodrigo because of the present crisis. This is the only reason he decided to apply for the scholarship, with the aim of not finding himself compelled to interrupt his labors.[90]

Falla had made such a strong and unusual display of interest, despite his habitual restraint and prudence in public relations, that the Count of Romanones replied at once, noting the "pressing interest" on Falla's part in favor of Rodrigo, as well the failure of Rodrigo to submit his application. Alarmed by this fact, Falla telegraphed Rodrigo in Valencia on the 22nd, although he had already left for Madrid, whence he replied, "I have not yet been able to submit my application in an official manner because they demand some papers, certificates, and strange things that keep one busy for so many days." In the same letter he expressed his concern: "One of the arguments they wield against me seems to be that I have already been abroad and have too many merits to receive a stipend. This is absurd and has left me stunned."[91]

Rodrigo had also written to Dukas to request a letter of support for his candidacy. Dukas, in turn, wrote to Falla on November 21 with great interest in the success of Rodrigo's application. Even Joaquín Turina wrote a letter of recommendation for him, in which he highlighted the "very sure and refined technique" of Rodrigo.[92]

With the deadline reached, there was a total of fourteen applications for the two music scholarships.[93] The Achilles' heel of Rodrigo's candidacy, leaving aside the rumors of his excessive merits, would lie in certifying his academic credentials, since he could only offer the document that the director of the École Normale de Musique had expedited for him, and this was not an institution where officially recognized studies were taught. But the support he had gathered was irrefutable. His main benefactors, Falla and Dukas, closed ranks in his favor. The two academicians with the most relevant musical activity—Pérez Casas and Fernández Arbós, as conductors of the main orchestras in Spain—also supported him from within the music section of the Academy of Fine Arts. The fact that Falla's letter was not in the file submitted by Rodrigo but instead placed directly in the consideration of the music section by the Count of Romanones, the president of the Academy, also had to be a deciding factor.

The session of the academy that took place December 31 made the decision public: the scholarship recipients proposed by the music section were Joaquín Rodrigo and the pianist María Teresa García Moreno.[94] For the first time by his own means, Rodrigo had guaranteed his subsistence during the following twelve months, with the possibility of extending this period to the year 1936.

The scholarship would be renewed for Rodrigo without any problems because during his stay in Paris, he bonded with the adjutant head of the Institut d'Études Hispaniques of the Sorbonne, Aurelio Viñas, who gave him unconditional support.[95] García Moreno, however, did not renew. Her scholarship became vacant at the end of 1935 and was offered in competition. There were nine applicants, and the winner—once again with Falla's support—was Ernesto Halffter, also very economically hard-pressed and armed with the project to move to Lisbon.[96] Thanks to Falla, both Rodrigo and Halffter found a way to support themselves at the most critical times of their lives. The convergences between the two young maestros go beyond the professional level. Both were married to foreign pianists in whose "domains" they enjoyed the "Count of Cartagena" Scholarship, and both were able to spend the Spanish Civil War (1936–39) far from Spain. Falla's support was for them an act of Providence.

Meanwhile, the Rodrigos moved to Paris in March 1935. The first work that Rodrigo probably finished there was his *Coplas del pastor enamorado* (Songs of the Shepherd in Love), with guitar accompaniment (though later arranged for piano). He dedicated the songs to Aurelio Viñas. The quality of this work is the first response to Salvador de Madariaga's prophetic observation of ten years earlier: "As I understand it, the Spanish *Lied* will come into being the day that Spanish musicians write guitar accompaniments for Spanish poems."[97]

Coplas del pastor enamorado did not display the usual couplets and refrain one expects. The title referred instead to its secular, amatory character, whose theme, like that of the *Cuatro canciones* (1934), is the absence of the beloved and the resolve to find her at any price. Yet what turned out to be significant is that in the context of *La buena guarda* by Lope de Vega, from whom Rodrigo had taken his text, the Shepherd is an allegory of Christ who wishes to recover Doña Clara, a wayward abbess who has left the convent. Rodrigo even avoided the final three verses of the shepherd's words ("Oh God, how weary I am! / What shepherd's crook can there be with strength / To endure this weight?"). His aim was to eliminate any religious connotation and cast his song in a secular light. In lieu of the final plea of the Shepherd in Lope's play, Rodrigo repeated the first four verses as a kind of ritornello to conclude his musical form.

And Rodrigo's reservoir of lyricism remained full. In 1935 he even finished two new songs, *Canticel*, on a Catalan text by Josep Carner, and *Fino cristal*, with a text by the Uruguayan poet Carlos Rodríguez Pintos. If we set aside the *Barcarola* (1934), with lyrics by his wife, these are his first songs on texts of contemporary poets. In fact, what Madariaga dreamed of in the text cited above was the convergence of new poetry and new music to guitar accompaniment.

In the three months of 1935 that Rodrigo spent in Spain before leaving for Paris, he inaugurated an occupation that he would cultivate with zeal in the future: lecturing. Hence, on January 30, in the Atheneum of Alicante, he gave a talk with musical illustrations (in which Rodríguez Albert also collaborated) entitled "Music and Valencian Musicians." The following day, the Chamber Orchestra, which had already performed his music on several occasions, played *Zarabanda lejana y villancico*. He gave the same lecture at the Bilbao Atheneum on March 5 en route to Paris, this time with the assistance of Jesús Arámbarri and his wife, the harpist and singer Josefina de Roda. On April 1, with Rodrigo already settled at the home of his in-laws in Paris, Arámbarri was playing *Per la flor del lliri blau* with the Bilbao Orquesta Sinfónica in the Nuevo Teatro de Vitoria.[98]

For Rodrigo, the study of music history was always a passion. In these years, it also became a possible professional outlet. During this stay in Paris, we know that he began broadening his background by attending the musicology classes of Maurice Emmanuel and André Pirro. Emmanuel's were held in the Conservatory, and Pirro's at the Sorbonne in a course devoted to Orlando di Lasso.[99] But what was most important for him would be that he could attend the final classes of Paul Dukas at the École Normale.

It is also possible that he had with him *Per la flor del lliri blau* and that some corrections appearing on the manuscript are the result of this meeting with Dukas. A reduction by eleven measures of the initial fanfare would be consistent with Dukas's concern for economy and his dislike of redundancies. In any case, this reencounter of Rodrigo with his teacher—better said, his good friend—was ephemeral: Dukas died 17 May 1935. Rodrigo, who attended the cremation of his mortal remains in the company of Nin-Culmell,[100] felt heartsick about it.

> For me it has been another sorrow of the many of these
> recent times, for while I felt admiration for the musician,
> I had even more for the man in the pure, great sense
> ·of this word. His judgment and serene criticism had no
> equal at that time, and with his death and the serious
> sickness of Ravel, French music enters its eclipse.[101]

Immediately Henri Prunières set in motion an issue of the *Revue Musicale* commemorating the first anniversary of Dukas's passing and slated to be published with the date May–June 1936. The issue contained a musical supplement to which nine musicians would contribute homages and memorials for piano. The composers would all be friends or students of Dukas: Florent

Press card to cover the 1935 Salzburg Summer Festival

Schmitt, Manuel de Falla, Joseph Guy Ropartz, Joaquín Rodrigo, Julien Krein, Olivier Messiaen, Tony Aubrin, and Elsa Barraine.

Rodrigo received the request for a piece while he was in Salzburg, where he had gone from Paris to attend the famous festival, which took place from 27 July to 1 September 1935. There he and his wife got settled in a boardinghouse on the outskirts and rented a piano, on which Rodrigo wrote his tribute to Dukas,[102] the first piano manuscript of his that we know Victoria Kamhi wrote out. Some months afterwards, he sent Falla a letter in which he told him, "I have written two brief pages with my heart for lack of a sharper quill."[103] Falla, driven by problems of health and time that were overwhelming him, delayed in answering this letter, as he had delayed in sending his work to the *Revue Musicale*. But in his answer to Rodrigo, he wrote, "I am wishing to know your [composition], and as soon as you tell me about it, I can also tell you about mine, since everything seems inadequate to me where a tribute to Paul Dukas is concerned, and very little is all that I have been able to do."[104] The two correspondents rejoiced that Nin-Culmell was the one assigned the premiere. This took place, along with that of the rest of the pieces of the *Tombeau de Dukas*, in the piano hall of the École Normale de Musique on 25 April 1936, in collaboration with the Sociétè Nationale de Musique,[105] with all the participating composers present except Falla. Messiaen selected the pieces of Rodrigo and Falla beside his own for a recital he gave in the Salle Béal of Lyon on 11 January 1937.[106]

Rodrigo's work, initially titled *Hommage à Paul Dukas*, eventually ended up with the title *Sonada de adiós*, which does not mean "Sonata" but rather "Sound" of Farewell. Max Eschig published it under this title in 1966,[107] and it has a noble, deeply felt, elegiac quality that perhaps can be better understood as a poetic tribute rather than as a final farewell. With some apparently simple procedures, such as a pedal and a recurring melody, Rodrigo achieved extraordinary emotional intensity, a depth of sadness without precedent in his piano works to that time or perhaps ever since. Written in the so-called Andalusian mode with a key signature of A♭ minor and a tonic of E♭, the melody has a strongly folklike character—deep and simple—which we could relate to a song of mourning for its repetitive character and the narrow melodic range in which it moves.

This melody floats over an ostinato pattern that alternates the tonic E♭ with a minor-second upper neighbor (F♭), producing an effect "like a tolling of bells," in the composer's own words.[108] Both the mode and the insistent flourish on the tonic immediately recall the *Hommage to Debussy* for guitar written by Falla for Debussy's *Tombeau* of 1920. A very diatonic work, Rodrigo's uses F♮ occasionally to produce strong dissonances and to join cadences—all different, surprising, and exceedingly beautiful—on E♭ major (see musical ex. 4.1).

At the precise midpoint of this piece there appears a great Andalusian cadence, a descending Phyrgian tetrachord on the scale degrees 4–3–2–1. This leads to the emotional climax of the work, one Wade memorably describes as "the territory of Rodrigo's anguish with sharp, painful dissonances shrieking chordally up to high trebles, an extreme moment which passes quickly."[109] This effect is achieved at mm. 50–61 as the second motive, E♭–F♭–D♭, which Rodrigo himself referred to as a "theme," accumulates into a kind of *stretto*. This is followed by a very condensed repetition of the main theme and a closing section.

This work's folklike theme, restrained nobility, and warmly modal harmonies also characterized the aesthetic of another great teacher of Dukas's period, Maurice Emmanuel, who wrote to Rodrigo to comment on his work as follows:

> I have read and reread your tribute to Dukas in the issue of the *Revue Musicale*, where I myself treated the works for piano of our dear friend.[110] Your piece is the *only one* that speaks to the heart; the rest is nothing but rhetorical wordiness without strength, without true grief. It is not with false notes nor with oddities with which one laments such a teacher, and I am sure that if he had to judge your piece for his tomb, he would have been grateful only to you for having moved him.[111]

Musical ex. 4.1: Cadences in *Sonada de adiós*
(mm. 25–27, 36–37; 47 [anacrusis]–49; 59–61)

During his first year with the Count of Cartagena Scholarship, Rodrigo served as correspondent for the review *Ritmo*
and later for the *Revista Musical Catalana*. This allows us once
more to gauge his unrelenting interest in being up-to-date
about premieres and, at the same time, in listening to works
from the canonical repertoire performed by the best interpreters. He reviewed the season from his arrival in Paris in March
until September 1935, and he took advantage of his prolonged

absence to adopt a more critical position in comparing the musical situation in Spain with that in France.[112] As for the most remarkable premiere of the season, he did not hesitate to choose Hindemith's symphony *Mathis der Maler*, conducted by Ernest Ansermet in the Salle Rameau (Pleyel) on May 31. According to Rodrigo, "it's about time for this personality to be well known in Spain." In fact, the Spanish public had had occasion to listen to a good number of Hindemith's works—very appreciated by Adolfo Salazar—and Arbós, with the Orquesta Sinfónica, had presented *Mathis der Maler* in Madrid on April 3, a month before Rodrigo heard it in Paris. But, apart from this small error, it interests us to see how the Spanish composer maintains an inner debate between his enthrallment with the German composer's technique, on the one hand, and his repulsion toward the "lack of poetry" and musical ideas "deprived of attractiveness, of beauty," on the other. Nonetheless, in this symphony, which Salazar described as "a romantic work,"[113] Rodrigo found sufficient beauty and musical emotion "to classify its author as one of the most interesting musicians of the present moment." Then too, Rodrigo mentioned the debut of the *Concertino* for saxophone and small orchestra of Jacques Ibert, "very pretty, very musical," and the *Sinfonietta* of Roussel, "good music that well characterizes its author, setting in relief his virtues more than his weaknesses."

Of the Parisian opera season, he highlighted a production of *Norma*, but a true glut of phenomenal opera productions took place in the months of July and August at the Salzburg Festival, where he attended operas by Mozart, Wagner, Verdi, Beethoven, and Strauss, as well as chamber music recitals. After the Salzburg Festival and starting on September 2, Rodrigo spent the fall in the small French locality of Mirmande (Drôme). Victoria Kamhi owned a modest country home there with her sister Mathilde, who took part in the artistic ambience created around a mansion of the cubist painter André Lhote. It was a happy time of vacations that, according to Kamhi, lasted until Christmas Eve.[114]

Newly in Paris, with his scholarship renewed for 1936, Rodrigo resumed his creative labor. Following his lyric inspiration, he wrote a series of songs in Catalan. In the first months of 1936, as he insisted on different occasions, he wrote the first drafts of what years later would be his *Quatre cançons en llengua cata-lana* and the *Tríptic de Mossèn Cinto*. They are two sets of pieces for soprano and orchestra, which would eventually premiere in 1946. In addition to the *Cançó del teuladí*, which he orchestrated at the end of 1934, and the orchestral version of *Canticel* (1935), the *Quatre cançons* incorporate two new songs, "L'inquietut pri-maveral de la donzella," on a sonnet of Josep Massó i Ventós, and "Brollador gentil," on a poem by Joan Maria Guasch i Miró. The *Tríptic* comprises "L'harpa sagrada," "Lo violí de Sant Francesc," and "San Francesc i la cigala," on three poems by Jacinto Verda-guer. No rough draft is preserved of this work. According to the composer, the bliss of these years of tranquility and relative eco-nomic independence is reflected in these works, which show his mastery of the art-song genre and the extraordinary richness of his harmonic palette.

Since his return to France, one of Rodrigo's main concerns was the publication of his songs. He did not achieve this, despite the fact that in Paris he was lucky enough to rely on a new interpreter, the soprano María Cid, for whom he orchestrated the *Cançó del teuladí*. She gave some important concerts of Rodrigo's music: one on 22 May 1935 took place in the Schola Cantorum, where, accom-panied by Joaquín Nin-Culmell, she became the first singer ever to perform the *Cántico de la esposa*.[115] Another concert, organized by the Société Nationale in the École Normale de Musique, was held 10 April 1936, when she premiered the *Coplas del pastor enam-orado*, accompanied by the French guitarist M. Lafont, of whom we have no further information.[116] They performed "7 Mélodies" of Rodrigo after Nin-Culmell had played the *Suite para piano* and the *Zarabanda lejana*.[117] In a letter no longer preserved, López-Chavarri must have told Rodrigo that the publication of songs was a complicated affair for everyone, to which Rodrigo responded with his own version of the problems and the solutions:

You are right about the business of songs, but the
suffering of many is the consolation of fools; in spite of
all my efforts and my public relations, all editors reject
my songs, and the devil take me, but they're not ugly
and they are a great success everywhere. But the time
has arrived for the publishers' penance, and for these
and everyone of us to purge the foolishness of editors,
authors, and critics by publishing it doesn't matter
what, and by seeing now that they have a heap of music
without anyone buying a note. [. . .] The only solution
would be a full new reorganization of the musical world,
beginning with schools, passing to the conservatories,
and ending with the swarm of editors, reducing the
prices, and finally, changing the structure of society.[118]

And right away he insists, "For the moment, *melodies* [songs]
are the most difficult thing to publish. In exchange, they ask
of me clear, easy things for piano." Although they are not such
clear or easy "things," it is significant that the other work that
Rodrigo was composing in 1935 was a set to which Victoria
Kamhi refers in her memoirs as *Cuatro danzas de España*.[119] Yet,
this piece would not be finished until several months later, and
under conditions quite different from the comfort in which the
composer lived when he began to write them.

He kept on sending his columns about musical life in Paris
to *Ritmo* in Madrid and the *Revista Musical Catalana* in Barcelona, stopping at the beginning of the 1935–36 season with
the concert version of the ballet *Sémiramis* by Arthur Honegger,
who, according to Rodrigo, "returns in this work to the harsh
musical language of some years ago." But he outdid himself in
praising Jacques Ibert, "the most musical composer [. . .] that
France brings to light at the present." For Rodrigo, his concert version of the ballet *Diane de Poitiers* is "a considerable
delight, very pretty and very attractive."[120] Yet he did not like
the Second Concerto for Violin, Op. 63, of Sergei Prokofiev that
Arbós had debuted with the Madrid Orquesta Sinfónica on 1
December 1935. Although he considered the Russian composer

one of the "most interesting of the present day," on hearing the work at its first Paris performance on 15 February 1936, he judged it as "extremely deficient," and added a shocking reflection about the composer of the *Classical Symphony*, Op. 25: "He is not a man capable of attempting an art of a classical type, to which his abundant nature does not lend itself. He wants to be pure, and he is overly bland: he wants to manipulate the old musical syntax, and his hand hesitates, because a sincere conviction does not move it, and a need of his turbulent feeling is not motivating it."[121]

The premiere taking place in Madrid of the Second Violin Concerto of Prokofiev gives proof that Spain, in those first months of 1936, had a certain relevance that would culminate in the simultaneous celebration in Barcelona of the Third International Congress of Musicology and the Fourteenth Festival of the International Society of Contemporary Music between the 18th and 25th of April 1936. It was a great event, inscribed into the annals of the history of music because it was there that the premiere of the Violin Concerto of Alban Berg took place.

The jury entrusted with selecting the works to form the festival programs had been chosen in 1935 by representatives of the sixteen nations then forming the ISCM and included Anton Webern, among other luminaries. This jury met in Barcelona from 28 December 1935 to 1 January 1936 to choose from among 150 compositions those that would make up the program for the Barcelona festival.[122] The Spanish section, which offered the program of performances that would be given in Barcelona, selected no work by Rodrigo, who consequently remained unrepresented in this important showcase of modern international music.

Arámbarri, who was in the festival and had just finished playing Rodrigo's *Cinco piezas infantiles* with the Bilbao Orquesta Sinfónica,[123] wrote him a private opinion that coincided with critical judgments like those that José Subirá published in the journal *Musicografía*:[124]

I tell you that I think that the *Cinco piezas infantiles* are worthy of having appeared in Contemporary Music in

Barcelona, since there was some trash, especially in national music. Any of your works, whether symphonic or chamber music, in my judgment, would have worthily represented Spain, whose contribution was chronically inferior.[125]

Surely exasperated because he did not take part in the festival, but at ease in Paris, Rodrigo probably spent the spring without paying much attention to composing. He collaborated on April 24 in the musical illustrations of the lecture "L'Esprit de la musique espagnole" given by influential critic and musicographer Alexis Roland-Manuel,[126] and he himself, commissioned by Aurelio Viñas, prepared a lecture that he delivered at the Institut d'Études Hispaniques (Sorbonne) on May 6 under the title "The Vihuela and the Vihuelists of the Sixteenth Century." This "erudite talk, nuanced with a pleasantness that at times verged on malice," according to the correspondent of the daily *ABC* in Paris,[127] relied on musical examples performed by the guitarist Emilio Pujol. Five months earlier, Pujol had discovered the vihuela preserved in the Jacquemart-André Museum of Paris—the first sixteenth-century vihuela ever found—and he ordered a reproduction of it from the guitar maker Miguel Simplicio. Pujol presented this instrument during a paper he gave in Barcelona April 23 during the Third International Conference of Musicology.[128] Several days afterwards, he played it to illustrate Rodrigo's lecture in Paris, and the composer wrote to Sainz de la Maza of the excitement he felt on hearing the *Fantasía que contrahaze la harpa en la manera de Ludovico* (Fantasy that Imitates the Harp after the Fashion of Ludovico), published by Alonso de Mudarra in his *Tres libros de música en cifras* (Three Books of Music in Tablature, Seville, 1546): "It is simply a wonder. Something that is almost two centuries ahead of that period, its thematic arrangement, its taste for modulation, the way of understanding development, is something new for its age, and its ending has truly astonishing things."[129]

With the Catalan songs only in a rough sketch and the dances for piano unfinished, the couple spent the winter, spring, and summer of 1936 in Germany. They decided to spend a few days at a hotel in Baden-Baden and then rent a little house with a piano in Freiburg am Breisgau. It certainly was not the best place for a study trip; nor did it seem a good idea for a Jewish family to summer in Hitler's Germany. Even so, Rodrigo, his wife, and his in-laws were willing to take a very comfortable vacation, and there they were living during the event that would alter the course of Spanish history in a decisive way: the military uprising of July 18 against the government-elect of the Republic. A political pronouncement set the Spanish Civil War in motion.

Rodrigo had received the fourth of six payments of the Count of Cartagena Scholarship, corresponding to the renewal of his scholarship at the end of July 1936. Nevertheless, the following transference of funds never arrived. On September 11 the Ministry of Public Education and Fine Arts ordered the cancellation of the scholarships and the immediate return of all recipients: "in these moments it is necessary for all useful elements outside of Spain to come back and work together."[130] Rodrigo decided not to return.

Spain at War, 1936–39

Few people supposed that the war following the military coup in Spain would last long, much less nearly three years. Through the joy and hope with which he greeted the Republic and the concern that the political instability of 1934 produced in him, Rodrigo could clearly see what was happening. In private, he showed as much very clearly. Hardly two and a half months after the beginning of the conflict, he wrote, "Everyone wishes this dreadful war would end. It would already have ended if not for the senseless stubbornness of the government, which is truly suicidal."[131] Seen from Germany, the denouement of the war seemed imminent and not favorable at all to the Republican government.

But Rodrigo did not only get information in Germany, along with the small colony of Spaniards residing in Freiburg and frequented by him. He also got downwind of current events during his trips to Switzerland. When he wrote the preceding letter, he had just come back from Zurich, where on September

21 he had given a lecture with musical illustrations—"at the gramophone and the piano"—organized by the Swiss Federation of Friends of Spain and Spanish America in the Hotel Carlton Elite. At the end of this lecture, a collection was taken "whose sum-total would go to the Auslandschweizer-Sekretariat [Secretariate outside Switzerland] in Bern to aid Swiss and Spanish fugitives coming from Spain and taking refuge in Switzerland."[132] A short time afterwards, he returned to Zurich, this time to take part in a concert at the Town Hall, attended, according to Victoria Kamhi, by the president of the Federal Council of Switzerland.[133] The Swiss governor would be present, attracted less by Rodrigo than by the fame of the flamenco star Carmen Gómez, *bailaora* and *cantaora* (flamenco dancer and singer), who went by the nickname "La Joselito," whom Rodrigo accompanied at the piano during some of her dances. The well-known leftist politics of La Joselito, along with the fact that Switzerland did not recognize the Franco government until February 1939, meant that this event would unavoidably acquire a political aspect favorable to the government of the Spanish Republic.

Rodrigo was attempting to find work for himself, or for his wife as a governess. He found nothing in Paris, but José Rolón from Mexico proposed something:

> [Manuel Ponce] and I have been chatting about the way
> to get you to come here in safe conditions. We have only
> come up with this means: you could get some letter
> of introduction from one of the important people of
> the government of Valencia for the Minister of Public
> Education here, Gonzalo Vázquez Vela, Esquire, for
> this official has always shown sympathy for Azaña's
> [Republican] government.[134]

Rolón had held a political position in the Secretariat of Education during the presidency of Abelardo L. Rodríguez, but when Lázaro Cárdenas came to power, he lost his influence. The only thing he offered Rodrigo, pending suitable recommendations, was a job at the National School for the Blind. It appears that Rodrigo quickly ruled out this possibility.

Nonetheless, alone in Freiburg—for Victoria Kamhi's parents returned to Paris at the end of 1936—the Rodrigos were lucky enough to find accommodations in the Blindenheim (Home for the Blind), a charitable institution devoted to the blind, giving asylum to a dozen elderly people and having workshops where other boarders made baskets, brushes, and other manufactured goods. The director, Otto Vanoli, also blind, along with his wife, welcomed the Spanish couple to a room with full board, and they collaborated as best they could in the labors of the institution. What seemed to be a transient arrangement lasted for over a year.[135]

There was a piano in the Blindenheim of Freiburg, and Rodrigo was able to complete some compositions. The most impressive is one of his *Cuatro piezas para piano* (also known as *Cuatro danzas de España*), entitled "Plegaria de la Infanta de Castilla." Its emotional intensity may well represent the tragedy that Spain was experiencing. That at least is how Joaquín Nin-Culmell understood it in 1937, when receiving a dedicated copy from the composer and writing him, "a huge hug of recognition and admiration for the dedication and composition of your *Plegaria*. I also hope that it will bring peace to Spain." Afterwards, he asked whether Rodrigo had plans for "the *rentrée*" (the reentry).[136] He had absolutely none.

There were many *infantas* (princesses) of Castile, but Rodrigo's work probably refers to the historical circumstances of Enrique IV, king from 1454 to 1474, whose succession gave rise to a civil war in the kingdom of Castile among the partisans of his daughter Juana and those of his half-sister Isabel. Although the composer never said so, we believe that here he represented the prayers for peace of the woman who would later become Queen Isabel the Catholic. Her prayer was also Rodrigo's for the peace of Spain: concerns about the prolongation of the war are clearly expressed in a composition that, like the *Sonada de adiós*, conjoins intellect and emotion in equal parts.

The work shows to what extent structures of a diatonic

character can be modernized by means of very sophisticated contrapuntal procedures. But beyond the technique, it also exhibits a strongly pessimistic sentiment. The unexpected tribute to the great zarzuelist Federico Chueca in "Caleseras" from the *Cuatro piezas para piano* could be interpreted as a less dramatic vision of the war. The quotes used by Rodrigo come from the number in which the protagonists of Chueca's hit *Agua, azucarillos y aguardiente* (1877), Pepe and Manuela, are reconciled after a quarrel typical of the *género chico* (zarzuela in one act).

In fact, the Rodrigos remained safely removed from the disasters of war in Spain. When good weather arrived, they enjoyed walks through the Black Forest and hikes up the Schauinsland mountain (4,213 ft.), with its stunning vistas. On those walks they used to listen to the cuckoo birds sing, and Victoria Kamhi wrote some simple verses with forced rhymes that Rodrigo raised to a lofty level of art in his *Canción del cucú*. This melancholy outpouring expresses longing for their homeland, which the music evokes in both rhythmic flourishes and modal colorings of an Andalusian sort, especially the cadential half step from F to E.

And yet, this work is far from humorless. The melody in E Mixolydian is accompanied by some arpeggios in which Rodrigo turns loose a whole flock of warbling cuckoos: many with the more common interval of a descending minor third (G to E) clashing with the G♯ of the main modality of E Mixolydian, but others also with intervals of a diminished fourth (C to G♯), presented next in enharmonic form as a major third (C to A♭), perfect fourth (F to C), and perfect fifth (D to G). As cuckoos mature, the downward interval of their "song" expands from a minor third to a perfect fourth, something the young couple noticed during their sylvan perambulations.[137]

Uncertainty about the future reflected in these naïve verses, so effectively bound together musically, became clear very shortly when the Rodrigos found themselves forced to make a decision that would be crucial. Victoria Kamhi narrates it thus:

TABLE 4.1 **Textual and harmonic correspondence in**
Canción del cucú

Cuckoo, cuckoo, sing, These are days for singing, Soon the harsh north wind Will run through the pine grove.	E Mixolydian (cuckoo G to E) (cuckoo E to C♯) G♯ major
Tell me if other woods I will see one day, If the distant land I will find very soon.	E Mixolydian Phrygian tetrachord on E (cuckoo C to G♯)
Tell me if through those worlds	Phrygian tetrachord on C (cuckoo C to A♭)
I will always wander, or if my errant life I very soon will cease.	(cuckoo C to G) Phrygian tetrachord on G F (cuckoo D to G)
Bird, good cuckoo Tell me if it's true: She says that always she will follow me.	E Mixolydian Phrygian tetrachord on B E
...	
Cuckoo, cuckoo, sing!	E Mixolydian

One afternoon, the institute director ordered us down
to his office for a very serious matter. We were petrified
to find out that there was an order for our expulsion.
"I would be truly sorry if you had to leave in these
circumstances," Herr Vanoli told us, "but the orders
are clear. You will have to leave the country within
24 hours, unless you exchange your passports for a
document issued by the Government of Burgos, for our
government does not recognize the Spanish Republic. To
obtain said passport, you would have to leave as soon as
possible for Berlin, where there is now a new consulate.
You have tonight to think it over, and must give me your
answer tomorrow."

That night neither Joaquín nor I closed an eye. For people as far removed from the political world as we were, it was a most difficult decision. [. . .] And if we made a false step, we might compromise our entire future: poverty, exile, and perhaps permanent separation, the end of our marriage, already so often threatened. I remember that all during the night the sound of the bell in the nearby cathedral seemed lugubrious and threatening.

When dawn came, I asked Joaquín, who waited anxiously for my decision, "Who was the French general who said: 'J'y suis; j'y reste'? [Here I am. Here I stay.] I think it was MacMahon. Anyway, here we are safe, under the protection of the compassionate Director of the Heim. Here we stay." And Joaquín agreed with me.[138]

In fact, in August 1937, the admiral of the Spanish Navy, Antonio Magaz, Second Marquis of Magaz, had taken possession of the Spanish diplomatic legation in the presence of Adolf Hitler in Berlin. The Rodrigos could no longer postpone what would be one of the most important decisions of their lives: to request the regularization of their situation as residents in Germany in the presence of Magaz, one of the shapers of Spanish foreign policy, called "national" policy, which was the one that, supported by Nazi Germany, was going to prevail in the Civil War.

Shortly after the Rodrigos returned to Freiburg with papers in order, Ambassador Magaz answered a letter that Rodrigo had sent him, backed by the diplomat who represented national-ist Spain in Vienna, Eduardo García Comín. Rodrigo apparently asked Magaz that he recommend him to the Spanish pianist José Cubiles—a very prominent musician in support of the uprising—and tell him to send a letter on his behalf. During the war, Cubiles had resided for some time in Germany, returned to Spain in May 1937, and a few months later, was named artis-tic director of the Radio Nacional.[139] Magaz examined this rec-ommendation and took advantage of the occasion to tell him, "I have learned with satisfaction about the program in your concert in favor of our national music, and we heartily congratulate you on it."[140]

The earlier letter possibly made reference to a concert that Rodrigo had given in the Margarete Ruckmich Haus in Freiburg, where he performed works of Soler, Granados, Albéniz, Falla, and Turina, besides some compositions of his own.[141] According to Victoria Kamhi, for several weeks, Rodrigo spent six hours a day at the piano studying these works, and it was on these days that he finished his *Cuatro piezas para piano*, which, along with "Plegaria de la infanta de Castilla" and "Caleseras," include the "Fandango de ventorrillo" and "Danza valenciana."[142]

All these pieces exhibit a much different style from the one he had cultivated up to that time. This leads us to suspect that these dances—the lightly Andalusian "Caleseras," the Castilian "Fandango," and the "Valencian dance"—had some relationship to the repertoire that he was studying so intensely. To be specific, the pianism of Rodrigo's "Fandango" exhibits a texture very similar to Scarlattian harpsichord technique and recalls the Fandango of Padre Antonio Soler, among the best-known Spanish keyboard works of the eighteenth century. Rodrigo's designation of this piece as a "country inn" fandango evokes the original ambience of this sort of lively, triple-meter song and dance, in a *venta* (or *ventorrillo*). These were little more than ramshackle structures made of stone and patronized by the commoners immortalized in Goya's famous painting *La riña en la Venta Nueva*, which depicts some local ruffians settling a dispute with their fists. *Ventas* also figure prominently in *Don Quijote*, as places associated with some of his celebrated exploits. Rodrigo was consciously mining a rich vein of Spanish heritage with this title, though his "Fandango" displays a distinctly Valencian pedigree in its rhythmic configurations, especially the use of a repeated-note anacrusis.

The "Fandango del ventorrillo," set down in the contract with Max Eschig signed on 14 June 1938 as "petite fandango," is a jewel with an eighteenth-century grace that inaugurates in the composer's catalogue something that much later would be labeled "neocasticismo," music rooted in tradition but open to modernity. He composed it during the first months of 1937, as can be gathered from a letter from Joaquín Nin-Culmell in which he recognized receipt of the manuscript and quickly asked him for another dance to premiere in a concert he had planned for May 26.[143]

This fandango exhibits a monothematic structure with frequent modulations, and consists of three repetitions of a series of four musical phrases. The first and third rotations move through the same circle of fourths, while the central rotation functions as a simple development.

The rhythmic flourishes and static bass lines of this piece strongly suggest the instrument that was habitually used to accompany a fandango: the guitar. In fact, its two-voice texture and idiomatic stylings have made it an attractive prospect for transcription as a guitar duet, by both Emilio Pujol and Pepe Romero. And yet, as an essay in sheer pianistic legerdemain, it has few rivals within his output.

TABLE 4.2 **"Fandango del ventorrillo,"** **harmonic and thematic process**

Rotation 1

A (mm. 1–12)	B (mm. 13–20)	C (mm. 21–30)	D (mm. 31–41)
F	B♭	E♭	A♭

Rotation 2

A (mm. 45–55)	B (mm. 56–60)	C + D (mm. 60–68)
C	A♭	D♭

Rotation 3

A (mm. 70–81)	C (mm. 82–90)	B (mm. 91–94)	D (mm. 95–105)
F	B♭	E♭	A♭

Finale

A (mm. 107–115)
F

After spending their second Christmas season in Freiburg, and celebrating New Year's Day there once more, in the first days of January 1938 the Rodrigos prepared for their return to Paris. Victoria Kamhi writes in her memoirs that the immediate reason for their departure from Freiburg was that she got food poisoning. She recovered in Paris, but their financial situation was not so easily remedied, and they endured actual hunger while staying in the room of a modest hotel very close to the Jardin du Luxembourg.

The persons closest to Rodrigo before and after the Civil War were always more sympathetic to the uprising than to the defense of the Republic: Joaquín Nin-Culmell, Ricardo Viñes, Leopoldo Querol, Federico Mompou, Emilio Pujol, Aurelio Viñas . . . but above all, Manuel de Falla, whose musical and moral authority was unassailable, grounded as it was in his independence and firm convictions. At the beginning of 1938, Falla published a revealing statement:

The National Uprising of Spain supposes for me the high hope that the blasphemies shouted through these streets, the martyrdoms, the sacrileges perpetrated in our temples and in our cemeteries, the destruction of those very temples, the stripping of our libraries and of our centuries-old treasure of art, and everything under the sign of the satanic effort [. . .] to snatch the eternal essence of the divine essence of the human consciousness away from it will never torment us again. This is what I feel, and this is what I say with all the Christian conviction that drives me to put God above all things and to hope, with the most fervent yearning, that there may come the day when Spain and all Nations can deserve the immense gifts of true Peace, of Clemency, and Equity, and the Justice of God.[144]

Although Rodrigo also rejected war, there is no obvious correlation between his own privately held religious beliefs and the public pronouncements of Falla on the subject of faith. Nor do we believe that it was a deciding factor for him that, at the start of the war, the Peasant Worker Associations of the Popular Front appropriated about thirty acres of tillable lands from his father.[145] He and Victoria shared a sympathy for social movements of a revolutionary character, but this had distanced him from his family. Further, he agreed as little with his father's conservatism as with the exacerbated Catholicism of one of his sisters and of Rafael Ibáñez. The Rodrigos were basically fighting for their survival, and their pragmatic decisions aligned them with persons with whom they had had good personal and professional relations. Soon, the authorities of the Spain that was winning the war would take him into account as nobody else in any place had.

Chapter 5

All about the
Concierto de Aranjuez
(1938–1940)

THIS IS THE story of the *Concierto de Aranjuez* for guitar
and orchestra. It is the central chapter of our book, and it contains information about the key with which Rodrigo opened the
door to the history of music and walked through it. A melody with
which he built the second movement, Adagio, crossed the border
between what is classical and what is popular, between élite art
and universal mass consumption. Here we examine the *Concierto
de Aranjuez* from the time Joaquín Rodrigo composed it in the
final years of the Spanish Civil War—between the end of 1938 and
the middle of 1939—until its 1940 premiere and dissemination.

More than a composition with some intrinsic musical values—
our main concern in this chapter—the *Concierto de Aranjuez* is a
complex phenomenon whose identity and reception have continued to evolve over the decades since its premiere. It was a challenge to compose and a singular achievement, which attained
renown in the halls of symphonic music for which it had been
conceived. But it afterwards occupied different musical spaces:

ballet, jazz, popular song, musical bands, and mass media. After becoming a widely recognized symbol of what was "Spanish," it ended up as a conventional musical ditty to sell luxury items like cars or perfumes and used in many film scores. We will trace the career of the *Concierto de Aranjuez*—where, how, for what purpose, and by whom it was used—thereby contributing to the growth of its fame, which would eventually become global.

The Summer Courses in Santander, 1938

During the first months of 1938, Rodrigo was preoccupied with simply surviving the circumstances in which he found himself, with making the sorts of decisions that would ensure the continuation of his creative life. He sensed that one of his most realistic options for finding work stemmed from his education as a lecturer, scholar, and popularizer of aspects of the history of Spanish music that he found interesting. After his first lecture at the Institut d'Études Hispaniques (Institute of Hispanic Studies) at the Sorbonne in May 1936 about the vihuela and vihuelists, he had gone deeper into the study of that preeminent musical instrument of the Spanish Renaissance, and he had completed a set of piano transcriptions with which to illustrate his talks. These are the *Cinco piezas del siglo XVI*: 1. *Diferencias sobre "El canto llano del caballero"* (Variations on "The Knight's Song") by Antonio de Cabezón (for organ); 2. *Pavana* by Luis de Milán; 3. *Pavana* by Luis de Milán; 4. *Pavana* by Enríquez de Valderrábano; and 5. *Fantasía que contrahaze la harpa en la manera de Ludovico* (Fantasy in Imitation of Ludovico's Harp) by Alonso de Mudarra.[1] Rodrigo probably debuted these transcriptions on his 5 October 1937 performance for Radio-Strasbourg.[2] But the first program in which the contents of the complete set are spelled out took place at a concert organized by the Académie des Lanturelus in Paris, an institution devoted to the union of historic and contemporary music. Rodrigo participated there 24 May 1938 by performing not only his pieces from the sixteenth century but also his *Zarabanda lejana*, *Pastoral*, *Preludio al gallo mañanero*, and *Serenata*.[3]

Several days thereafter, Rodrigo and his wife crossed the border at Irún on their way back to Spain. It was July 6, and he had been invited to give a series of lectures as part of the Summer Course of Studies for Foreigners in Santander, between July 1 and August 25. Spain was still at war, and the three great cities that Rodrigo had frequented before 1936—Madrid, Barcelona, and Valencia—remained under the control of the Republican government. More than a summer course to teach Spanish to foreigners, what was organized in Santander during the summer of 1938 was the first plenary conference to feature the most important cultural elements of the Nuevo Estado (New State) now taking shape. Rodrigo's role consisted in giving three concert lectures, on July 21, 22, and 23, in the Atheneum of Santander, under the title "Instrumental Music in the Imperial Courts of Spain."

Rodrigo was able to establish connections with people who would become influential and provide him with support and collaboration. He met the aristocrat and theater manager Luis Escobar, a seminal figure in the reorganization of the Spanish theater as head of the National Department of Theater during the postwar period. Escobar was preparing a production of *La vida es sueño* by Pedro Calderón de la Barca with the company of the National Theater of the Falange (the Spanish fascist party), which commissioned music by Rodrigo. He recycled the orchestral arrangement of the *Zarabanda lejana* and wrote two new numbers, "Fanfare" and "Rebelión." The debut of the production of *La vida es sueño* with Rodrigo's music took place on 7 December 1938 at the Teatro Principal de Burgos, in a gala show presided over by none other than Carmen Polo, wife of General Franco. However, the composer himself was not in attendance because he had already gone back to Paris.

During the Santander course, Rodrigo began to send out feelers to find work that would allow him to return to and settle in Spain. The Jesuit Nemesio Otaño, who in the 1940s would become the factotum of Spanish academic musical life, wrote to the chapelmaster of Granada's cathedral, Valentín Ruiz-Aznar, on 6 September 1938, "Rodrigo, the blind man, has come here, and I consider him a very good musician. I met him in Paris and I saw several of his things. He has no financial resources, and let's see how we can find him a job."[4] Otaño and other people with influence in the new regime would help Rodrigo, but the one who first came to his aid with greatest decisiveness, influence, and firmness was again Manuel de Falla.

Within a few days of Rodrigo's return to Spain, he wrote Falla to congratulate him on his nomination to be president of the Institute of Spain, created by the Franco government as a "Senate of Spanish Culture," into which all the Royal Academies flowed together.[5] Falla was not able to respond quickly, but when he finally did, he was extremely affectionate, expressing the joy that it gave him to have word of Rodrigo and to find him in Spain. He also indicated how much he esteemed him: "I give thanks to the Lord for having in you a friend whose heart is of such a rare and fine quality as his art."[6] In the next letter that he sent to Falla, dated Bilbao, September 8, Rodrigo broached his main concern:

> I will not conceal from you, Don Manuel, that I came back
> to our country to stay indefinitely, while contributing
> my modest collaboration to the reconstruction of our
> beloved homeland. But despite all my efforts, I have not
> managed to obtain any nomination to National Radio [or]
> any conservatory, nor have I even received a permanent
> nomination as interim professor of the National College
> for the Blind, as I had done in 1935. All this has caused in
> me a certain bitterness and pain. [. . .] I find myself needing
> to return abroad to keep struggling with the enormous
> difficulties now put in the way of foreign musicians.
>   I have come to think that everyone harbors mistrust
> of my musical preparation, and for that reason I dare to
> beg you, dear Don Manuel, in case you think it opportune
> and it does not trouble you in the least, that you apply
> pressure to Mr. [Alfonso García] Valdecasas, Subsecretary
> of National Education, a person who has seemed very
> good and cultivated to me; Mr. Tovar, Director of National
> Radio, who takes an interest in me; and perhaps also Don
> Eugenio d'Ors, national Head of Fine Arts, who professed
> a great deal of kindness to me. I want nothing more than
> to return to Spain [Rodrigo was writing from Spain in his

way back to Paris], settle here definitively, and end this nomadic life that is so opposed to my way of being.[7]

Mastering his illnesses, Falla set to work to write to the powerful Eugenio d'Ors with a clear recommendation of Rodrigo: "He is a composer with very complete technique and exceptional *inspiration* in the whole true value of this word. [. . .] Dukas, who was his teacher, esteemed him as his favorite pupil. Are we who so lack *true* musicians going to lose him?"[8] Some days afterwards, Falla wrote directly to the Minister of National Education. This letter is a document of great importance, because in it Falla singles out Joaquín Rodrigo and Ernesto Halffter as the main composers on which the new Spain could rely:

> In these days, I have written to Eugenio d'Ors asking
> him to find a way to obtain for Joaquín Rodrigo (whether
> on the radio, a conservatory, etc.) some well-remunerated
> office that allows him to continue in Spain, as he desires.
> If not, we would lose one of the few positive treasures on
> which our music can rely, since he is a composer of great
> worth, both for his technique and for his inspiration.[9]

Sainz Rodríguez took only two days to respond: he could offer Rodrigo a contract for a course as a professor at the Conservatory of Seville or at the Conservatory of Granada for a total salary of 5,000 pesetas. Aware that this was too little, he added, "If besides this I could find something else to offer him, I would get in touch with you. Make the offer to your friend, and if he accepts this nomination, I will send you the authorization with great pleasure."[10]

Falla, who had undergone a surgical operation at that time, dictated to his sister a letter of gratitude to Sainz Rodríguez and another letter in which he conveyed the news to Rodrigo, asking him to answer the minister. But Rodrigo was no longer in Bilbao. Not having found adequate employment, he had returned to France, and it would be several weeks before he received news of the result of Falla's efforts on his behalf. On this trip occurred something that would completely change the course of his life.

The Meeting in San Sebastián
and *En los trigales* (1938)

In the final days of September 1938, Victoria Kamhi indicated in her memoirs the date of the Munich Accord in which Hitler and Mussolini, meeting with the French and British prime ministers, approved the annexation of the Czechoslovakian Sudetenland to Germany.[11] With this pact, which merely postponed an unavoidable confrontation, there disappeared for the Spanish Republic any possibility of receiving aid from France or Great Britain. En route to Paris, Rodrigo stopped in San Sebastián and spent time with Regino Sainz de la Maza, who had also taught at Santander that summer. At the invitation of Luis de Urquijo, future Marquis of Bolarque, the Rodrigos and Sainz de la Maza had lunch at the Nautical Club of San Sebastián. It was here that the possibility was raised of Rodrigo's composing a concerto for guitar and orchestra. Rodrigo later related details of their conversation in some notes from 1943:

> Suddenly, Regino, with that tone between fickle and
> resolute that so well characterizes him, said, "Man,
> you must come back with a concerto for guitar and
> orchestra." To soften me, he added in an emotional
> tone of voice, "It is my dream of a lifetime." To further
> ingratiate himself to me [. . .] he went on, "You are the
> one meant to do it, something like a *chosen one*." I
> emptied two glasses nonstop of the best Rioja wine, and
> I exclaimed with the most convinced voice in the world,
> "Man, that's as good as done."[12]

Sainz de la Maza and Rodrigo were united in an old friendship. The last time that they had seen each other was in the Valencian port of Grao in 1934. Sainz de la Maza was now embarking on a trans-Atlantic tour. Two years later, just before departing on another tour, Rodrigo wrote him a promise: "On my word of honor, on returning from America, you will find a work of mine for guitar."[13] Rodrigo kept his word, and on reuniting with the

guitarist in Santander on this early fall day of 1938, he must have
taken to him a new guitar piece. It was "Amanecer en los trigales"
(Dawn in the Wheat-Fields), the first movement of a planned
suite for guitar entitled *Por los campos de España* (Through the
Fields of Spain).

Instead of the usual suite of brief pieces commissioned or
received by the great Segovia following the model of the *Suite
castellana* by Moreno Torroba, Rodrigo had proposed to make a
geographical suite: a trip through Spain from Castile to Andalusia. Nevertheless, he would delay almost twenty years in resum-
ing this long journey *Por los campos de España*, begun in 1938
with the piece mentioned for Sainz de la Maza, which he finally
entitled *En los trigales*. This time Rodrigo matched the work's
technical demands to Sainz de la Maza's abilities, and the guitarist was able to prepare it in just two months. He premiered it
in a concert that took place in the Gran Kursaal Theatre in San
Sebastián on 3 November 1938.

Rodrigo's mastery of the technical possibilities of the guitar
is really quite impressive. The piece is so idiomatic that, unlike
his previous contributions to the repertoire of that instrument,
he did not transcribe it for any other performance medium.
Nevertheless, it clearly derives from the "Fandango del ventorrillo" of the *Cuatro piezas para piano*, with which it shares the
very characteristic beginning of its main theme. In fact, *En los
trigales* seems to be made with scraps that Rodrigo had left
over from the composition of "Fandango del ventorrillo" (musical ex. 5.1).

Musical ex. 5.1: Motives of *En los trigales* and "Fandango del ventorrillo"

The piano piece has a more elaborate formal organization, but what *En los trigales* lacks in this respect it more than makes up for in spontaneity. Its harmonic development is much more direct and less inflected. Hence, of the 144 measures that Rodrigo wrote, the majority are found within a diatonic harmony of G minor, with frequent use of the harmonic-minor scale (with F♯) and occasional use of the melodic-minor scale (E♮ and F♯). The harmonic structure is reduced to a series of brief modulations between mm. 56 and 88, moving through A♭ major, F♯ major, and B♭ minor. Thereafter, an enharmonic shift from G♭ to F♯ paves the way for a return to G minor. Save for the introduction of the first sixteen measures, practically the whole piece is repeated, though between the two repetitions there is a central section of thirty measures in the relative major (B♭ major). This scheme exhibits a very theatrical quality, which Rodrigo described in the following way: "In contrast to the virile dance of the first part, a kind of recitation follows, with the faraway sound of bells, similar to a rest or respite during the difficult work of the harvest."[14] Besides the recitative and bells, in this part there also appears an echo of the main motive, a veiled, disfigured reminiscence that offers only the characteristic rhythm and nothing of its melodic outline.

Yet, during the meal with Urquijo and Sainz de la Maza at the Nautical Club, nothing was said of this work, which was already on the music stand of the guitarist. Other projects were more interesting, especially one that in those days would have seemed positively whimsical: a concerto for guitar and orchestra. As Victoria Kamhi noted in her memoirs, the plan was for Sainz de la Maza to debut it in Madrid, still under Republican control, with Arámbarri conducting.[15] Paradoxically, a premiere seemed more feasible than the actual creation of such a novel work.

A Concerto for Guitar and Orchestra?

The idea seemed nonsensical, as no one remembered such a thing ever being attempted. A guitarist as renowned as Miguel Llobet had never suggested the idea, and leading performers like Emilio Pujol and Daniel Fortea agreed with their teacher

Francisco Tárrega that, unlike a piano or violin, the soft-spoken guitar could not compete with a full orchestra and was therefore not suitable as a concerto instrument. Throughout the nineteenth century, the piano had sidelined the guitar, which, unable to compete with that "kingly instrument," had managed to survive by cultivating a specific, devoted audience organized around local societies. Professional guitarists and passionate devotees of the instrument, which always had a large number of fans, generated an entire poetics of the guitar as a different instrument, mysterious and residing on the limits of what is perceptible.

From a practical standpoint, the intimate volume of the guitar was an impediment in competing with a modern orchestra, though there was actually a long history of earlier concertos featuring plucked-string fingerboard instruments. Antonio Vivaldi's Mandolin Concerto in C Major (1725) and his Lute Concerto in D Major (1730s) are examples of such works well known today but completely forgotten in the 1920s. With the advent of the modern classical guitar in the late 1700s, leading virtuosos such as Mauro Giuliani and Ferdinando Carulli composed concertos for the instrument during the early nineteenth century. But the orchestral forces these called for were slight by twentieth-century standards and consisted mostly of strings. Moreover, the concert venues for which they were intended were more intimate than their modern counterparts.

Though these early works for guitar and orchestra lay in obscurity around 1900, there were some precedents in the early twentieth century, especially the decade of the 1930s. There was the *Concertino* of Mexican guitarist Rafael Adame, composed in 1930 and debuted 5 February 1933, with the Mexican Ensemble Orchestra directed by Julián Carrillo. After its premiere, though, it fell into oblivion until its rediscovery at the end of the twentieth century.[16] In Madrid, on 8 December 1934, the Orquesta Filarmónica brought two guitarists to its platform. One was the composer Ángel Barrios, who debuted a *Suite madrileña* by Conrado del Campo, with interludes for two guitars. It did not appeal to critics, who singled out the guitar part as the worst element.[17]

Following a similar model, but now in a concerto-like way, was the "Spanish rhapsody" *Guitarra andaluza* of Quintín Esquembre, composed in 1928 for orchestra and arranged in 1938 for orchestra and two guitar soloists. Esquembre was a composer and a self-educated amateur guitarist. He clearly saw that to find an acceptable balance with the orchestra, it was necessary to employ two guitars, which usually play in unison or double an octave apart. This piece was studied in the 1940s by flamenco guitarist Matilde Cuervas and her husband Emilio Pujol. They belonged to the circle of friends closest to the Rodrigos during their final months in Paris, but they did not premiere the piece.[18] Still, it was the first or among the very first concertos for one or more guitars composed in Spain.

These precedents give a good idea of the difficulties of writing a composition for guitar and orchestra, and the reluctance of critics and the public, orchestras and their patrons, to welcome such a thing. From the beginning of the 1920s, there were other guitar concertos in the works, encouraged by Segovia, who had become the most celebrated guitarist of the time and one of the most sought-after performers on the international circuit. One of those projects would materialize at the same time that Rodrigo was composing the *Concierto de Aranjuez* and would be debuted more than a year earlier: the *Concerto per chitarra i orchestra* No. 1, Op. 99, of Mario Tedesco-Castelnuovo (1895–1968).

Segovia's persistence in cajoling his closest composers—the Mexican Manuel Ponce, the Italian Mario Castelnuovo-Tedesco, and the Spaniards Federico Moreno Torroba and Joaquín Turina—to write a concerto for guitar and orchestra was no secret. When Rodrigo attended Segovia's Paris premiere of Ponce's *Sonata romántica* in 1929, the celebrated guitarist urged Ponce to write such a guitar concerto. Ponce got stalled in the concerto project, but even Castelnuovo-Tedesco, who was always Segovia's best bet in such endeavors, had many doubts: "I could not imagine (without ever having listened to it), the 'association' of the guitar with the other instruments of the orchestra. [. . .] It was a problem both of quantity and quality of sound, which frightened me, and I didn't dare to face it!"[19] Some months after Rodrigo's meeting at the Nautical Club, Castelnuovo-Tedesco got to work. In January 1939 he finished the entire work and sent it to Segovia, who would debut it in Montevideo on October 28 of that year.

Rodrigo, who would encounter more difficulties debuting his composition, confronted the same problems and harbored the same doubts as the Italian composer. In some notes published during the period of his concerto's premiere, Rodrigo underscored that, among the many challenges the enterprise posed, "It was necessary to achieve an orchestra of duralumin, resistant enough to give consistency to the phantom of sound that the guitar is, and at the same time, so light that it would not cover the subtle vagueness of the Spanish instrument."[20] Sainz de la Maza recognized the same thing: "The great difficulty that the writing of this concerto presented was in overcoming the natural imbalance of sonority between the guitar and the orchestra." He added, "Rodrigo found the solution."[21] To that end, Rodrigo drew on what he had learned from Dukas about orchestration. Yet, when and how did he reach *his* solution?

The Rodrigos set out for France in fall 1938, and in Paris, they were lucky enough to find lodging at the home of a Spanish professor, Amalia Carrasco, who lived in the Latin Quarter. She gave them a room with a bath and small kitchen, besides allowing them the use of her piano. They soon received a letter from Falla, informing them of the fruits his contacts with highly placed authorities had borne. Rodrigo responded to him that he would immediately write to the minister to learn the nature of the work offered him at the conservatory, whether of Seville or of Granada. Some weeks afterwards, Rodrigo wrote to Falla that he had communicated to Minister Sainz Rodríguez and Subsecretary García Valdecasas his acceptance of the post that they were offering him, but he added, "Until now I have received no reply, owing perhaps to the great commotion that always prevails in the Ministries."[22] Actually, the offer to hire him for an academic year made no sense insofar as the school year had already begun.

In the same letter, Rodrigo informed Falla that he had gone back to his routine of attending concerts, and that the only thing he had seen of interest had been the *Passion According to*

206 · A LIGHT IN THE DARKNESS

Saint Matthew, "sung by the Chorale of Leipzig." The choirs and soloists of Saint Thomas Church in Leipzig were joined by the Orchestra of the Philharmonic Society of Paris, all under the baton of Saint Thomas cantor Karl Straube. On Thursday October 27, they performed the first part of the Passion, and two days afterwards, the second part.[23] This date takes on special significance in light of what the composer himself recalled about the concerto's initial genesis:

> I also recall, I don't know why (everything concerning
> the *Concierto de Aranjuez* has remained in my memory),
> that one morning, two months after [the luncheon of 26
> September 1938 in San Sebastián], when I was standing
> up in my small study on the Rue Saint Jacques, in the
> heart of the Latin Quarter, vaguely thinking of the
> concerto, since I had taken a liking to the idea by dint of
> its very difficulty, I heard singing within me the complete
> theme of the Adagio, with a jolt, without hesitation and
> almost identical to the one you are about to hear.[24]

The famous melody must have occurred to him around 26 November 1938, less than a month after the impression made on him by the great Bach Passion. He wrote to Falla on December 21 that that was what had most interested him since his arrival in Paris at the end of October. In the Adagio of the *Concierto de Aranjuez* there is the affect of extreme dignity in the plea of an aria like *Erbarme dich, mein Gott* (Lord, have mercy upon me). The two melodies share the same key of B minor, and what Rodrigo wrote about his Adagio in some program notes could be perfectly applied to the pulse that governs Bach's aria: "a deep, uninterrupted striking, four beats per measure, maintains the entire sonorous edifice of this movement."[25]

Further, the notion of looking back to the Baroque was something that Stravinsky had made fashionable in Paris of the early 1930s, with works like the *Capriccio pour piano et orchestra* (premiered December 1929), the Violin Concerto in D (October 1931), and the "Dumbarton Oaks" Concerto (June 1938). The first two of these works are concerto-style compositions that offer a return to the Baroque in their slow tempos. To be sure, Rodrigo's focus completely differs from the stringent, objective character of Stravinsky's neoclassicism. Our composer's point of view is indebted to the *nouveau lyrisme* that Dukas had championed and that Rodrigo favored in the homage *Sonada de adiós* (1935).[26] In making this leap to the eighteenth century, Rodrigo did not seek so much the form, sonority, or mechanics of the music of the High Baroque as he did rather its expression, something that he could have found closer to his own epoch.

The conception and gestation of the *Concierto de Aranjuez* begins with a melody of ten measures created around 26 November 1938. This melody must have been very similar to the one performed by the English horn in the initial measures of the second movement (musical ex. 5.2).

Taking their cue from Kamhi's memoirs, many commentators have maintained that the creation of this melody resulted from a tragic event that occurred during the final months the Rodrigos spent in Paris, before returning to Spain. Victoria Kamhi had become pregnant between the months of November and December 1938, but after seven months of pregnancy, in June 1939, she suffered a miscarriage and was hospitalized for a short time in critical condition. According to Kamhi,

> While I was in the clinic, Amalia [Carrasco] took care of Joaquín, trying to comfort him in his tremendous disappointment. Later she would tell me how he would

Musical ex. 5.2: *Concierto de Aranjuez*, second movement, mm. 2–16 (English horn's main theme)

spend the long hours of the night at the old piano,
unable to sleep, and that she heard from her room a
melody as full of sadness and longing that it truly gave
her chills. This melody would become the "Adagio" from
the *Concierto de Aranjuez*. He was playing it for the first
time, wrapped in darkness.[27]

The story is emotional, but it is also fictional. The pregnancy
and the creation of this musical theme must have occurred practically at the same time, between November and December 1938,
and when the miscarriage came seven months afterwards, the
concerto was nearly finished. Apart from the hopes and dreams
produced by the pregnancy, the Rodrigos spent their winter in
privation and uncertainty. It was "the hardest and most distress-
ing period of our lives," according to Kamhi, who also noted in
her memoirs how, on Christmas Day 1938, the only luxury that
she and her husband could afford was to fill their stove full of
firewood and share a great Yule log that Aurelio Viñas had given
them. Kamhi then wrote, "One morning, Joaquín, to my great
surprise, announced that he already had two movements of his
concerto for the guitar: the second—which was to attain such
fame—and the third. Furthermore, he hoped to have the first
ready very soon."[28]

The composer's own recollections corroborate his wife's memoirs when he indicates that soon after composing the theme of
the Adagio, he wrote that of the final movement: "this one absolutely equal to the one appearing in the work." And he added,
"Quickly I realized that the work was done. Our intuition does
not deceive us in this. I sketched the form governed by the two
respective themes and wrote the guitar part with a first very
rough and tentative outline of the orchestra part."[29]

Soon after inventing these themes, Rodrigo wrote the guitar
part and sketched the orchestration. On March 11, Sainz de la
Maza wrote to him and revealed that he already knew of Victoria Kamhi's pregnancy and the progress being made in composing the new concerto. "I am dreaming of the Concertino [little
concerto] and I am promising myself great excitement from

it."[30] Despite the efforts the composer was making to earn some money, the concerto for guitar was his main musical undertaking in these first few months of 1939, as it had been in the final months of 1938.

Nonetheless, the first movement still remained to be composed, and Rodrigo wrote the following about it:

> While something like inspiration, that irresistible, supernatural force, led me to the Adagio and the final Allegro, I arrived at the first movement through reflection, conscious thinking, and will. It was the last movement of the three. I finished the work where I had begun it. Therefore I had no full awareness of it except on writing that movement, the first. In a few months it was finished; and that orchestra that, needing to form a tissue around the most elusive of instruments, to form part of it, to wrap around it, to be in it, was basically resolved. It was the spring of 1939. Joyous spring.[31]

Everything seems to indicate that the concerto was finished in Paris by spring. Kamhi's memoirs are clear on the point: "We arrived in Spain [28 August 1939] with only two suitcases, containing old clothes and some books and scores, among them the finished manuscript of the *Concierto de Aranjuez*."[32] Yet the composer on several occasions pointed out that something was concluded in Madrid: "The *Concierto de Aranjuez* was composed in Paris in the winter and spring of 1939, and definitively finished shortly afterwards in Madrid."[33]

While in Paris, he probably completed the manuscript in Braille and later committed it to conventional notation. But analysis of the surviving Braille manuscripts of the *Concierto de Aranjuez* has yet to be undertaken. Further, there is a set of handwritten sources in conventional notation among which stands out a rough copy written in pencil on the guitar part.[34] This source seems to prove that there was a process of negotiation between the initial and final versions that was the responsibility of Sainz de la Maza, a guitarist noted for exceptional virtuosity. Rodrigo seems to suggest as much when he wrote: "It is well enough for fantasy to have its day. Afterwards, reality will come, the struggle with matter in an often futile fight and the satisfaction if only one of those fantasies has come into being. Sainz de la Maza's art has done the rest face to face in a treacherous but premeditated hand-to-hand tussle. He has made the guitar sound as Stravinsky would say it sounded: penetrating and faraway."[35]

Ultimately, the composer gave very little ground in this negotiation, so Sainz de la Maza bravely faced the premiere of a supremely difficult work, one that would extend the technique of guitar playing in so demanding a way that it became for several generations of guitarists the ultimate test of their technique and musicianship.

Obstacles on the Road and *Homenaje* a *"La Tempranica"* (1939)

Something that on 26 September 1938 had been nothing but a harebrained idea, arising in the flush of good Rioja wine in the Nautical Club of San Sebastián, was now a reality. Barely six months after that meeting, Rodrigo, who for many years had tried to write a concerto for piano and orchestra, had practically composed a concerto for guitar. Only an idealist (or a visionary) could have been obsessed with composing anything similar. It could not have either the impact or the outcome of a piano concerto. In 1939 there were only two guitarists in the world willing to place themselves with their instruments in front of an orchestra, and it still remained to be seen whether there was some orchestra willing to place itself behind a guitarist. Even so, the concerto was his main compositional task during the months in which he also had to accept some other assignments that promised actual income.

One of these assignments was the orchestration of some of Albéniz's piano music for a new ballet number titled *La Serenata de Don Juan*, to be written for the Sakharoffs, a duo of ballet dancers formed by the German ballerina Clotilde von der Panitz and the Russian Alexander Sakharoff. We have found no trace of these arrangements, which were Rodrigo's first entrée to the world of ballet, a world that was going to interest him so much in the future. We do know, though, that in his final months in Paris, before returning to Spain, he had been working on a ballet with a plot by Roland-Manuel about the Spanish vihuelists.[36] Further, he wrote a piano piece he never published, the *Danza de la odalisca*, which a group of students danced to on 10 June 1939 at the École Normale. The ballerinas had been students of Elvira Viñes Soto, ballerina and ballet teacher in Paris and the niece of pianist Ricardo Viñes. Antonio Gallego was the first to catalogue this piece, though he remarked with scorn about its trite Alhambrism, offering a folk feast of "Christians and Moors."[37] Rodrigo had used this theme to create an exotic ambience, but the *Danza de la odalisca* is a piece of incidental music without any other purpose than accompanying thirteen "steps" indicated in the score, of between four and eight measures each, with castanets ("Crotales") on the fourth step. Rodrigo also dedicated to Elvira Viñes a more substantial piece: the "Caleseras" of his *Cuatro piezas para piano*, which she herself danced in the recital in which her pupils debuted the *Danza de la odalisca*.[38]

Rodrigo's financial need in these fall and winter months of 1938–39 was so excruciatingly great that he departed from his elitist comfort zone and approached styles that had more popular appeal. First he made some arrangements of Albéniz's *Sevilla* and Falla's "Fire Dance" from *El amor brujo* for the delightful little jazz orchestra "Manolo Bel y sus *symphonic boys*." Established by violinist Manuel Bel, this group performed in the best Parisian nightclubs, gracing suppers and evening parties of the well-to-do in cafés on the Champs-Élysées. We have found no trace of these curious arrangements, but there does exist an original *pasadoble* by Rodrigo entitled *Torerito* (Little Bullfighter), dedicated "to the Bel Orchestra with the greatest respect." The orchestration of this piece—two violins, two clarinets, three saxophones, two trumpets, a trombone, two percussionists, a banjo, bass, and piano—corresponds to the ensemble of the little orchestra of Bel in the 1930s, which billed itself as a group of twelve Valencian musicians of the highest caliber.

Rodrigo's next efforts within the realm of popular music were two light songs: *Chimères*, with lyrics by Victoria Kamhi, and *La chanson de ma vie*, on a text signed by "Joc," the pseudonym of the French Hispanist Jean Camp, whom the Rodrigos often visited during these final months in Paris. *Chimères* is a tango, while *La chanson de ma vie* is a *cuplé* employing the habanera rhythm. They are excellent pieces within the popular genre, featuring sparks of finesse that evince the expert hand of the composer. Both pieces were published by Max Eschig in 1939. Had a gifted performer like Edith Piaf interpreted them, thereby "creating" them, these simple songs would have achieved an important success. But that was not to be, and they did not interest any French *chanteuse*; instead, according to Victoria Kamhi, "This yielded us no profit at all. It was a fiasco!"[39]

What did give them a brief time to relax was a very unexpected commission: music for a movie that the great French filmmaker Abel Gance wished to direct about Christopher Columbus. Rodrigo was hired at the beginning of 1939 by the head of Max Eschig, Jean Marietti, and he received 10,000 francs in advance. The European War put an end to this interesting project, which could have been accomplished in the early years of "talkies" and in Technicolor. Of whatever Rodrigo might have written for the Columbus film, there remains only the *Canción del grumete* (Song of the Cabin Boy), based on a Sephardic folk ballad that the composer set in the mode of C♯ Phrygian, with a refrain that represents the back-and-forth motion of the waves transformed into a hypnotic kind of Siren's song. On the other hand, the ethnic roots of the song that Rodrigo borrowed can be interpreted as an allusion to the hypothetical Sephardic origin of the navigator, which at that time was asserted by no less an authority than the historian Salvador de Madariaga. Although the project did not prove fruitful, the composer made quite a lot of money from this song, because besides the advance that he earned from Max Eschig, it won a prize of 5,000 pesetas in a 1942 song contest, which awarded Rodrigo the same amount for his *Canción del grumete* as it did to Jesús Guridi for his lengthy ballad *La novia del rey* (The King's Bride).[40]

Unfortunately, all of these divertissements delayed completion of the guitar concerto. Furthermore, Rodrigo added to his catalogue at that time *Dos miniaturas andaluzas*, a diptych formed by a "Preludio" and a "Danza," of which he wrote several versions. One for piano was debuted by the composer himself in a picturesque concert of Austrian, Spanish, Hungarian, Czech, and Peruvian music, graced by a talk given by Jean Camp on 6 February 1939 in the Salle du Foyer International de Etudiants. Another version was written for a string orchestra and bore the French title *Deux miniatures andalouses*, dated Paris, 8 January 1939, and dedicated to "Madame Jane Evrard," who debuted it with her Orchestre Féminin de Paris in a radio broadcast on 27 March 1939.[41]

The main version—the only one now in the composer's catalogue—is for symphony orchestra. Its title, *Homenaje a "La Tempranica,"* alludes to the zarzuela by Gerónimo Giménez (1852–1923), one of the jewels of Spanish operetta, with its close ties to urban folklore. In Valencia on 25 October 1930, Rodrigo had attended a performance of Federico Moreno Torroba's operatic transformation of this work, entitled *María La Tempranica*. It impressed him favorably, as he informed his then fiancée Victoria Kamhi.

According to the composer, his work is "a kind of small overture to our most representative zarzuela," and it begins with "a small but very characteristic melodic phrase of the masterpiece of Giménez."[42] In a review of the Madrid debut of the version for large orchestra on 15 November 1939, a seasoned zarzuela expert, Víctor Ruiz Albéniz, found Rodrigo's piece an "evocation of *La Tempranica*, perfectly fashioned, but very far from the genially Spanish inspiration that characterizes the great score of Gerónimo Giménez."[43] Rodrigo could have very serenely titled his work *Dos miniaturas andaluzas*, as he had at first. For in fact his work uses no recognizable quotations from *La Tempranica* but is instead only a distant echo. On the other hand, we can understand why critics received Rodrigo's work with misgivings, for his modernist aesthetic could well remind them of the recent past. In fact, the version for string orchestra was more moderate

Musical ex. 5.3: *Homenaje a "La Tempranica,"* mm. 1–4
(Rodrigo's piano reduction)

in its use of dissonance than was the orchestral version premiered in Spain, though the principle of systematic opposition of the keys of D and A is the same. This opposition appears in a brusque form in the very appearance of the main theme of the prelude, which concludes with a ninth chord (D–F–A–C#–E; musical ex. 5.3).

Even though it is true that there is no direct quote from *La Tempranica*, what Rodrigo does reap from it is the unabashed sentimentality of the zarzuela, while at the same time elevating it to a symphonic level. Here, even more than in "Caleseras," we find the foreshadowing of what the composer would later define as *neocasticismo*, a modernized Spanish style. The emotion of the prelude and several rhythmical traces of the dance are very characteristic elements also found in the *Concierto de Aranjuez*. Indeed, Rodrigo considered this composition as "something torn away from the *Concierto de Aranjuez*," and he explained this beautifully: "In the same way as in the faraway world of the stars, there exists in this world of music scraps detached from great compositions that spin in the same orbit as those: they are like parentheses in the work schedule of the author that could not escape his first and more important concern."[44] In other words, the *Homenaje a "La Tempranica"* is a satellite torn away from the *Concierto de Aranjuez* and composed practically at the same time. Hence, if we consider the fact that the version for string orchestra of *Deux miniatures andalouses* is dated January 8, here we have one more sign that Rodrigo was deeply involved in the composition of his concerto during the Christmas season of 1938–39. The fact that he finished it in the spring of 1939 is something that Rodrigo insisted upon several times. Furthermore, the accident of the miscarriage, which probably occurred around the month of June, would not have offered a propitious time for creative work.

Aranjuez?

When this misfortune occurred, the concerto was already practically composed, and the Rodrigos decided to spend the summer in Mirmande. With Victoria Kamhi still convalescing, they left Paris in the first days of June. They would not return to the French capital for many years. After almost two months in Mirmande, they entrained to Hendaye, where they spent a few days at the home of a friend, the great blind organist André Marchal. It is noteworthy that Rodrigo, educated by the organist Antich as well as being a friend of Marchal's, would only dedicate to the organ two late pieces integrated in the *Cánticos nupciales* (1963), the impressive ostinato "Entrada" and a brief "Fughetta."

The Rodrigos crossed the border at Irún on August 28, with all their possessions in two suitcases. These contained the Braille manuscript of the guitar concerto, which Rodrigo hoped and dreamed would establish his career on a firm foundation when he returned to Spanish musical life. Sainz de la Maza was growing impatient, and a few days before he had written him, "I imagine that you are in the middle of things with the music on Columbus and finishing off my concerto. Send it soon because I want to give it in Madrid at the start of the season and to depart throughout the world at once to play it with the best orchestras. You will see."[45]

What we see is that the concerto "of" Sainz de la Maza still had no name. Rodrigo insisted on several occasions that he had composed it "in spring near the Garden of Luxembourg in bloom while the students were happily singing."[46] We recall that the park was next to their modest flat on the Rue Saint-Jacques. The Rodrigos would often stroll through there, hopeful about Victoria Kamhi's pregnancy while contemplating the commotion of children that filled the area in the evenings, playing on the esplanade in the winter snow and sailing rented boats on the pond in the spring. On their leisurely walks through this park, the couple would recall the history of the palace of Luxembourg, from the shady political intrigues of Marie de' Medici to the libertine parties of the Duchess de Berry, Marie Louise Élisabeth d'Orleans, known, among many other nicknames, as the "Venus of Luxembourg."

The fact that Rodrigo at last gave his concerto the name of another palace and other gardens with a great Bourbon history—but having nothing to do with the birth of his work—is something that has important implications of a different kind, but no importance of a purely musical character. The name of Rodrigo would remain forever united to Aranjuez, such that in 1991 the king of Spain granted him the aristocratic title of Marquis of the Gardens of Aranjuez, and his mortal remains rest in the Municipal Cemetery of Aranjuez. Therefore, it must be understood that this is a delicate affair, but we cannot avoid the fact that the gardens near the birth of the concerto were those of Luxembourg, and the riverbanks along which the Rodrigos walked with the concerto newly composed were those of the Rhône, not those of the Tagus.

The linkage of the concerto with Aranjuez, its gardens, its palace, and its history, occurs a *posteriori*, as the composer's program notes for its premiere make clear: "With the concerto conceived, it was necessary to situate it in an era and even more in a place."[47] The place was going to be Aranjuez; the era, for the monarchs cited in the notes—Charles IV, Ferdinand VII, and Isabella II—belonged more to the nineteenth century than to the eighteenth. This was not the epoch of J. S. Bach or Domenico Scarlatti, when Farinelli relieved Philip V's melancholy with his songs at parties in the Palace of Aranjuez, and Scarlatti adorned the princely court of María Bárbara de Braganza and Ferdinand VI with his musical confections. But Rodrigo insisted that this was only false scenery: "Although this concerto is a piece of pure music without any programmatic element, its author, on situating it in a place, Aranjuez, has wanted to mark out a time for it: the end of the eighteenth and beginning of the nineteenth centuries, courts of Charles IV and Ferdinand VII, a subtly stylized ambience of *majas* and bullfighters, of *sones* [tunes] returned from Spanish America."[48] Aranjuez was a framework proposed for the interpretation of what the music was able to represent. "And what did it represent?" Rodrigo asked. His response stressed the same thing: "What each of us may posit on listening to it, within the suggestive picture in which the author placed it and aimed to situate the audience, that is, a suggestion of past times, the beautiful gardens of Aranjuez, its fountains, trees, birds [. . .] all that and, unfortunately, none of that."[49]

The *Concierto de Aranjuez*

The setting given to the *Concierto de Aranjuez*, which seems not to harmonize with the pre-Classical musical references of the second and third movements, fits well with the first movement. This is especially relevant to the so-called *sones de ida y vuelta* (tunes of departure and return)—music developed in the Spanish-American colonies based on Spanish models and afterwards popularized in Spain. In fact, the generative idea that sets the *Concierto de Aranjuez* in motion is not a melody (as in the second and third movements) but rather a rhythmic motif, which Rodrigo writes in 6/8 meter, marked "Allegro con spirito." A repeated sequence of accented sixteenth notes, that is, two groups of three followed by three groups of two, >- - >- - / >- >- >-, takes place within the alternation of two beats in triple meter and three in duple meter, that is, 2 x 3 and 3 x 2. This rhythmic motif, often written by alternating measures of 6/8 and 3/4, is characteristic of the flamenco *guajira*, derived from the "*punto* of Havana" or "Cuban *punto*," which in turn is related to sarabandes like those found in the *Metodo mui facilissimo para Aprender a tañer la guitarra a lo español* (Paris, 1626) by Luis Briceño.[50] This rhythmic impulse is present in other well-known flamenco *palos*, or styles of song and dance, including the *petenera* and the *soleá*. To be sure, these differ from the major-key *guajira* in their tragic affect and consequent modalities: the *petenera* is in minor, while the *soleá* is in the so-called Andalusian mode (explained below). Another analog might be the *bulería*, which features persistent hemiola at a brisk tempo and can be played in any mode or key, though it is usually in the Andalusian mode. But despite their differences, these and other *palos* exhibit the sort of hemiola metrical structure that has become a dependable marker of "Spanish" music.

This eminently rhythmic theme with which the concerto begins (A; musical ex. 5.4) situates it well within the spatial locale suggested by the work's title, as do the elaboration and implications of its form. As for its elaboration, what stands out is the fact that the three-bar theme exhibits a very clever construction, both rhythmically and harmonically. The first measure presents the driving rhythmic motive of an eighth note, two sixteenths, and an eighth. This lively rhythm, however, contrasts with a static harmony on the tonic chord of D major. The second measure is far simpler rhythmically, but the harmonic pace picks up with a change of chord on each of the three downbeats: I, ii, V, over a D pedal. The third measure essentially sums up the previous two, presenting the initial motive on a D-major chord followed by the three chords of the second measure in rhythmic diminution, changing on each eighth note rather than every other one. This distinctive alternation of rhythms and chords provides an extraordinarily propulsive force to set the concerto in motion (musical ex. 5.4).

Concerning its formal implications, Rodrigo decided to begin with the guitar. Concertos of the Classical period nearly always began with an orchestral exposition, followed by the entrance of the soloist restating the principal themes, a formal procedure often called a "double exposition." However, this process began to change in the early 1800s, and Beethoven's Piano Concerto

Musical ex. 5.4: *Concierto de Aranjuez*, first movement,
Allegro con spirito, mm. 1–3

rasgueado

No. 4 and Mendelssohn's Violin Concerto are conspicuous examples in which the concerto begins with the soloist. Rodrigo here follows in their footsteps by leading off with the guitar front and center. However, he immediately faces the problem of imbalance between the volume of the guitar versus that of the orchestra.

It is obvious that a traditional double exposition would underscore the contrast between orchestra and guitar, as well as the reduced dynamic range of the soloist. Instead, with the rhythmic base in the previous example upon a tonic pedal in the double basses, Rodrigo elaborates an entire crescendo with the guitaristic technique of *rasgueo*, or strumming. While the double basses continue playing *sempre pianissimo*, the guitar goes from *pianissimo* to *fortissimo* on a tonic D-major chord, revoiced in ascending registers (musical ex. 5.5). This tonality functions especially well on the guitar with the employment of scordatura tuning, in which the lowest string is tuned down from E to D, giving the instrument added resonance. This tuning, typical of the *guajira*, was something new in Rodrigo's output for guitar, and here it allows him to utilize the three lowest strings, D-A-D, in open position, greatly enhancing the guitar's sonority. The message of this beginning is clear: the guitar arises from the orchestra.

Rodrigo has thereby avoided the problem of the guitar going *mano a mano* with the orchestra. Indeed, the orchestra is soon compelled to imitate the idiomatic strumming patterns of the guitar. Hence, the string section employs *ricochet* bowing to simulate the natural effect of guitar strumming as a perfectly recognizable cliché. Further, the arrangement of the chords in the orchestra matches that on the guitar, except on the third chord. While in the guitar part there are three octaves of

Musical ex. 5.5: *Concierto de Aranjuez*, tonic harmony on the guitar (Allegro con spirito, mm. 1–18)

difference between the bass and the upper voice in this chord, the strings are retained within the range of two octaves. It is clear that Rodrigo does not want the orchestra to violate any necessary constraints.

Between the two themes previously played on the guitar (A, B), the first *tutti* interpolates a third theme (C) presented by the first violins with the oboe. This theme adheres to what has come before when it appears with an accompaniment that is the initial rhythmic motif. Therefore, in our scheme (table 5.1 below), we call it C(+A). Thus we see how Rodrigo is taking care that in this moment of thematic exposition, in which a variety of materials are to appear, there are elements of unity. What is more, the three themes are related by a slight melodic turn of phrase in the initial rhythmic gesture (musical ex. 5.6), and almost all of the subsequent thematic development is related to theme C—almost all, that is, because one theme (D) is still missing, the one that displays the most conspicuously national character in this movement.

As can be seen in musical example 5.6, the guitar begins its second solo in measure 61 by adapting theme C, which the orchestra had introduced. The guitarist does so using a texture of song and accompaniment that it had not deployed in the two previous themes. The accompanimental use of the four lowest open strings (D, A, D, G) gives volume to the guitar part and gradually prepares the entrance of the orchestra: first, the violins

Musical ex. 5.6: *Concierto de Aranjuez*, first movement, Allegro con spirito. Motivic relationship of the main themes (A, B, and C)

with chordal sonorities and the flutes, and afterwards the rest of the instruments. The woodwinds reinforce the guitar part with the bassoon doubling the low register, and the oboe, the central register. An echo effect in the clarinet evokes the song of the cuckoo, Rodrigo's musical signature.

The part in which the woodwinds (and the first horn at the end) support the guitar is an expansion of theme C, which the orchestra had introduced. This expansion (mm. 69–74) is basic to the movement's form, because it makes way for a series of three rotations that will lead from the lengthily prolonged tonic to the second ritornello, in this case in the dominant minor. That ritornello (mm. 115–126) would mark the end of an exposition section and the beginning of an area of development. In fact, what follows is clearly a development, but the preceding exposition does not exhibit the thematic function of expositions of the Classical and Romantic periods, namely, principal theme group, transition, cadence, secondary theme group, and codetta. On the contrary, it is a continuous exposition, built with a procedure very much utilized in the Baroque and defined at the beginning of the twentieth century as *Fortspinnung* (spinning-forth).

It is not likely that Rodrigo was familiar with this term, but he clearly knew the procedure. In lieu of destabilizing the tonic in a more or less gradual process, he uses a series of brief modulations. In this case, we have three modulations, with all three centered around a phrase of four measures in the so-called Andalusian mode typical of flamenco: in the first, F♯ Phrygian; in the second, A Phrygian; and in the third, E Phrygian.

Those steeped in common-practice ways of thinking about tonality can imagine the Andalusian mode as a half cadence in the minor, for example, cadencing on E major in the key of A minor. The mode uses a harmonic-minor scale when ascending (with G♯), and a natural-minor scale when descending (G♮). The basic chord progression derived from this is what we call a descending minor tetrachord: A minor, G major, F major, and E major. Because E functions as the tonic, we might think in terms of E Phrygian, but the G♯ falls outside that modal designation. The prominence of G♯ (leading tone to A minor) and the resulting augmented second interval between it and F♮ is a virtual cliché of flamenco, and Spanish music in general. It strikes us as very "oriental" sounding, and it gives *Carmen's* "death motive" its "Gypsy" quality. But it is the half step between E and F, and their corresponding triads, that defines the Andalusian mode, insofar as F functions as the "dominant," preceding as it always does the E "tonic."

A close examination of Rodrigo's harmonic procedures reveals that he had a deep understanding not only of flamenco harmony but also the idiomatic resources of the guitar, including chord progressions typical of the instrument. What is most interesting is that these three modes correspond precisely to three of the four basic "finals" of flamenco:[51] the mode called "de taranta" (F♯), the mode "por medio" (A), and the mode "por arriba" (E). Along with one more mode, "de granaína" (B), these are the traditional modes with which the flamenco guitar accompanied singing and from which it gradually developed its capacities as a solo instrument. Therefore, they are the tonal areas in which the guitar functions naturally and effectively, with the simplest positions in the left hand. But Rodrigo would not be seeking technical simplification in this case. Tuning the sixth string down to D completely changes the positions, and playing "por arriba" (E) loses its main purpose, which is to have the tonic on the open sixth string. Rodrigo's intention seems to be more rhetorical than practical: to allude to the harmonic essence of flamenco, which is complementary to the allusion in theme A, one of flamenco's most characteristic rhythmic patterns. Thus, those measures play simply and insistently with the alternation between the tonic and its modal dominant, which has the peculiarity of being constructed on the second degree of the scale.

Vis-à-vis the most cultivated and refined use of flamenco, which would place the dominant in the bass, Rodrigo prefers leaving the tonic as a kind of pedal. Since this sound corresponds to the seventh of the modal dominant chord, it functions well to give it tension, and it sounds, furthermore, very germane to the guitar. In musical example 5.7, we transcribe for guitar what the orchestra does in these modulations, and we stress the structures of the tonic and dominant chords of each modulation. Between brackets we indicate the structures of the dominant within the "academic" tradition of flamenco.

The final modulation concludes with the prolonging of a dominant-seventh chord of A minor with an added fourth (mm. 109–114). In measure 115 this chord settles on a *tutti* that reaffirms the area of the dominant of this first movement. The first cello here has its moment with the introduction of theme C in the minor mode and an elegant adornment (mm. 117–126). As opposed to what happened at the beginning, in this section the orchestra enters first, and the strategy that Rodrigo uses to emphasize the entrance of the guitar consists of introducing it in the major mode of the same key (mm. 126–129). Thus begins an area of development based on theme C, which extends to measure 166, wherein a new ritornello recovers the main key of D major. The final ten measures of the development, with their chain of dominant sevenths, can be considered as a retransition.

After the third ritornello, there comes the recapitulation of the Phrygian modulations belonging to the *Fortspinnung*. However, these modulations remain in the tonic instead of preparing the dominant. In this part, theme B is not recapitulated but rather left for a coda in which the main key is affirmed (mm. 220–243). In the coda also appears theme C, transformed into a final fanfare (mm. 220–228) with the orchestra at full volume. The guitar can only give a reply by being used to render some *rasgueos* (mm. 232–235), and the movement closes with the reappearance of themes A (mm. 240–243) and B (mm. 236–240)

Musical ex. 5.7: *Concierto de Aranjuez*, first movement, Allegro con spirito. Reduction for guitar, mm. 75–77, 91–93, and 105–107

in reverse order, as in some symphonies of the *galant* period. In table 5.1 we offer a scheme of the form and harmonic process of this movement.

Rodrigo insisted that this first movement was the last one he composed. He did it, he indicated, as an exercise of "reflection, calculation, and willpower."[52] The formal planning is clear, and his models can be situated in orchestral music immediately prior to Viennese Classicism. This becomes evident through the somewhat conventional interpretation of sonata form, the prominent use of the dynamic effect of crescendo at the start of the movement, and the slow harmonic rhythm, 40 percent of the time in the tonic and 15 percent in the dominant. Among the main strengths of the movement is its careful balance between the soloist and an orchestra that Rodrigo did not want to be small. It is clear that by reducing the number of instruments of the orchestra, the main problem could easily be solved. But the challenge meant not avoiding but rather resolving it. Rodrigo, a gifted orchestrator, did not want to diminish the palette of instrumental colors available to him. In that sense, despite the moment in which the difficulties are evident in letting the guitar be heard above the orchestra with horns and trumpets, Rodrigo's work was intelligent, extremely precise, and very imaginative in its solutions.

In any case, what is noteworthy in this first movement is the effective way in which Rodrigo culled the essence of a popular art form, flamenco, by means of a commonplace rhythm and a very characteristic harmonic procedure. By what means did he obtain so detailed a knowledge of flamenco guitar? In fact, he had a very reliable source of information nearby, because among the closest persons to the Rodrigos during these difficult times in Paris were the renowned husband-and-wife guitar duo of Emilio Pujol and Matilde Cuervas. We have already referred to Pujol on several occasions, first, with respect to the printing of the *Zarabanda lejana* in 1934 within the collection of guitar music that Pujol directed for the Max Eschig Publishing House, and second, in relation to the lecture on the vihuela delivered by Rodrigo at the Institut d'Etudes Hispaniques in 1936, a presentation relying

TABLE 5.1 *Concierto de Aranjuez*, I, Allegro con spirito, formal scheme

Ritornello

				Exposition		
Solo 1	**Tutti 1**			**Solo 2**		

A	B	A	C(+A)	B	C	D	
1–18	18–26	26–43	44–53	53–61	61–75	74–79	
D						**F# Phrygian**	
					E[C]	D	
					78–82–87–91	90–95	
					D Bb	**A Phrygian**	
					E[C]	D	F[C]
					94–96–101–105	104–109	108–115
					F Db	**E Phrygian**	V7/a **a**

Ritornello	**Development**
Tutti 2	**Solo 3**

C+A	A	X[C]		X[C]	X[C]	X[C]	
115–126	126–129	129–133	133–412	141–143	143–145–147	147–150–151	151–156
a	A	a		**F**	**Ab** ab **B**	b	

(retransition)
F[C]
155–160–162–164–166
V7/F# V7/b V7/d **D**

Ritornello	**Recapitulation**
Tutti 3	**Solo 4**

C+A	C	D
166–172	178–180	179–184
D		**F# Phrygian**
	E[C]	D
	183–187–191–196	195–200
	G Eb	**D Phrygian**
	E[C]	D	F[C]
	199–201–205–210	209–214	213–220
	Bb Gb	**A Phrygian**	V7/d **D**

Coda

Tutti 4		**Solo 5**		
B+C	GB	GB	B	A
220–228	228–232	232–235	236–240	240–243
D				

on the musical demonstrations of Pujol. Pujol was also a worthy composer of guitar music, and perhaps his hallmark composition, though not his best, is the *Guajira* (Paris: Joseph Rowies, 1926). Often titled *Guajiras gitanas*, this piece appeared time and again in Pujol's recitals. It is written in the traditional key of D major, with the sixth string tuned to D. It concludes with a scalar flourish that clearly recalls the one that elegantly makes way for the orchestra after the first solo of the Rodrigo concerto (musical ex. 5.8).

Rodrigo would not have been very interested in Pujol's nationalistic musical style, but he was certainly intent on learning about flamenco-guitar technique from Cuervas. Although she had classical-guitar training, Cuervas was also an accomplished flamenco guitarist, educated in her native Seville by musicians like the patriarch of the legendary Habichuela family of flamenco performers.[53] In the 1920s and '30s, Cuervas and Pujol gave recitals in which they alternated duets with her flamenco numbers and his classical repertoire. Among the additions they made in the 1930s to their repertoire was the arrangement of the first dance from *La vida breve* of Falla. But what is most important is that Pujol made an arrangement for two guitars of Rodrigo's "Fandango del ventorrillo" from the *Cuatro piezas para piano*. Although Max Eschig did not publish this arrangement until 1965 (M.E. 7589), it is probable that it had been made in the 1930s and that Cuervas and Pujol had played it in London in a radio concert broadcast by the BBC on 20 July 1939.[54] In that very recital Pujol played his *Guajira*, and no doubt Rodrigo, who often visited their house in Paris during that time, knew their repertoire well.

In addition, we can learn much from the recollections of

Musical ex. 5.8: Emilio Pujol, *Guajira*, mm. 14–17

Cuban guitarist Isaac Nicola, who met and began to study with Pujol in Paris in February 1939, before following him to London. We know that Nicola spent the month of August in Nice; therefore, the following statement of his probably dates to before mid-July 1939:

> I became acquainted with the Concierto de Aranjuez before the birth of the entire work. On one occasion, while I was in Paris, Pujol invited me to go one Sunday with him to the home of a young composer who was doing something very interesting for the guitar. We arrived at the home of Joaquín Rodrigo, a young man. I was twenty-two or twenty-three years old at the time, and Rodrigo was ten years older than I. He had already composed for guitar—I knew his Zarabanda lejana. He was with his wife, a very pleasant woman who always wrote his music down, and after conversing awhile, he sat down at the piano and began to play. He would say, "Here the guitar does so-and-so," and he would play it on the piano; and afterward, "The orchestra does something else," and he also played it on the piano. From the first moment on, as has always turned out, the most important thing for me was the second movement, of which so much has been said, that it is impossible to say anything new.[55]

Certainly much has been written about the second movement of the Concierto de Aranjuez, but it is always possible to say something new. We have done as much with respect to the history of its composition and everything referring to it; now we will attempt to contribute something from an analytical viewpoint. This movement (the Adagio), which became one of the most celebrated compositions of the twentieth century, is organized entirely around the melody played by the English horn at its beginning (musical ex. 5.2). That theme occupies no fewer than forty of the movement's one hundred measures. Bearing in mind that the soloist's cadenza (mm. 57–83) is largely elaborated around that theme, it is clear that its appearance in the movement is even more notable. The movement—as can be seen in the scheme of table 5.2—is arranged around three appearances of this principal theme (P1, 2, 3): at the beginning, toward the middle, and toward the end, as a powerful climax. In each place it shows up in a different form and in a different key, providing welcome variety. Moreover, musical episodes D–G provide contrasting material that keeps the principal theme's predominance in this movement from becoming tedious.

First it appears in B minor, the key of the beginning two-part section (AABB), which the English horn performs in dialogue with the guitar. Rodrigo achieves a memorable effect here in that the guitar accompanies the English horn in its initial presentation of the main theme. It is hard to imagine this exchange working quite as well with any other instrument in the orchestra. The English horn has a somber, even lugubrious tone quality, and its range is roughly comparable to that of the guitar. Sibelius employed its distinctive color to good effect in his tone poem *The Swan of Tuonela*, and this has no doubt influenced the way we perceive and interpret its sound. The fact that it evolved out of the eighteenth-century oboe da caccia makes it even more appropriate in a concerto named after an eighteenth-century palace.

The guitar takes up the main melody and elaborates on it by means of diminution or coloration. This form of adornment was codified in the Renaissance, but it has a medieval origin, and a broad development as well during the Baroque. It helps to maintain our interest in the melody, but it also serves a very practical purpose. The sound of the guitar has a very steep "attack and decay" envelope, meaning that a note or chord produced on the guitar begins to die away almost immediately after it is played. Since the guitar cannot sustain sounds in the same way as the wind or bowed instruments, what Rodrigo does is to divide the long sounds into repeated shorter ones, in order to create the sensation of longer note values. At the same time, he always preserves the outline of the original melody, even though he does so in shorter rhythms or in light rhythmic displacements. Hence the first five measures in the English horn consist of forty-four notes, while the guitar plays the same melody in

TABLE 5.2 ***Concierto de Aranjuez*, II, Adagio,
formal scheme**

P1

solo

A	1–6	b			
B	7–11				
B	12–16				
B	17–22				

tutti

C	22–25	b – V⁷/f♯	f♯ – vii⁷/F♯ – F♯ = V⁷/B	
		22 – 23	24	25

$\mathrm{b} - \mathrm{V}^7/\mathrm{f}\sharp \quad \mathrm{f}\sharp - \mathrm{vii}^7/\mathrm{F}\sharp - \mathrm{F}\sharp = \mathrm{V}^7/\mathrm{B}$

solo

$\mathrm{D_1}$	25–28	V^7/B – B = V^7/E – E		
		25 26 28		
$\mathrm{D_2}$	28–31	V^7/A – A = V^7/d – d		
		28 31		
$\mathrm{D'_3}$	31–33	V^7/g – g		
		31 33		
$\mathrm{D'_4}$	33–35	V^7/c – c		
		33 35		

tutti

K	35–37	V^7/B – B = V^7/e – e		
		35 36 37		

P2

solo

A	37–42	e
B	42–46	
$\mathrm{E_1}$	46–49	V^7/a
$\mathrm{E_2}$	49–52	V^7/g

tutti

$\mathrm{F_1}$	52–53	V/f – f
		52 53
$\mathrm{F_2}$	53–54	V/g – g
		53 54
K	54–56	

solo

cadenza	57–58	g♯ Phrygian

P3

tutti

A	84–88	
B	88–93	f♯
C	93–94	
		C♯

solo

K	95–101	c♯ – F♯ – B
		95 98 100

eighty-six notes. In the second period of five measures, vis-à-vis the forty-six notes of the part of the English horn, the guitar plays 140, which require one more measure. In other words, in its first response the guitar practically doubles the number of notes on the English horn, and in the second response triples it.

There is another subtle detail Rodrigo uses to set the guitar in bold relief, even in the moments in which it accompanies the entrance of the English horn with slow arpeggiated chords, four per measure. Besides allowing the guitar to begin alone during the first measure, in the second part of the melody, Rodrigo introduces a countermelody above the accompaniment. In contrast, when the orchestra accompanies a melodic elaboration in the guitar, it does so with triads in root position, followed by tonic and dominant-seventh chords in the cadence.

Subsequent movement in the harmony provides a bridge (C in table 5.2) from the melody to a series of modulations in the manner of *Fortspinnung*, a German term that literally means the "spinning out" of ideas (D_1–D'_4 in table 5.2). The procedure has the same function as in the first movement: to achieve a secondary tonal area. In this case, E minor is confirmed with the second appearance of the main theme, now in the solo guitar. Rodrigo writes the guitar part in two staves, with the song in the lower staff for the three lowest strings of the guitar. Now there is little diminution of the original melody, which the English horn introduced, for the guitar is "singing" in its most sonorous register, accompanied by itself (musical ex. 5.9).

This is the first time in the entire concerto thus far that the guitar has played alone, without any orchestral accompaniment. Thus, sometimes this section is considered as a cadenza. Its function, however, is rather that of a ritornello of the main theme, one that makes way for an area of development (E_{1-2} and F_{1-2} in table 5.2). Here Rodrigo once again utilizes the same strategy of *Fortspinnung*, with two pairs of modulating sequences (mm. 46–52 and mm. 52–54).

The last sequences, performed by an orchestral *tutti*, move via secondary dominants to F minor and G minor, respectively, joined by a reappearance of the guitar. This is a magnificent

Musical ex. 5.9: *Concierto de Aranjuez*, second movement, Adagio, mm. 37–46

detail of Rodrigo's compositional craft. After reaching F minor (m. 53), the guitar plays the notes F♯–G–E–F♯. After attaining G minor (m. 54), it plays G♯–A–F♯–G♯. This form of climbing a semitone over the key to which it has arrived is precisely the way Rodrigo manages to set in relief the imminent guitar cadenza. After the previous G minor, the cadenza is written in G♯ Phrygian. Moreover, that motive, formed by a minor second–minor third–minor second, is a reworking of the main motive of the first movement. When this motive rises from the low register of the guitar to its greatest height in the trumpets and flutes, with a subsequent echo of the clarinets, it appears transformed with a resonantly diatonic sequence of notes, D–E–C–D. In a cyclical fashion, then, this form establishes a clear relationship with the main themes of the first movement (musical ex. 5.6). Immediately afterwards, the bassoon brings the motif back to the key of G minor, but the reference to the motive of the first movement has been unmistakable (musical ex. 5.10).

From this point onward, the guitar begins its cadenza with the momentum that it acquires from starting a semitone above the preceding key. In its twenty-six measures, three different

Musical ex. 5.10: *Concierto de Aranjuez*, second movement, Adagio, mm. 54–56

areas are distinguishable. The first eleven measures present the basic motive of this movement, which is the shift of the major second descending and ascending. The following eight measures are organized around the descending minor tetrachord in the Andalusian mode (C♯–B–A–G♯). The last seven create melodic and harmonic tension that leads to the climax in which the orchestra returns to the main theme, this time in F♯ minor (musical ex. 5.11).

The intensity of this climax is achieved by reaching the dominant key united to the orchestral *tutti* in a *fortissimo*, while the woodwinds repeat the main motive time and again, like an insistent echo. This stirring climax is followed by barely nine *pianissimo* measures. Though there is a loss of inertia here, indicated by the markings *piu tranquillo* and *rallentando*, the B-major tonality does not give us much of a sense of closure, as it is not articulated very strongly and disappears into thin air as the guitar plays an ascending arpeggio in artificial harmonics, ending on the dominant note, F♯. This gives the cadence a tentative, transient quality and prepares for the concerto's continuation.

Musical ex. 5.11: *Concierto de Aranjuez*, second movement, Adagio, mm. 84–93

The conclusion of the Adagio and beginning of the Allegro gentile take us on an emotional roller coaster, from a grief-stricken *cri de coeur*, to resignation and acceptance, to the jaunty high spirits of the final movement. Rodrigo skillfully manages this transition by beginning the final movement in B major (mm. 1–20), then moving directly to D major.

Just as he conceived the theme of the second movement in the key of *Erbarme dich, mein Gott* (B minor), so the theme that he had initially sketched for the third movement was most likely the one that the orchestra presents in D major (first violins and first oboe), between mm. 20 and 40. In an arch form recalling the melodic contours of the Adagio, the third movement is based on a similarly pre-Classical thematic structure. It features very astringent harmonies, but these are merely surface color and do nothing to conceal a very conventional extension of the tonic and modulations of four repeated measures: A (mm. 20–24, 24–28) and B (mm. 28–32, 32–36), which are motivically very similar. These materials appear in addition to the repetition of the first group of four measures (A', mm. 36–40). However, this group now has a more conclusive character, achieved by the movement of the basses through an ascending octave in the D-major scale.

This theme, which we know that Rodrigo composed immediately after the Adagio, is the refrain of a rondo (musical ex. 5.12),

Musical ex. 5.12: *Concierto de Aranjuez*, third movement, Allegro gentile, mm. 20–40 and the end of its first phrase already foreshadowed the principal motive with which the main themes of the first movement were to be constructed. In the formal organization of this final movement, the refrain appears five times. The first two times and the last, it appears in the tonic, the third the subdominant, and the fourth in the dominant (table 5.3), mirroring the I–IV–V harmonic motion of the first movement. Among the refrains appear four episodes in which Rodrigo shows his ability to combine material, working with different thematically related modulations in which the harmonic development of the composition occurs.

The relationship that we have pointed out between the Adagio and the first movement, through a motive whose origin can be found in the main theme of the Allegro gentile, is a sign that the final phase of the orchestration was completed in Spain. Then it would seem fairly clear that Sainz de la Maza was going to debut the concerto. What was not known was where or with what orchestra. The original idea of doing it in Madrid under the direction of Jesús Arámbarri was still uppermost in the mind of composer and soloist, but in postwar Spain nothing was going to be simple or certain.

La rentrée

On 28 August 1939, three days before the German invasion of Poland, Rodrigo and his wife left France. On the border at Irún

TABLE 5.3 **Concierto de Aranjuez, III, Allegro gentile, formal scheme**

A	B	A	C		A
1–40	40–53/53–69	69–98	97–105	105–139	139–165
(B) D	D / E	D ...	c♯–C♯	B/E/a♯	G

D	A	E	A	Coda
165–185 / 189–209	208–229	229–292	292–311	311–322
CDeD / GAbE	A	A–(b)–D	D	

Portrait of Rodrigo, Bilbao, 1930s

they obtained a pass to go to Bilbao, San Sebastián, and Madrid, spending two weeks with the Arámbarris in Bilbao before continuing on. The Civil War had ended on April 1, and the first stage of a new period in the political history of Spain was beginning. The democratic, pluralistic Republic that the Rodrigos had left behind four years earlier was now a country devastated by war and subordinated to the government of a general who had come to power by force of arms. This was a country in the process of building upon two pillars: Catholicism and anti-communism.

In those months after the end of the Civil War, many had departed from Spain to escape the repression of the Franco regime, and very few of them ever came back. Those favoring

Franco had managed to return before the end of the war to place themselves at the disposition of those who were about to take control. Rodrigo, nonetheless, only returned when he was conscious of a greater danger he faced in a northern Europe on the brink of a general war, and once the Spanish authorities assured him the means for his subsistence. It is clear that in the new Spain, there was a notable effort to reintegrate him—in response to the confused situation of Ernesto Halffter, who had never managed to return, and the imminent departure of Falla for Argentina, which took place on 2 October 1939.[56]

Rodrigo always regretted not having had the opportunity to reunite with Falla and show his gratitude for all that he had done for him. Almost a year before, Falla had urged the Minister of National Education to grant Rodrigo a well-remunerated position in radio or in a conservatory. That effort was rather hurried, and Rodrigo did well to turn down the opportunity to incorporate himself into a provincial conservatory. Now, however, things had cleared up, and what they proposed to him was very interesting.

In the first place, he was offered a post on Radio Nacional, which in those years had become the means of communication with greatest impact. It was a post directly designed for him by the director of that institution, Antonio Tovar, Subsecretary of Press and Propaganda. Rodrigo's function as "musical assessor" of the weekly review Radio Nacional was to coordinate its musical contents. That position gave him a certain relevance within the profession because it would allow him to assign remunerated articles to persons in his circle. He was also assured a space to publish his own writings on the most varied themes of music history and current musical affairs, and to expand his presence through radio talks. Hence, on November 1, Radio Nacional broadcast a lecture by Rodrigo and, the following day, a piano recital by him in what would be one of his first public appearances after his return.[57]

In the second place, in the month of October, Rodrigo was named interim professor of folklore at the Conservatory of Madrid, but he took little interest in these classes.[58] As he made clear in a letter to López-Chavarri, in principle the idea was for him to be named professor of harmony, but he ended up "in that business of folklore, which of course is infinitely more comfortable and good for feigning knowledge that one does not have."[59] Some days afterwards, he wrote what he wanted his program of studies to be; not surprisingly, it was based on the curriculum of the École Normale de Paris:

> I intend as a first step and strictly to make the kids study or, better said, harmonize chorales, which they may well need. So for now let's not waste time doodling. Later I intend to pass to the study of harmonization of folksongs and even later we will do something about the nationalist schools and we will attempt to study the forms which the application of folklore has been able to originate. That is what I am thinking, because in the whole blessed conservatory there was no plan of studies or anything.[60]

Although the radio and the conservatory would be his main occupations, Rodrigo was also named head of the Section of Art and Propaganda of ONCE (National Organization for Spanish Blind Persons), an institution that played an enormous role in assisting and educating the blind under the direction and control of the blind themselves. Affiliated with this important institution as of 1 October 1939, Rodrigo was one of its first directors and attended its first national conference, which took place in Seville 17–18 December 1939.[61]

According to Victoria Kamhi, the Spanish authorities had also committed themselves to making the two monthly payments still owed to the couple for the Count of Cartagena Scholarship, as soon as they returned to Spain. With that money they could face the difficult task of finding an apartment to rent in Madrid and coping with the rationing of basic commodities. They found lodging thanks to a friend of theirs, the blind musician Julio Osuna Fajardo, one of the founders of ONCE. It was a fifth-floor apartment, with a coal stove and without an elevator, in which they stayed for a short time. There Victoria Kamhi realized that she was again pregnant, and Joaquín suffered a serious health crisis.[62] We do not yet know what sickness afflicted him, but the sanitary conditions in Madrid were very poor. That autumn there were simultaneous epidemics of smallpox, diphtheria, and typhoid fever.

Despite everything, the Rodrigos came out ahead, and the composer began to get situated in the musical ambience of the capital, which, with the departure of Adolfo Salazar to Mexico, had completely changed. Sainz de la Maza was now also a music critic for the Madrid daily *ABC*, and he was well connected. He introduced the composer to a promising young man with a university education and musical calling, who had spent the war in the fifth column of the Republican Army and was soon to acquire extraordinary fame and influence. His name was Federico Sopeña. As critic of the daily *Arriba*, official newspaper of the Franco regime, he adopted Rodrigo as "his own" musician, just as in the preceding period Salazar had adopted Halffter. It is somewhat ironic that after the war, *Arriba* occupied the same building as had *El Sol*, the Republican daily for which Salazar had written. Sopeña narrated as follows his discovery of Rodrigo:

> There is no great critic without a *new man* to discover,
> I told myself as of the autumn of 1939. Situated next to
> the delightful daily labor of Joaquín Turina, comfortably
> imprisoned in an admiration without reservations, I
> needed a more problematic dialogue, more replete with
> unknowns, to excite my pen. Regino [Sainz de la Maza]
> told me at once that yes, the musician of our times was
> already among us [. . .] and that his masterpiece was a
> concerto for guitar and orchestra.[63]

That concerto for guitar and orchestra could not be debuted during the entire season of 1939–40. Meanwhile, despite the precariousness of Spanish musical life, Rodrigo was making himself known. The ballerina Manuela del Río included the "Valencian Dance" from the *Cuatro piezas para piano* on a recital program at the Teatro Español, accompanied by pianist Javier Alfonso. Sainz de la Maza wrote that the "Valencian Dance" "can appear with dignity at the side of the [Four] *piezas españolas* of the excellent maestro Manuel de Falla."[64] Leopoldo Querol, for his part, began to include *Preludio al gallo mañanero* in his concerts and debuted this piece in Madrid on 6 December 1939. Conservatory professor Conrado del Campo, teacher of the main Madrid composers of Rodrigo's generation, referred to this work as "succulent, animate, overflowing with humor and freshness, qualities mainly characterizing up to now the musical personality of this interesting composer."[65]

In March 1940, Madrid audiences once again heard *Per la flor del lliri blau,* in a performance by the Madrid Orquesta Sinfónica under the direction of Manuel Izquierdo. According to Sainz de la Maza, "The public intuited that it was in the presence of an exceptional work and gave a deserved tribute to the musician, present in the theater box."[66] A few days later, on April 1, during a celebration of the first anniversary of the "liberation" of Madrid, the same ensemble appeared in a gala concert at the Teatro Español, attended by the highest political and diplomatic echelons under the *Caudillo* himself, Francisco Franco. In this concert, Izquierdo conducted the two great orchestras of Madrid, the Sinfónica and the Filarmónica, first separately and lastly together. With the Sinfónica, he once more performed the symphonic poem of Rodrigo, who was the only representative of the composers of his generation. The other composers selected were Falla, Turina, Granados, and Albéniz; as a finale, the two orchestras performed "Preludio y pantomima," from the third act of *Las golondrinas* by José María Usandizaga, and the prelude to *La revoltosa* by Ruperto Chapí. The gesture of uniting the two orchestras, which had always been bitter rivals, was as symbolic as the canon of Spanish classics that the program proudly presented.[67]

In this first season of his return to Spain, Rodrigo had a premiere, but it was not of a new work. It was a version for large orchestra of his *Homenaje a "La Tempranica,"* presented as an intermission during a dance program by the Sakharoffs.

It was first performed at the Teatro Argensola in Zaragoza on 3 November 1939 and twelve days later at the Teatro Calderón in Madrid. The orchestra was most likely an ensemble called the Orquesta Patriótico-Sinfónica de Zaragoza, conducted by César de Mendoza Lassalle.

This connection between Rodrigo and Mendoza Lassalle, which dated back to his passage through Bilbao and San Sebastián before going to Madrid, is important because, in September, the conductor proposed to the composer that he write a ballet on a plot taken from either *La Celestina* by Fernando de Rojas or the *Novelas ejemplares* of Miguel de Cervantes. It was for a Spanish ballet company that Mendoza Lassalle wished to create with the dancer Vicente Escudero, in order to take on tour *El amor brujo* by Falla, *Goyescas* by Granados, and the new piece by Rodrigo.[68] This interesting project did not come to fruition, but it offered a good idea of the enterprising character of the conductor, who was very active in the first months of the postwar period, and it was crucial for the premiere of the *Concierto de Aranjuez*. In fact, rather than "a premier," we should speak of two pre-premieres followed by the actual premiere.

The Premieres

Mendoza Lassalle was always aware of the fact that he was not Rodrigo's and Sainz de la Maza's first choice to conduct the premiere of the *Concierto de Aranjuez*. That would have been Arámbarri with the Orquesta Municipal (Municipal Orchestra) of Bilbao. In the month of August, they were even speaking about rehearsing the concerto with this orchestra, but the Sociedad Filarmónica (Philharmonic Society) of Bilbao passed up the opportunity because of a lack of confidence in the project. Its president, the Count of Superunda, Ignacio de Gortázar, admitted as much in a letter to Rodrigo: "We sin from a lack of faith and we are penitent: in our sin we bear the penance, which consists of the shame of having let escape from our hands the honor to have it premiered here, in our home, a work that will travel the whole world in triumph."[69]

Sainz de la Maza collaborated with Mendoza Lassalle in a May

1940 concert at the Teatro Guimerá of Santa Cruz de Tenerife. There, between the Symphony No. 7 of Beethoven and the *Sinfonía sevillana* of Turina, the guitarist played several solos and the guitar part of a certain "Third Quintet of Boccherini," which must surely have been the Quintet in E minor, G. 451, of Luigi Boccherini.[70] The "rarity" of the guitar repertory that Sainz de la Maza had played for the first time in 1937, though seldom afterwards,[71] should have convinced Mendoza Lassalle about the concert potential of the guitar. Several months after the concert in Tenerife, the conductor was organizing a series of programs at the Palau de la Música of Barcelona, and he wrote to the guitarist, "It is a question of your cooperation for one of our concerts in Barcelona with the Orquesta Filarmónica, and in it would be premiered Rodrigo's Concerto. The dates of these concerts will be during the month of November, God willing. Once I have your acceptance, in principle we will deal with a definitive date and your fee."[72]

Sainz de la Maza answered quickly: "I think that the concert will require special care, but if we turn out a good result, as I expect, it will be something sensational. You'll see."[73] Later, to prepare the work, he secluded himself during the months of August and September in the house he owned in Santander. The technical difficulties that the music of Rodrigo posed and the uncertainty of the result in tandem with a symphony orchestra adversely affected the guitarist's health. His wife, Josefina de la Serna, then wrote to Rodrigo, "His skinniness and sick face are alarming. [. . .] He is crazy about the concerto and despite my prohibitions studies it more than he should."[74]

The task that lay ahead of him was titanic for a guitarist of his time, but he could no longer turn back. He was negotiating his contract with Mendoza Lassalle, promoter of the concerts he would also conduct. It is surprising, nonetheless, to what extent the premiere was still up in the air. We deduce this from what the conductor wrote to him from San Sebastián on 17 September 1940:

The musicians, as always, whether from Madrid or wherever, always do what they please, and at this time I don't know if I still have any orchestra at all. As soon

as I've refused to let myself be bamboozled, as they had
the habit of doing, all the accommodations disappear
and the objections begin. Nonetheless, I am willing to
give the concerts on the Saturdays of October 26 and
November 2, 9, and 16, if not with last year's musicians,
then with others. But the concerts will be given. I have
firm contracts with Thibaud, Arthur Honegger, with Else
Scherz and Franz Josef Hirt, Benedetti, Quiroga, Viñes,
Maurice Maréchal. I can hire you for one of the first four
concerts that will take place on the dates that I indicated
to you before, and the fee that I can offer you is 1,200
pesetas, the same that I pay Benedetti, Viñes, etc. If in
the final analysis it proves impossible for me to give the
concerts with an orchestra, one thing I'm sure about
setting up as soon as I get to Barcelona in the first days
of the month is that your concert would take place in a
recital, since I would open a subscription on the same
dates for four recitals. Of course, if it is with an orchestra
and you accept this fee, we will play Rodrigo's concerto.[75]

The fee offered was practically equivalent to three months
salary for Rodrigo in the conservatory, but the guitarist only
reluctantly accepted it:

I am sorry that the musicians behave so poorly with
you and upset the plans. As I don't want to heap on you
any worry about me, I relieve you of your first offer, and
I accept the new fee that you propose to me without
it serving as any precedent [for future negotiations]. I
rejected that very fee from the Cultural [Society] last
season. Now then, I think you should include me in that
first subscription to the recital, and afterwards perform
Rodrigo's concerto if, as I expect, the musicians agree to
rational reasons and stop playing around like asses.[76]

The conductor managed to organize an orchestra with the
grandiose name of the Barcelona Philharmonic, although it was

Program from the premiere of Concierto de Aranjuez

ultimately a thrown-together ensemble, and the *Concierto de Aranjuez* was premiered at the Palau de la Música Catalana on 9 November 1940. This premiere took place under the watchful eye of the very authorities who had firmly contributed to Rodrigo's settling in Madrid. According to a press notice, Subsecretary of National Education Jesús Rubio came "expressly from Madrid along with different hierarchies of the Party to attend the debut."[77]

Rodrigo and Sainz de la Maza traveled together by train, but Victoria Kamhi could not go with them because her pregnancy

was so advanced. Many years after, Rodrigo recounted an anecdote related to that trip. To all appearances, he could not sleep,
and he awoke the guitarist to express to him the worry that
obsessed him: "And what if tomorrow, in the rehearsal, the guitar would not be heard?" From that moment on, neither one of
them could sleep a wink.[78]

Certainly that was the great question, and the composer himself, in the notes to the work that went with the program of the
premiere, had wished to lower the audience's expectations a bit:
"It would be unfair to ask that this concerto be powerful, and in
vain would great sonorities be expected of it; that would be the
same as falsifying its conception and bastardizing the instrument made of subtle vagueness. Its strength has been sought in
its lightness and in the intensity of the contrasts."[79]

That mix of lightness and power, of grace and energy, is the
most beautiful and concise definition possible of a work that
from its birth caused rivers of ink to flow about it. Rodrigo was
not even credited as the author of the program notes. The hero
of the program was Sainz de la Maza. That remains very clear
from the fact that his biography extends for twenty-two lines,
while Rodrigo's is polished off in only five.

Among the reviews published in the Catalan press, there
were some good ones and some lukewarm ones. Among the com-
plimentary ones, that by composer Xavier Montsalvatge in the
Barcelona weekly *Destino* has always been singled out. In it the
Concierto de Aranjuez was hailed as a milestone in the history
of Spanish music of the twentieth century, on the same level as
Falla's *Concerto per clavicembalo*:

[W]e stand before a music that, like Falla's [*Concerto*]
previously mentioned, brilliantly solves the problem
of the national element in the art of sounds. No one
can deny in the work of J. Rodrigo the existence of a
diffuse southern luminosity and of an ancestral racially
national Spanish strength, projected outward, much
more efficacious, vis-à-vis European music, than that
possessed by many other works of apparently national

flavor, but with a narrow background, provincial or even urban horizons. Neither can anyone find limitations in the language employed in it, [as it is] rich and new in its universal intelligibility.[80]

Among the lukewarm criticisms, one attributed to guitarist Alfredo Romea opined that "The struggle of the guitar with the orchestra is impossible. But the composer has hit the mark on arranging, almost always, for the guitar to dialogue with the orchestra. In the moments that it fuses in the instrumental mass, the guitar is not heard."[81] A similar estimation was expressed by the critic writing for La Vanguardia Española.[82] The tradition-bound aficionados of guitar music, represented by Romea, kept on failing to understand or even to accept the idea that their instrument could concertize with an orchestra. A week after the Barcelona debut, the Concierto de Aranjuez arrived at the Teatro Arriaga in Bilbao, with the Orquesta Municipal conducted by Arámbarri. The Barcelona pre-debut and the concert in Bilbao served to prove that the composition worked. With that much acknowledged, on December 11 it achieved the honor of being performed by the Orquesta Nacional de España, under the direction of Arámbarri, at the Teatro Español. Thus would it be introduced to the public and the critics of Madrid. This was something different. Despite all its initial deficiencies and contradictions, the Orquesta Nacional de España (National Orchestra of Spain) was now called upon to be the flagship of Spanish music, and this was its first important premiere.

The repercussions in the press were enormous, and there was virtual unanimity in acclaiming the work. Reviews by Gerardo Diego and Federico Sopeña (who was cutting his teeth as the music critic for Arriba) positively glowed with enthusiasm. Diego certified the work's success while admitting that it continued to arouse misgivings among some segments of the public: "The balance of pitches, the coherence and clarity of the finest sonorous atmosphere, surprised those who harbored mostly a priori skepticism."[83] Sopeña, for his part, wrote a long article dedicated to the great premieres of the 1920s. But some criticism did not fail to sneak in amidst so much praise. Víctor Ruiz Albéniz, for instance, made it clear that since the premiere of Falla's *Noches en los jardines de España*, this had been the most important historical moment in Spanish music. But he stressed that the orchestra was too large, that "[the concerto] would gain much if in future it were performed with guitar and small orchestra."[84] The identical recommendation is to be found in the criticism of orchestra conductor and composer José María Franco.[85]

In fact, Rodrigo was composing for an "ideal" instrument, to which he referred at the beginning of his program notes to the premiere: "a strange instrument, a phantasmagorical instrument, gigantic and multiform, idealized by the heated fantasy of an Albéniz, a Granados, a Falla, a Turina. It is an instrument that would have the wings of a harp, the tail of a piano, and the soul of a guitar."[86] That instrument dreamed of by Rodrigo would have the strength to compete with a big orchestra, the lightness to fascinate the audience, and the depth to move it. Rodrigo had written, with no concessions, the first work for this imaginary instrument that, from that time on, guitarists have bravely tried to convert into reality.

In Spain the *Concierto de Aranjuez* was heralded as the first concerto ever written for the guitar. We have already shown that this was not so. Indeed, after its 28 October 1939 premiere in Montevideo (Uruguay), Andrés Segovia took Castelnuovo-Tedesco's guitar concerto on a tour of Latin America, including the capital cities of Mexico, Peru, Chile, and Argentina, between February and May 1940. It is hardly likely that there would have been no word of these concerts in Spain, but diplomatic relations with the Spanish-American countries were strained at the time. Further, Andrés Segovia's loyalty to the Franco regime was ambiguous. He did not return to perform in his native country until 1952, and he continued his concertizing in the 1940s by frequenting countries hostile to Spain.[87]

On 22 December 1940, the music critics of the main Madrid dailies met with Rodrigo and Sainz de la Maza to celebrate the success of the *Concierto de Aranjuez*: "Much was said about music and Spanish musicians, and vows were taken so that Sainz de la Maza and Rodrigo might come back soon to give occasion to fair and heated praises, reflections of the public opinion of their colleagues in music criticism."[88] They were in fact colleagues, because besides the fact that Sainz de la Maza was the music critic of *ABC*, Rodrigo had been hired in June 1940 as music critic for the new daily *Pueblo*.[89] This was another vocation that would reaffirm his presence within the most influential elite of Spanish music, and it would help him to maintain a comfortable existence. Nevertheless, these various jobs would soon leave him with little time for his main occupation, composition.

The year 1940, year of the *Concierto de Aranjuez*, was reaching its end when Rodrigo received for his work the prize of the Sindicato Nacional del Espectáculo (National Union for Performing Arts), alongside the Orfeón Donostiarra (San Sebastián Chorale) and the Agrupación Nacional de Música de Cámara de la Orquesta Nacional (National Group of Chamber Music of the National Orchestra). There is no doubt that the Orquesta Nacional and the Orfeón Donostiarra were two emblems of Spanish musical culture used as propaganda by the Franco regime. It is also clear that at that moment an attempt was being made to situate Rodrigo on the same level. It is quite a different matter whether such an attempt bore fruit. The composer had accepted the posts offered to him so that he and his wife could live in Spain. And he utilized them while they lasted, which was not long, in order to follow his creative path even as he tried to maintain a certain independence within a country that was being subjected to a remorseless purge of political dissent. To continue composing while evading attempts to make him a tool of politics was not going to be an easy task.

Chapter 6

The Postwar Years

(1941–1949)

Family and Friendships: Rodrigo and the Falangist Cultural Milieu

Nothing mattered more in Rodrigo's life than the birth of his daughter, Cecilia, a blond little bundle of joy who came into the world on 27 January 1941. Her parents' obsession was to know whether the baby had good eyes. Hers were perfect and very blue, like the composer's. That evening was filled with anxiety because a number of complications had kept Victoria Kamhi in bed for over a month. So, Rodrigo spent much of it in the company of his friend Federico Sopeña, who had found in the composer a man to admire in that "hour of tense loneliness."[1]

Sopeña and the woman who was his fiancée at the time, the soprano Lola Rodríguez Aragón, served as Cecilia's godparents. Her baptism in February was followed by a celebration in the apartment where the Rodrigos had settled: an attic with a great terrace in the centrally located Calle Villalar, beside the Buen Retiro Park. In a small salon that day there gathered together, besides the new parents and the godparents, several

With his daughter, Cecilia

musicians—Joaquín Turina, Nemesio Otaño, and Bartolomé Pérez Casas—all of whom were among the "top brass" in Spanish music during the first years of the postwar era.[2]

In Falla's absence, Turina became the patriarch of Spanish music, and he occupied the post of Comisario General de la Música (General Commissioner of Music) from 1940 until his death in 1949. He first formed a triumvirate with Otaño and the pianist José Cubiles and, from 1941, occupied the chief position by himself.[3] Rodrigo, who quickly forgot the indifference toward his early works in some of Turina's music reviews, affectionately recalled his frequent visits to the commissary to share with the Sevillian maestro his conversation and a glass of Manzanilla wine.[4]

Father Otaño, a Jesuit priest, had enormous power in the early 1940s as president of the Consejo Nacional de la Música (National Council of Music), in which Turina, as general commissioner, occupied the post of secretary.[5] Otaño headed the Madrid Conservatory from 1940 until 1951, and he shared the Chair of Folklore with Rodrigo. They were not close friends, but they got along alright.

With regard to Pérez Casas, we already noted his pre–Civil War interest in Rodrigo's music; afterwards, he underwent a difficult period when accused of having collaborated with the Republic. But at Otaño's insistence, the charges against him were dropped, and with the decisive support of Turina, he conducted the new Orquesta Nacional de España from 1943 until his retirement in 1949, when he was kicked upstairs to succeed Turina as General Commissioner of Music.[6] In his debut as the head of that institution, he conducted the first performance in Spain of Rodrigo's *Concierto heroico* for piano and orchestra.

It was Antonio Tovar, Subsecretary of the Press and Propaganda, who now found a position for Rodrigo as a consultant for the Radio Nacional.[7] Tovar's friendship with the editor-in-chief of the daily *Pueblo*, Jesús Ercilla, had probably also paved the way for Rodrigo to become music critic of that newspaper. Before the war, Tovar had begun a brilliant academic career by broadening his studies in 1935 in Paris (where Rodrigo also happened to be) and in 1936 in Berlin. His political adventure lasted a short time, and he left his subsecretarial position in May 1941.[8] However, his extraordinary erudition and great love of music enabled him to appreciate Rodrigo's artistic and personal traits. Whenever circumstances allowed, he would favor the composer. To reciprocate, Rodrigo dedicated to him and to the Subsecretary of National Education, Jesús Rubio García-Mina, the *Gran marcha de los Subsecretarios* in B minor, for piano duet.

Written in the first half of 1941, the *Gran marcha de los Subsecretarios* is a surprising composition related to the carefree world of *Les Six* and to Erik Satie's *Sonatine bureaucratique* (1917). Lasting a little over four minutes, Rodrigo's piece has flair and an ironic character, representing all the weight of the bureaucratic apparatus of the state. The tempo markings, "At a good pace, but without haste" for the first part and "ministerial tempo" for the trio, and the apotheosis of the lengthened final cadence in B major, evince the descriptive meaning of this parody.

The composer's closest friends were all moving in the environment of the Germanophilic Spanish fascist movement, the Falange. They were drawn to German culture and the politics of the Third Reich, and they had their moment of maximum influence from 1938 until about 1943, when the war began to go poorly for the Axis. It is known that though he was not assiduous in doing so, Rodrigo frequented the discussion group, or *tertulia*, at the Lyon d'Or Café in Calle Alcalá, led by Manuel Machado and José María de Cossío. This was one of the meeting places of intellectuals with an affinity for Falangism: a bubble in the middle of a desolate Madrid in which a few men (women could not attend), as Francisco Umbral noted with great accuracy, "exercised vital optimism in an age with no future."[9] Rodrigo, of course, could not lose hope: his life, as the father of a family and as a professional musician, had just begun.

The Falangists' academic instrument of diffusion was the review *Escorial*, founded in November 1940. In its ten years of existence, this journal characterized an era of Spanish culture. Rodrigo also had relations with the so called "group of the *Escorial*." On 15 March 1941, he took part in the tribute to Ricardo Viñes held in the salons of the review to celebrate his return to Madrid after over twenty years of absence. Presiding over the occasion that day were the two philharmonic subsecretaries to whom the composer dedicated his march; Pedro Laín Entralgo, subdirector of the review, served as host; Sopeña lectured on the distinguished pianist Viñes; Gerardo Diego recited sonnets dedicated to Beethoven, Schubert, Schumann, and Stravinsky from his book of poems *Alondra de verdad* (1941); Viñes gave a recital in which he included Rodrigo's *Deux berceuses*; and Rodrigo himself, "while Viñes took a short break, played with singular mastery his [Prelude to the] *gallo mañanero*, [. . .] earning the affectionate ovations of the audience."[10]

Among those attending were the pianists José Cubiles and Leopoldo Querol, by the side of a well-represented number of musical critics, including Turina (from the weekly *Dígame*), Sainz de la Maza (from the daily *ABC*), Antonio de las Heras (from the evening paper *Informaciones*), and Víctor Ruiz Albéniz (*Hoja del Lunes de Madrid*, or the Madrid Monday weekly), besides Sopeña (*Arriba*, the Falange daily), and Rodrigo himself (*Pueblo*). The tribute ended with a visit to the Lyon d'Or.

In the auditorium of the review *Escorial*, on 24 June 1941, there took place an artistic evening of music in which were exhibited four paintings of Ignacio Zuloaga. Rodrigo closed this program by performing his recently published *Cinco piezas del siglo XVI* (Five Pieces from the Sixteenth Century, 1937).[11] Everything took place in the presence of the Falangist minister Ramón Serrano Suñer, Franco's brother-in-law and Minister of External Affairs, among many other personalities of Falangist politics and letters.[12] And several days later, on July 1, there took place in the office of *Escorial* a concert dedicated exclusively to songs by Rodrigo, performed in order of composition by the soprano Lola Rodríguez Aragón, accompanied at the piano by the composer, who also played some of his piano works.[13] At the concert was debuted the *Canción del grumete* by Rodrigo.

The same political and cultural ambience of the discussion circle at the Lyon d'Or and the review *Escorial* promoted relations with Nazi Germany; moreover, during this period, there were intense musical interchanges between Spain and Germany.[14] The performances in Madrid of conductors like Herbert von Karajan in 1940 and Karl Böhm in 1941 with the Berlin Philharmonic served to solidify Spanish symphonic life, as did the visits of German conductors to lead the Orquesta Nacional de España. As for Rodrigo, his *Concierto de Aranjuez* was performed for the first time outside Spain on 16 July 1941, at the climax of the first Hispano-German Festival of Music (Deutsch-Spanisches Musikfest). This took place in the German resort city of Bad Elster and was attended by a large Spanish delegation, though Sainz de la Maza was not at all satisfied with the performance of the *Concierto de Aranjuez* by an improvised orchestra and a mediocre conductor like Eduard Martini.[15]

On 5 November 1941, Rodrigo attended the 150th anniversary of Mozart's death as a guest of the Reich's Ministry of Public Enlightenment and Propaganda in Vienna. The Spanish delegation was flown to Vienna in a Lufthansa four-engine plane. This was the first time that Rodrigo had traveled by plane; the account he published on his return not only gave proof of his "baptism by air" and of the hospitality of his hosts, but also stressed his reencounter with the Vienna Philharmonic: "The lightness of their bowstrings at times makes me shudder, and the woodwinds seem softer and better shaped than ever. What can I add about the trumpets, which give the sensation of playing a keyboard for the accuracy and neatness with which they attack the score?"[16] But what most impressed him was being immersed in Mozart's operas with conductors like Knappertsbusch, Krauss, Böhm, and Richard Strauss. He was also greatly impressed by Mozart's *Requiem* conducted by Wilhelm Furtwängler. And Rodrigo had the opportunity to see once more two of the main French men of music who attended the celebrations as representatives of their country: Florent Schmitt and Arthur Honegger.

Besides being very well connected with the cultural and political elites of the Falange, Rodrigo was also wooed by its social bases. Thus, the Sindicato Nacional del Espectáculo (National Union for Performing Arts), directly tied to the Falange, awarded the *Concierto de Aranjuez* its prize in 1940 and presented it to Rodrigo in a public ceremony on 4 May 1941 at the Teatro Español.[17] Also related to the Falangist social movement were the prizes organized in February 1942 by the Delegación Nacional del Frente de Juventudes (National Delegation of the Front for Youth Groups), desiring to select a hymn for the male section and a song for the female one.[18] Rodrigo anonymously presented his hymn *Pequeños arqueros* for the male category and the *Canción del grumete* for the female one. Each song won a prize of 5,000 pesetas, a generous sum that was equal to Rodrigo's annual salary at the Conservatory.[19] The hymn *Pequeños arqueros* was an outstanding contribution to the rich Falangist songbook. Although it is not included in his catalogue, there are readily accessible versions that show its quality.[20] It is easy to understand his removal of it from his catalogue, because by the early 1940s Franco was demobilizing the Falange, which subsequently lost much of its power and political influence, even before the collapse of German and Italian fascism in 1945. Many of its troops lost their lives fighting on the Russian front, and the leading intellectuals who had belonged to that movement shifted to a stance against the Franco regime and its perpetuation by forming an educated opposition that would play a major role in the 1970s, during Spain's transition to democracy. At that time, the most reactionary political sectors, nostalgic for Francoism, appropriated Falangist symbols.

The authorities of the Nuevo Estado (New State) trusted and favored Rodrigo, and in the 1941–42 school year, the Conservatory of Valencia passed him (with a grade of superlative) in all the classes he needed to attain the title of professional composer. Many held high hopes for Rodrigo and believed that the music he had composed to date certified him as a leading figure in Spanish musical life, especially in the realm of symphonic music. Alas, the year 1941 and a great part of 1942 went by with Rodrigo composing hardly any new music, and Sopeña sent out a clear warning:

> [Ernesto] Halffter's *Portuguese Rhapsody* and the
> *Concierto de Aranjuez* have been the two recent Spanish
> works that have reaped the triumph over Spain and
> Europe. Yet, we wish to leave these names behind with a
> respectful warning. Given the present-day heartbreaking
> condition of our composers, the labor of both [Halffter
> and Rodrigo] appears to be sluggish.[21]

Sopeña was partly right, because in 1941, Rodrigo had to adapt to his new situation as a man with many responsibilities: he had just begun fatherhood, his summer vacations (which previously enabled him to devote himself to composition) had turned out to

Writing on his Braille machine

be relatively unproductive, and afterwards Victoria Kamhi fell ill and had to be admitted to a sanatorium.[22] However, by this time he had acquired a machine on which he could type his musical inspirations in Braille. He would then read the Braille back to an assitant, who would commit it to conventional notation. This would be his standard method of composition for the remainder of his career.

In addition to the *Gran marcha de los subsecretarios*, in 1941 he finished his *Tres danzas de España* ("Rústica," "Danza de las tres doncellas," and "Serrana"). These were three miniatures inspired by some poems of the critic and academician of Fine Arts Víctor Espinós, and Rodrigo dedicated them to three pianists of his time: Nikita Magalov, who debuted them in Madrid in April 1943, as well as Gonzalo Soriano, and Gabriel Abreu.[23] Several months later, Abreu was to offer musical examples for a prominent lecture given by Rodrigo at the Atheneum of Madrid about the music of Manuel de Falla.[24]

The dance dedicated to Abreu, "Rústica," is something like the Galician dance called a *muñeira*, and it expresses the essence of that genre, its rhythm and melodic beginning. Yet, it stays on a dream level from which it does not awaken. Just at the moment it seems to want to develop with a modulation to the relative minor (F♯ minor), two measures end it abruptly with a sonorous cadence in A major. Since Abreu did not make the professional grade of pianist, Rodrigo seems to be musically portraying the dedicatee of his work.

For a better understanding of the "Danza de las tres doncellas," it is fitting to compare the perfect cadence of the first two measures (with their upbeat) and their reformulation in the final measures of the piece. This cadence, formed by the joining of five chords, articulates the formal structure of the dance and demarcates the process of chromatic saturation of the harmony by means of which emotional intensification is achieved. "Serrana" has a three-part form in which the third part is a repetition of the first but an octave higher, and the second part is a variation of the first.

There is a surprising contrast between the difficulties that Rodrigo had experienced in writing the two dances between 1929 and 1930, on the one hand, and these *Tres danzas de España* that seem written with a single penstroke, showing a composer who has achieved real maturity. The crucial ingredient was time, especially now that he was focusing on the piano concerto of which he had dreamed in 1930 and which he was planning to write as of 1933 or '34 in honor of Leopoldo Querol. Still, in 1941, Querol wrote him, "Several days ago, I spoke with Mendoza Lassalle by phone from Barcelona, and he told me that he had seen you in Madrid and that you had spoken about debuting your piano concerto in Barcelona. Is it possible that you are working on it? I won't believe it until I see it."[25] Querol's lack of confidence is not surprising in view of almost a decade of unfulfilled promises, but things were soon going to change.

A Disputed Contest

On 21 April 1942, Sopeña left the General Commission of Music with a piece of news that he hastened to share with Lola Rodríguez Aragón: "I am very happy, because yesterday I offered Rodrigo a wonderful opportunity to earn 10,000 pesetas. I received a call from Lozoya [Juan de Contreras, General Director of Fine Arts], and he told me to establish what kind of composition would be demanded for the national prize for music for this year. As you know, Joaquín is finishing a piano concerto, and this has been the theme that I have established."[26]

The contest announcement, not officially published until June 30, specified as its theme "a concerto for piano and orchestra, divided into three or four movements." This offers another sign about the leaning toward Rodrigo that Sopeña pointed out, as he probably knew that the composer's project was a work in four movements. The period for handing in the work was set between September 15 and 30.[27] If Sopeña notified Rodrigo at the end of April, he gave him a nine-week head start to complete his composition—two months more than the three allotted by the contest announcement to the other competitors. When, on July 15, the public was informed that the jury was to be composed of Joaquín Turina, Leopoldo Querol, and José María Franco,[28] Rodrigo must have seen that events greatly favored his winning the prize, for the concerto he wished to write was to be for Querol, a friend of his since adolescence. Though he therefore had a built-in advantage, there was also a dauntingly persistent problem: he would have to finish his piano concerto after tussling with it for about ten years and just when he had the least time to devote to it. The dénouement was going to resemble that of the *Danzas* that had resulted in a mental block at the beginning of the 1930s, only to emerge from his imagination with the greatest of ease a decade later.

That Rodrigo was being served the prize on a silver platter was not something that went unnoticed in the narrow Spanish musical milieu of the post–Civil War era, especially given the stiff competition he faced. Rodrigo himself recognized as much: "There are those who think that this selection was made to my measure because I had a piano concerto. That is not so. What is more, I wrote it with feverish effort in the final month of the time set by the contest rules."[29]

Sopeña's indiscretion shows us that the theme of the prize was chosen while thinking about Rodrigo. The designated jury was favorable to him, but the composer himself clarified matters when he said that he did not have it already composed when the contest was officially announced. He confessed that he had a first movement completely orchestrated in the winter of 1935, and a second movement written during the weeks he passed in Salzburg the summer of that year, but he discarded them: "What I had written up to then, more than half the work, did not appeal to me, and more than not appealing, did not satisfy me. I wanted to make another work, and in spring 1940 began to make notes for nothing less than a *heroic concerto*." According to him, the composition process took place "in less than half the summer of '42."[30] We can only add two things here: first, that that manner of composing—swiftly, at the last moment, and in a feverish state of concentration—was completely in agreement with Rodrigo's *modus operandi*; second, that the music writer Ángel Sagardía, who had been Rodrigo's copyist for years and whom the composer would receive every night from 10 to 12:30 to write his works in ink, offered some details about how the second movement, Scherzo, must have been completed by Rodrigo after the deadline, because he had had no time before then.[31]

The jury was unexpectedly inundated with concertos, and because the works were delivered signed, it noted that among the contestants were some very accomplished musicians. The jury finally delivered its verdict on December 31, and the prize went to Rodrigo's concerto, but with "honorable mention" going to several other contenders as well, who were awarded the publication and performance of their works.[32]

The "heroic" subtitle of this work has stimulated a lot interpretive speculation since the concerto's premiere. Of course, there was ample precedent for "heroic" music, the most conspicuous example being Beethoven's "Eroica" Symphony No. 3 in E♭ major. That this is a concerto with roots in the nineteenth century is further evidenced by Rodrigo's deployment of four rather than the traditional three movements, an innovation of Brahms in his second piano concerto. What also reminds us of Brahms is the symphonic conception of this work, in which the orchestra plays a role of equal importance and into which the piano is incorporated as an element. This is the closest Rodrigo ever came to writing a symphony, one for piano and orchestra, and some scholars view the work as more of a symphonic poem than a concerto.[33] The large orchestral forces provide further evidence of this, as the score calls for three flutes and two each of piccolos, oboes, clarinets, bassoons, and trumpets, as well as four horns and three trombones, along with the usual complement of strings and a large battery of percussion: snare and bass drums, bells, cymbals, and triangle. It is also the longest of his works, taking about half an hour to execute. In another gesture reminiscent of the Romantic symphony, he inverts the inner movements so that the scherzo is second and the slow movement is third. One thinks, for instance, of the ninth symphonies of both Beethoven and Bruckner in this regard.

Thus, the thematic material and the dimensions of this concerto are of truly heroic stature, but also conspicuous is the muscular character of the solo writing, the post-Lisztian thunder and lightning that require an extraordinary level of virtuosity to execute. If we are in search of heroes to celebrate here, we need look no further than the soloist, who is the real general leading an orchestral army. As Rodrigo himself explained it, "I also wanted the piano to be the hero, and the orchestra [. . .] to be [. . .] its stimulus, its impulse to visualize its pianistic deed."[34]

The first movement has a march-like quality and, appropriately, begins with the "general" soloist leading the way, yet another nod to nineteenth-century concerto conventions on display in, for instance, Beethoven's Fourth Piano Concerto and Mendelssohn's Violin Concerto. The tempo marking is *Allegro con brio*, and the metronome marking is high enough to give the bravest pianist second thoughts. The *Alla marcia* theme at m. 33 (musical ex. 6.1) is what establishes the character of the first movement and indeed the entire work, as it generates thematic ideas throughout the concerto. Iglesias suggests that it is a musical symbol of the "sword," and that each succeeding movement will have such a symbol: the spur, the cross, and the laurel of victory.[35]

This music has a military character, and the addition of piccolos

Musical ex. 6.1: *Concierto heroico,* first movement,
principal theme, mm. 33–43

is a Beethovenian flourish that adds a martial patina to the ensemble, while the clarion call of the principal theme sets the mood. This movement exhibits the sonata form—exposition-development-recapitulation—one expects in the first movement of a symphony. Rodrigo disdained the so-called double exposition of the traditional concerto, in which primary thematic materials are presented first by the orchestra and then by the soloist. Here, the soloist and orchestra are equal participants in the deployment, variation, and restatement of musical materials.

The Scherzo may not be in the traditional place within a four-movement sequence, but it is in the traditional ternary form: ABA or scherzo-trio-scherzo. The word *scherzo* is Italian for a joke or jest, but during the nineteenth century, while it retained the upbeat tempo and lively rhythm of its eighteenth-century predecessors, it often took on a serious character. If the first movement was a sword according to Iglesias, this one is a spur. Again, we hear trumpet calls and a march-like mood, which differentiates this scherzo from others, which are normally in triple rather than duple meter.

The Largo conveys a mood of medieval religiosity, hence its designation by Iglesias as the Cross. This affect is conveyed in part by the use of medieval modalities. According to Igelesias, this was the movement most lauded by critics and which most moved the public. Its structure is simple binary, ABAB-coda, with a cadenza at the end of the first B section.

The concluding *Allegro maestoso* exhibits perpetual motion in E minor and is symbolized by the Laurel of Victory, according to Iglesias. This recalls the heroic mood of the first movement but exhibits an unusual formal design, one not akin to the traditional rondo typical of many concertos: ABABABB'A-coda. Once again, Rodrigo evades being reduced to a rule.

This work shows Rodrigo's intention to unify the score not only through the interrelationship of motivic ideas among the four movements but also with an overarching tonal scheme among the movements. This is built on fifths between the principal tonalities of the first three movements, then a return to the original key: E major, B major, F♯ major, and an E-major coda in the fourth and final movement, in conjunction with a cyclic return of the *Alla marcia* theme.

Many commentators have been inclined to interrogate the meaning of the "heroico" adjective and to find political significance in it. Rodrigo himself insisted in the program notes that "There is no literary suggestion at all, not even implicit allusions; it only obeys the concept its title imposes, and what Europe is currently undergoing."[36] So the "heroic" designation had no specific programmatic content. It was simply a reference to the epoch through which Europe was then passing, in which, presumably, heroism was a trait exhibited by people on all sides of the conflict. Had Rodrigo wanted to extol and eulogize the Caudillo explicitly, such a tribute would have ruffled no official feathers. But he made no such specific claim. So, this was simply a concerto whose affect was one of heroism. In the end, he chose to let others interpret "heroico" as they saw fit.

As Moreda-Rodríguez observes, "The fact that the concerto was first performed in Lisbon, in the context of a musical expedition controlled by the Comisaría de Música and aiming to promote further friendship with Portugal, reinforces the view that the work was understood as a national asset, as an export product representative of the image which the Franco regime wished to present abroad."[37] Many critics were quick to acclaim the work as a fitting encomium for the Maximum Leader and the forces under his command, whose collective heroism had saved Spain from Bolshevism. Víctor Ruiz Albéniz did not mince his words in this regard:

> Being as he was in the prime of life, it was natural for
> this young composer to feel in himself the vibration of
> the impulse, of the enthusiasm, of the brave sacrifice
> made by the best among Spanish young men to preserve
> our civilization, our beliefs and our patriotic sentiment.
> [. . .] He is, has been and will always be a spiritual
> fighter, a fighter in heart and soul to defend Spain's
> greatness to liberate our country from the shame of the
> Marxist hordes."[38]

An anonymous correspondent writing for *Informaciones* in Lisbon chimed in, asserting that "Rodrigo thinks of the Spanish young men who, under the Caudillo, have achieved a better fatherland with their faith and their military and heroic sentiments, typical of the best Spain of all times." Critic Rafael Villaseca declared that the concerto was nothing less than "the musical consequence of our Crusade."[39]

Rodrigo never assented to these interpretations, but neither did he deny them. As Moreda-Rodríguez points out, "Rodrigo generally avoided open praise of the Franco regime or explicit criticism of its enemies."[40] But over time, many observers came to view the work as an expression of right-wing political sentiments and evidence of his collaboration with the *franquista* government. The controversy continues to rage even to this day, though the second edition of the work, in 1995, changed the title to *Concierto para piano y orquesta*, in an effort to change the subject, so wearisome had it become. But the Spanish historical memory is long, and the debate persists.

Thus, though Leopoldo Querol was dedicatee of the first edition, in the 1995 edition Rodrigo changed the dedication to "Sagunto, my hometown, to whose ruins I have dedicated this concerto." This could evoke the siege of Sagunto in the second century BCE by the Carthaginians under Hannibal, and that interpretation became more common in the 1990s. But between 1937 and 1939 the town was reduced to rubble by Franco's forces, while members of Rodrigo's family were still living there. Certainly the composer was aware of that fact. So, perhaps Rodrigo's dedication was an encoded condemnation of Franco's destruction of the city. In the opinion of Moreda-Rodríguez, this is an interpretation more like Picasso's *Guernica*, as a protest against Franco's crimes, and a reading "more consonant with modern sensibilities in Spain than was the original interpretation of the concerto as a celebration of Franco's victory."[41]

As in the case of the *Aranjuez*, one can choose to interpret the work and its subtitle any way one wants. We could easily see it as an expression of the heroism that Rodrigo exhibited every day of his life, facing a complex and dangerous world with fearless creativity and a will to persevere in spite of all obstacles. In the end, the heroism this concerto expresses is not Franco's, Sagunto's, or even the pianist's but rather that of Rodrigo himself. And how could it be otherwise? He could hardly contrive such a bold musical statement without having personally experienced the emotions that reside within every bar of the score.

The *Concierto heroico* premiered on 5 April 1943 in Lisbon with Leopoldo Querol as soloist and Ernesto Halffter as

*With Cecilia during the summer in which he was
composing the* Concierto de estío, *1943*

conductor of the Orquesta Nacional. Some days afterwards, it
was repeated in Oporto. Although in the reception of Rodrigo's
work it is necessary to take into account the political tensions
of the moment,[42] it is fitting to consider here an observation
of the influential Portuguese composer Fernando Lopes-Graça,
who around this time was a member of the Portuguese Communist Party. Lopes-Graça emphasized the singularity of this
work within Rodrigo's catalogue, though it is certain that the
Concierto heroico, a "poor Titan" strangled between two butter-
flies, as the composer referred to it,[43] is not the work that best
represents him, despite its many virtues.

A Series of Works for Violin (1942–45)

In the summer of 1943, the Rodrigos spent two months in Benicasim (Castellón province), where the musician found the peace

of mind to compose his *Concierto de estío* (Summer Concerto) for violin and orchestra, completed in Madrid in early 1944. His first idea was to be able to debut it in January, but at the end of October he had still not begun the process of having it copied. The composer then wrote to Sopeña, who had left behind his brilliant career in Madrid for the Diocesan Seminary of Vitoria to pursue a vocation as a priest: "It will not be able to be performed in January; we will leave it for April. I also think that it will be prettier."[44]

The exchange of letters in these years between Sopeña and Rodrigo reveals that Rodrigo retouched his works up to the moment of dictating them to his copyist, when they acquired their final form. Hence, between the composition and the definitive copy, at times a considerable amount of time would elapse.[45] In the present case, the composer was in no hurry, because in February he wrote, "It's about time that I busy myself with my piece on *Summer*, since otherwise it will never have its debut. The worst thing that can happen in these cases is to think that it is all done when actually all that you have is a rough copy, and when the time has arrived to make decisions about the score, there are nothing but unexpected doubts and wastes of time."[46]

One movement was already copied, but Rodrigo had to interrupt his work because he traveled with his family to Barcelona, where they had prepared for him his first important tribute with a concert in which the *Concierto de Aranjuez* and the *Concierto heroico* would be played together on 22 February 1944, with the Orquesta Filarmónica conducted by Josep Sabater.[47] Hence, by mid-March, the concerto continued to be uncopied. The Comisaría General de la Música decided that the debut of the *Concierto de estío* should take place during a second trip to Portugal by the Orquesta Nacional, in April. There was no time to lose: Rodrigo completed the part for violin, handed two complete movements to Pérez Casas, and devoted some days to finishing the orchestration of the first movement. As he wrote to Sopeña, "Now it truly can be said that it's almost finished."[48]

The *Concierto de estío* was dedicated to Infante José Eugenio de Baviera, who was then the member of the Spanish Royal

House best integrated into Franco's regime. He had affinities to the Falange and was a fine pianist. This concerto completely contrasts with the *Concierto heroico*, lacking any reference or relationship to anything outside the music itself. The naming of the three movements, "Prelude," "Siciliana," "Rondino," makes this clear, as does the statement of the author himself in the introduction to the 1993 published score:

> We should not seek or imagine we can find in it,
> [. . .] preconceived ideas or direct allusions. But the
> suggestiveness and even the conscious or unconscious
> intention which the adoption of a general title inevitably
> implies, together with the fact of resorting in the
> three movements [. . .] to expressions unequivocally
> symptomatic of a style, a form or even a particular
> age—all this reveals the composer's intentions, and the
> aesthetic stance of a concerto influenced by symbols
> beloved of Vivaldi and familiar in his works.

He goes on to say that only in the "Rondino" is there suggestion of "popular motifs," of a "certain Catalan affiliation." "The second theme of the 'Preludio,' played by the woodwinds, also has a certain popular colouring. In spite of these delicate folk elements [. . .] the *Concierto de estío* is created from the purest elements, refined and dignified by long use in the most aristocratic forms of music. As far as its structure is concerned, the work faithfully follows concerto form in the first movement, from which I have eliminated the double exposition, as in my previous concertos." This is an interesting connotation of "purity" (contrasted with use of folk elements = lower classes = impurity) and exaltation of the aristocratic (= purity), one that throws interesting light on the aristocratic pedigree of the *Aranjuez*. In any case, the composer makes clear his desire to infuse "new life into the concerto form from before the era of Haydn and Mozart." He does so in part by adhering to the traditional fast-slow-fast sequence of movements and by deploying an orchestra of modest dimensions featuring the double winds that typified the eighteenth-century ensemble: two flutes (with piccolo), two oboes, two clarinets, two bassoons, two horns, two trumpets, and strings.

Rodrigo endows his 1933 *Tocata* for guitar with new life here, orchestrating it for violin and orchestra, as the first movement "Preludio" of the *Concierto de estío* written ten years later. As the principal scholar of this concerto, Eva León, observes, it is a "Neoclassical work with Spanish flavor." Rodrigo combines "typical Spanish rhythms and minor-key lyrical melodies [to] create the Mediterranean flavor so often associated" with his music.[49] Rodrigo disdained the "double exposition" characteristic of the Classical concerto and does so again here, preferring a straightforward sonata form, consisting of exposition, development, and recapitulation. His penchant for economical use of musical material is immediately in view, as the motive from the opening four measures will be repeated throughout the movement. The overall tonal scheme in the exposition is not typical of the 1700s, moving instead from tonic to dominant to subdominant in the exposition, and from there to the mediant in the development. The recapitulation brings us back to the tonic key of E minor. Ever present is Rodrigo's love of dissonance for surface color, which never undermines the fundamentally tonal character of his harmonic language. He is especially fond of chords made of fifths but sometimes revoiced to include seconds, for example, E–B–F♯ to E–F♯–B.

The "Siciliana" that follows is lightly related to the one Rodrigo composed in 1929 for cello and piano, but this one makes more obvious the digressive character of that piece, which Casals adjudged "a bit long." As the composer himself observed in the Preface, "The Siciliana develops a single theme, and here one can perceive the general preference for the variation form latent in my work, and clearly present in the *Concierto heroico*. Here a complex relationship exists between the theme of the Siciliana and the first theme of the work [Prelude], an interplay which is resolved in the cadenza." Again we note his love of organicism. As we have mentioned earlier, the siciliana was a sort of pastoral music popular during the Baroque period, in 6/8 or 12/8 meter, with characteristic use of dotted rhythms. The simple harmonic language and predilection for drones here suggest rustic instruments like bagpipes and hurdy-gurdys. The first theme is cast in a binary structure, developed, and then restated. This exposition is followed by three variations. Then there is a "cadencia," in which there is an interplay between the main theme of the "Preludio" and that of his *Capriccio (ofrenda a Pablo Sarasate)* for unaccompanied violin (see below). The movement is tied off with a coda. As León notes, the simple harmonic language is enriched with dissonances and modulations that clearly place it in the twentieth century.[50] The overall tonal design is exposition, B–D; development, F♯–A–C–E; recapitulation, B; variations, B–D; cadenza, D–E; coda, E–B.

In the composer's own words, "The 'Rondino' [. . .] is the most consciously composed of the three movements." The main theme is followed by ten variations, or, as Rodrigo labels them, "variants," expositions without episodes and no real variation, "since the word 'variation' seems rather pretentious in this case." Instead, "my intention was to trace with its theme a kind of harmonic and formal circle: that is, that the refrain should circle around a preestablished pattern. [. . .] The violin pirouettes upon harmonic bases made up of tonic, subdominant and dominant foundations, around which the other instruments ride in sudden flights to sometimes distant keys, though contained within the imposed tonal orbit."

Whether these melodic ideas are variants or variations, they elaborate the main theme in all its parameters: rhythm, melody, harmony, dynamics, and instrumentation. "The length of each variation is different due to these elaborations."[51] Traditional harmonies are enlivened by dissonance, including added-note sonorities and even bi- and polytonality. Moreover, the dynamics, textures and registers provide formal clarity as well as contrast.[52]

One of the problems that Rodrigo had to face with his devotion to concertos was battling the soloist's ego. Sainz de la Maza found it difficult to allow other younger, more capable guitarists to play the *Concierto de Aranjuez* when his exclusive rights to perform it for almost a decade after the 1940 premiere expired.

Although we have no knowledge of Sainz de la Maza's paying anything for this privilege, we do know that Rodrigo offered Querol an exclusive right to play the *Concierto heroico* for 2,000 pesetas, and the pianist refused it.[53] Nonetheless, Querol was upset when Pilar Bayona, one of the best pianists of the time, expressed her wish to play Rodrigo's concerto, a wish that never came true. Indeed, despite its promising initial success, the *Concierto heroico* has lacked performers and performances.

Hence, to avoid wounding sensitivities, the debut of the *Concierto de estío* was raffled off between the two most important violinists of the Orquesta Nacional, Enrique Iniesta and Luis Antón, by using a large lottery roller that belonged to ONCE (National Organization for the Spanish Blind).[54] Iniesta drew the winning ticket, and thus it was he who performed the debut on the second tour of the orchestra through Portugal on 11 April 1944, under the direction of Pérez Casas. Later, it was played in Oporto, and it finally made its Spanish premiere at Madrid's Palacio de la Música on May 3.

In Lisbon, Lopes-Graça showed more satisfaction with this concerto—"a work finely fashioned and perfectly performed"[55]—than he had with the piano concerto. But there was one critique that greatly upset the Spanish delegation, authored by the musicologist Santiago Kastner, whose political orientation was diametrically opposed to Lopes-Graça's. Apparently, what most infuriated Kastner was the carefree, jovial humor of this concerto. Lopes-Graça would also have preferred from Rodrigo music with a more tragic sense of life, but he accepted the option taken by the Spanish composer. Kastner, on the other hand, absolutely rejected it as something redolent of Parisian frivolity in the period between the two world wars, and he proffered severe demands for "Latinity."[56] This "Latinity" aspired to conform with the ideology of the Falange's founder, José Antonio Primo de Rivera, whom he confessed he had known personally.

Rodrigo had one more bitter pill to swallow on account of the *Concierto de estío*. Although the composer, straining his ingenuity, had managed to avoid conflict between the Madrid violinists, the Barcelonese debut was a source of friction between Iniesta and Mariano Sainz de la Maza, the guitarist Regino's brother. This struggle greatly upset the composer and began to alienate him from Regino.[57] The resulting discord threatened a musical confrontation between Madrid and Barcelona, with Rodrigo situated on the side of Madrid, though he had always enjoyed a warmer reception in the Catalan capital. As a consequence, it was necessary to postpone the Barcelona debut of the *Concierto de estío*. When the tempest subsided, it was Mariano Sainz de la Maza who presented the work, with Toldrá conducting the Orquesta Municipal, on 1 June 1945.[58]

Flanking the composition of the *Concierto de estío* are two works for violin by Rodrigo with a very different character: *Rumaniana* (1942) for violin and piano and *Capriccio (ofrenda a Pablo Sarasate)* (1945) for solo violin. The memoirs of Victoria Kamhi are the only source we have to date the composition of *Rumaniana* to June of 1942, apparently commissioned "for the contests of the Madrid Conservatory."[59] The work is a display of musical exoticism based on some melodies that Victoria Kamhi recalled by memory, and they can be loosely traced to Ravel's *Tzigane* and its phenomenal flair that so impressed Rodrigo in 1928, when he heard it in Ravel's concerts in Valencia. The "exotic" character of the thematic matter provided by Kamhi and the dramatic intensity of Rodrigo's version—a kind of prayer, fantasy, and grotesque dance—can be related to the Rodrigos' concern about Victoria Kamhi's mother and sister, to whom they fruitlessly tried to give refuge in Spain. They finally had to remain in Mirmande, with hardly any resources and in constant peril. In any case, the Rodrigos kept Victoria Kamhi's Sephardic origins discreetly hidden in those years, following Sopeña's recommendation that she pass for a practicing Catholic: "I would like one thing, dear Joaquín: that on Saint Cecilia's Day, you three go to Mass and that you remember me. You and Wiky [Victoria] should take communion, while confessing with Fr. Félix (what sins will Wiky have committed?)."[60]

During the summer of 1944, Rodrigo composed his only piece for solo violin: *Capriccio (ofrenda a Pablo Sarasate)*, commissioned by Radio Madrid to commemorate the centennial of the birth of the great Navarrese violinist, although he did not conclude it until the first days of January 1945. The virtuosity and scope of this work could point once again to *Tzigane*, but in this case, Rodrigo described this composition as an attempt to bring to the violin the piano of Albéniz's *Iberia*. In fact, the relationship with the guitar is also relevant, because the structure of this *Capriccio* can be compared to the *Tocata*, from which emerged the first movement of the *Concierto de estío*. Thus, it is important to note the climax prior to the final dénouement, which in the guitar piece was achieved with the repetition of an eleventh chord. This powerful gesture, which did not pass from the *Tocata* to the lengthier first movement of the concerto, nonetheless is reformulated in this *Capriccio*, which Rodrigo was to consider the most important work that he composed for a solo instrument after the *Preludio al gallo mañanero*. Enrique Iniesta debuted the *Capriccio* on 8 January 1946,[61] but three years went by before any other violinist played it.[62]

On 16 December 1944, the announcement of a national contest was published to choose "the composers and writers of Spain who prove before a competent jury that they have performed the most efficient, the deepest, and the most fruitful labor to advance our music since the end of our War of Liberation [the Spanish Civil War]."[63] Rodrigo himself proposed the "creation of four prizes to reward the labor of those composers who have garnered the most distinction in symphonic music as of the end of the Movement [i.e., the Civil War] to the present." He added, "Let the devil take me if I did it for myself, although I think that no one can dispute me for the first prize."[64] In fact, Rodrigo received this new Premio Nacional de Música (National Music Prize) of 10,000 pesetas for his contributions in the area of symphonic and chamber music between April 1939 and December 1944.[65]

Musical Tributes and Professional Setbacks

With three concertos debuted and now in circulation, Rodrigo was able to relax a bit and return to less risky, if also less profitable, areas of creativity. Hence, the main works he wrote after the *Concierto del estío* were, like the *Capriccio*, devoted to various types of musical tributes: A l'ombre de Torre Bermeja (1945) for piano is a posthumous tribute to Ricardo Viñes; the Dos piezas caballerescas (1945) for an orchestra of cellos celebrated the twenty-fifth anniversary of the cellist Juan Ruiz Casaux's chair in the Madrid Conservatory; and Invocación y danza (1947?) for guitar was a tribute to Manuel de Falla, who died in Argentina in November 1946.

Viñes's death in Barcelona in the early morning of 29 April 1943 went largely unnoticed in Paris. That city, to whose musical splendor the Spanish pianist had contributed so much, was suffering from the humiliation of a German occupation that Viñes was unwilling to witness. In Spain, where he had been received with honors, his unexpected passing caused general commotion and upset Rodrigo, who was very fond of him. Viñes had formed part of his history: first, as one of the main inspirations that he experienced in his adolescence, and afterwards as witness to his "birth" as a composer in the Paris of 1928. Throughout the following years, Viñes gave Rodrigo the gift of debuting some of his works, and the composer dedicated to him the Preludio al gallo mañanero because he was one of its earliest performers. They were friends, and Rodrigo enjoyed whenever possible the delicate and kind interaction with the pianist.

Rodrigo has left us a beautiful sketch of the pianist with several recollections: "His friends thought that Ricardo would never die; he was the youngest of us all. He laughed and enjoyed like a child, his conversations were endless; his unexpected comments, filled with genial insights, with grace, irony, and humor, would interrupt his lessons."[66] As a consequence, the musical tribute that Rodrigo gives to this fascinating personality could not be mournful, and it is not. Its title mixes into an almost absurd expression, consistent with Viñes's humor, the shadow (ombre) of Torre Bermeja (Vermillon Tower) and the man (hombre) of Torre Bermeja: A l'ombre de Torre Bermeja, an extravagant mix of Castilian and French. This is reflected in a music that evokes Viñes as a bridge with three arches that go from Albéniz to the avant-garde of the 1920s and '30s, passing through Debussy and Falla.

Rodrigo was a great admirer of Isaac Albéniz, the first of

the internationally renowned Spanish nationalists whose lineage continued through Granados, Falla, and Turina, culminating in Rodrigo himself. Rodrigo hailed Albéniz's music as being "of supreme importance internationally for the piano" and as the "richest music written for the Spanish piano." He credited him as representing "the incorporation of Spain into Europe, or more correctly, the reincorporation of Spain into the European musical world."[67]

Just as the *Sonada de adiós* was a musical homage to Rodrigo's beloved teacher Paul Dukas, so *A l'ombre de Torre Bermeja* is his stirring tribute to Albéniz; however, as piano scholar Douglas Riva points out, though "Torre Bermeja" is a reference to architecture, the title "wants to convey that he was composing 'in the shadow' of Albéniz, not the tower." Even a cursory exposure to Albéniz's "Torre Bermeja," the final piece of the *Doce piezas características* for solo piano (1888–89), followed by Rodrigo's piece, reveals that the latter is essentially an extended and quite ingenious riff on the former. It is, in fact, "a kind of commentary or paraphrase" of the original, not a direct quote, but an elaboration of materials generously provided by Albéniz.[68]

It is always assumed that Albéniz's title refers to the Vermillon Tower of the Alhambra in Granada. A great lover of that city, he evoked it in some of his most celebrated compositions. However, any tourist who has had a close encounter with the Torre Bermeja knows full well that there are two towers, not one. As it turns out, there is another Torre Bermeja, and it is located on the Playa de Barrosa in the province of Cádiz, a region with which Albéniz was familiar. It is situated on a cliff overlooking sand and surf, and it formerly served as a defensive fortification. This may well have been the original inspiration for Albéniz's piece, though he said nothing to that effect and we may well never know.

In any case, both Albéniz and Rodrigo were indisputably attempting to evoke not a tower but rather Andalusian music, in particular flamenco, especially in the use of triple meter. The opening triplet arpeggiations in Albéniz's work and imitated by Rodrigo suggest figurations typical of an introduction played on the guitar, in preparation for the singer's *salida*, or entrance. And the use of E as a tonal center (whether major or minor) is consistent with the tuning of a modern guitar. Not surprisingly, then, Albéniz's work is most often heard by concert audiences in transcription for the guitar, the instrument it so obviously suggests. In fact, many of Albéniz's piano solos imitate the strumming and plucking patterns of the guitar, as well as its idiomatic harmonic devices. Both composers had a rudimentary level of playing skill on the guitar, but only Rodrigo actually composed music for the instrument. Albéniz wrote guitar music for the piano, which guitarists have dutifully "retranscribed" for their own performance medium.

Use of a macaronic title, blending Spanish and French, was something that Rodrigo thought typical of Albeniz's titles, though piano scholar Douglas Riva could find no examples.[69] What one finds is that Albéniz's compositions were often published with either Spanish or French titles, but not with a mélange of the two. Thus, his *Cantos de España* was also published as *Chants d'Espagne*, not the "Cantos d'Espagne" or "Chants de España." According to Rodrigo, his aim was "that Ricardo [Viñes], at least ideally, rest in the shadow of that tower [Torre Bermeja], but wrapped in roses from France, those very roses that Claude Achilles [Debussy] plucked in his whimsical wandering through his dreamed Iberia." Thus, according to the composer, his work "breaks out strolling [. . .] with guitar arpeggios, friezes of Torre Bermeja" in a clear allusion to Albéniz's little masterpiece. In m. 37, he introduces a theme that he said he would feel "happy if someone on listening to it thinks it belonged to that blessed first epoch of Isaac's."[70]

The accompaniment to the previous theme in E minor is restated in E major as of m. 80, and in m. 84 there appears the motive that Debussy utilized in the second movement of *Iberia* (1905–12), introduced by the first trumpet, "sweet and melancholy" (rehearsal 43 in the full score). This motive articulates the final part of "Les parfums de la nuit," played on the first violin with the bassoon "faraway and expressive," and "even further away," there reappears on the flute, within the finale of *Iberia*,

"Le matin d'un jour de fête," to bond the night of the previous movement with the first rays of dawn. More than a quote, what Rodrigo does is to incorporate Debussy's motive into his own musical discourse.

The structure of this enchanting piece exhibits an alternation of "guitar" interludes and "vocal" outbursts. The introduction and first theme strongly resemble Albéniz's themes, while what ensues is conspicuous in its use of chordal planing in the Impressionist manner, something that was not present in Albéniz's pre-*Iberia* works like "Torre Bermeja" but employed here to suggest Albéniz's beloved Paris, also beloved by Viñes and Rodrigo himself. As Iglesias puts it, this section in particular evokes "a sad and melancholy world," in contrast to the "luminous and happy" music that preceded it.[71]

The work concludes in that same despondent mood, with a perfunctory statement of the dominant and tonic, very much in the fashion of Albéniz's evocative vignettes. It folds over itself symmetrically with the captivating theme of Albéniz's piece and its arpeggiated guitar-like "friezes of the Vermillon Tower," finished off with a condensed statement of the two main themes heard between slow resonances of the untuned bells of the tower. As the composer described it, "They toll for Ricardo, without pain, without sorrow. One does not mourn when a big child rises to heaven [. . .] and everything is snuffed out on the cadence that Isaac loved so well: the bass notes B down to E below the staff in the left hand. It is the 'rest in peace' said to Ricardo."[72]

Rodrigo must have had a good time composing the *Dos piezas caballerescas* (1945), titled "Madrigal" and "Danza de cortesía," as he had the opportunity to write for an ensemble of twenty cellos, his favorite instrument. This was offered as part of a tribute that the Madrid Conservatory was organizing to honor Juan Ruiz Casaux for his twenty-five years of service as professor of cello. Nor would Rodrigo take much time to complete it. His contribution displays interest in the music of the seventeenth century, an interest that was to recur in the following years and that would lead him to compose important works like the *Cuatro madrigales amatorios* (1947) and the *Fantasía para un gentilhombre* (1954) for guitar and orchestra. Despite their good humor, these pieces mark Rodrigo's farewell to the Conservatory. For when the tribute to Ruiz Casaux was celebrated on 27 May 1945, Rodrigo had already abandoned his chair. The director, Nemesio Otaño, was determined to reorganize the institution by announcing state examinations for almost all specialties. Rodrigo signed up right away,[73] but when he found out that the tests had a practical part that he could not perform, he had to desist from presenting his candidacy.[74] Shortly thereafter he wrote to Sopeña, "It was already preestablished that one of the exercises consisted of transcribing the notation of medieval cantigas [songs] to modern notation. All right, patience. We will not take part in the illustrious cloister of professors. I am sorry, but not about the meagre salary to be earned."[75]

"His" place was won in that state examination by Aníbal Sánchez Fraile,[76] a priest with a mediocre record as a musician and folklorist. The Madrid Conservatory thereby lost with Rodrigo the opportunity to have on its staff a name that would have given it international prestige. And that was not his only professional disappointment. In September 1946, at the beginning of the concert season, he found that he had been replaced at the daily paper *Pueblo*, which he had served since its founding in 1940. This led to a lawsuit resolved in the composer's favor along with an indemnity, although he did not recover the position.[77]

In the spring of 1946, Sopeña finished the first-ever book-length biography of Rodrigo, but the composer was not satisfied with it. Certainly the book was written from the author's heart, but it suffered from a paucity of reflection, analysis, and understanding of Rodrigo's work. Further, it lacks the photographic illustrations on whose inclusion Victoria Kamhi had insisted. The result was a disappointment, though Rodrigo was careful not to offend his friend. Still, he must have told him something in a letter that was not preserved, one that merited a bitter reply from Sopeña.[78]

Finally, he experienced one more disappointment: the poor reception of a piece of lightweight musical theater in collaboration with Federico Moreno Torroba, author of some of the best zarzuelas of the 1930s. The work debuted by Rodrigo and Moreno Torroba on 22 May 1946, at the Teatro Calderón of Madrid, was the operetta *El duende azul* (The Blue Elf). In it, Rodrigo recycled *La chanson de ma vie* (1939) and a few other numbers presented in 1943 to the star Celia Gámez (1905–1992) that she never sang.[79] The musicians, in their self-critique, were wondering the same thing that zarzuela aficionados in Madrid were no doubt asking: "Torroba and Rodrigo, operetta composers?" The authors themselves had an answer: "In art, the work matters as much as the genre. Whoever disagrees shows he is not enough of an artist. In art there is also another heaven in which all genres, large and small, fraternize when they are good."[80] They had bad luck, and Rodrigo confidentially wrote to fellow composer Rafael Rodríguez Albert, "The music went over very well, but that did not stop the critics from treating us poorly. [. . .] the show has had to fold after twenty-five performances."[81]

After Manuel de Falla's death in Argentina on 14 November 1946, the Spanish government made it an affair of state to repatriate his remains.[82] The intense labor of Spanish diplomats was successful thanks to the support of Argentine president Juan Perón, who had emerged in the postwar era as one of Franco's principal allies, while the United States and the European powers marginalized Spain for its Germanocentric "neutrality" during the war. Indeed, Spain's fragile political stability depended greatly on the support it received from Argentina, especially the two merchant ships that transported tons of wheat every month to Spain. One of these ships also transported Falla's body to the port of Santa Cruz de Tenerife, in the Canary Islands, after which an army frigate completed its journey to Cádiz on 9 January 1947. On that very day, Falla's corpse was interred in the crypt of the cathedral, with the greatest honors of the Spanish state. Franco did not attend the funeral, perhaps to make his displeasure known about the composer's attitude in his final years. But Rodrigo traveled to Cádiz to pay his last respects to Falla, for as he wrote to Mompou, "I did not wish to fail to do my duty for the person who on two occasions of my life had done for my sake all that he could."[83]

Rodrigo must have composed *Invocación y danza* for guitar around this period, although it would not debut until many years later. In 1961, the composer rescued his work from Sainz de la Maza's possession and sent it to the contest "Coupe de la guitar," announced by the Office de Radiodiffusion-Télévision Française (ORTF). Rodrigo won first prize, and in a stroke of irony, second prize went to the *Homenaje a la guitarra* by Eduardo Sainz de la Maza, another of Regino's brothers.

The *Invocación* is marked *lontano* (distant) *ad libitum*, and the *pianissimo* dynamic level together with poignant dissonances and the use of artificial harmonics create an air of mystery and suspense. Especially striking is the bimodal juxtaposition of D Lydian in the bass with A Aeolian in the treble melody. The consequent cross relations between F♯ and F♮, along with the prominent tritone between G♯ and D, may seem strikingly novel in Rodrigo's harmonic language, until we recall exactly this sort of bitonal procedure in the "Preludio" of his *Suite para piano*. Here, however, the effect is merely disquieting rather than obstreperous. He soon repeats this procedure (mm. 14–21), but transposed to A Lydian in the bass and D Aeolian in the treble. At this point there is a clear reference to the main theme of Falla's ballet *El amor brujo*, within a bimodal context, which can be understood as a kind of sonorous enchantment. But Rodrigo does not dwell on this reminiscence for long, and in mm. 27–34, he emphasizes a minor-second motive derived from the Andalusian scale and that recalls the main theme of Falla's *Homenaje a Debussy* for guitar, which in turn is based on the initial theme of Debussy's "Soirée dans Grenade," from *Estampes*. What we have here, then, is a quotation of a quotation. Rodrigo's use of bimodality in these first two sections of his *Invocación* reproduces and brings up to date the enchantment that Falla derived from Debussy's use of the Andalusian mode in works that evoked Spain.

More than merely two successive movements without transition, *Invocación y danza* could be defined as a fantasy with a complex structure articulated by the recurrence of a *danza* that Rodrigo calls a *polo*, a traditional Andalusian song and dance in lively triple meter. This appears three times, as an interruption within a rhapsodic discourse. In its first appearance, the "Polo" is in B minor (mm. 67–86); the second time, in F♯ minor (mm. 97–116); and the last time, in D minor (mm. 176–194). The symmetrical phrasing of this dance (two phrases of 4 + 4 measures plus another of 4 measures at the end), its clear tonal definition, and its resolution by means of Andalusian cadences in the corresponding Phrygian modes (F♯, C♯, and A) point to a kind of *copla* (dance song) separated by *falsetas*, virtuosic scalar runs and rapid glissando-like arpeggios on the guitar. The overall harmonic structure exhibits a juxtaposition of D major and minor with A Phrygian, though the work concludes quietly on an A chord without a third. The hollow fifths and fourths are a time-honored rhetorical device suggesting the absence of life.

This level of compositional sophistication and technical detail was virtually without precedent in the guitar repertoire, and it speaks to the profound respect that Rodrigo paid to Falla in this tribute. Indeed, some of the techniques here would be considered "extended" in comparison with guitar works typical of the 1940s, and all of it lay far beyond the capacities of Sainz de la Maza. Once more, as in the *Preludio al atardecer* and the *Tocata*, Rodrigo had imagined and created a music for the guitar of the future. Fortunately for him, on this occasion he was able to attend the debut of *Invocación y danza*, when the Venezuelan virtuoso Alirio Díaz interpreted it for the first time in 1962, at the Mai Musical de Bordeaux (May Musical of Bordeaux).

Voice and Orchestra

In the last five years of the 1940s, Rodrigo revealed the confluence of his calling as a composer of art songs and the mastery he had achieved as a symphonic composer. He paid tribute to an audience that had always welcomed him better than the one in Madrid, by debuting in Barcelona the seven songs in Catalan with orchestral accompaniment, divided into two sets: *Quatre cançons en llengua catalana* and *Tríptic de Mossèn Cinto*. The *Quatre cançons* are two compositions from the 1930s, the *Cançó del teuladí* (1934) and *Canticel* (1935), which in their transcription from piano to orchestra attain a suitable and powerful broadening.

They are completed with two other songs, apparently conceived from the start with orchestral accompaniment: "L'inquietut primaveral de la donzella," on a sonnet of Josep Massó i Ventós, and "Brollador gentil," on a poem by Joan Maria Guasch i Miró. Rodrigo was clearly referring to "L'inquietut primaveral" when he wrote, "There exists one poem out of the four which is a little bit Verlainian-Catalanesque-Debussyan-Rodrigan."[84] It has all these components and also introduces a quote from the second phrase of the *Cançó del teuladí*, giving this set the appearance of forming a cycle.

Tríptic de Mossèn Cinto is a song cycle with orchestral accompaniment, one whose sketches and notes date from the mid-1930s. The Rodrigos left these behind in Paris, where Antonio Iglesias recovered them. Hence, the composer could devote the summer of 1946 to the completion of this new masterpiece in his symphonic catalogue.[85] It is a work that goes back to a moment of earlier creativity, separated from the debut by only a few years, but with the historical break of the Civil and World War II. That explains the traits in "L'inquietut primaveral de la donzella" so characteristic of the Franco-Spanish avant-garde between the world wars. These reminiscences are even clearer in the kinship in sonority of the second movement of the *Tríptic de Mossèn Cinto*, "Lo violí de Sant Francesc," to the *Sinfonietta* (1925) by Ernesto Halffter. The orchestration of three songs forming this triptych displays savoir faire in its abundance of descriptive details and the great demands made on the orchestra interpreting it.

Much of the success that these songs enjoyed at their debut was due to their exaltation of the Catalan language and one of its most eminent figures, Jacinto Verdaguer. They appealed to the acute cultural sensitivity of the Catalan people, whose independent streak was strongly suppressed by the Franco regime. Another factor contributing to that success was the performance at the premiere by Catalan soprano Victoria de los Ángeles, then at the start of her professional career. For Rodrigo, her great interpretative gift was her capacity to intuit the intentions of the composer, beyond what was written down. Her first truly important debut was the *Tríptic de Mossèn Cinto*, which was dedicated to her and performed at the Palau de la Música in the inaugural concert of the 1946–47 season, with the Orquesta Filarmónica under the direction of Juan Pich Santasusana. Thereafter the *Tríptic* made its Madrid debut at the Palacio de la Música, once again with Victoria de los Ángeles as soloist, and the Orquesta Nacional de España conducted by Ataúlfo Argenta, on 7 November 1947.

Rodrigo perhaps planned the composition of his *Romance del Comendador de Ocaña* for the National Music Contest of 1945, whose theme was "a poem for orchestra and song on a poem by a Spanish writer of the seventeenth century."[86] However, Rodrigo's composition for soprano and orchestra, not completed till 1947, used instead verses from Lope de Vega's play *Peribáñez y el Comendador de Ocaña*, rearranged by the philologist Joaquín de Entrambasaguas in the form of a ballad.

In this work in A Phrygian, Rodrigo once again makes a show of sophistication in harmonic organization. The mode serves as a basis for a completely syllabic song with the fluidity and repetitive character of traditional ballads, reinforced by the disciplined reiteration of one eight-syllable line of text for each measure with eight notes (with the first and the final two longer, and with the penultimate lightly ornamented). The composer nonetheless avoids monotony by introducing some very discreet madrigalisms, such as those appearing on the words "cabalgando" (galloping), reinforced by the brass, "halcón" (falcon), where the soprano achieves the highest point of her song, and "florido" (florid), over which there appears the longest melisma in the form of a quintuplet, successively imitated by the clarinet, oboe, and flute. This piece calls for brilliance both on the part of the soloist and the orchestra. Rodrigo dedicated the work to Lola Rodríguez Aragón, who would premiere it in the Spanish capital with the Orquesta de Cámara de Madrid conducted by Argenta.

One of the main final responsibilities of Rodrigo as a consultant of Radio Nacional de España consisted of forming a chamber orchestra.[87] This initiative culminated with the formation of the Orquesta de Cámara de Radio Nacional (National Radio Chamber

Orchestra), made up of performers of the Orquesta de Cámara de Madrid, under the direction of Argenta. On 29 May 1945, the Orquesta de Cámara of the Radio Nacional gave its inaugural concert with Argenta. Turina's *Oración del torero* was to precede Rodrigo's *Tres viejos aires de danza* on the program. More important was the inaugural program of the Radio Nacional broadcasts for America on the morning of 21 June 1945. On that occasion, after a speech by Franco, Argenta conducted Rodrigo's *Concierto de estío*, with Iniesta as soloist.[88] Rodrigo's intuition and experience were decisive in the initial phases of Argenta's career, and he went on to become the leading Spanish conductor of his time.[89]

However, the Orquesta de Cámara de Radio Nacional was short-lived. One month after its first appearance, there was a shake-up within the Spanish government, which, during the course of the Second World War, had swung from a Falangist orientation to a Catholic one. The change was transmitted to all levels of the state, and it reached Rodrigo in his position at Radio Nacional, where he was replaced by Leopoldo Querol. The composer did not forgive Querol, and what had been a friendly relationship changed as of the 1940s into an open hostility that affected the performance of the *Concierto heroico*, from which Rodrigo erased the dedication to the pianist. The changes affected as well the radiophonic orchestral group, which dissolved, giving way, through Querol's initiative, to the Orquesta Sinfónica de Radio Nacional (National Radio Symphony Orchestra). Argenta continued his work as conductor of the Orquesta de Cámara de Madrid, which, on 5 April 1948, at the Teatro Español of Madrid, debuted the *Romance del Comendador de Ocaña*, with Lola Rodríguez Aragón as soloist.

Rodríguez Aragón, besides being an extraordinary soprano who specialized in art song, was also a great teacher.[90] Two months before she sang Rodrigo's ballad, on 4 February 1948, four female students of hers had debuted the original version with piano accompaniment of his *Cuatro madrigales amatorios*, at the Círculo Medina of Madrid. The same sopranos—Blanca María Seoane, Celia Langa, María de los Ángeles Morales, and Carmen Pérez Durias—would be featured along with the bass

Chano Gonzalo at the debut of Rodrigo's tone poem *Ausencias de Dulcinea*, the work which, along with the *Concierto de Aranjuez*, Rodrigo held in highest esteem.

The *Cuatro madrigales amatorios* retain the character of sixteenth-century music on which they are based, but at the same time bring that music into the twentieth century and transform it into a small cycle on love. Rodrigo did not indicate their origin probably because of the extend of his modifications.

When the madrigals debuted, Rodrigo was finishing a composition intended for the contest announced by the Ministerio de Educación Nacional (Ministry of National Education) to commemorate the fourth centennial of Cervantes's birth. The contest offered three texts by Cervantes on which the composers might base their works.[91] Rodrigo took the verses that Don Quijote wrote during his penance in the Sierra Morena ("Trees, grasses, and plants"),[92] and he decided to compose his work for bass and four sopranos, besides the "large orchestra" called for in the contest rules.

However, in the summer of 1947, Rodrigo had suffered an acute inflammation of the right eye, "with fever and severe pain,"[93] and he lost any remaining ability to distinguish light and dark. That affliction and the composition of the *Cuatro madrigales amatorios* took up much of the time he needed to create the Cervantine composition. Hence, waiting until the last minute as always, in January 1948 he wrote to Sopeña, "I go out only a little, very little, and I don't go to concerts since I am deep in the middle of Don Quijote."[94]

Rodrigo was a man of letters as well as notes. An avid devotee of literature, his tastes were wide-ranging (though some of his preferences are predictable). Among these was *Don Quijote* by Miguel de Cervantes. Thus, when the competition was announced, he hoisted his lance and charged the windmill, not necessarily because he believed so much in competitions per se but because the creative challenge proved irresistible. The text Rodrigo had chosen was the poem recited by the knight errant in chapter 26 of part I, and he completed it in about six weeks. Table 6.1 presents the original with a modern English translation.

TABLE 6.1 **Poem recited by Don Quijote,
Part I, Chapter 26**[95]

Árboles, yerbas y plantas	Trees, grasses, and plants
que en aqueste sitio estáis,	That stand in this place,
tan altos, verdes y tantas,	So lofty, green, and many,
si de mi mal no os holgáis,	If my ill does not gladden you,
escuchad mis quejas santas.	Listen to my sacred plaints.
Mi dolor no os alborote,	May my pain not alarm you,
aunque más terrible sea;	However terrible it may be;
pues, por pagaros escote,	Since, to pay you his share,
aquí lloró don Quijote	Here lamented Don Quixote
ausencias de Dulcinea	Absences of Dulcinea
del Toboso.	Del Toboso.
Es aquí el lugar adonde	Here is the place
el amador más leal	The most loyal lover
de su señora se esconde,	Of his lady is hiding,
y ha venido a tanto mal	And has come to so much evil
sin saber cómo o por dónde.	Without knowing how or where.
Tráele amor al estricote,	Love gives him a rough time,
que es de muy mala ralea;	For love is quite a lowlife;
y así, hasta hinchar un pipote,	And thus, until he filled up a keg
	[with tears],
aquí lloró don Quijote	Here lamented Don Quixote
ausencias de Dulcinea	Absences of Dulcinea
del Toboso.	Del Toboso.
Buscando las aventuras	Looking for adventures
por entre las duras peñas,	From amidst the hard boulders,
maldiciendo entrañas duras,	Cursing hard hearts,
que entre riscos y entre breñas	For among crags and among rough grounds
halla el triste desventuras,	The hapless one finds misfortunes,
hirióle amor con su azote,	Love wounded him with his whip,
no con su blanda correa;	Not with his soft strap;
y en tocándole el cogote,	And while he touched his nape,
aquí lloró don Quijote	Here lamented Don Quixote
ausencias de Dulcinea	Absences of Dulcinea
del Toboso	Del Toboso.

These comically clumsy verses reveal three essential aspects of the don's psyche: the valorous knight errant, the lovelorn poet, and the delusional lunatic. Rodrigo's challenge, then, was to find the musical means to express and reconcile all three of these personality disorders within fifteen minutes, alternating and eliding grandeur and irony. By any aesthetic standard, he succeeded, and the judges were unanimous in awarding him that year's prize.

Nelson Orringer states that the poem is made up of six *quintillas*, stanzas with five octosyllabic lines and usually rhymed ababa. This was a popular poetic form during the Siglo de Oro, Spain's Golden Age, of which Cervantes stands as perhaps the chief representative. Fernández Bahillo analyzes it somewhat differently, as three *décimas* (ten-line stanzas) and a final refrain, each with the structure ababa-cdccd. He further deems the use of unpoetic words like *estricote, alborote, pipote, escote,* and *cogote* as forced rhymes that deliberately poke fun at the conventions of Renaissance love poetry.[96] As is always the case with Rodrigo's text settings, the words are not merely hooks on which to hang the music; rather, the music is "organized around expressing the contents of the poem, the tempos, vocal registers, dynamics, and instrumentation to express agitation, insanity, grandeur, heroism, sublime amorous contemplation, and mystic exaltation."[97] All of this bears some resemblance to the so-called doctrine of the affections that governed Baroque music.

As we already saw in chapter 2, Rodrigo made no secret of the inspiration he drew from Falla's puppet opera *El retablo de maese Pedro*, based on a comical episode from Cervantes's novel, which was composed and premiered a quarter of a century earlier. As in that work, the part of Don Quijote is sung by a bass. Here, the externalized voice of Dulcinea is given to four sopranos, as "Rodrigo himself explained his use of four sopranos 'because neither to the north, to the south, to the east, nor the west will Don Quijote find that phantom that is Dulcinea.'"[98] The substantial orchestra includes not only the usual complement of strings but also ample brass and woodwind sections, along with percussion and two harps. The voices and instruments together provide Rodrigo with all the sonic pigments he required to paint both the exterior and interior realities of this poetic vignette.

Just like Falla's opera, this work begins with a brass fanfare, in this case proclaiming the age of chivalry of which Don Quijote is a notorious representative. Notably, there is a familiar motive of three short notes followed by a longer note, likely an allusion to the opening of Beethoven's Fifth Symphony and in the same key of C minor. Don Quijote is nothing if not a man of destiny, even if that destiny has brought him to this unhappy pass.[99] The woodwinds will soon serve to convey his stature as a knight errant, while the strings suggest his avocation as a poet in love. The dual harps convey the world of his vivid imagination, which veers into insanity, especially in their delirious glissandi. Rodrigo also employs harmony, texture, and tempos to express the dramatic situation.

Rodrigo's penchant for archaism finds an appropriate outlet in modal harmonies that comport with the period in which the story takes place, the late Renaissance and early Baroque. Fernández Bahillo also points out that not only do modes convey an earlier epoch, but they also connect Don Quijote with the real world by their correspondence with a historical musical language. This is especially true of a brief but poignant refrain that tenderly expresses his love for Dulcinea and whose modality is "from the epoch" and thus "of the real world" (musical ex. 6.2).[100] This cell always appears in the same key of C minor, the prevailing tonality in this work, except at the end, when it is in B minor. That choice of tonal center was probably no mere coincidence, as the medieval B mode is also known as "Locrian": B–C–D–E–F–G–A. Traditionally it was associated with madness because of the prominence of the tritone between the "tonic" and "dominant" of B and F.

The sopranos are the musical manifestation of the otherwise immaterial Dulcinea, presenting the poetic refrain "Dulcinea del Toboso" in contrapuntal textures that harken back to the

Musical ex. 6.2: *Ausencias de Dulcinea*, Love motive, mm. 17–19 madrigals of the late sixteenth century. (El Toboso is a town in the province of Toledo, Castile-La Mancha, central Spain.) But their wayward chromaticism, though it might find a precedent in the madrigals of Carlo Gesualdo, also suggests a disconnection from corporeal reality, ultimately telling us more about Don Quijote's mental state than about her. Strident dissonance is used throughout the work to express his psychological instability. This is reinforced by the numerous changes in tempo that correspond to the knight's shifting moods. As Fernández Bahillo sums them up, "*Adagio maestoso* for the proclamation, *Molto tranquillo* for declarations of love and lyric sublimation, *Tranquillo* in moments of exposition or description, and *animatos* or *agitatos* with their respective *piu* for moments of major excitation, insanity, or anguish."[101]

In addition to these, dramatic changes in dynamics and registers also take the knight's emotional temperature. Especially evocative are Baroque-style echo effects that create a sense of the mountainous landscape in which Don Quijote has sought hermitic refuge. On a more metaphorical level, these effects may also intimate a contrast between reality and imagination as a mere echo of the real world. As the sopranos fade out at the end of the work, we sense Dulcinea's ephemerality, as she disappears into nothing at all, the same nothing whence she came, since she does not actually exist outside of Don Quijote's cerebrum. But even as nothing more than a "verbal sign,"[102] she has real power to influence the knight's inner and outer lives.

Another evocation of the natural world is Rodrigo's signature cuckoo call in mm. 45 and 161–164. This has multiple meanings, not only as the composer's signature, but also both the physical reality Don Quijote inhabits and his lunacy.[103] But this brings us to a bird's-eye view of the work and Rodrigo's philosophy of composition in general. As Nelson Orringer points out:

Joaquín Rodrigo wrote that music arose in response to the human need to make an image of the surrounding world. Affected by [philosopher José Ortega y Gasset's] view of life as the interaction of self and circumstance, Rodrigo would eventually attribute to music enough

subtlety to paint even [living] beings in the artist's
ambience with perceptible properties. [. . .] Rodrigo
applies that conception to music itself when making his
musical setting of Don Quijote's quintillas on Dulcinea's
absence. Hence, the work becomes an exercise in music
making a statement on music itself.[104]

And thus, Rodrigo may well have seen something of himself
in Don Quijote, for just as Dulcinea was an invisible presence who
could only be suggested through verbal and musical symbols,
so the exterior world of physical objects, as he imagined them,
was something to which he gave symphonic substance in this
work—a work that for all its archaisms could have originated
only in the twentieth century and still sounds strikingly modern.

Concerto in modo galante (1949) and International Projection

After a visit that the great cellist Gaspar Cassadó made to the
Vitoria Seminary in 1946, Sopeña wrote to Rodrigo, "He has been
very affectionate with me and showed a great interest in seeing me [. . .] and an even greater interest that I influence you to
make a cello concerto. This proposal seems very important to
me: it is the first occasion that a genuinely international performer approaches you."[105] Several days before, the composer, in
his function as critic, had referred to Cassadó as "the great voice
of the Spanish cello."[106] That voice was also capable of confronting the hostility of Pablo Casals, his teacher, regarding the political situation in Spain. All this, united to Rodrigo's passion for
the cello, smoothed the way for the union of the composer and
the performer in what would be the finale of a series of works for
cello soloist and orchestra that debuted in the 1940s.

As Sopeña wished, Rodrigo agreed in 1946 to write Cassadó
a work for cello and orchestra, but on one condition: that it not
be a concerto. Thus, he began to think about calling it "Tres
fragmentos sinfónicos" (Three Symphonic Fragments), but this
produced nothing more than a mental block. He then began to
think of it as a sinfonía concertante, and, in the same way that

the "foundational" theme of the *Concierto de Aranjuez* had come to life, there arose with the stroke of his pen the main theme of a work that, as the composer immediately understood, could no longer be a *sinfonía concertante*. It was a full-fledged concerto.

Furthermore, the same theme situated the piece in a very definite time and mood: the eighteenth century's *style galant*, a transitional phase from the Baroque period to the Classical. According to Rodrigo, "If the theme seemed gallant, appropriate for a concerto, for a gallant concerto, and if it was proper for the voice and manners of the cello, then cello, elegance, or gallantry and concerto had to take us close to an epoch and, carrying things to their extreme, to one musician: Boccherini. Boccherini, Italian and Spanish, composer and cellist."[107]

In his reluctance to tackle yet another concerto, Rodrigo was once more leaning, as in the *Concierto heroico*, toward a form with descriptive elements that one suspects are also related to the cellist, who not only commissioned the composition but also made a copy of it. Thus he shared for some summer days moments of intimacy with the Rodrigos in their chalet in Torre-lodones, northwest of Madrid. There, according to Kamhi, illumined at times by one lone candle due to electrical restrictions, "in the idyllic calm of the country, interrupted only from time to time by the scream of some nocturnal bird, the two friends stayed up working until four in the morning."[108] And there they would talk nonsense about a theme that later recurs time and again in their correspondence: the "flirt," the English word for Spanish *galanteo*. "Don't do too much *flirting*, [. . .] for Vicky [Kamhi] is not willing to tolerate the *genius* of the great composer" ("No hagas demasiado *flirt* [. . .] que Vicky no está dispuesta a aguantar la *genialidad* del gran compositor"), Cassadó wrote him.[109] And as in the composing of the guitar concerto, the last part of the cello concerto that Rodrigo composed, even after the days in which he worked with Cassadó in Torrelodones, was the first movement, whose main theme derives directly from the concerto's second movement, the Adagietto.

Though Rodrigo conceived of this work as a set of "symphonic fragments" instead of a concerto, he was never prepared to discard tradition entirely, and it features the traditional fast-slow-fast sequence of movement tempos. And the eighteenth century peeks through in other ways, especially in a clear thematic debt to Luigi Boccherini and borrowings from Domenico Scarlatti, two preeminent Italian musicians who made their careers in Madrid and whose works often evoke Spanish folklore, in the use of typically Spanish bolero-style rhythms and the alternation of compound duple and triple meters (6/8 and 3/4), or hemiola.

The concerto begins with the solo cello presenting an accompanimental pattern in an ostinato rhythm, marked *Allegretto grazioso*. The principal theme does not actually appear in the cello until m. 32, marked *con galantería* and featuring a Baroque-style "walking bass" in the orchestra. Rodrigo's love of orchestral color is soon apparent in the deployment of horns, trumpets, and clarinets, and this emphasis on winds instead of strings is definitely a neoclassical trait. The secondary theme is marked *cantabile* and *dolce*. Though the motor rhythms stop, it has in common with the first theme an eighth-and-two-sixteenths motive. The principal theme was in F major, while this secondary theme is now in A, revealing an attraction to third-related keys atypical of the Classical period. Riotous dissonance adds harmonic spice to Rodrigo's development, and after the cadenza, a recapitulation offers varied restatements of the principal and secondary themes. The coda reprises the introductory material and brings the movement to a breathtaking climax with some very virtuosic bowing on the cello.

The second movement is in a kind of rounded-binary form: ABA'B'. It is in D minor and thus its tonic, in tandem with the F and A tonal centers of the first movement, forms a D-minor triad. This kind of tonal planning is typical of the composer. The orchestra commences with an introductory "frame" followed by the cello solo, which presents the A theme (musical ex. 6.3). Marked *nostalgico ma semplice*, it is clearly something new, but it shares in common with the first movement a motive of an eighth note followed by two sixteenths. It is characteristic of Rodrigo to unify his score in this way.

There is also a similar alternation of duple and triple meters. The B section commences at m. 67 and is marked *Allegretto rustico (senza affrettare)*. The solo part features a drone, giving the harmony a suitably pastoral effect. And when the melody moves to the orchestra, the cello accompanies it with drones played in harmonics. Thus, a certain folklike simplicity prevails here that offers welcome contrast from the previous animation. But that energy will not remain suppressed for long, and the frenzy soon returns, rife with comically strident dissonances in multiple stops. The A material reappears at m. 209, and there is a brief reminiscence of the B theme at m. 240. First lively rhythms and then "distant" (*lontano*) harmonic drones in the cello bring the movement to a satisfying conclusion, in D major rather than minor.

The third movement is a kind of rondo, featuring hemiolas in 6/8 meter, a time signature we usually associate with the gigue, though here the rhythms evoke the Spanish *zapateado*. As it was in the beginning, the cello soloist presents the main theme right at the outset. There is some furiously virtuosic bowing that exudes the same riotous good spirits we heard in the last movement of the *Aranjuez*. Tonally we have come full circle, as the music is once again in the F major of the first movement. As Ana Llorens points out, there are some formal anomalies here, as the third statement of A also inserts the B theme at m. 180, right before the D section. She speculates that the composer wanted to avoid being quite so predictable, to "avoid the marked

Musical ex. 6.3: *Concerto in modo galante*, second movement, A theme, mm. 5–7

sectionality of the form."[110] The overall form, then, could be dia-
grammed as ABACA(B)DA.

To the *Concierto de Aranjuez* for guitar, the *Concierto heroico*
for piano, and the *Concierto de estío* for violin was now added
the *Concerto in modo galante* for cello, which Cassadó debuted
on 4 November 1949 at the Palacio de la Música in Madrid with
the Orquesta Nacional directed by Argenta.[111] Some days afterwards, Eduardo Toldrá with Cassadó and the Orquesta Municipal
de Barcelona presented it to the Catalan public. It enjoyed great
success, but Rodrigo could not attend these concerts because he
was in Buenos Aires with his wife. Spain's need to come out of
the isolation to which it had been subjected at the end of the
Second World War was pressing, and the main avenue of escape
from this isolation passed through the Argentina of Perón,
whose presidency was a lifeline to the Franco regime.[112] Joaquín
and Victoria were aiding in that escape.

The Rodrigos had already managed to break the diplomatic
siege in May 1947 by traveling to Paris to pick up Victoria Kamhi's mother, who, after spending the war in France, was going
to live with them in Spain. By taking advantage of the family
reason for the trip, our composer was able to give a concert
for the Institute of Hispanic Studies at the Sorbonne, which
the correspondent of *ABC* celebrated in his news report of May
8 as the "heartfelt inauguration of cultural relations, renovated and never expired between the two nations."[113] This is
the first indication of Rodrigo's duties in the realm of cultural
diplomacy, but the appreciation of the correspondent was premature, as France kept its border with Spain closed until February 1948. Rodrigo would not be able to return there until the
following year.

Rodrigo returned to France in his second departure from
Spain after World War II. Accompanied by his wife and the soprano
Consuelo Rubio, he gave a recital of his works at the College of
Spain of the Parisian Cité Universitaire on 20 May 1949. Shortly
before, Sopeña had written him with very Falangist nostalgia,
"God willing, this trip will be fruitful, and you will set the bases

to stay there when necessary. Here, musically speaking, there is nothing to do, Joaquín: the beautiful times of hopes, dreams, and community have passed."[114] What had definitely passed was the time of the Falange and its fascist dreams; what remained behind, however, was the ossified totalitarian state, anticommunist and Catholic. None of this prevented Spain's increasing consolidation within the Western bloc, with help from the Vatican. But this integration proceeded in ironic conjunction with the dictatorial singularity of its political regime.

While the terms of that integration were mainly being defined and instituted by the United States, there remained Argentina, whither went Rodrigo in 1949 with his wife, in a rather improvised trip that was as much an artistic tour as it was a diplomatic mission on behalf of the Institute of Hispanic Culture.[115] They arrived in Buenos Aires on September 12, and on December 1 they returned via the port of Bilbao.[116] They had spent two long months of intense activity: recitals, lectures, radio programs, cocktail parties in their honor, and a great Hispano-Argentine festival at the Teatro Colón on November 7, during which *Ausencias de Dulcinea* and the *Concierto de estío* were performed. It was a fine culmination of a decade of Rodrigo's creative activity, one that prompted Sopeña's title for him in 1949 as "the musician of these years."[117]

The *Concierto de Aranjuez* in the Decade of the 1940s

The *Concierto de Aranjuez* did not go with Rodrigo on his Argentine excursion, but Sainz de la Maza had already debuted it in Buenos Aires on 26 June 1947.[118] It was the first journey out of Spain for Rodrigo's guitar concerto since its 1943 performance in Lisbon. Six long years of being locked up did not manage to snuff out its fire; on the contrary, it seems that there was increasing interest in this concerto.

An exceptional witness to the Buenos Aires debut of the *Concierto de Aranjuez* in 1947 was Andrés Segovia, who had had in his possession a reduction of the score with an accompaniment of the work since 1946. Segovia wrote to Rodrigo,

The *Concierto de Aranjuez* is delightful, and I am going
to work on it with zeal. In Washington, two years ago, a
version for guitar and piano was handed to me, [. . .] but
the coordination of the first movement was mutilated
and the rest of the copy had obscene errors. I thus did
not form an exact judgment until I listened to it in
Buenos Aires. And naturally, I held myself back from
taking any step toward it, while considering it almost
the property of its performer. It seemed legitimate to
me that, with such a good passport, Regino [Sainz de
la Maza] travel the musical world. [. . .] It's a pity that
the performance of such a graceful composition has
remained confined for years and years to the musical
life of Spain. But, in the end, as regards the possibility
of exporting it, I will try to make up for lost time. [. . .]
I think that I am going to take the liberty of revising
the guitar part, so that it may achieve a fuller sonority
in some passages. When I see the score, I will follow or
abandon this resolve.[119]

Despite the warm enthusiasm for the work that he conveyed
to Rodrigo, Segovia never played the *Concierto de Aranjuez*.[120] In
fact, it was Ida Presti who gave it a Parisian premiere, at the Salle
Pleyel on 24 March 1949, with an orchestra of young university
students.[121] Sainz de la Maza's exclusive rights to the *Concierto
de Aranjuez* had expired, and a new generation of guitarists
was now prepared to relieve him and take that composition to
new audiences.

What indeed had great repercussions was the arrival of the
Concierto de Aranjuez into the capable hands of Narciso Yepes,
a young guitarist with enormous technical facility, one whose
international career would be launched in the 1950s precisely as
a result of his interpretation of Rodrigo's increasingly renowned
concerto. His debut with the Orquesta de Cámara de Madrid
under the baton of Argenta took place at Madrid's Teatro Español
on 16 December 1947. It was a great event, one attended by both
Sainz de la Maza and Rodrigo in their capacity as music critics

for *ABC* and *Marca*, respectively. Rodrigo, who had to be delicate with Sainz de la Maza, limited himself to predicting the "great triumphs" that Yepes would have in his long concert career.[122]

With Yepes, the *Concierto de Aranjuez* was to enter a new phase. Sainz de la Maza, however, had the privilege of making the first commercial recording of this work, with the Orquesta Nacional de España directed by Argenta in 1947 and occupying three 78-rpm records on the Columbia label (RG 16066, 16067, and 16068). This format, prior to the microgroove, with discs of 30 centimeters in diameter, only allowed for four minutes of recording on each side. Hence, each movement of the concerto was shared between the two sides of one record. This fact had an important implication in the interpretation of the famous "Adagio," which, at its original tempo, lasted over ten minutes. Argenta and Sainz de la Maza found it necessary to speed up their version of this movement to cut off the two minutes that exceeded the capacity of the 78-rpm record.[123]

Rodrigo was aware of the importance of such recordings in disseminating his music. Thus, when the review *Ritmo* took a poll among musical and cultural personalities in December 1945 about what would be their wishes for the next year, several of them expressed their interest in the publication of their music. Rodrigo, however, showed that he was ahead of them when he answered, "What I most desire is that at last there be an organism that publishes and makes impressions of Spanish music on records, without which most efforts of musicians in composing their works, and those of the different organisms in creating orchestras, conservatories, etc., will be irrevocably lost."[124]

The 1947 recording of the *Concierto de Aranjuez* satisfied the composer's wishes. Although it did not begin to appear in Columbia's catalogue until 1948, 78's of the *Aranjuez* were already in circulation in the summer of 1947.[125] Still, on 2 March 1949, Argenta and Yepes made a non-commercial recording of the *Aranjuez* on four 78's in the studios of Radio Genève, with the Orchestre de la Suisse Romande.[126]

Now the only step left to be taken was to publish the score of the *Concierto de Aranjuez*, without ceding rights to any publisher.

Rodrigo counted on the support and backing of Luis de Urquijo, who had just inherited from his father the title of Marqués de Bolarque and, with it, the presidency of the Sociedad de Estudios y Publicaciones (Society of Studies and Publications) that belonged to the financial framework of the Urquijo Bank. There, in 1949, three volumes were published: one with the reduction for guitar and piano for 90 pesetas per copy; the orchestral score for 200 pesetas; and another with complete materials for orchestra that cost 800 pesetas. The total cost of the edition was 31,248 pesetas.[127] Never in the history of twentieth-century Spanish music had so costly an edition been made of a musical composition. And this was just the beginning.

Chapter 7

Between Creation and Depression

(1950–1962)

Academician of Fine Arts

The Academy of Fine Arts admitted Rodrigo as an academician on 18 November 1951, only four days before his forty-ninth birthday. For him it was a great day, although more than one among the academicians came out doubting whether a madman had come into their midst in so illustrious an institution. Such was the shock caused by the dissonances that Rodrigo had unleashed on the piano in that solemn ceremony, such the surprise and dismay, that our composer regained the mischievous smile of the *enfant terrible* that he displayed in early youth, when he enjoyed provoking the conservative Valencia public by following to the letter a recommendation of Falla's: "may everyone follow his own tastes and tendencies; in that fashion, whether he amused the others or not, he will at least manage to amuse himself [. . .] which is no small undertaking. [. . .] [W]hoever amuses himself by sticking to his job has many possibilities of amusing others as well."[1] The

The day of his admission as academician of Fine Arts

academicians who were amused that evening, and the friends of
Rodrigo accompanying him—among them, the new Minister of
National Education, Joaquín Ruiz-Giménez—would understand
that the musician's gesture this time was not so much a provo-
cation as a declaration of the principles that had elevated him to
the official elite of Spanish art.

With the death of Antonio Fernández Bordas in February 1950, the vacancy that the distinguished violinist left in
the Academy of Fine Arts was an opportunity for Rodrigo to
strengthen his position at the apex of Spanish music. Hence,
Rodrigo was institutionally recognized as the successor of Falla

and Turina. A year and a half after his election, he honored the institution with a memorable entrance into it. The musician took this very seriously: at the 1951 investiture, besides delivering a speech entitled "Técnica enseñada e inspiración no aprendida" (Taught Technique and Unlearned Inspiration), one of his best essays and one of the keys for knowing his ideas as a composer, he debuted on the piano his five *Sonatas de Castilla (con toccata a modo de pregón)* (Sonatas of Castile with a Toccata in the Manner of a Street Vendor's Cry). Rodrigo's speech defines his position and his aspirations within the history of Spanish music. Yet, at the same time, it expresses his frustration as a creator and confesses his inability to find a path toward a new Spanish music, one diverging from the blending of traditional folklore with classical forms. At this intersection of what is local and what is global, "Albéniz grows impatient and burns out; Falla feels anguish and grows sterile; Turina accommodates himself and languishes."[2]

At the same time that he set down these reflections, he was completing his catalogue of piano music and, in response to his creative crisis, he divided it into two diametrically opposed sets: his *Cuatro piezas andaluzas* ("El vendedor de chanquetes," "Crepúsculo sobre el Guadalquivir," "Seguidillas del diablo," and "Barquitos de Cádiz"), beautiful, virtuosic pieces, with a warm, picturesque element, though filled with details of the composer's mature style; and the *Sonatas de Castilla*, which served as the culmination of his speech, leaving the audience openmouthed.

Rodrigo's best music arises precisely from the tension between what is "Spanish" and what is "universal." Hence, the speech arose from the recollection of a phrase uttered by Falla and cited in the prologue to the *Abbreviated Encyclopedia of Music* by Turina, which Rodrigo now paraphrased: "Technique is learned, but not taught."[3] Although he errs in quoting Falla's sentence, Rodrigo hits the mark in its meaning: true art has no rules but rather creates them in an introspective process of learning; it does not assimilate them by reproducing models or by following teachings that can be compiled in textbooks. "Taught" art would be a dogmatic creation of little value. What is taught is the trade.

The mistake would arise by confusing technique with the trade, or, in the terms utilized by Falla, the art with the artifice.

Having distinguished between art and trade, between creating and teaching, Rodrigo concludes his speech by expressing the concern that Spanish composers, himself included, may be "building a music on a false premise": the confluence of taught techniques originating in the Central European musical mainstream with inspirations insufficiently grounded in the Spanish musical heritage. The problem seems to be the peripheral position of Spain, both in its geography and in its history; the symptoms of that position were the scarcity and intermittence of Spanish contributions to the history of music and the lack of a future. "Something is missing from our music. What is it? I think that if—as Romain Rolland was sharp enough to point out—'Italian music lacks weight, German music air, and French coal, that is, heat,' I would venture to say that Spanish music lacks horizons." This lack of a future is attributed by Rodrigo to finding oneself gripped, on the one hand, by European tradition—taught technique which is consequently not original, acquired by the composer by means of study—and, on the other hand, by Spanish music itself, like an exotic, barbarian, or semi-barbarian tradition, one quite unknown. "For to tell the truth, we know nothing about its origins, laws, or derivations." Rodrigo's conclusion is that the horizon will become clear the day that Spanish musicians are capable of creating an original technique, new, belonging to them, and adequate to their musical uniqueness.[4]

As the next part of the program, Prince José Eugenio de Baviera y Borbón replied to Rodrigo's speech with a brief biography of the composer. Rodrigo wanted to finish off the occasion with the premiere of a series of works in which he gave an example of untaught technique and learned inspiration (just the opposite of what he had dealt with in his speech): the polytonal technique that he himself had developed in the creation of works in an unmistakable style, without any model and without theorizing, as Milhaud had done, and the inspiration in a form like the sonata that he had learned and to which he gave some thematic contents that gather together essences of Castilian music, both traditional and historic.

The composer then sat down at the piano and attacked the "Toccata a modo de pregón," which led the way to the premiere of his *Sonatas de Castilla*. The surprise must have been overwhelming; the piano of the great institution had probably never been submitted to so severe a "disinfection." The first eight measures utilize the entire chromatic scale within a bitonal harmonic context juxtaposing A major (the key signature of the piece) with G♯ minor. The ensuing eight measures follow in this harmonic complex with a somewhat lighter texture that leads like a bridge to the repetition of the eight initial measures a fourth lower, suggesting a traditional "modulation to the dominant," now pitting E major against D♯ minor, confirmed with a change of key signature from the three sharps of A major to the four of E major. There is a period of closure for sixteen measures, in which Rodrigo limits himself to pounding out the two tonics *fortissimo*, and with a very simple distribution of rhythms and pitches: E in the left hand and D♯ in the right. The piece afterwards proceeds to a developmental section with a simple contrapuntal texture that unfolds a cycle of fifths in sequences of five measures: E major–B major (mm. 41–47, 48–52, 53–57, 58–62), F♯ major (mm. 63–67), C♯ major (mm. 68–72), and G♯ major (m. 73). In measure 79 we reach a tonal center adjacent to but very distant from E major, that is, E♭ major, which is the enharmonic equivalent of D♯, thereby continuing the succession of fifths. As of this point, there begins the harmonic withdrawal of this digressive section, which concludes with a prolongation of B major (mm. 91–100), from which the recapitulation is launched. The eight measures of the main theme and the eight of the bridge passage are repeated; however, instead of leading to the main theme in the dominant area, as in the first part, they make way for something like a variation of that material between measures 117 and 127 to continue with 25 measures of A in the left hand clashing with G♯ in the right, while unsuccessfully aiming to assert the double tonic A–G♯ through repetition.

Aside from the fact that several of the motives used by

Rodrigo in this "Toccata a modo de pregón" could be repeated in loops, seemingly anticipating minimalism, the "science" (without too much art) that this piece displays was quite novel. It was nothing but a street-vendor's cry (pregón), dedicated to the academician Federico García Sanchiz, who strolled through the world as a lecturer and hawker of "Spanishness." Rodrigo met him in Buenos Aires, and the writer publicized the labors of the musician with a series of news stories published in the daily paper *Madrid*.

After the severe twenty-five measures of the Toccata's finale, Rodrigo paused to begin the first sonata *piano* and with the same key signature of three sharps. A motive of two measures, delicate and subtle, opens this composition in F♯ minor, while auguring a rest for the academicians's ears. But the grace of this motive lies in the unexpected turn taken in its last note: G♯ in the right hand with B♯ in the bass.

The composer recovers in this fashion the reference to the conflicting keys of the toccata with the relative minor of A major (F♯ minor) and G♯ major in relation to the preceding G♯ minor. This sonata, dedicated to José Cubiles, is the most Scarlattian of the series in its texture, form, keyboard treatment, the makeup of its motives, and the restatement of sounds and small phrases of two measures, which are individualized by means of immediate repetition. In a letter to Federico Mompou, Rodrigo offered another key for the historical interpretation of these *Sonatas de Castilla*: "It seems to me that after them, thank God, the Spanish piano in the style of Scarlatti was all finished. [. . .] Or if you prefer, go to hell, Scarlatti."[5] In these sonatas, Rodrigo wished to mine the Scarlattian vein that had obsessed Falla and that had so deeply affected the young composers of the Generation of 1927, especially Ernesto Halffter.

For reasons as obvious as the lack of a clear cadence in the first part on F minor and the finale in the key of F major, Rodrigo avoided mentioning the key in the title of the first sonata. Nonetheless, the following piece in the series, dedicated to Antonio Iglesias, was titled, "Sonata in F♯ Minor." In its slow tempo and tonal likeness, it forms a diptych with the previous piece, in the same way that some of Scarlatti's sonatas form pairs. In his works with sonata forms of a pre-Classical character, Rodrigo often united the bridge passage with the secondary theme, as in the first sonata. He also united the repetition of the main theme in the dominant tonal area with the development, as in the second sonata.

In the center of the set, Rodrigo positioned a sonata that was probably the one he had been thinking for years of writing for Luis Galve. We find the first mention of this in a letter from Federico Sopeña dated 1943.[6] A few months later, the composer wrote him, "I am seriously beginning to think about the sonata that Galve insists I write for him. Let see what emerges."[7] Nothing emerged, because in another letter Rodrigo wrote, "I am also trying to finish the piano sonata."[8] He did not finish it then either, but these documents show that he had been reflecting on the piano sonata as a musical form for over five years, and the first consequence of these meditations was the Sonata in D, the third of the five *Sonatas de Castilla*. It is a composition with a more brilliant piano technique than the other sonatas, less compact because it introduces new material into the development, and it offers a complete recapitulation of the exposition. Nonetheless, the measures that recapitulate the main theme and the bridge passage are not literal. Besides being condensed, they are so bound up with the development that they could be considered its finale.

The "Sonata como un tiento" that follows, dedicated to Frank Marshall, shares its key signature with the previous "Sonata in D" but features a slower tempo, in the same contrasting manner as the first two. More a *tiento* (a free-form keyboard genre of the Baroque) than a sonata, starting in the key of B minor, it is structured by means of four identical cadences but in different keys: F♯ major, B major, G major, and E major. Between the last two cadences there is the suggestion of a recapitulation with a variation on the theme as it appeared in m. 9, now in E minor. This suggests that the first eight measures in B minor were something of a false start harmonically. As noted before, Rodrigo's works often exhibit an overall tonal scheme, and this sonata perfectly functions as a "bridge" between the third sonata in D major and the final one in A major, in other words, D–E–A, or IV–V–I.

Another proof of a large-scale tonal design in the *Sonatas de Castilla* is that Rodrigo concludes the contrived first theme of the final Sonata in A, dedicated to Pilar Bayona, with his musical signature: the song of the cuckoo, from C♯ down to A, which jokingly imitates the tense conclusion of the main theme at the same time that it anticipates the beginning of the second theme of the tonic area, which, in this sonata, is prolonged to measure 34. The development of this sonata also introduces new material, like the Sonata in D; but this time the interpolation is a quote from the famous zarzuela *La Revoltosa* (1897) by Ruperto Chapí.

In this event, Rodrigo had shone as a lecturer, a performer, and especially as a composer. Leaving aside the fact that some certainly found the abundance of dissonances annoying, while others did not see any references to Castile other than the bolero-style tune that permeates the third sonata, everyone must have recognized Rodrigo's efforts and the extraordinary significance of his admission to the Academy. In her memoirs, Victoria Kamhi recalled little of the importance of this moment in the artistic development of her husband, but she recorded that the noble ceiling of the Academy was leaking water and that drops were falling on the hat she was wearing for the first time that evening.[9] Looking beneath the gleaming surface of the most distinguished Spanish institution devoted to the arts, one could see the grime of an exhausted, dilapidated, and isolated country. Rodrigo fulfilled his task as best he could, but he knew that the future lay beyond a Europe still recovering from world war. The new center of cultural and economic gravity was the United States, which had become the driver of development, leaving Spain marginalized and excluded from the European Recovery Program, the Marshall Plan.

Between External Politics and the International Projection

The doors began to open when the U.S. secretary of state, Dean Acheson, took a step back in the struggle of President Truman against Francoist Spain. In a text published in the *New York Times* in January 1950,[10] Acheson publicly recognized the failure of Resolution 39(I) of the General Assembly of the United Nations, which in December 1946 culminated in isolating Spain. This resolution excluded Spain from all organisms of the United Nations and recommended that member states close their embassies in that country, something done by all except Argentina, Portugal, the Dominican Republic, and the Holy See. The unworkability of Resolution 39(I) was something the government of the United States noted from its inception, and in 1948, Secretary of State Frank Marshall agreed with the U.N. delegates of France and the United Kingdom that if that resolution were raised again in the General Assembly of Paris, they would vote against it.[11] It was not raised, but diplomats of the so-called Spanish Lobby brought about its nullification in 1948.[12] Two years later, in November 1950, Resolution 386 of the U.N. General Assembly revoked the main sanctions on Spain and paved the way for the immediate reestablishment of normal diplomatic relations.

Even before political solutions came into play, cultural relations had somewhat eased the way. A note in the press was countlessly repeated in many U.S. newspapers concerning some statements made by Rodrigo, who was clearly regarded as a visiting dignitary, one whose opinions on government assistance to the arts were universally relevant: "Rodrigo said government aid and encouragement to orchestras never has been so great as at present. However, he added, composers 'do not have sufficient help to carry on their artistic tasks.'"[13] The orchestra of Louisville, Kentucky, announced an initiative that seemed to respond to Rodrigo's demands: "The Louisville Philharmonic Society, which will present six pairs of subscription concerts this season under the direction of Robert Whitney, has announced a departure from the accepted 'star-soloist' system of programming.

The orchestra now intends to build its season around the composer."[14] According to one of the first news items published with regard to this plan, "The innovation announced represents not only a break with tradition but a notable step forward for the creative musicians."[15]

The Louisville concert season of 1948–49 would feature six contemporary composers. Each was contracted to compose a work about ten minutes long for $500, and it was proposed to invite them to attend the rehearsals and conduct their debut.[16] The composers included the Americans Virgil Thomson, Roy Harris, and Claude Almand, the Frenchman Darius Milhaud, the Italian Gian Francesco Malipiero, and Joaquín Rodrigo. Further, the orchestra boasted that for that season only three soloists were to be hired, all very young. Among them, the Spanish coloratura soprano Marimí del Pozo debuted in the United States with the premiere of the orchestral version of the *Cuatro madrigales amatorios* on 9 November 1948, the first concert of the season, with Robert Whitney as conductor, in Louisville Columbia Auditorium.

That was a memorable event in the history of modern classical music, and not just in the United States, because the policy of hiring composers inaugurated by the Louisville Orchestra continued during the following seasons, and in 1953—when debuts of Hindemith, Honegger, and Martinů were being launched alongside premieres of Rodrigo, Villa-Lobos, Milhaud, Malipiero, and a long list of American composers—it received a subsidy of $400,000 from the Rockefeller Foundation.[17] The enterprise became an example of how seasons devoted to living composers and the creation of new works, without the attraction of great performing stars, could be successful. This is something that Rodrigo had always encouraged as a good way to offer composers resources to accomplish their work. It is not certain that he actually received the $500 commission.[18] He did benefit, however, from a good introduction to the U.S. public at a historical crossroads in American classical music.

Marimí del Pozo again sang the *Cuatro madrigales amatorios* on December 29 in a concert of the Symphony Orchestra of El Paso, conducted by Hine Arthur Brown.[19] In the summer of 1949, she made a recording of that work—the second orchestral piece by Rodrigo phonographically recorded—in England with the Philharmonic Orchestra conducted by Henry Warwick Braithwaite for His Master's Voice (2EA 14108–9). Already in the early 1950s, the renowned African American coloratura Mattiwilda Dobbs included the *Cuatro madrigales amatorios* in her repertoire in the original piano-vocal version.

At the beginning of 1950, Rodrigo, intended to travel to the United States, in the role of cultural ambassador.[20] Although he was unable to organize this trip, the Coros y Danzas de la Sección Femenina—flagship of Spanish musical propaganda—performed at the Hollywood Bowl in August 1950. The Bowl's general manager, Karl Wecker, then spent several weeks in Spain under the auspices of the Institute of Hispanic Culture.[21] Asked by the editors of *La Vanguardia* about the possibility of inviting the Choruses and Dances once again, Wecker affirmed, "I would also like to take the Orquesta Nacional and the most outstanding artists of Spain. Everything Spanish arouses ever more interest daily in the United States."[22]

In contrast with Rodrigo's rising fortunes in the United States, things were not going well for him in Europe. The *Concierto de Aranjuez*, which had languished in an isolated Spain in the hands of guitarist Sainz de la Maza, was finally arousing interest in the author's work, but it also contributed to creating a rather slanted image of the composer as a conservative nationalist. While all doors were opening to the *Concierto de Aranjuez*, Rodrigo missed a few important opportunities to present his music at European festivals of great renown. The first was the Biennale of Venice in 1950; the second, Mai Musical de Bordeaux in 1951.

The possibility of presenting Rodrigo in the Venice Biennale had to do with Sopeña. Established in Rome as a priest in the Spanish Church of Montserrat, Sopeña lost no time in promoting the music of Rodrigo. With the mediation of Domenico De'Paoli, he arranged for the 1950 Biennale that a symphony be premiered of which Rodrigo had spoken to him years before, though no such work would ever see the light of day. For that reason, the planned premiere was traded for a performance of *Ausencias de Dulcinea* under the baton of the great Polish conductor Paul Kletzki. The concert was set for September 11, and Rodrigo was to share the program with Ildebrando Pizzetti, Arthur Honegger, and Paul Hindemith, who would conduct their own works.

Nonetheless, little more than a month before the projected date, the organization canceled Rodrigo's participation without providing a convincing explanation. Sopeña conveyed the bad news to Rodrigo along with the following evaluation: "I imagine that that affair is nothing less than a boycott of a political type."[23] Shortly afterwards, he added, "I think that all this has a communist twelve-tone basis,"[24] associating dodecaphony with Marxism. Neither did Gaspar Cassadó, already familiar with the ways of the Italian music world, discount the influence of politics in this affair. He pointed out that the director of the Biennale, Ferdinando Ballo, belonged to the Communist party, "and consequently both the festivals of Venice and those of the International Society of Contemporary Music are not free of politics."[25] Although Rodrigo and Sopeña were careful not to publicize this project, fearing a possible backlash, the press reported a chat with García Sanchiz in which the political issue was connected with Kletzki: "In the recent festival of Venice the announced composition of maestro Rodrigo was not played because the orchestra conductor, a Pole, refused to promote the work of a Spanish author."[26] Kletzki's family had been murdered in Nazi concentration camps; hence, he needed very little cause to deny his support to any initiative supporting Spain.

Nevertheless, in 1956, Kletzki conducted the Orquesta Nacional in the premiere of Rodrigo's *Concierto serenata* (1952) for harp with Nicanor Zabaleta as soloist. Despite the fiasco of his participation in the Biennale, Rodrigo traveled with his wife to Italy in January 1951. Once in Rome, they at last had occasion to hear in person the *Concerto in modo galante*, performed by Cassadó with the orchestra of the Accademia Nazionale di Santa Cecilia, conducted by Argenta. But what they heard they disliked very much. Cassadó wanted to shorten the work in a way that Rodrigo wanted to avoid. After the premiere in Madrid on 11 April 1949, Cassadó made some modifications to Rodrigo's

original, mostly in the first movement. Afterwards, before playing the concerto in Barcelona on 11 November 1949, he broadened
the omissions. The changes were so numerous that Cassadó had
to pay for a copy of a new score and some new orchestral parts,
with which he performed the *Concerto in modo galante* (1949)
in Baden-Baden on 18 November 1950, under the direction of
Fernando Previtali.

When Cassadó informed Rodrigo of the success of the performance, he added a "general opinion" of individuals he considered objective enough to judge the work: "Some repetitions
could be suppressed; [. . .] the same thing could be said with
more brevity."[27] On 7 January 1951, Rodrigo heard the work in
person.[28] Cassadó had alerted him, "The author has no more duty
than to listen to the botched job that the soloist and orchestra
conductor feel like doing. [. . .] My God, how cruel is the fate of
the composer!"[29] According to Victoria Kamhi's memoirs, "Joaquín complained bitterly about seeing his work mutilated."[30] In
May 1952, the composer agreed to make a revision of the *Concerto in modo galante*.[31] This version would be the one played in
Valencia on 25 June 1952 and the one intended for publication.
Some leading publishing houses showed interest, but the nego-
tiations led nowhere, and in 1956, Rodrigo published at his own
expense a piano reduction by Cassadó. This concerto followed a
long road until its publication by Salabert in 1970.

As he approached fifty years of age, Rodrigo was aware of
his place in the history of Spanish music. It was hard for him to
accept "lessons" about his creative labor. When he had to represent Spain, he did it with aplomb, whether in Buenos Aires
in 1949 or in London between February and March of 1951,
where he was invited by the British Council.[32] If he had to write
a march for the Frente de Juventudes (Youth Fronts, the most
characteristic institution of Francoism for the young), like the
one published by the daily paper *Arriba* on 1 April 1951, *Tambores
de primavera* (Drums in Springtime), he did so, though it does
not appear in any of the catalogues of his works.[33]

It was difficult for him to admit that he was sidelined from
events he considered important for the performance of his music.

In his office in the 1950s

When he found out that in the concerts that Argenta was going to give with the Orquesta Nacional de España in the Mai Musical de Bordeaux of 1951 the only work of his would be an orchestral arrangement he had made in 1936 of his *Deux berceuses*, he wrote a letter of protest to his old friend, still Subsecretary of National Education, Jesús Rubio García-Mina.

Perhaps what Argenta was seeking was to give his program a veneer of modernity that could only be found with difficulty in other music of the Spanish classical repertoire. Yet, all that these pieces could convey that was new in 1951 was but a reflection of Rodrigo's early career. The *Berceuses* were more than twenty years old, and Rodrigo preferred to be represented by more recent compositions, such as *Cuatro madrigales amatorios* and *Ausencias de Dulcinea*, both from 1948. Unfortunately, neither of these later works was easy to program. Rodrigo had prioritized creating what he considered artistically necessary at every moment, rather than focusing on "practical" considerations. Now it was a politician, Rubio García-Mina, who reminded him with great bluntness, "Only one thing I celebrate, among so many disagreeable things, and it is that this incident can encourage you to write compositions exclusively for orchestras, much easier to take everywhere than those that are complicated with the interventions of soloists or groups of soloists, always difficult to get and manage."[34]

The contrast between the disaffection of this subsecretary and the affection with which Rodrigo had been received in Buenos Aires by Antonio Tovar, the other dedicatee of the *Gran marcha de los subsecretarios* (1941), highlights two of the factions into which the Falangists split after the fall of Germany: on the one hand, the old guard fanatically defended the Franco regime; on the other hand, the old liberal, enlightened sectors sought the modernization of the country, political change from within the system, and convergence with the Western democracies. Rubio García-Mina was closer to the former, while Tovar aligned himself with the latter. Rodrigo definitely favored the liberal faction, because of his understandable interest in disseminating his works beyond Spain.

In the early 1950s, Rodrigo moved toward a person with political influence both in Francoism and in the transition to democracy: Joaquín Ruiz-Giménez. A cultivated man who had studied philosophy and literature after earning his law license, Ruiz-Giménez was president of the international Catholic organization Pax Romana. The prestige and international contact obtained by Ruiz-Giménez in Pax Romana enabled him to pursue a brilliant political career that began with his appointment in 1946 as first director of the Institute of Hispanic Culture. In December 1948, he was designated Spanish ambassador to the Holy See. In that post, with Sopeña's mediation, he met the Rodrigos in January 1951 and arranged a private audience for the couple with Pope Pius XII.

Hardly six months later, Ruiz-Giménez was named Minister of National Education. Rodrigo, disenchanted as he was with the

Lecturing to a class at the University of Madrid in the 1950s

outgoing minister, hastened to congratulate him. We do not have Rodrigo's letter to him, but we do know the minister's reply: "The Caudillo [Leader] has placed a heavy burden on my shoulders, but with God's help and collaborations like that of our exemplary Federico [Sopeña], I trust I will be able to lend some service to Spain. For everything musical, I count as fully as possibly on you. Agreed?"[35]

Ruiz-Giménez played his cards well and brought about a notable renovation in his ministry. He discharged Rubio García-Mina, recovered Antonio Tovar by naming him rector of the University of Salamanca, made Pedro Laín Entralgo rector of the University of Madrid, replaced Nemesio Otaño with Sopeña at the head of the Madrid Conservatory, and named as Director of Fine Arts the mayor of Granada, Antonio Gallego Burín, who organized in 1952 the International Festivals of Spanish Music and Dance of Granada.

To a great extent, the old group of the review *Escorial*, who had supported Rodrigo in the early 1940s, came back to power a decade later and would strongly support him again. But the ren- ovating project of Ruiz-Giménez lasted only a short time and had a major weakness precisely where it had most strongly implanted itself: in the University of Madrid (now the Universidad Com- plutense). Revolts and confrontations between the Falangists and students led to the resignation of the rector Laín Entralgo. On 16 February 1956, Ruiz-Giménez resigned. The most that Rodrigo derived from Ruiz-Giménez's ministry, apart from being named to the executive committee of the reorganized National Council of Music,[36] was the strengthening of his position in the univer- sity, where he remained until his retirement in 1978.

Rodrigo and the University

Joaquín Rodrigo resumed teaching music at the University of Madrid in 1948, but it was Ruiz-Giménez, through his Ministe- rial Order of 6 March 1952, who regulated that teaching activity through the creation of the "Manuel de Falla" Chair, for which the rector, Laín Entralgo, at once designated Rodrigo.[37] As dis- tinguished from his teaching position between 1948 and 1952, the "Manuel de Falla" Chair had a small financial endowment and supported the organization of concerts. Of all the labors that Rodrigo had undertaken, this was the most pleasant for him. A whole series of his compositions, produced in this decade of remarkable fecundity, is attributable to the university and the academic environs in which Rodrigo performed, including the Academy of Fine Arts.

In this context we examine the *Dos canciones sefardíes del siglo XV* (Two Sephardic Songs of the Fifteenth Century, 1951) for mixed chorus and the immediate forerunner of these songs, the choral composition *Triste estaba el rey David* (Sad Was King David, 1950). Grouped in the composer's catalogue as *Tres canciones sefardíes*, the first two originated from the Sephardic *Romancero* (Book of Ballads), but *Triste estaba el rey David* is from the *Tres libros de música en cifras para vihuela* (Three Books of Music in Tablature for Vihuela, 1546) by Alonso de Mudarra. *Triste estaba el rey David* is an important piece, and Rodrigo showed great enthusiasm for it. In a letter to López-Chavarri, he referred to some "harmonic audacities" that he had taken into the terrain of choral music but with a result that seemed to him "stupendous, very difficult, with a great effect."[38] Certainly, *Triste estaba el rey David* is a piece very characteristic of Rodrigo's style, and so complex that it remains a *tour de force* for any chorus that tackles it. The composer wrote it for the Coral de Cámara de Pamplona, an excellent ensemble founded by Luis Mocoroa in 1946 with singers who came from the Orfeón Pamplonés. In the choral group's debut at the prestigious International Cultural Weeks of l'Abbaye de Royaumont, on 25 June 1950, it premiered Rodrigo's work, alongside a set of pieces of the exiled Adolfo Salazar and works by two composers marginalized by the Franco regime: Fernando Remacha and Arturo Dúo Vital. When he received the work of Rodrigo, Mocoroa consulted with Remacha, who found much to admire in it: "The work is very pretty, and you have made a great acquisition. [. . .] All of it, although it seems innocent, obeys a very refined taste, and all the ideas are very mature, with nothing arbitrary, even though at times it seems otherwise."[39]

The *Dos canciones sefardíes del siglo XV*, "Malato está el hijo del rey" and "El rey que muncho madruga" ("The King's Son Is Sick" and "The King Who Rises Very Early"), are very different. They have an epigrammatic brevity and a technical simplicity that exemplify Rodrigo's harmonization of a melody with a folk origin or, as he put it himself, the reconciliation of a "light" folk melody with "heavy" vocal polyphony. The National Chorus of the Spanish University Union premiered them on 3 May 1952 in the main hall of the Faculty of Philosophy and Letters of Madrid, where ten days later the composer was to inaugurate the music classes of the "Manuel de Falla" Chair.[40] The songs had stemmed from the compilation of Sephardic ballads collected by Manuel Manrique de Lara at the start of the twentieth century in Central Europe. They are therefore original, unpublished documents of Sephardic folkloric tradition, and Rodrigo undertook to harmonize them from a critical perspective, which he clearly explained in a text accompanying their appearance in the review *Sepharad*, published by the Consejo Superior de Investigaciones Científicas (Higher Council of Scientific Research). Also in relation to this institution, one of the most important cultural projects of Francoism, Rodrigo wrote his *Doce canciones populares españolas* (Twelve Spanish Folk Songs, 1951) with piano accompaniment.

Premiered in the Madrid Atheneum by Marimi del Pozo, to whom they are dedicated, with Victoria Kamhi at the piano, the *Doce canciones populares españolas* were written on a commission from the Departmento de Musicología of the Consejo Superior de Investigaciones Científicas. The director of the Institute, Higinio Anglès, who also directed the Roman Pontificium Institutum Musicae Sacrae, had met Sopeña in Rome and entrusted to him the section of modern music of the Instituto Español de Musicología (Spanish Institute of Musicology). The series of publications in which the songs of Rodrigo appeared likely stemmed from the relationship between Sopeña and the Instituto Español de Musicología.

In the archives of that institute is to be found a copy of the letter in which its secretary, musicologist Miguel Querol, communicated the commission to Rodrigo and sent him "15 melodies that Father Donostia has selected from among the many we have from the provinces of León, Cuenca, and Ciudad Real," so that he might choose twelve, while requesting of him that the accompaniment he would write should not be difficult.[41] Rodrigo fulfilled this commission rapidly, as he possessed the necessary knowledge and experience, acquired when he taught the course on folklore at the conservatory. In December 1951, he had already completed this important set of songs, which he "autographed" with a cuckoo song in the accompaniment of the final two verses of the "Canción de cuna," which concludes the cycle. He wrote to Querol, "I have tried to give to each song its particular atmosphere, or an atmosphere, since the norms you suggested [. . .] forbade me from launching experiments that probably would not have been opportune."[42] In other words, the problem he posed in the introduction to the *Dos canciones sefardíes del siglo XV* is perfectly applicable to his *Doce canciones populares españolas*:

In spite of what is often assumed, the harmonisation of a popular song is not easy. One is faced immediately with the grave problem involved in reconciling a "light" musical form with a more "serious" one. [. . .] The answer, if it exists, would seem to be to prefer "atmosphere" to something academic. That is, to try to situate the song in what seems to be its milieu, to place it there by recreating its world, aims which are more feasible when we accompany the song with one or more instruments than when we try to adapt it for a choir of singers, in spite of what we might at first think.[43]

What Rodrigo expresses and exemplified in the *Doce canciones populares españolas* is nearly identical to what Manuel de Falla did in his *Siete canciones populares españolas* (1914), which can be considered the precedent for Rodrigo's work. However, whereas Falla was at liberty to select the folk models, manipulate them, and determine the difficulty of the accompaniment, in Rodrigo's case these aspects were predetermined. And in Falla's songs, there is more interaction between the voice and the piano, while in Rodrigo's there is a general tendency to separate the voice from the piano. Nonetheless, the style of Rodrigo's "Una palomita blanca" (A Little White Dove) and "Adela" resembles that of Falla's "Nana" (Cradle Song), just as the former's "Porque toco el pandero" (Because I Play the Tambourine) reminds us of the latter's "Canción" (Song). For that reason, Rodrigo ought to have complained when he saw that in the edition published by the Spanish Institute of Musicology he was only credited with "arranging" the piano accompaniments. Finally, Rodrigo published the work to his own taste in 1959 with Schott & Co., with texts translated into English by the Hispanist Nigel Glendinning. This time they were titled simply *Twelve Spanish Songs–Doce canciones españolas*, whereby they were distinguished from Falla's collection by eliminating "popular" from the title.

Música para un códice salmantino

The work best representing Rodrigo's link with the university community is his *Música para un códice salmantino* (Music for a Salamancan Codex). In 1953, Rodrigo was invited by his friend

Antonio Tovar to compose a cantata celebrating the 700th anniversary of the founding in 1253 of the Universidad de Salamanca, where Tovar was now the rector. Rodrigo readily acceded to this request and chose a poem by one of Spain's most important modern philosophers and poets, Miguel de Unamuno (1864–1936), who had himself served as rector of this prestigious and venerable institution. Rodrigo's creative choice invites much speculation,[44] especially insofar as Unamuno's poetry has rarely been set to music. However, as Rodrigo himself observed, "Although Unamuno was certainly not a lyric poet, it cost me no effort at all to set him to music."[45] The work lasts about eleven minutes and is scored for solo bass, mixed chorus, and eleven instruments. It is one of the composer's most distinctive and inventive works.

Rodrigo finished his composition in Torrelodones on 19 September 1953, after about two weeks of effort. This was such a short period of time that he himself was surprised: "It is the work that I have accomplished most quickly. Only toward the end I suffered a two-day mental block, but it wasn't Unamuno's fault; it was mine."[46] As Unamuno scholar Nelson Orringer has explained to us, "Although famously antimusical, Unamuno confesses to having passed through a transitory period of anticlassicism, during which he imitated ancient poets in employing the Sapphic ode, thought to be originally a form of sung verse. Rodrigo was attracted to Unamuno's Sapphic ode 'Salamanca' precisely for the musicality of its lines."[47]

Unamuno was a major figure in the cultural and intellectual renaissance in Spain around 1900. He was a leading member of the so-called Generation of 1898, a group of writers who sought to define or redefine Spain's place in the modern world in the wake of its disastrous war with the United States and subsequent loss of the remnants of its overseas empire. Unamuno's view was that Spain had much to contribute to global culture but could do so only by mining its heritage for those aspects that were distinctive and relevant, what he called its "tradición eterna" (eternal tradition). As an eminent man of letters, he not surprisingly found Spain's literary heritage to be of immense value. But he celebrated not only the conspicuous cultural monuments of Spain's past but also something he called "intrahistoria," the events in the lives of ordinary people that generally do not find their way into history books.

This combination of the monumental and the quotidian characterizes much of his poetry, in particular the ten strophes of his celebrated *Oda a Salamanca* (Ode to Salamanca, 1904), a poetic *tour de force* that reveals the depth and breadth of his erudition. It consists of thirty-one stanzas in all, though Rodrigo chose only ten of them to set to music, the first seven and final three. As Orringer points out, "Not only do the classical references [. . .] display his knowledge, but also the form of the poem itself. Each strophe contains three unrhymed verses, the first two hendecasyllables and the third a pentasyllable, in accordance with the conventional Sapphic ode,"[48] named after Sappho, the sixth-century BCE Greek poetess from the isle of Lesbos whose poetic effusions were intended to be sung while accompanied on the lyre.

Orringer wonders how Rodrigo "dared to give musical permanence to the ode during the Franco era, when the controversial Rector of Salamanca had aroused animosity as a heretic in the view of the Spanish church."[49] Though there is a strongly traditional streak in Unamuno's philosophy, his heterodox theology ran afoul of Catholic dogma, and he made no secret of his opposition to the militarism and fascism of the Franco faction. Rodrigo must have felt that his professional situation was sufficiently secure that he could now "dare," even as he had dared already in the 1940s, to set Catalan texts to music, in defiance of the regime's active suppression of the Catalan language.

Rodrigo's composition can be thought of as having three levels—evocative, narrative, and related to the ambience. The three levels are respectively linked to the instrumental group, the soloist, and the chorus. The most prominent of the three, the one that serves to articulate the work and refer it to the ancient time of the university's foundation, is the canon of the instrumental group with which it begins. In his own analytical preface to the edition of the work, Rodrigo declared his intention "to evoke" in music the meaning and images in the poem.[50]

He resorts to standard though imaginatively deployed rhetorical devices: descending minor arpeggios in the strings suggest the setting of the sun behind Salamanca's towers (mm. 69–70), while a cadence in A♭ major conveys the sun's gilding of the cloudscape with its rays (mm. 74–75), and the bass voice reaches its high point on E♭, invoking the sun's fire (m. 77). The use of brass instruments at this juncture intensifies the effect. Elsewhere, the soprano voices and the sound of the harp have their association with "the love of the students." And his signature cuckoo bird will make an appearance as well (mm. 131–135).

Rodrigo suggests that the work's structure resembles a "motet." The motet had its origins in the thirteenth century, but based on the form here, Rodrigo clearly had in mind the Renaissance motet, with its characteristic bipartite structure: prima pars and secunda pars. The "prima pars" of this motet-cantata is highly evocative. It is labeled "Introito," but, unlike the Introit of the Mass, this introduction is purely instrumental, at least in terms of the scoring. In fact, the melody (musical ex. 7.1) has a very lyrical quality, and Rodrigo himself said it had "*cantiga* inflections."

A *cantiga* is a medieval song type, the most famous belonging to the thirteenth-century collection of *Cantigas de Santa María*, troubadour-style songs that sing the praises of the Virgin. So, Rodrigo's opening gambit is an instrumental evocation of medieval song, suggestive of the university's medieval origins, and it is further the subject of a canon at the unison (or octave). This is accompanied by a drone, which suggests a folk instrument of some kind. One thinks first of bagpipes, which are still played in the northwest regions of Spain, though there was also a large

Musical ex. 7.1: *Música para un códice salmantino,* "Introito," mm. 1–9

sort of medieval hurdy-gurdy called an organistrum, immortalized in the Pórtico de la Gloria of the cathedral of Santiago de Compostela. Drones were also typical of organum, an early type of polyphony. Rodrigo further explains that this was the sort of melody that might have been the inspiration of the organist whom King Sancho IV of Castile (1258–1295) appointed to teach music at the university. Incidentally, Sancho was the son of Alfonso X, "The Wise," who sponsored the creation of the *Cantigas de Santa María*. All of this was clearly on the composer's mind as he wrought this tribute.

The lengthy Introit is followed by the entrance of the bass voice singing the selected portions of Unamuno's poem. As Pitt-Brooke points out about the subsequent structuring of the vocal section,

> While Rodrigo's setting is by no means strophic,
> he always acknowledges the ends of stanzas with a
> harmonic and melodic formula, which I call the Stanza-
> end formula: three root-position chords descending by
> step from *do* to *la* with the vocal melody descending by
> step to the tonic. [. . .] The last chord of this formula is
> often the first of another trio of downwards-stepping
> root position chords. [. . .] The Stanza-end formula is
> sometimes supplemented by an echo of the first phrase
> of the *Introito* subject. This recollection gives a deeper
> level of formal articulation, and also becomes symbolic of
> the act of remembrance.[51]

This device provides formal unity while allowing the text to take the music where it will. Textural changes suit his evocative purposes, for in addition to imitative polyphony and homophony, in the sixth stanza antiphonal exchanges between the bass soloist, choir, and instruments harken to the psalmody of an earlier epoch. Though Rodrigo's harmonic language is resolutely tonal, he resorts to modality and passages of bitonality, in order to add color and nuance to his setting. Indeed, the final sonority pits a Db major chord against Ab minor. Insofar as the poem itself is laden with "images of late afternoon and sunset,"[52] this rather ambiguous close in the orchestra and sopranos is presented *pianissimo* and *perdendosi* (dying away).

The Salamanca celebrations took place between 8 and 12 October 1953. Forty-four countries participated and thirty-two rectors attended, besides delegates of numerous national and foreign academic institutions and representatives of UNESCO, the Organization of American States, the International Association of Universities, and the Union of Latin American Universities. It was an event intended to signal the end of Spain's international isolation. The festivities culminated on the morning of October 12, the *Día de la Hispanidad*, with a theatrical and colorful parade. After the parade, there took place in the auditorium an academic ceremony over which Ruiz-Giménez presided, with almost 800 personalities in attendance, including Rodrigo, whose new cantata opened the session. It was performed by Joaquín Deus and the Radio Nacional chorus along with the Cuarteto Clásico featuring soloists from the Orquesta Nacional. Odón Alonso served as conductor.

Tovar also wanted this extraordinary occasion to exalt the figure of Unamuno, three times rector of the University of Salamanca—the first time, during the monarchy; the second, during the Second Republic; and the last, for several months at the start of the Civil War, in a Salamanca controlled by the rebels. Because of his independent thinking and his permanent spiritual crisis, he was an unsettling personage for all the political regimes through which he lived. The entente between Unamuno and Franco lasted only a short time. Hardly was he restored as rector when he was dismissed and placed under house arrest. Remaining practically in isolation, he passed away on 31 December 1936, a month and a half after he had confronted the insurrectionists. From that point on, his place in Spanish postwar culture was problematic.

Rodrigo situated his cantata in his already extensive output within a line that runs from the *Cantiga: Muy graciosa es la doncella* and passes through *Cántico de la esposa* and *Ausencias de Dulcinea* up to *Música para un códice salmantino*. And we note the important experience he acquired in the treatment of the chorus in *Triste estaba el rey David* (1950) and the direct kinship with *Ausencias de Dulcinea*, "twice the sister of *Música para un códice salmantino*," according to Rodrigo, who added, "But I judge that they resemble one another in the least possible way."[53]

And while we are on the subject of resemblances, the work we now introduce, *Concierto serenata* for harp and orchestra, is clearly in line with the *Concierto de Aranjuez*. Whereas *Música para un códice salmantino* gathers up the academic experience and the most elevated, serious reflection on the hallowed halls of the University of Salamanca, the *Concierto serenata* suggests the rambunctious classrooms of an upstart University of Madrid, in which the composer gave his classes. This concerto is, as Rodrigo himself wrote, "like a message to youth."[54]

Rodrigo finished this work in 1954 on a commission from the harpist Nicanor Zabaleta, who had returned to Spain in 1952 after a twenty-year absence, during which he developed an important international career. Rodrigo seems to have begun with the final movement, a rondo that he entitled "Soirée," whose main theme plays, like the first movement of the concerto for guitar, with binary and ternary subdivisions of rhythms in 3/4 meter, in effect alternating 3/4 and 6/8 (hemiola).

Rodrigo sent this movement to Zabaleta in September 1953, and the harpist wrote him, "It goes perfectly well with the harp. You have captured the type of writing for the instrument, and what changes it needs will be small modifications without any importance. Hence, up and at 'em."[55] Thus encouraged by Zabaleta, Rodrigo composed the first movement, "Estudian-tina" (a university-student group made up primarily of plucked instruments and voices), which begins, like his earlier concertos, with the soloist presenting the main themes without a preceding orchestral ritornello. This "Estudiantina" contains an intertextual reference to his own version of "De los álamos vengo," from the *Cuatro madrigales amatorios*, as well as a very naturalistic quote from the "Caleseras" from *El barberillo de Lavapiés* (1874) by Francisco Asenjo Barbieri (1823–1894), which is one of the jewels of the *zarzuela grande* (three-act zarzuela). The main difficulty that this concerto posed to Rodrigo was managing to make everything "light, clear, merry, like the childlike soul of the harp."[56] This movement is diaphanous, devil-may-care, airy, exulting, and possessing a humor that recalls the first of his *Cinco piezas infantiles*, "Son chicos que pasan," with all the harsh parts of that piece softened and with a lighter orchestration that at every instant protects the delicate sonority of the harp.

The movement that took him the most time to compose was the second, "Intermezzo con Aria," which has a profoundly Baroque affect, though perhaps not as original or as spontaneous as the second movement of the *Concierto de Aranjuez*. Rodrigo's interest in counterpoint and recurring fugue in these years followed the second centennial of the death of Johann Sebastian Bach, on whose works he gave countless lectures throughout Spain. Hence, after a creative process that extended for more than a year, the *Concierto serenata* was completed in spring 1954. Zabaleta immediately had 15,000 pesetas sent to Rodrigo for the commission, and wrote him that "the concerto is precious and I am sure that it is going to have a great success. After working on it I think it unnecessary to make any cuts in it."[57] Zabaleta premiered the *Concierto serenata* on 9 November 1955 in Madrid's Palacio de la Música, with the Orquesta Nacional de España, conducted by Paul Kletzki. He further informed Rodrigo that "I am very much looking forward to the recording we will make at the end of this month. You know that with the Germans one can collaborate very well, and I am sure that the record will come out magnificent."[58] True to his word, Zabaleta made a recording for Deutsche Grammophon (SLPM 138, 118) with the Berlin Radio Symphony Orchestra. After so many heartaches with the performers of his concertos, Rodrigo had no complaints at all about Zabaleta, and his relationship with the harpist, more professional than personal, lasted as long as both lived.

Return to the Guitar: Andrés Segovia and Beyond

Like Zabaleta, Andrés Segovia returned to Spain in 1952 after almost two decades of being away. His reappearance was a main event and concluded the First Festival of Spanish Music and

Dance of Granada, which took place June 15 to 24. His concert career had flourished during the years abroad, and thus he generously ceded to a local charitable institution in Granada the phenomenal sum of almost 60,000 pesetas (equivalent to $1,500 at that time), which he was paid for his two stellar appearances at the festival.[59] Rodrigo, nonetheless, did not attend this showcase of Spanish music, during which the Orquesta Nacional de España, conducted by Argenta, gave four concerts that included *Concerto in modo galante*, performed by Cassadó, and *Tríptic de Mossèn Cinto*, sung by Consuelo Rubio.[60]

The relationship between Segovia and Rodrigo, until then centered around the frustrated project of having the guitarist perform the *Concierto de Aranjuez*, was gradually turning toward the composition of new music. The first time that Rodrigo mentioned his aim to write a piece for Segovia was in a letter of 1949: "As soon as I finish a concerto that I am writing under contract to Cassadó, I intend to try to make a work for you. A small orchestra and guitar. I call a violin, viola, and cello, and a wind quartet or trio a small orchestra—in sum, seven or eight instruments and guitar. It seems to me that the guitar calls for more incisive pitches of woodwind and brass; at least that has given me a good result in the *Concierto de Aranjuez*."[61] A year later, Segovia wrote to Rodrigo:

> I repeat to you again the request I made of you on another occasion, and now do so peremptorily. Does it enter into your plans to write a quintet for guitar—for guitar and string quartet—with a Hispanic character? If you feel that way, set yourself to writing it without delay, and begin sending me what you've written for me to study it. I intend to perform a very important concert in Chicago and am already studying a precious quintet that Castelnuovo-Tedesco has just composed for me.[62]

Since these projects never materialized, in 1952 the guitarist formally commissioned Rodrigo to compose a "Suite, Sonata, Fantasy or whatever may please you for solo guitar." Segovia offered him 200 U.S. dollars while kindly asking him to grant him total discretion, because, as he wrote, "Neither to Castelnuovo (who is rich, on the other hand), nor to Ponce, nor to Tansman, in short, to nobody, to no composer who has written for me have I ever handed over the least amount." The reason that Segovia gave for this extraordinary offer had to do with his perception of the social and cultural situation of the country: "Now that I have come to Spain, I realize the atrocious difficulties that anyone must endure if they wish to maintain a home in a decent fashion. This applies even more if they devote themselves to affairs of the spirit and not to selling smuggled goods. I consider it a duty to help you compose that work with certain peace of mind."[63]

Rodrigo quickly responded: "You don't know how grateful I am to you for this. As soon as I finish the concerto I'm attempting to write for harp, I will write for you with greatest pleasure a guitar suite. You are right, it is more worthwhile that we begin with something for solo guitar; it is more practical and I can more easily find time for it." At once, he amicably declined the pecuniary component of the commission: "Having you play it and especially like it is pay enough for me; let's not talk about it any more."[64]

Another year went by, and Segovia was interested in the state of the suite, according to a letter that offers us the first notice we have about Rodrigo's project to write for him a work for guitar and orchestra "about—or in honor of—Gaspar Sanz."[65] Then things began to pick up speed as Segovia showed great interest in Rodrigo's early guitar pieces, intending to include some of them in a series of recordings that he was making in spring 1954 for Decca. Though he did not know if it was an old piece or the beginning of the promised suite, after receiving the *Tiento antiguo* from the composer, Segovia wrote, "It is fine and has a poetic ambiance."[66] Shortly thereafter, he received the edition made by Emilio Pujol for Max Eschig of the *Zarabanda lejana*, and this work immediately charmed him: "I am laboring tenaciously so that [. . .] it may be possible for me to record it on one of the next records. [. . .] It is very beautiful."[67] Finally, he included it in one of his most famous productions: the album *Bach: Chaconne* (Decca, DL 9751), released in 1955.

The widespread dissemination of Segovia's recordings must have encouraged Rodrigo to complete in the summer of 1954 the works he had promised. Segovia first received the "Passacaglia," in which the composer for the first time brought to the guitar his interest in contrapuntal forms with a clearly Hispanicized neo-Baroque character. This is apparent in the fughetta of its finale, marked "rítmico como un fandango" (rhythmic like a fandango). Segovia was delighted with it and wrote, "It is very beautiful," though cautioning Rodrigo to "Be careful with the dissonances, especially in the lively movement. [. . .] Those of the 'Passacaglia' are possible—and spicy—because the movement is slow and takes advantage of certain open strings."[68] However, Rodrigo defied the guitarist's recommendations about dissonances in the fast movements. Indeed, the "Fandango" began and ended with a completely dissonant outburst, while the "Zapateado" (a dance featuring intricate footwork) posed technical difficulties that Segovia had scant time to master between one tour and another.

As far as anyone knows, Segovia never gave a public performance of these *Tres piezas españolas*, as Rodrigo entitled them, which formed a triptych in three modes on E: the "Fandango" in major, the "Passacaglia" in Phrygian, and the "Zapateado" in minor. In the event, he premiered only the "Fandango," at the Teatro Colón in Buenos Aires on 29 June 1957.[69] During that same tour, he performed it in a concert at the Festival Hall in London, before a packed house of some 4,000 spectators. According to the *ABC* correspondent, it was "one of the most applauded pieces on a night of ceaseless acclaims."[70] When the guitarist recorded the "Fandango" in January 1958 in New York (Decca, DL 710034), shortly after playing it in the Orchestra Hall in Chicago,[71] it became clear that he had renounced playing the "Passacaglia" and the "Zapateado." By then, Segovia had Rodrigo's new work for guitar and orchestra ready to premiere.

In a letter dated 24 September 1954, where Segovia conveyed to Rodrigo his first impressions of the "Fandango" and the "Zapateado" of the *Tres piezas españolas*, he added, "Get to work on the *Fantasía* for guitar and orchestra."[72] Less than a month later, Rodrigo wrote, "When I got your letter, I shut myself up in Torrelodones under lock and key; I said that I was away on a trip, and in two weeks I have composed for you the fantasy under the title *Fantasía para un gentilhombre*."[73] It was rather a suite than a fantasy, and the "gentleman" was Segovia. But "Suite for Segovia" did not sound as enticing as *Fantasía para un gentilhombre*, the "fantasy" element being the elaboration of material that Rodrigo had borrowed from the small pieces for Baroque guitar of Gaspar Sanz (1640–1710). Rodrigo wrote the first movement of the concerto using Sanz's *Villano* and *Ricercare*. Sanz's *Españoleta*, introduced by the *Fanfarria de la caballería de Nápoles* (Fanfare of the Naples Cavalry), came second. The sixteen measures of the *Danza de las hachas* (Dance of the Axes) gave him enough material for the 120 measures of his third movement. Sanz's lively *Canarios* informs the fourth and final movement of the *Fantasía para un gentilhombre*.

Gaspar Sanz's eminence in the history of the Spanish guitar was well known, and in the first half of the twentieth century some of his pieces had entered into the repertoire of guitarists like Emilio Pujol, Sainz de la Maza, and Andrés Segovia himself. Nevertheless, the original source of Sanz's music, the three books that formed his *Instrucción de música sobre la guitarra española* (1674–75), was only published in facsimile edition in 1952.[74] This was not the edition Rodrigo, or rather Victoria Kamhi, consulted. As Rodrigo himself revealed: "Vicky, who as you know is an excellent pianist, was able to extract the most appropriate themes with her infallible musical accuracy."[75] She got them from the *Cancionero musical de la provincia de Zaragoza* (Musical Songbook of the Province of Zaragoza), published in 1950 by Ángel Mingote, which ended with the transcription of nineteen pieces by Sanz made by Gregorio Arciniega, pioneer in the study and revival of the Baroque guitarist's music.[76] The *Fuga por primer tono al ayre español* (First Tone Fugue in the Spanish Fashion), edited by Mingote, was the origin of the "Ricercare" of the first movement of the *Fantasía para un gentilhombre*, and all the pieces that Rodrigo utilized to elaborate his work are found in that compilation. What is more, Arciniega's transcriptions for piano, edited by Mingote, take certain liberties with the originals that subsequently found their way into Rodrigo's version.

The result is a fine work, the summit of Rodrigo's activities with respect to the Spanish musical heritage, though he had some misgivings about Sanz's music: "When I stop to consider Gaspar Sanz's material up close, I saw how feeble that material was. In fact, it could hardly be played such as he left it, reduced to some themes with rather simple improvisations."[77] Segovia agreed with him: "I didn't want to say anything to you, but, knowing as I did the work of Gaspar Sanz, I found the basis of the labor that you were going to undertake much too feeble. All the better that, like a spider, you took out of yourself the thread with which to weave the work."[78] Of course, finishing off the *Villano* with a brief *fughetta* fashioned from Sanz's theme propelled the initial movement forward. It was something else to introduce into the *Españoleta* the patchwork of fanfares of the Neopolitan cavalry, thereby prolonging the emotion of the slow movement, which closes with a rhetorical figure of *anabasis* (arrangement of elements in ascending order), similar to that utilized at the end of the second movement of the *Concierto de Aranjuez*. In the same way, the *Canarios* of the last movement introduces, with the signature of the cuckoo, a cadenza that structures and expands Sanz's original while conserving its essence.

From the first moment, Rodrigo clearly saw the model he wished to follow: "After meditating about all this material, before beginning, and while composing, I have believed that, at least in this case, it was not wise to adulterate this material, and I was a bit inspired by the arrangement that Respighi had made of the *Ancient Airs and Dances* that has had so much success."[79] Certainly the kinship was obvious between the anonymous "Siciliana" of the third suite of the *Antiche arie e danze per liuto* (1932) by Ottorino Respighi and the *Españoleta* of Sanz-Rodrigo, and Respighi's manner of freely handling the historical originals was an excellent model for Rodrigo to follow.

While the procedure of stretching out the meager material of Sanz was ingenious and effective, no less so was his development and manipulation of the themes. The skillfulness of Rodrigo's orchestration always allows the guitar to be heard, thus taking advantage of Segovia's legendary sound. As he told Segovia, "It is fitting to let the guitar, especially yours, sing like a cello."[80] While the *Tres piezas españolas* was more to his own liking than to that of its dedicatee, in the *Fantasía* Rodrigo strove to please the almighty Segovia. That responsibility came to overwhelm him: "My hair stood on end, because not only the compromise of writing for Segovia, as almost all contemporary composers have done, but also the difficulty of writing for guitar and orchestra, made the task that much harder."[81] Rodrigo became worried when the premiere of the *Tres piezas españolas* kept being put off without any explanation, and his anxiety increased when years passed before Segovia debuted the *Fantasía*.

Little more than a month after the announcement of its completion, Segovia received the *Fantasía para un gentilhombre* in San Francisco. From there, where he was about to perform Ponce's *Concierto del Sur* and the Concerto in D Major by Castelnuovo-Tedesco under the direction of Enrique Jordá,[82] he sent Rodrigo a check for 200 U.S. dollars "to compensate for the costs of copyist, paper, the trip of being shut up in Torrelodones, and whatever else." In the same letter he added, "I have given the score to Jordá, who wanted to study it, and the result is that we have decided to include it in the symphony concert of next season and both of us to make a long-playing record out of it, either for Decca or for RCA."[83]

An old friend of Rodrigo's from Paris of the 1930s, Jordá was a man of great culture and extraordinary charisma, who had just been elected in 1954 by the public and by the directorate of the San Francisco Symphony to succeed his historic predecessor, Pierre Monteux, choosing him over conductors like Steinberg, Solti, Fricsay, and Szell.[84] Jordá wrote to Rodrigo, "I had the pleasure of reading your *Fantasía para un gentilhombre* when Segovia was in San Francisco last November, and your work seemed to me the composition of a gentleman with fantasy."[85]

Despite the distress that Segovia's slowness to premiere the *Fantasía para un gentilhombre* caused him, Rodrigo's year 1957 went by very swiftly. In February he was in Paris, giving concerts and lectures. In March he went to Venezuela as the delegate of Spain in the Second Festival of Iberoamerican Music.[86] From Caracas, he flew in April to Puerto Rico, where he reunited with Casals and attended the festival named after the cellist.[87] From Puerto Rico he went to New York. Shortly after Rodrigo returned to Spain in May, Jordá announced to him that the committee of the San Francisco Symphony had approved contracting Segovia for the 1957–58 season, and that their intention was absolutely to give the premiere of the *Fantasía para un gentilhombre.*[88] Finally, on 27 February 1958, the composer and his wife left for San Francisco to attend the premiere on March 5, 6, and 7 at the War Memorial Opera House, with Segovia and the San Francisco Symphony conducted by Jordá.

The recording of this work was made by Segovia and Jordá, but with the Symphony of the Air. With a graceful cover design representing a stylized gentleman of the eighteenth century, at the foot of a staircase underneath Segovia's name in capital letters, this record (Decca DL 10027) featured on the flip side Ponce's *Concierto del Sur.* Insofar as the month of June marked the fiftieth anniversary of the June 1908 Granada concert that Segovia considered to be his debut, these two recently recorded concertos and the "Fandango" of Rodrigo's *Tres piezas españolas* were included in the triple album "Segovia Golden Jubilee" (Decca DXJ-148), which marked an epoch in the history of guitar recordings.

The *Fantasía para un gentilhombre* soon began to enter the repertoire of great guitarists. Segovia performed it on a dozen occasions, almost all during his European tour of 1958. In 1962, Narciso Yepes added it to his repertoire just as Segovia ceased to perform it. Rodrigo remained very grateful to Segovia because, at the Madrid premiere on 24 and 26 October 1958, with Jordá conducting the Orquesta Nacional de España, our composer obtained a truly memorable triumph. The very day of the second concert, he wrote to Segovia, "I have no other farewell word than the word that, for the first time in my life, with great emotion, I said to you at the end,

'THANK YOU.' To you I owe the greatest success of my career before the public."[89] To be sure, the Madrid premiere was not an unqualified triumph, as the critique of Antonio Fernández-Cid was fairly lukewarm: "Pretty music, well-made, amicable, not excessively ambitious."[90]

During the years around this initial history of the *Fantasía para un gentilhombre*, Rodrigo composed some other important works for guitar. First and foremost, he continued the journey through Spain that he had begun in *En los trigales* with a song and dance titled *Bajando de la meseta* (Descending from the Plateau, 1954), whose initial melody, in B major, features a practically atonal resolution. The dance that follows it, in "tempo de seguidilla," seems to try to restore the tonal framework undone at the end of the song by means of an episode that starts in the key of G major, develops in the key of E major, and is resolved with a V–I cadence in a final section, written in the main key, B major.

Rodrigo continued his journey by completing in 1956 his next composition for guitar, *Entre olivares* (Among Olive Groves), which has an Andalusian flavor. His guitar works until then had been inspired more by Castilian rather than Andalusian folklore, but this arrival in Andalusia was going to extend to the end of his career. *En los trigales*, *Bajando de la meseta*, and *Entre olivares* form the suite *Por los campos de España* (Through the Fields of Spain), but Rodrigo did not interrupt his journey there; instead, he continued it by crossing Andalusia from Granada to Cádiz, with two pieces dedicated to Siegfried Behrend and Luise Walker, guitarists who played a major role in the international diffusion of his works. To Behrend he dedicated *Junto al Generalife* (Near the Generalife, 1959), which features the tremolo technique typical of the *toque por granaínas* (Granadan style of flamenco guitar). For Walker he wrote *En tierras de Jerez* (In the Lands of Jerez, 1960), a beautiful *copla* introduced and strongly varied after the fashion of *falsetas*, which signal Rodrigo's evocation of flamenco guitar, though with a harmonic richness that flamenco guitarists would not incorporate into their music for several years yet. The composer referred once to the first works of the series as a "suite after the fashion of Kodak," that is, photographic memories of a journey with a more modern finish than that of the "paintings" of the previous century.

Two important compositions for guitar close the decade we treat in this chapter, both begun in 1959. The first, in response to a commission from the English guitarist Julian Bream, was the *Sonata giocosa* (1959), his first sonata in three movements, a format that would typify some of his best works of the 1960s and '70s.[91] The second was the impressive *Tonadilla* (1959–60) for two guitars, written for the duo of Ida Presti and Alexandre Lagoya.

Bream and Rodrigo first met in 1957. Besides the *Concierto de Aranjuez*, the English guitarist had in his repertoire the *Zarabanda lejana* and *En los trigales*. It appears that it was Rodrigo who offered to dedicate a new composition to him. In January 1958, Bream wrote to Victoria Kamhi suggesting that the work exhibit a character different from those he already knew: "more in the form of a three-movement sonata or sonatina. This would also be most agreeable since many pieces for guitar, however charming, tend to be rather short."[92] Bream wished to receive the composition in May to debut it in the festival Benjamin Britten was organizing in Aldeburgh, in a recital "paying homage to Spanish music." Although it took him a year to complete, Rodrigo followed Bream's recommendation regarding the work's layout. In April 1959, he sent him his *Sonata giocosa* in three movements. The English guitarist's response was surprising: "To be honest, I was a little disappointed with the *Sonata*, not that it hasn't got charm and pleasant textures, [. . .] but for all that, I found it a little empty, and quite frankly lacking in invention [. . .]."[93]

Yet, the *Sonata giocosa* has grace, emotion, and is a mature example of Rodrigo's creative experience. In particular, it is odd that the deep, moving lyricism of the second movement, of an evocative sadness, compelling yet distant, fading away instead of concluding, would not touch Bream's heart. But the guitarist had committed to detaching the guitar from Spanish tradition, an outlook apparent in the following remarks:

The Spaniards are by nature, one might say, an old-fashioned and conservative people. [. . .] So I don't think you should be surprised that they write conservative music; and perhaps the very identification of the guitar with Spain and with Spanish folk culture, which Segovia naturally encouraged, may have held up the guitar's progress toward a more universal musical integration.[94]

One wonders how a culture as "old-fashioned and conservative" as Spain's could produce Pablo Picasso, the most revolutionary artist of the twentieth century, or Federico García Lorca, a leading-edge poet and playwright. Bream's essentializing polemic stops short of considering such anomalies. The stubborn fact remained that the Hispanic tints of Rodrigo's *Sonata giocosa* and the similarity of the third movement to the "Canarios" of the *Fantasía para un gentilhombre* went against Bream's modernist grain. Hence, although Bream offered to finger the work, Rodrigo broke off all communication with him. He sent the *Sonata giocosa* to Renata Tarragó, and it was with the fingering of this guitarist that it was published in London in 1960.

Ida Presti's attitude was the exact opposite of Bream's. Ten years after premiering in Paris the *Concierto de Aranjuez*, Presti asked Rodrigo to write her a guitar duet which she could play with her husband, Alexandre Lagoya. She suggested to him a "Spanish concerto" for two guitars and orchestra.[95] The composer, conscious of the international recognition of the Presti-Lagoya guitar duo and also pleased that Presti had included in her repertoire his recent guitar piece *Junto al Generalife*, unhesitatingly offered them a concerto, although he asked them to be patient.[96] Presti then requested a composition for two guitars for her next concert tour, and her confidence in the result was so unshakable that she only needed Rodrigo to supply a title that she could convey to her impresario.[97] Although the title that Rodrigo had initially improvised was "Music for Two Guitars," in September, while participating in the courses at Santiago de Compostela, he had already decided to entitle his work *Tonadilla*.[98]

The duo began its season in the Opera House of Lille on

November 9. With the month of October well under way, Lagoya asked Rodrigo if it would be possible to have his composition by the end of the month.[99] On October 21, Presti wrote to ask if she should change the program because she still had not received Rodrigo's duet.[100] The first movement was already composed. Rodrigo dictated it against the clock, and Kamhi corrected the manuscript, which reached its performers November 4.[101] In barely five days, the guitarists prepared Rodrigo's piece and premiered it in Lille. Some days afterwards, they wrote with enthusiasm, "Thank you, bravo, it is very beautiful, magnificently written for two guitars, we are very happy."[102] Apparently, the public received this first movement of *Tonadilla*, "Allegro ma non troppo," very well. In it Rodrigo used once more, with great efficacy, the polytonal language that had characterized his first important compositions of the 1920s. Between May and June 1960, Rodrigo completed this type of suite with a brilliant "Allegro vivace," preceded by an ironic, neoclassical "Minuetto pomposo" (including a trio), in which the guitarists detected an evocation of the era of Luigi Boccherini.

The plan was to debut the complete *Tonadilla* during the performance of the duo at the Festival of Aix-en-Provence on 15 July 1960. We do not know whether this premiere took place, but Presti and Lagoya played Rodrigo's work in many of their recitals, recorded it on their album *Musique espagnole pour deux guitares* of 1963 (Philips, 641.729 LL), and arranged for its publication by Ricordi with contractual stipulations that were very favorable to the composer. Meanwhile, Rodrigo made great efforts to find the time and inspiration to write the concerto he had promised. Nevertheless, the difficulties he encountered in completing this new composition in the first half of the 1960s gave proof that something was going wrong.

At the same time that Segovia was launching the *Fantasía para un gentilhombre* on its career in 1958 with performances in San Francisco, Granada, and Madrid, Rodrigo experienced a crisis of nerves that Victoria Kamhi related in the following terms to the guitarist: "Excessive work, worries, and disappointments of the last few months have had a horrible influence on his nerves."[103]

It was a serious condition that had arisen some time earlier and would recur several times in the years to come. Rodrigo's physician had diagnosed his ailment as a "depressive state with a very good prognosis."[104] This crisis would explain why, in the years 1957 and 1958, he hit a dry spell after finishing a soundtrack for the film *El hereje* (1957) and a pair of lesser works—*Música para un jardín* (1957), which reutilizes *Deux berceuses* of the 1930s, and *Folías canarias* (1958) for voice with guitar accompaniment. What was the cause of the exhaustion that his depression had unleashed on this occasion? It was surely an accumulation of factors: extended travels, the empty-nest syndrome stemming from his daughter's departure to study in London, and professional disappointments, among other things. But it could also have had to do with the intense devotion of those years to incidental and stage music, which we will examine in the following chapter.

The *Concierto de Aranjuez* in the 1950s
In the early 1950s, Rodrigo still harbored the hope that Segovia would incorporate the *Concierto de Aranjuez* into his repertory. Segovia insisted on modifying the guitar part, something to which the composer gracefully acceded. Rodrigo mentioned to Segovia the possibility of having the concerto performed at the Festival of Aix-en-Provence as well as for the BBC. And in case Segovia was interested, Rodrigo would reserve these opportunities for him.[105] He was also willing to reserve for him the premiere in the United States during the concert season 1949–50.

However, the guitarist ended up by desisting from tackling a composition that in the 1950s followed a path diverging from his interests as a performer. Hence, it was another Spaniard, Narciso Yepes, who presented the work in Paris, on 7 May 1950 at the Théâtre des Champs-Elysées and with the Orquesta Nacional de España directed by Ataúlfo Argenta. It was a concert over which Miguel Aguirre de Cárcer presided, several months before this diplomat reopened the embassy of Spain in France. It was therefore a relevant act of cultural propaganda, and Rodrigo considered this the initiation of his concerto's global career. The international reputation that Yepes held and the success of his recordings of the *Concierto de Aranjuez* converted him into its main performer during the 1950s.

Instead of Segovia or Yepes, the guitarist who first performed the concerto on a BBC broadcast was Julian Bream, on 21 April 1951, with the BBC Orchestra under the direction of Stanford Robinson.[106] However, according to one critic close to Bream, "Julian was unfortunately balanced with the orchestra so that despite the usual volume he can produce, he was overwhelmed far too frequently."[107]

Sainz de la Maza, for his part, succeeded in premiering the concerto in Mexico. That country had welcomed thousands of Spanish refugees after the Civil War and tenaciously resisted granting legitimacy to the Franco government. But the expatriates were receptive to the *Concierto de Aranjuez*, thanks to the support of three important figures of Spanish music in exile: Adolfo Salazar, Jesús Bal y Gay, and Rodolfo Halffter.[108] The three were old friends of Sainz de la Maza and left aside their political differences with respect to Spain in order to take the opportunity to get together in Mexico. The premiere took place at the Palacio de Bellas Artes in Mexico City on 22 and 24 August 1952, with the Orquesta Sinfónica Nacional conducted by José Pablo Moncayo. Among the critics, there was less unanimity in support of Rodrigo's work than among the exiled Spanish musicians, and Gerónimo Baqueiro Foster referred to it as "hardly meaningful, anachronistic, and corny."[109]

In 1952, Rodrigo finally yielded to demands for performing the *Concierto de Aranjuez* outside the concert hall. It appeared as incidental music in the film version of the play *Don Juan Tenorio* by José Zorrilla, directed by Alejandro Perla with scenery by Salvador Dalí. The climactic scene of this famous theater piece, "¿No es verdad, ángel de amor . . . ?" (It Is Not True, Love Angel . . . ?) unfolds using the music of the concerto's Adagio. Also in 1952, Pilar López's choreographic version was a great success when it debuted in Barcelona on April 12 with soloist Luis Maravilla, who was more of a flamenco than a classical guitarist. With this version, Rodrigo's concerto entered a different dimension of popularity, about which Segovia had clearly warned Rodrigo, "You do very well to refuse the metamorphosis of the *Concierto de Aranjuez*. If Russian and Spanish dancers popularized it, [. . .] the level of its artistic dignity would vanish. And although the tickets of the new version may cost more, do not forget that it is at the expense of the originality, the beauty, and the moral value of the work."[110] Nonetheless, the choreographed version contributed to the diffusion of the *Concierto de Aranjuez* with its success at the Edinburgh International Festival in September 1953,[111] just before it was presented onstage at the Stoll Theatre of London, where one perspicacious critic observed that the *Concierto de Aranjuez* was a kind of *Noches en los jardines de España* for guitar, "with a very poetic nocturne."[112] This association was no mere coincidence, because the first long-playing record of the *Concierto de Aranjuez* appeared on the market with Falla's *Noches* on the other side.

As already seen, Segovia said he had plans in 1951 to record the *Concierto de Aranjuez*. At that time, the only commercial recording was the one made by Sainz de la Maza in 1947, on three 78-rpm records. Nonetheless, in 1952 Yepes and Argenta, with the Orquesta de Cámara de Madrid, made the first long-playing recording for the Alhambra label (MCC 30054). These recordings were the best means for propagating music that could gain only limited exposure in concert halls. In 1957, five years after their first recording, Argenta and Yepes, with the Orquesta Nacional de España, made a second phonograph record for Alhambra (MCC 30054)—the first in stereo—which had an extraordinary international impact. It was this recording that inspired Miles Davis to employ the famous middle-movement melody as the basis for his 1960 LP *Sketches of Spain* (Columbia, CS 8271), though he did so without requesting the composer's permission. Rodrigo successfully sued him for a portion of the royalties, which were considerable. With this arrangement of the Adagio, Rodrigo and his *Concierto de Aranjuez* entered another dimension of celebrity, which we explore in the final chapter.[113]

Chapter 8

Theatrical Adventures and Misadventures

(1951–1960)

Rodrigo WAS AN impassioned lover of opera. He also liked the theater and, to a lesser degree, cinema. For years, he had planned to write a ballet. Yet in the first thirty years of his career, he hardly ever wrote for those genres. Instead, he specialized in concert music and fared very well in that arena. Once the most difficult years of the postwar had elapsed, he managed to buy an attic apartment in Madrid, a seaside cottage in the outskirts of Villajoyosa (Alicante province), a good Bechstein grand piano in 1959, and, in 1962, a Renault Dauphine.

However, he often complained of how little the performances of his works earned him in view of his legal rights as author. He must have envied Falla, whose economic independence stemmed from the success of his ballets, as well as Federico Moreno Torroba and Pablo Sorozábal, who lived very well on the income of popular lyric works mostly premiered in the 1930s. Could he not also achieve success in those musical genres, including not only ballet and zarzuela but also opera? And why had he been overlooked to undertake the lucrative exercise of composing music for the flourishing Spanish film industry of the 1940s and 1950s? Juan Quintero, Jesús García Leoz, and Manuel Parada had made a fortune writing this kind of music, as had Ernesto Halffter. We now explore Rodrigo's efforts in all these directions.

A Tableau That Was Never Seen

Everything about the *Retablo de Navidad* by Joaquín Rodrigo is very complicated, and it was a work that never premiered in its original form. In the composer's catalogue it remained divided into two independent sets: *Villancicos y canciones de Navidad* for soprano, baritone, choir, and orchestra, and *Tres villancicos*, with versions for soprano and orchestra, piano, or guitar accompaniment. *Retablo* had originated as a commission from the Madrid Atheneum for Rodrigo to compose music for a Christmas tableau written by Gerardo Diego. To help finance Rodrigo's labors, the Atheneum announced a contest of Christmas carols in December 1952, with three prizes provided by the General Directorate of Film and Theater.[1] Rodrigo entered the contest and won first prize for the collection of Christmas carols he submitted.[2]

The Atheneum contest, though publicly announced, had the aim of rewarding the tableau music composed by Jesús García Leoz, on the one hand, and the efforts of Rodrigo, on the other. The problem arose when Gerardo Diego claimed half the prize won by Rodrigo: "It is only fair that we split the 15,000 pesetas in two equal parts. My labor on the *Tableau* is equivalent in importance and rank to yours. I have done it completely and you only halfway. [. . .] I have to stick to the only manner of compensation offered and claim through it the part to which I am fairly entitled."[3]

Rodrigo did not yield to the poet's claim, and the latter made a drastic decision that he conveyed to him in writing: "I declare my collaboration with you at an end in this letter, of which I am sending a copy to the [General] Society [of Authors], so that it remains crystal clear that I will not authorize the performance, publication, or printing of any lyric of mine with any music of

TABLE 8.1 **Music for film and stage by Rodrigo between 1951 and 1960**

Year	Title	Genre	Co-authors
1951	El desdén con desdén (A. Moreto)	Incidental music	Luis Escobar (director)
1952	Sor Intrépida	Soundtrack (in collaboration with Juan Quintero)	Rafael Gil (director)
1952/1964	Retablo de Navidad	Songs and choral pieces	Gerardo Diego/ Victoria Kamhi (literary collaborators)
1953	La guerra de Dios	Soundtrack	Rafael Gil (director)
1953	Soleriana (orchestration of eight sonatas by Antonio Soler)	Ballet	Antonio Ruiz Soler (choreographer)
1954	La vida es sueño (Calderón de la Barca)	Incidental music	José Tamayo (director)
1954	La destrucción de Sagunto (J. M. Pemán)	Incidental music	José Tamayo (director)
1954/1964	El hijo fingido	Zarzuela	Libretto by Jesús María Arozamena on a text by Lope de Vega with corrections by Victoria Kamhi
1955	Cyrano de Bergerac (E. Rostand)	Incidental music	José Tamayo (director)
1955	Pavana real	Ballet	Plot by Victoria Kamhi
1956	Tiestes (J. M. Pemán)	Incidental music	José Tamayo (director)
1956	Juana y los caldereros	Ballet	Plot by Victoria Kamhi
1957	El hereje	Soundtrack	Francisco Borja Moro (director)
1957	Música para un jardín	Orchestral music	José María and Manuel Hernández Sanjuán (directors)
1960	La Azucena de Quito	Oratorio (originally conceived as an opera) unfinished	Libretto by José María Valverde

yours."[4] It appears that for the *Retablo de Navidad*, the composer had written four songs on original texts by Diego that he later replaced with others by Victoria Kamhi. She, in turn, made an adaptation of the plot that is preserved in the Archive of the Victoria and Joaquín Rodrigo Foundation. Using this source, we may propose the following reconstruction of Rodrigo's *Retablo de Navidad*:[5]

Scene 1:
1. "Preludio" (instrumental)
2. "Pastorcito santo" (poem by Lope de Vega)
3. "La espera" (text by Victoria Kamhi adapted to the music that Rodrigo composed for the "Letrilla de la Virgen María esperando la Navidad" by Gerardo Diego)

Scene 2:
4. "Cançoneta" (likely the one he composed in 1933)
5. "Duérmete niño" (duet for soprano and baritone adapted by Victoria Kamhi to the music written by Rodrigo for the poem "La cuna" by Gerardo Diego)
6. "Cantan por Belén pastores" (text by Victoria Kamhi)
7. "A la clavelina" (for chorus on a poem by Lope de Vega)
8. "A la chiribirivuela" (chorus to a text compiled in the *Cancionero español de Navidad* by Adolfo Maíllo)
9. "Giga" (presumably the "Giga" from Rodrigo's *Tres viejos aires de danza* of 1929)

Scene 3:
10. "Aire y donaire Air and Grace" (text compiled in the *Cancionero español de Navidad* by Adolfo Maíllo)
11. "Coplillas de Belén" (text by Victoria Kamhi adapted to Rodrigo's music for Gerardo Diego's "La palmera")
12. Unspecified orchestral music

Despite the misfortune of this project in its stage version, among its melodies is one of the most famous and beautiful songs of the composer's catalogue, *Pastorcito santo*.

Soundtracks

Rodrigo began to compose music for film precisely when José Forns (1897–1952) passed away. A member of the Academy of Fine Arts, director of the Society of Film Authors and afterwards of the Film Section of the General Society of Authors of Spain, Forns was a clear and open enemy of Rodrigo. This enmity probably dated back to when they were at the Madrid Conservatory, where Forns occupied a chair of Aesthetics and History of Music, the post to which Rodrigo and Sopeña had aspired. The mention of Rodrigo by Forns in his *History of Music*, widely circulated in Spanish conservatories, put his hostility on public display during the doldrums in which Spanish music criticism seemed to languish: "[Rodrigo is] among the most prolific present-day composers, [. . .] just as he dominates the lyric note of simple and delicate faux folklorism, for the more ambitious enterprises to which he has sought to rise, he is lacking in vigor and personality, although some may come to see in him, with patent exaggeration, as the best Spanish musician of today."[6] Forns was also a jurist specializing in intellectual property, and he passed away in Geneva, where he had traveled in 1952 to represent Spain at an important meeting of UNESCO intended to regulate authorial rights.

In that same year, Rodrigo first collaborated on the soundtrack of a Spanish film, *Sor Intrépida* (Sister Intrepid, 1952), directed by Rafael Gil. *Sor Intrépida*, with its plot about a fashionable singer who becomes a virtuous missionary nun, was financed by the National Delegation of Pontifical Missionary Works. Rodrigo was limited to composing some fragments, among which two religious choruses stand out: "Aleluya," "Quia tu es, Deus, fortitudo mea," and the "Música para el tránsito por el corredor" (Music for the passage through the corridor), which accompanies a moment of great dramatic intensity.[7]

Gil commissioned him to compose the soundtrack of his next production, *La guerra de Dios* (God's War, 1953), one more piece of National Catholic propaganda from the team formed by Gil with the screenwriter Vicente Escrivá and the producer Aspa Film, which was founded by Gil and Escrivá with the sponsorship of the bishopric of Madrid. Rodrigo composed the roughly forty numbers comprising the soundtrack. He took advantage of the opportunity to experiment with the manipulation of a twelve-tone theme that he used time and again throughout his score (musical ex. 8.1). Some years later, speaking about this, he stated, "Twelve-tone style? It seems that those who practice it have a good time. [. . .] I find it simple, too simple, since it seems like a mathematical procedure."[8] However, *La guerra de Dios*, with its strongly doctrinal, dramatic, and social character, is not a simple film. By means of the manipulations to which Rodrigo subjects his twelve-tone theme, the music represents deviousness, social conflict, darkness, and death.

He only employed serialism on one other occasion, in his enigmatic song *La grotte*, a tribute to Debussy for voice and piano setting French verses of Louis Emie and written on a commission of Mai Musical de Bordeaux in 1962, in which it premiered along with the *Invocación y danza* for guitar performed by Alirio Díaz.

Concerning the intensity of his labor on *La guerra de Dios*, the composer recognized that "The nervous excitement produced by long hours of work deprived me of almost all sleep, and that made me resume my work at once."[9] This was clearly a symptom of worsening health. In any case, Rodrigo stressed that "the material compensation afforded by film is higher than any other. And this is an aspect not to be overlooked at all."[10] So great was his compensation that, according to Victoria Kamhi, they were now able to purchase rather than merely rent the property of the attic apartment on Calle Villalar.[11]

Rodrigo wrote the soundtrack of only one other film, the Hispano-Italian co-production *El hereje* (The Heretic) by Fran-

Musical ex. 8.1: Twelve-tone theme of Rodrigo's soundtrack for *La guerra de Dios*

cisco Borja Moro, adapting a tale of José María Sánchez Silva.
Though filmed in 1957, it did not premiere until October of 1958.
It received very negative reviews; however, this did not extend
to the music. The score includes some fragments as long as the
ten minutes accompanying a scene entitled "The Calvary," and
it was based on a texture of growing density which, according
to Antonio Gallego, "would deserve to be heard a second time."[12]
Because of his health problems, Rodrigo delegated part of the
orchestration to Albert Blancafort. Blancafort, who was the
only real disciple that Joaquín Rodrigo had, wrote to his father,
Manuel Blancafort, also a composer, "He trusts me so much that
he doesn't revise my work. He tells me, 'You orchestrate this with
the brass and woodwinds that form the background. And I cope
with this.'"[13]

Finally, *Música para un jardín* (1957), written for a documentary by the brothers José María and Manuel Hernández Sanjuán
about the passing of the seasons in the Madrid park El Retiro,
cannot be considered incidental music. It is instead the filming
of the music of Rodrigo in which the images follow the rhythm
of the composition. He built the work by adding to his *Deux berceuses*, one of fall and the other of spring, two others belonging
to summer and winter, plus a prelude and a postlude. All this
creates his personal version, epigrammatic and dreamlike, of the
four seasons.

In 1959 the composer made the following assessment of his
complete work related to film:

I have already written music for many films. It is true.
I collaborated on *Sor intrépida*. I wrote the score for *La
guerra de Dios*—a difficult, harsh, and long score. Even
more difficult was *El hereje*, where I was to follow the
hero's spiritual transformation step by step, expressing
the hope that little by little invades the protagonist's
soul. My final score was that of a documentary, *Música
para un jardín*—this time, the Madrid park El Retiro—
with which I was to evoke, through the murmur of

its plants, the successive metamorphoses of the four seasons. [. . .] To write music that says something for film and is not a simple background—at times useless or bothersome—is difficult. Film music should stress the voices, gestures, sentiments, and thoughts of the performers. It should express what neither words nor landscapes come to express completely. Ah! And to frame it in a coherent architecture.[14]

In fact, he did not take part in very many films. His devotion to musical composition for theatrical pieces was more intense, mainly in the mid-1950s, even though much less remunerative.[15]

Music for the Theater

Rodrigo collaborated on important productions like the staging of *La vida es sueño* (Life Is a Dream) by Pedro Calderón de la Barca for the Lope de Vega Company, directed by José Tamayo, who represented Spain at the First Sarah Bernhardt Festival of Dramatic Art, in Paris in 1954. This performance, which was not very well received by the French critics, was financed without regard to expenses by Spain's General Directorate of Film and Theater, the General Directorate of International Relations, and the Ministry of National Education. Rodrigo wrote thirteen brief pieces for a chamber ensemble of woodwinds, harp, percussion, strings, and a mixed group of voices. Earlier, he had supplied music for a production of *El desdén con desdén* (Disdain with Disdain) by Agustín Moreto, which premiered on 16 November 1951 at the María Guerrero Theater, under the direction of Luis Escobar, another of the Spanish-theater greats with whom Rodrigo had already collaborated years earlier. The theater critic of *ABC*, Luis Calvo, stressed Rodrigo's work in this production: "He has composed some very beautiful measures, replete, filled with nostalgia, and others, full of merriment, for the songs that Moreto inserted with abundance in his work."[16] In this case, Rodrigo wrote for a small instrumental group comprising flute, violin, and guitar.

Immediately after the performance in Paris of *La vida es sueño*, José Tamayo and his company performed the tragedy *La destrucción de Sagunto*, a grandiose theatrical project to exalt Spain and Spanishness, debuting in the Roman Theater of Sagunto on 8 June 1954. José María Pemán and Francisco Sánchez-Castañer wrote the text, and José Tamayo was general director. Sigfrido Burmann was director of scenery, Manuel Muntañola, Vicente Viudes, and Emilio Burgos collaborated on the illustrations, while Alberto Lorca was choreographer. The cast included close to 400 actors, among whom was the cream of Spanish theater. No effort or expense was spared, and it was completely financed by the Ministry of Information and Tourism—all for a spectacle that was to be very ephemeral and difficult to reproduce. Rodrigo composed an abundance of music for the production, scored for a large complement of wind instruments, percussion, harp, and chorus.

The musical collaboration of Rodrigo with the Lope de Vega Company of José Tamayo continued with the opening production of the 1955–56 season—*Cyrano de Bergerac* by Edmond Rostand—and the following year with the tragedy *Tiestes* of Pemán, which debuted on 7 June 1956 at the Teatro Romano of Mérida, where there was another production of *La destrucción de Sagunto*, though less extravagant.

Pemán and Rodrigo collaborated once again in 1960 in the contest announced by the National Council of Spanish Catholic Action to compose a hymn. That prominent association was in a state of extensive reorganization, and as a strategy to reinforce the cohesion of the diverse groups it embraced, it sought to impose a common hymn upon them. The 10,000-peseta prize for the author of the text, with 25,000 pesetas for the composer of the music, was quite substantial. According to the rules of the contest, the composition had to be "for chorus singing in unison and with an organ." The music had to be "popular, vibrant, melodious, and easy to assimilate and interpret among the masses." The brief text had to express the "ideals and sentiments of Catholic Action." The compositions were to be submitted unsigned before October 31. The jury consisted of the composers Jesús

Guridi, Julio Gómez, and José María Franco, the soprano Lola Rodríguez Aragón, José Perera as leader of the group Cantores de Madrid (Singers of Madrid), four representatives of Catholic Action, and the music critic Juana Espinós as secretary.

The jury selected eight proposals tape-recorded by the Madrigalistas de Madrid, and discarded four. A vote was taken on the four finalists, and the hymn of Pemán and Rodrigo won the prize.[17] Certainly the jury realized that Rodrigo and Pemán had entered the contest, as there was no other duo of musician and lyric-writer that could compete with them. In any case, Pemán gave his winnings to a religious institution from Cádiz, "since not for a single instant would I want anyone to think that I had any lucrative interest in this contest."[18] Rodrigo pocketed his prize money without any qualms because he had ceded the work's copyright in perpetuity to Catholic Action. Moreover, his creation brilliantly solved the difficult problem of composing a popular hymn, and it fulfilled point by point the requirements of the contest. Without sacrificing an ingenious harmonic elaboration, Rodrigo put together a melody that was easy to sing and also vibrant in reaching a melodic climax in the last phrase of the refrain, "For the glory of a better world!"

The movement of Spanish Catholic Action reached the apex of its social influence in the late 1950s, and it began to decline in the following decade. With its commitment to social justice, it was out of step with the ecclesiastic hierarchies and political powers. The strikes in 1962 of Asturian miners, supported by the young brotherhoods and associations of workers connected with Catholic Action, clearly showed a divergence of many Catholics from the Franco regime and the ecclesiastical hierarchy that supported it unconditionally.

The relationship of Joaquín to religion was quite complex. He was not a man who went to Mass every day, or even every Sunday. But neither did he fail to go to church when he considered it opportune, and he always went with his spouse. She observed Jewish customs and traditions in private, and in the same way she would go to synagogue and get involved with Jewish associations in Madrid. But she also had on her nightstand an image of the Virgin. The couple had no conflict in this respect, and when the time came to educate their daughter at a period when the state had ceded educational matters to the Church, they first took her to the French Lycée and then to the Colegio Estudio. The latter, a lay school, was an anomaly within the single-mindedly religious instruction that prevailed during the Franco period; it had carried on the practices of the Institución Libre de Enseñanza, which had been suppressed in the postwar period, at the Colegio Estudio, Cecilia Rodrigo, who had debuted in public as a ballerina in the "Danza de los tristes augurios" (Dance of the Sad Auguries) from *La destrucción de Sagunto* (1954),[19] was able to develop her interest in dance, to the point that after finishing high school in 1957, she enrolled in the Royal Ballet School of London.

Spanish Ballet and Dance

The idea of composing a ballet had intrigued Rodrigo as early as during his years in Paris. Yet, except for the incidental *Danza de la odalisca* for piano composed in 1939 and the orchestrations of Albéniz's music made in the same year for the Sakharoffs (now lost), not until well into the 1950s did Rodrigo complete his first orchestral work for dance. The first such work involved missteps and misunderstandings, and was never performed as intended. It was the orchestration of eight sonatas of Padre Antonio Soler, compiled into a kind of suite, with each sonata given a title related to dance: "Entrada" (Sonata No. 6 in F♯ minor), "Fandango" (Sonata No. 7 in D minor), "Tourbillon" (Sonata No. 11 in G minor), "Pastoral" (Sonata No. 8 in G minor), "Passapied" (Sonata No. 5 in D major), "Fandango a lo alto" (Sonata No. 10 in F major), "Contredanza" (Sonata No. 9 in D♭ major), and "Boleras" (Sonata No. 12 in F♯ major).[20] Two of these sonatas, the fifth and the eleventh, had achieved success in the repertoire of Antonio "El Bailarín" (Antonio Ruiz Soler) starting in 1952, when he danced them in the film *Duende y misterio del flamenco* by Edgard Neville.

Antonio had returned to Spain in 1949 as a noted celebrity after twelve years in the United States and various Latin Ameri-

can countries, where he had developed a major career with performances at Carnegie Hall and in some popular films like *Ziegfield
Girls* (1941) and *Hollywood Canteen* (1944).[21] Encouraged by the
success of the choreography of Soler's sonatas, which he danced
to piano accompaniment, Antonio wished to broaden the set and
give it greater theatrical relief with an orchestral arrangement.
In light of the popularity achieved by the version of the *Concierto
de Aranjuez* choreographed in 1952 by Pilar López, Rodrigo was
aware of the advantage of having his music associated with this
buoyant generation of Spanish dancers, and he seized this excellent opportunity to orchestrate the sonatas selected by Antonio. This choreographed version debuted at the Second Festival
of Spanish Music and Dance of Granada. From the very beginning, it must have been obvious how difficult it was to play and
dance to the very challenging orchestration that Rodrigo had
prepared. Fernández-Cid, in his critique, sounded an alert about
the "excessive optimism" of the composer with respect to the
"orchestras that in this world are to play his version."[22]

In fact, Rodrigo's approach was hardly realistic, and the dancer
immediately saw the difficulties of adjusting his art and his castanets to the composer's orchestral arrangement. He asked him
first to revise his orchestration, and afterwards replaced it with
another by Ángel Currás, the pianist of his company. This new
orchestration was presented at the Teatro Español of Madrid on
13 November 1953. Rodrigo did not attend this premiere because
he was abroad in Greece and Turkey, where the director and
composer Cemal Reşit had organized a festival with his music.
But when he returned to Madrid, there was an unpleasant surprise awaiting him. According to Rodrigo, "When I came back,
my good friend Fernández-Cid pointed out to me that when
Antonio had appeared in Madrid with his show, he had used the
Sonatas de Padre Soler adapted by me but without mentioning
my name."[23]

Rodrigo went to the Sociedad de Autores, where he learned
that Ángel Currás was collecting royalties for the arrangement
of the sonatas of Soler that Antonio was dancing. Rodrigo did
not get in touch with Antonio and Currás because they were on

tour in Europe, with the result that a process of amicable resolution was begun by the Sociedad de Autores. But there arose a greater problem when Rodrigo made statements to the press that offended Currás, who filed a claim against him for slander, seeking an indemnity of 500,000 pesetas. In the event, the contretemps was quickly resolved because the orchestration that Antonio was dancing to was different from Rodrigo's. But the judicial trial was not resolved until 1956, with the composer being absolved and the 25,000 pesetas that he had had to leave as bond returned to him.

Rodrigo's orchestration in a concert version was premiered by the Berlin Philharmonic Orchestra under the direction of Hans von Benda on 22 August 1953. On 22 January 1954, the Orquesta Nacional, under the direction of Argenta, performed this work in the Palacio de la Música of Madrid. It is listed under the title *Soleriana* in the catalogue of Rodrigo's symphonic music, and it is a *tour de force* for orchestras that perform it. This orchestration of Soler's sonatas must have been a good preparatory exercise for the labor Rodrigo was about to undertake in the fall of 1954 with respect to the music of Gaspar Sanz in the *Fantasía para un gentilhombre*.

Rodrigo at once made plans for a much more ambitious undertaking. It would be a ballet with scenery by Salvador Dalí and choreography by Léonide Massine. Though these plans came to naught, Rodrigo very soon began on two new ballets with original music of his own: *Pavana real* (Royal Pavane, 1955) and *Juana y los caldereros* (Juana and the Tinkers, 1956), both based on stories written by Victoria Kamhi. They did not have much success either: *Pavana real* has been staged only three times; *Juana y los caldereros* never had a premiere, and Rodrigo left its music unorchestrated.

Pavana real, the most ambitious ballet composed by Rodrigo, derives from an idea that arose in Paris in 1939 when he and Alexis Roland-Manuel proposed to write a ballet on a theme related to Renaissance Spanish vihuelists. That project fell through, but Victoria Kamhi now took advantage of the creative euphoria experienced by her husband just before sinking into depression and began to draft a plot derived from *Il cortegiano* (The Courtier, 1561) by Baldasarre Castiglione. The story is situated in the viceroyal Valencia of the Duke and Duchess of Calabria, about which the composer had so often lectured. The main characters are the vihuelist Luis de Milán himself, the Duke of Calabria, his wife Germana de Foix, and Doña Mencía de Mendoza. Divided into three acts—*El deseo* (The Desire), *La cacería* (The Hunt), and *Fiesta de mayo* (May Festival)—the work consists of twelve musical pieces, among which the initial fanfare, "Ricercare a modo de Diana," exhibits a strongly imitative character. A charmingly unaffected and very melodious "Cantiga de pastor" (Shepherd's Song) functions as an interlude, followed by *La cacería*, exuding a very dynamic character and great musical energy. This holds true both in the "Danza de cazadores" (Hunters' Dance) and in the "Escena de cetrería" (Falconry Scene), for which Rodrigo recycled the folk theme of "Els tres tambors" that he had earlier used in his tone poem *Per la flor del lliri blau*, though treated here very differently. The act ends with the ballad "Durandarte," which appears in the vihuela book *El Maestro* (1536) by Luis de Milán, and it is performed in pantomime by the viceroy's wife, accompanied by the vihuela player. In the introduction to the *Romance de Durandarte*, Rodrigo quotes the initial phrase of Milán's ballad but later proceeds with his own original music. This is the only piece in the ballet that digresses from the orchestral score as a song with guitar accompaniment, or as a solo guitar piece. Where Rodrigo did utilize a piece by Milán was in the "Danza del Heraldo y Cupido" in his third act, which derives from the orchestration and variation of *Pavana VI* by Milán.

The association of the guitar with the character of Milán, situated at the center of the plot, turns out to be quite effective, although to facilitate programming the work, Rodrigo wrote a part for harp to substitute for the guitar if necessary. In the end, it was not necessary because this ballet is seldom performed, despite its attractive music. Unfortunately, Rodrigo did not assemble a suite of pieces from the ballet that could be

performed by symphony orchestras, so the music is not featured
on concert programs either.

Pavana real, composed in spring 1955, was premiered at the
Gran Teatro del Liceo in Barcelona on December 19 of that same
year. Joan Magriñà was the choreographer and also acted the
part of the Duke of Calabria. The other actor-dancers in the
main ballet roles were Aurora Pons, who played Doña Mencía and
would later direct the Ballet Nacional de España, and Alexan-
dra Dimina as Germana de Foix. The guitar part was played by
Renata Tarragó. Xavier Montsalvatge noted in his critique what
was perhaps the Achilles' heel of the performance, which nonetheless enjoyed a respectable success:

> The costumes individually were not bad, but taken
> together did not form a set. The two stage sets were
> horrible. If care had been taken with the plastic element
> of this work, using curtains and illustrations ordered
> for refined scenery, we would today hail the creation of
> one of the most beautiful and suggestive Spanish ballets,
> with the indisputable quality of its music, that has been
> staged in recent years.[24]

According to Victoria Kamhi, stage sets from Meyerbeer's Les
Huguenots had been repurposed for this production,[25] revealing
not only the poverty of the staging but also a certain hurried-
ness that no doubt impeded getting the work off to a strong
start. After its Barcelona premiere, Pavana real was produced
at the Teatro Colón in Buenos Aires in 1959, with choreography
by Antonio Truyol in a performance that he presented shortly
afterwards in Lima, Peru.

In the summer of 1956, while on a vacation with his wife in
Vienna, Rodrigo wrote to Antonio Iglesias,

> Probably as a result of the effort that I had sunk into
> Pavana real or because this happens to me with definite
> regularity, it is certain that during the months of
> February and March [. . .] I fell into one of those periods

with lack of appetite, depressions, laziness. [. . .] This
had happened to me last summer with the symphony
in which, to be sure, I am quite advanced. [. . .] In April,
when the crisis, laziness or idiocy, whatever you want to
call it, was already over, I began taking trips that are still
going on. But since I am a cyclothymic man, there you
have it: these trips have not stopped me from composing.
[. . .] I have written a ballet that Pilar López already has
in her possession, and she will debut it in the fall.[26]

The symphony was an old project, very sought after by
Sopeña, but it never materialized; the ballet that he had finished
in the summer of 1956 was *Juana y los caldereros*. The plot, newly
written by Victoria Kamhi, was based on the skit *El calderero y
vecindad* (*The Tinker and Neighborhood*, 1777) by Ramón de la
Cruz (1731–1794), for which Rodrigo had written nine new musical numbers occupying about twenty minutes. This would have
been his contribution to the flourishing of Spanish ballet in the
mid-1950s, which boasted compositions by Mompou, Montsalvatge, Ernesto Halffter, and Pablo Sorozábal.[27] Nevertheless,
Pilar López did not manage to choreograph *Juana y los caldereros*. Rodrigo's health was quite poor, and although his own diag-
nosis of cyclothymia (bipolar disorder) could have been accurate,
he had still not been clinically evaluated in a competent way, nor
had he received any form of treatment.

A Zarzuela and an Opera Project

During the second half of the 1950s, the shadow of depression
greatly affected Rodrigo's creative output and would also affect,
though unevenly, his two most ambitious theatrical works: the
zarzuela *El hijo fingido* (The Impostor Son), composed and revised
between 1954 and 1960 but not debuted until 1964; and *La Azucena de Quito*, an opera that later became an opera-oratorio and
remained an unfinished oratorio, from which one of the arias,
entitled "Despedida de Azucena," was debuted in 1960.

El hijo fingido proved to be one more mishap. He wrote it
for a national contest of zarzuelas announced in May 1954.[28] A

first prize of 100,000 pesetas and a second of 50,000 were to be shared between the authors of the libretti and the music. Rodrigo probably saw this as a good opportunity to enter the realm of popular lyric theater; nevertheless, he did not win the contest.[29] In fact, his work did not even receive mention from the jury. To be sure, the fact that the libretto of *El hijo fingido* was an adaptation from classical theater (arranged by Jesús María de Arozamena and based on the play *¿De cuándo acá nos vino?* [1612–14] by Lope de Vega) meant that, according to one of the contest rules, it entered the contest at a disadvantage, with "lower merits." Futhermore, Arozamena's libretto bore witness to his lack of experience in the zarzuela genre.

One of the main problems faced by musicians interested in composing zarzuelas was acquiring a good libretto. In general, successful librettists were reluctant to give their works to composers inexperienced in musical theater, and in particular they had many misgivings about classical composers apt to go outside the limits of an essentially popular genre. Nonetheless, given his great stature in the world of Spanish music, Rodrigo was able to approach the best team of librettists available: Federico Romero and Guillermo Fernández-Shaw. Hence, after the failure of the operetta he had written with Moreno Torroba, *El duende azul*, in 1948 Rodrigo spoke in the press of a libretto that Romero and Fernández-Shaw would have written for him—"a revision, not a review, of our Madrid of yesteryear and the day before yesteryear."[30] Later, Rodrigo and Fernández-Shaw contemplated the possibility of collaborating on a ballet based on a comedy by Tirso de Molina, *Don Gil de las calzas verdes* (1615), for the Ballets de Monte Carlo.[31] Neither the zarzuela nor the ballet got beyond the planning stage, but Rodrigo kept in touch with Fernández-Shaw, and in 1950 he wrote a song based on one of his poems, *Primavera* (1950). This is essentially an aria for coloratura soprano like those introduced in lyrical plays by Romero and Fernández-Shaw after the success of *Doña Francisquita* (1923), with music by Amadeo Vives.

Precisely what zarzuela of the 1950s needed was a "new" *Doña Francisquita*, a smash hit that would revive a dying genre as Vives's score had done thirty years before. And that was what

Rodrigo attempted. Rather than a frivolous zarzuela, what would have served his purposes was a work of higher caliber, one based on comedies of intrigue from the Siglo de Oro. Therefore, he understandably showed interest in the libretto that Arozamena offered him in summer 1954, and in a few weeks he completed a score, with more than the usual quota of musical numbers, upsetting the normal balance between sung and spoken parts.[32] This feature, added to the fact that his zarzuela lacked any choral numbers, prejudiced the jury against it. Arozamena, who had named his libretto a "comic opera," and Rodrigo, who referred to his work as a "lyric comedy," had proposed a kind of opera buffa with spoken parts, in two acts, preceded by a prologue. This model was something he clarified in an interview when asked to which genre he would ascribe his work: "I think it is a musical comedy in the style of opera buffa."[33] That response clarified nothing, and the work fell into oblivion for almost a decade. It was revived when Lola Rodríguez Aragón, godmother of Cecilia Rodrigo, took charge as *empresaria* of the Teatro de la Zarzuela between 1958 and 1960. She encouraged Rodrigo to make a revision that would include choral numbers.[34] As Arozamena had lost all interest in *El hijo fingido*, Victoria Kamhi undertook the revision of the libretto, and the work at last rose to the stage of the Teatro de la Zarzuela on 5 December 1964 with an excellent cast and production staff. In a self-critique published the day before the debut, Rodrigo offered some important keys to the focus he had given to his work: "Everything is melody. I have tried as much as possible to avoid my classical technique and habits to work in an orchestra that is like a small footstool, placed in the service [. . .] of the sparkle and enhancement of the voices."[35]

The reception of *El hijo fingido* was very uneven, but the negative critiques focused mostly on the libretto. Those aligned with the musical avant-garde, like Enrique Franco, wrote that the adaptation was naïve and anachronistic,[36] while Fernando Ruiz Coca considered the plot inadmissible for a twentieth-century setting.[37] Other critics closer to Rodrigo, like Federico Sopeña and José María Franco, stressed that what was truly worthwhile in *El hijo fingido* was Rodrigo's music.[38] Yet not even these favorable critiques of the music seemed good enough to the Rodrigos. Their ill feeling was so intense that the close relationship with Sopeña was seriously damaged. But in the end, this work, like the concerto for cello, remained in limbo. The *Concerto in modo galante* lay between a concerto and a *sinfonía concertante*, just as *El hijo fingido* was situated somewhere between a *zarzuela grande* (three-act zarzuela) and an opera buffa with spoken dialogue. Neither fish nor fowl, it lacked a clear identity and has not endured.

What happened with *La azucena de Quito* was even worse, because most of it remained unwritten. Nonetheless, its history turns out to be interesting for the zeal with which Rodrigo for many years tried to find a way forward with this composition. Further, he depended on José María Valverde, a writer who would have a major impact on the literary culture of his time. Valverde's ideological embrace of a kind of Christianity bordering on Marxism leaned toward liberation theology, making him a good candidate to write the libretto of *La azucena de Quito*. It deals with Mariana de Jesús (1618–1645), an Ecuadorian saint, canonized in 1950, revered by the people, and remembered, among many other things, for the songs she sang while accompanying herself on the guitar. The project was generously financed by Juan March through the foundation that he had established in 1955.

Yet the year 1957, which he should have dedicated to this project, literally went flying by as he embarked on a series of trips to Paris, Venezuela, Puerto Rico, and New York from February to April. Further, he devoted much time to the soundtrack of *El hereje*. Claiming that he had poorly calculated the time it would take him to compose the opera-oratorio, Rodrigo was granted a yearlong extension. It was the worst moment to shackle himself to an undertaking of this magnitude. First, he had to make an exhausting trip to attend the premiere of the *Fantasía para un gentilhombre*, which had him crossing the United States from coast to coast during the months of March and April 1958. Second, he fell into a serious depression. Rodrigo even attempted to return the money that the Juan March Foundation had awarded him, and in 1960 he abandoned the project altogether after having composed only a few scenes from the first act. To settle his debt, in 1963 he handed in to the foundation the unpublished score of *El hijo fingido*, still undebuted at the time.[39] It was a bad period for Spanish lyric theater in general.

Chapter 9

The Final Years

Florescence, Fame, and Legacy
(1963–1999)

T HE YEAR 1963 was a particularly eventful and significant one in the life of the Rodrigos, as well as the world at large. On January 19, they celebrated their thirtieth anniversary, but the most momentous occasion that year was the marriage of their daughter Cecilia to Agustín León Ara, a violin virtuoso originally from Tenerife in the Canary Islands who was now active in Brussels, where Cecilia had a dance academy. These newlyweds would spend many happy and productive decades together, and they produced two children of their own: Cecilia in 1967 and Patricia in 1970. The nuptials took place on April 6 in Madrid's Iglesia de la Ciudad Universitaria (Church of University City). Rodrigo friend and biographer Federico Sopeña, her godfather, delivered a speech for the occasion, while the proud father of the bride offered a new work especially for this ceremony, the *Cánticos nupciales* for three sopranos and organ, utilizing texts from the book of Tobias, Psalms 31 and 128, and the Gospel of St. John.

In May, Joaquín and Victoria Kamhi journeyed to Cullera, on the Mediterranean coast about twenty miles south of Valencia, where they were building a chalet facing the beach "in a leafy grove of pine trees."[1] This would provide them with a summer retreat from the heat of Madrid. However, the highlight of this particular summer would not be a retreat in Cullera but rather a trip to Puerto Rico, where Joaquín had been engaged by the Universidad de Río Piedras to teach a course on the history of music. Both were touched by the "warm hospitality" shown them there.[2] A notable manifestation of this high regard was a Rodrigo Festival that took place on November 6 in the Grand Theater, to honor the visiting musical dignitary. The selection of his works included the *Fantasía para un gentilhombre*, with Narciso Yepes as soloist, a concerto now entering the mainstream of the guitar repertoire only five years after its San Francisco premiere by Andrés Segovia.

However, this joyous event was soon overshadowed by the assassination of John F. Kennedy on November 22, which coincidentally was the maestro's birthday. Kamhi vividly recalls the "ear-splitting screams" of a neighbor who delivered that tragic news of the president's death. "There was an outpouring of sympathy and emotion, followed by days of anxiety and sorrow in the entire country."[3] The world looked on in horror and trepidation, as the West's Cold War with the Soviet Union was at its height, and no one could say what the implications of the assassination would be for that. Kennedy's all-too-brief presidency had witnessed the disastrous Bay of Pigs invasion in 1961, a vain attempt to overthrow the Castro regime, and then the Cuban Missile Crisis in fall of 1962, during which the world teetered on the brink of a nuclear holocaust. Kennedy's murder raised suspicions of communist involvement—Cuban, Soviet or both—and it was obvious that the end of the Cold War was nowhere in sight; in the event, it would get hotter before it ended, as the United States' involvement in Vietnam deepened with the ascent of Lyndon Baines Johnson to the presidency.

Yet, Franco's Spain benefited from its ardent anti-communism, and it was reliably on the side of the United States and its allies in opposing the Soviet Union. This meant the inflow of economic assistance from the International Monetary Fund and World Bank. But Spanish diplomacy was cultural as well as geopolitical, and it was increasingly the works of Rodrigo that defined Spain to the outside world, as it was music that actually sounded Spanish. And the works that gained the most traction in this respect were, not surprisingly, for the guitar. Rodrigo became a sort of cultural ambassador, one whose *Concierto de Aranjuez* was now the most recognized composition by a modern Spanish composer. After the release of Miles Davis's *Sketches of Spain* in 1960, it found its way into mainstream popular culture around the world.

In the 1960s, liberalization of the Spanish regime took place gradually and at many levels, and it was greatly aided by the steady improvement in Spain's economy that occurred over that period. In fact, its impressive rate of growth was matched by no other country except Japan.[4] It was driven to a large extent by tourism, which in turn stimulated economic modernization and liberalization. As Spain became more industrialized and urban, it also experienced the growing strength of labor unions and demands for greater political freedom. Strikes occurred with increasing frequency, and young people in particular were less content with the status quo.[5]

Franco's government waged a charm offensive in the 1960s to maintain the support and confidence of the United States and Western Europe. This project was largely cultural, to show that despite the dictatorship, Spain was a modern country and sufficiently tolerant to merit continued assistance. Thus, the liberalization of culture "lent a patina of credibility to the regime."[6] After all, a too-rigid, too-brutal dictatorship would have made it politically difficult for democratic regimes to lend it aid. Franco's Spain had to put its best foot forward on the international stage if it was to continue on its upward trajectory, and to conceal as best it could its continued opposition to regionalist forces, labor unrest, and political dissent, especially among students and intellectuals—who nonetheless led the way toward reform.

In 1969, Franco designated as his successor Juan Carlos de Borbón, grandson of Alfonso XIII. He thought this young man sufficiently conservative and dedicated to authoritarianism that the regime would be safe with him. Instead, King Juan Carlos was dedicated to the opposite of autocracy, and thus the old dictator's determination to restore the aristocracy would have unforeseen and unintended consequences. With Franco's death in 1975, the attendant ideology of *franquismo* was finally bereft of any residual *raison d'être*. Moreover, "during the final years of the Franco regime, the vast majority of Spaniards saw it as normal that the political future of the country should be similar to the present of other European countries [. . .] [young people] could not conceive of a future which was not similar to their neighbors.'"[7] Thus, dictatorship in Spain ended with a whimper, not a bang. The first free and fair general elections since 1936 were held nineteen months after Franco's death, on 15 June 1977, and brought a significant number of socialists into the parliament. In 1982, Felipe González was elected Spain's first socialist prime minister since the days of the Second Republic.

All of these developments had far-reaching implications for Spanish culture. The 1978 Constitution heralded a new era of press freedom. The Ministry of Culture recovered and promoted the cultural legacy suppressed by Franco, celebrating the work of exiled artists and intellectuals. The socialist government was determined to build on these advances and bring the resources of the government to bear on promoting the arts. And as Kamhi noted, Queen Sofia was a big fan and attended concerts of Rodrigo's music: "Her love of music is proverbial, and it is well known that she never misses a good concert."[8] Queen Sofia became a leading patroness of Spanish arts, which underwent a dramatic transformation during the second half of the twentieth century.

The Spanish Avant-garde in Music

Though Franco and the avant-garde made for very strange bedfellows, the artistic avant-garde's aesthetic goals meshed perfectly with the regime's *realpolitik*. As Luis Marzo observes, "Spain's abstract expressionists were not only palatable to

Franco's regime, they unwittingly served its interests. Franco's state wanted art that could be exported as proof of the regime's spiritual values, but that did not carry any overt political criticism. Abstract expressionism was perfectly suited to this purpose."[9]

The same could be said of avant-garde music. By the mid-1960s, composers within Spain such as Luis de Pablo had long since embraced the international avant-garde. Luis de Pablo and his progressive contemporaries are collectively referred to as the Generation of 51, and they formed ensembles and institutes devoted to the performance of avant-garde music. The contrast between Rodrigo and this new generation of composers is illustrated by considering the initial concert by Zaj, a group founded in 1964. The first work on the program was John Cage's *4'33"* (1962). This was later followed by Cage's *Variations III* (1963) for prepared piano.[10] During the 1960s, another major influence on Spanish composers was Darmstadt and Karlheinz Stockhausen. At this same time, Rodrigo had not yet written his *Concierto andaluz* (1967) or *Concierto para una fiesta* (1982). In the age of hip-hop, such distinctions may seem trivial, but at the time, these two radically different approaches to composition demarcated radically different worldviews. Rodrigo summed up his own perspective when he referred to contemporary music as "excessively cerebral" and called for a music that was more "humane, more attentive to natural sensibilities, more expressive and less driven by a desire for novelty, and above all more independent of what many have called the 'tyranny of modern art.'"[11]

In fact, one must say that, despite the flowering of the Spanish avant-garde in the 1960s, the outside world continued to focus on the older compositions of Rodrigo, especially those resting on the Spanish musical heritage such as *Cuatro madrigals amatorios* (1948) and *Fantasía para un gentilhombre* (1954). These provided the musical equivalent of the tourism on which the Spanish economy became increasingly dependent in the 1960s, with their appealing and accessible evocations of Spanish monuments and places, songs and dances. The inability of the Spanish avant-garde to displace the traditionalists at home resulted largely from a lack of domestic enthusiasm for experimental music.

Yet, if one compares this to the way that avant-garde music was suppressed in the Soviet Union, denounced as decadent and formalistic, insufficiently relevant to the proletariat, one can see why atonal music became a useful ace in the hole in Cold War poker. It did not matter whether the Franco regime and the Spanish public liked it. All that mattered was that it made them *look* better than the Bolsheviks. And just as abstract painting posed no iconographic threat to either the Church or the regime, so atonal music was safely apolitical. It deployed no hymns or songs associated with any oppositional political movement, and its disdain for folklore made it mute in matters of regional separatism. It made no attempt, had no real ability, to mobilize the masses or inspire insurrection. The relative indifference of the Spanish public to that sort of thing made it harmless enough.

In fact, at the same time the regime capitalized on and claimed as its own the triumphs of the musical avant-garde, it was benefiting from the overseas success of the progressive Spanish artists. It projected this renovated image outward to rehabilitate its reputation and to stimulate the tourist industry, which would in turn help to stabilize and legitimize the regime. Rodrigo's music projected a positive image of Spain, and that served both its cultural and geopolitical purposes.

The Same Old Busy Routine, but Different New Vocal Works

And it was not only Spain that was in a period of stability and growth it had not known for decades. Rodrigo's life exhibited a similar trajectory, and these last three and a half decades present us with a sort of paradox. Even as his domestic life settled into an established routine, centered in Madrid, economically secure, and unthreatened by civil conflict or world war, his professional life became more and more hectic. He remained productive as a composer, one with an increasingly large reputation thanks in large measure to his hugely popular guitar concertos. Leading musicians were lining up to commission works from him, especially concertos, and not solely for the guitar. He was in nearly constant demand as a professor, guest lecturer, and visiting dignitary, often in the role of cultural diplomat. Thus, his travels spanned the globe as he attended Rodrigo Festivals from Mexico City to Tokyo and Puerto Rico to London. It was as if every time the phone rang or they turned on the radio or television, there was news of some award or honor conferred upon him. As the years progressed, he became something of a cultural icon, one whose diminutive physique, dark glasses, and unruly white hair were recognizable to ordinary people who had seen him on television and recognized him on the street. Autograph seekers were not shy in requesting his signature. Few composers have enjoyed within their own lifetimes the degree of celebrity he achieved. Clearly, this confluence of events would not have been possible in earlier, more tumultuous decades of Spanish and world history.

For both the momentous and quotidian goings-on of these years, the ensuing narrative is deeply indebted to Kamhi's memoirs, of which she noted that "Since 1942 I had jotted down something almost every day about the vicissitudes of our busy life and the most important events of the Madrid musical scene."[12] Kamhi described 1963 as commencing with "the same busy routine as always: visits and visitors, interviews and concerts."[13] In some respects, this sums up their existence, domestic as well as professional, during the final four decades together. Their lives had settled into a routine, one that would facilitate rather than impede their creative endeavors. And routine notwithstanding, there was still plenty of excitement.

After a festival of Rodrigo's music in Puerto Rico in early 1964, the composer and his wife returned to Madrid on February 2, and a little over two months thereafter, on April 9, they received news of another distinction bestowed on Rodrigo, an honorary doctorate from the University of Salamanca, among Spain's oldest and most prestigious institutions of higher learning. The year culminated with the premiere of the composer's lyric comedy *El hijo fingido*. If anyone required proof that there was nothing a blind composer could not compose, this ill-fated zarzuela was it.

The following year, Rodrigo reverted to his traditional metier, writing a concerto requested by the phenomenal guitar duo of Ida Presti and Alexandre Lagoya, the *Concierto madrigal* (1966), though Presti's tragically premature demise in 1967 at the age of 42 prevented them from premiering the work. That privilege was later given to Pepe and Ángel Romero in 1970. After his earlier collaborations with Sainz de la Maza and Segovia, Rodrigo would soon develop a close friendship and musical collaboration with the Romero family of guitarists, to which we shall shortly return. A subsequent trip to Tenerife concluded with Rodrigo's completion of the *Cuatro canciones sefardíes* (1965), a musical testament to the high esteem in which he held his wife's cultural heritage as a Sephardic Jew.

Rodrigo's fascination with the Sephardic tradition had already manifested in *Triste estaba el rey David* (1950) and the *Dos canciones sefardíes del siglo XV* (1950) for mixed chorus. Further inspired to honor her cultural heritage, Rodrigo soon thereafter composed a set of four songs, for soprano and piano, based on anonymous texts preserved by Menéndez Pidal and adapted by Victoria Kamhi.[14]

1. "Respóndemos" (dedicated to the memory of his father-in-law, Isaac Kamhi)
2. "Una pastora yo amí" (dedicated to Prof. M. J. Benardete)
3. "Nani, nani" (dedicated to Pilar, a painter, and her husband, Walter Rubin, director of the Spanish Program for the American military base at Torrejón de Ardoz and subsequently professor of Spanish literature at the University of Houston)
4. "Morena me llaman" (dedicated to Isabel Penagos, a singer and friend of the Rodrigos)

These premiered at the Ateneo de Madrid on 18 November 1965, with Fedora Alemán, soprano, and Miguel Zanetti, piano.

Rodrigo utilized the traditional words and melodies in these settings, but he fashioned the accompaniments himself. He commented on the difficulties inherent in harmonizing a popular song, which requires nothing more than a "light support, a diminutive escort, but should nonetheless breathe new life into old numbers."[15] The first of these numbers is a psalm-like invocation of a religious character, while the second is a pastoral love song. The third is a lullaby exhibiting "intelligent tenderness."[16] The fourth song takes up a time-honored motif of the dark-hued woman ("Morena"), commonly found in traditional Spanish songs. It provides a high-spirited conclusion to the cycle. In terms of the compositional technique, these songs respect the originals while bringing something new to the musical table. Rodrigo opts for strophic form in all four songs, and the tempos range from *Lento* (1 and 3) to *Andante moderato* (2) to *Allegretto grazioso* (4), thus avoiding extremes. The tonal-modal organization is worth noting, as it progresses from E Aeolian to G Aeolian, then to B minor and G minor, thus spelling out an E-minor chord.[17] This kind of overarching harmonic plan gives the cycle a sense of coherence and is a technique favored by our composer.

In this same prolific year of 1965, he composed yet another impressive collection of songs. *Cantos de amor y de guerra* (Songs of Love and War, 1965) is a cycle with a clearly stated thematic thrust.[18] The title immediately reminds one of Claudio Monteverdi's eighth and final book of madrigals, *Madrigali guerrieri, et amorosi* (Madrigals of War and Love), published in Venice in 1638. These songs characterized Monteverdi's *stile concitato*, or "agitated style," replete as they are with expressive and often strident rhythms and harmonies. Though Rodrigo made no allusion to Monteverdi's work in his own commentary on these songs, given his avocation as a music historian, he cannot have been unaware of the inevitable comparison. He had madrigals on his mind at that time, as evidenced by the aforementioned *Concierto madrigal* of 1966, based on a Renaissance madrigal by Jacques Arcadelt.

The five songs were originally composed for soprano and orchestra but were later arranged for voice with piano accompaniment by the Valencian composer Vicente Asencio (Kamhi later revised the reduction). These songs were preserved in a variety of sixteenth-century collections, called *cancioneros*, and the texts were freely adapted by Victoria Kamhi. The set is dedicated to the composer's daughter, Cecilia.

1. "Paseábase el rey moro."
2. "¡A las armas, moriscotes!"
3. "¡Ay, luna que reluces!"
4. "Sobre Baza estaba el rey."
5. "Pastorcico, tú que has vuelto."

The initial orchestral version was premiered by soprano Ana Higueras and the Orquesta Sinfónica de Radio Televisión Española on 15 March 1968, at the Ministerio de Información y Turismo in Madrid.

Three of the songs (1, 2, 4) deal with themes of war, and two (3, 5) are love songs. The subjects of the war songs pertain to conflicts with the Moors during the Middle Ages. Number 1 is a ballad in imitation of Arabic poetry dating from the early 1300s and may pertain to the 1482 battle of Alhama, in which the Christians defeated the Muslims. The lyrics of number 2 urge Christianized Moors, *Moriscotes*, to take up arms in their defense. Number 4 is narrated from the perspective of King Fernando I of León in the mid-1000s as he surveys his vast army, having enjoyed repeated success in battling the Moors. Of the love songs, number 3 is a simple utterance of praise to the moon's reassuring light. The final song in the collection is a pastoral lament for a lost love.

The melodies often remain true to the original, though the ingeniously contrived accompaniments are clearly products of the century in which the composer lived and make no attempt to mimic early harmonies. Their purpose is to accentuate the meaning of the text; however, as the composer makes clear in his commentary on them, he uses sparse instrumental resources, despite the deployment of an orchestra consisting of flute, oboe, 2 clarinets, snare drum, and strings.[19] He hardly ever resorts to *tutti* passages, and chooses his timbres carefully, so as never to overwhelm the voice. In his own words, he wanted to preserve the "atmosphere" of the romances by keeping the harmonization "simple" and the orchestration "sober."[20] Indeed, the strings only appear in the first two songs, and the third song utilizes only flute accompaniment. Its melody is the only one in this cycle that he freely composed, rather than relying on the original. The fourth presents harp, flute, oboe, horn and trumpet, while the final features only brass and snare drum.

Perhaps the most fruitful development at this time, however, was the advent of his *Himnos de los neófitos de Qumrán*, a work begun in 1965 and completed in 1974. This final set of songs we examine reveals the composer's ongoing passion for exploring Jewish history, but extending long before the Expulsion or any meaningful reference to Sephardic Jews. In this case we go back to biblical times and a community of believers in an imminent apocalypse, a community centered on the shores of the Dead Sea at Qumran.

The *Himnos de los neófitos de Qumrán* for voices and chamber ensemble is a singular work in the catalogue of Joaquín Rodrigo. It displays none of the composer's characteristic referencing of Spain's cultural legacy, indeed of Spain at all. Gone are any and all allusions to the *Siglo de Oro* or to folklore. And also gone is *neocasticismo*.

This is a work that takes us to another dimension, not just in the composer's output but in time and space. The *Himnos* transport us to a realm of thought and feeling as alien to Andalusia as the moon, and the musical language Rodrigo invents to convey this sense of the alien is similarly far removed from boleros and fandangos. On a personal level, the work may well represent a sort of juncture of Christian and Jewish traditions, just as Rodrigo's marriage in 1933 to Victoria Kamhi represented a union of Spanish Catholicism and Sephardic Judaism. And the open expression of this union in so experimental a work was consonant with the zeitgeist of the 1960s and '70s, during which there was a marked liberalization in Spain's political life and increasing religious tolerance in the wake of the Second Vatican Council (1962–65). Of course, the work would not have been possible at any time without the fortuitous discovery of the Dead Sea Scrolls in 1946–47.

About two millennia ago, these scrolls were placed in clay jars and hidden in caves near the Dead Sea. The fragments of papyrus, leather, and even copper, numbering over 100,000, coalesce into about 900 documents in Hebrew, including books from the Hebrew Bible as well as certain Apocryphal writings accepted by Roman Catholicism and Eastern Orthodoxy, though not by Jews and Protestants. There are also nonscriptural writings, such as the Manual of Discipline and the Damascus Document, which were also part of the library of a group of Jews who inhabited the caves at Qumran and organized themselves into a religious community that practiced celibacy and other spiritual disciplines. Most scholars believe that Qumran was a monastic outpost of the Essenes, a prominent sect of Jews preparing for the Apocalypse.[21] Kamhi described these texts as the "hymns which the novices used to sing, in a solemn ceremony, on the day of the admission into the community."[22]

Rodrigo wrote the first *Himno* for the 1965 Semana de la Música Religiosa (Week of Religious Music) in Cuenca, and it premiered at the Iglesia de San Miguel on 15 April. The premiere went well but left many in the audience feeling that the work was too short, so he amplified it by adding a couple of strophes and by composing two more *Himnos*. The three *Himnos* together premiered a decade later, at the 1975 Semana de la Música Religiosa in Cuenca, on 25 March. Shortly after the 1965 performance, the Rodrigos traveled to Israel, and in the Archeaology Museum in Jerusalem they were able to view the actual Dead Sea Scrolls. "When we landed at Lod airport, my nerves were in such a state that I scarcely recognized the friends and relatives who had come to welcome us! It all seemed like a dream!"[23]

In Rodrigo's personal library, located in the Fundación Victoria y Joaquín Rodrigo (Madrid), Nelson Orringer located the sixth edition of the book *The Dead Sea Scrolls*, written by John Marco Allegro and published in 1961.[24] The work was heavily annotated by Victoria Kamhi, who was so excited to read it that she even made a handwritten list of its illustrations.

When Victoria Kamhi read Allegro's text, she conceived the idea that her husband could set the hymns to music. The text itself quoted the words of two hymns taken from the *Canon of the Community of Qumrân*, and these hymns were to form the second and third *Himnos* composed by Rodrigo.[25] The lyrics of the first *Himno*, in Orringer's opinion, are a poetic composition by Kamhi herself, made in imitation of the style of the lyrics of the other two hymns, which in turn imitated well-known biblical passages and the Hebrew liturgy. In this first *Himno*, whose lyricism and stylistic flexibility surpass those of the others, Kamhi appears to paraphrase the prose text of Allegro's conjectures about the daily life of the Qumran community.

In his commentary on the *Himnos de los neófitos de Qumrán*, Rodrigo stresses the enigmas of the universe, rendered even more enigmatic by his attempt to reconcile Jewish with Christian symbols. His three sopranos symbolize the three archangels (Gabriel, Michael, and Raphael) of the Judeo-Christian tradition. His four-part male chorus (TTBB) represents the neophytes of Qumran, who he says include ascetics, sages, and observers of the stars and the heaven, with their "eternal mystery for the human being."[26]

Rodrigo's chamber orchestra consists of two flutes, bassoon, timpani, crotales (small antique cymbals), xylophone, vibraphone, timpani, tam-tam (gong), celeste, harp, violas, cellos, and basses. There are no brass and no violins, oboes, or clarinets. Concerning his orchestration, he notes his striving for "extreme sobriety," minimized to give emphasis to the text, loaded as it is with symbols. This subordination is a tenet of the "New Liturgy" mentioned in Rodrigo's commentary, by which he was referring to the extensive liturgical reforms that emerged from Vatican II (1962–65).[27] The humbling of the musician to the liturgy would explain the relegation of instruments to the lowly rank of a mere utensil, for the greater glory of God.

The composer gives special symbolic value to the number three and multiples thereof: he speaks in his program of three numerical symbols, with the first standing for his (original) nine-note scale, about which we will have more to say below; the second, for the repeated calls of the celeste, as if invoking the greatness of God, as do Kamhi's lyrics repeatedly; and the third, for the invocation of the three archangels.

The number four relates to the cardinal points, north, east, south, west, and is therefore associated with the terrestrial domain. Thus, though there are dozens of gospels, only four are deemed canonical, as they represent the revelation of Jesus's life and mission to those who inhabit this world. It is apparent, then, that both the numbers three and four have sacred significance in Judaism and its offshoot, Christianity. Their sum is seven, which is especially significant within the ancient Jewish numerological system, as it corresponds to the number of days in the week, culminating in the Sabbath. Their product, however, is twelve, which corresponds not only with the tribes of Israel but also with the canonical number of Jesus's disciples.

As to the second and the third hymns, with his reverence for the number three, Rodrigo stated his wish to form a kind of "triptych," a notable anachronism, as these three-paneled altarpieces only began to be used in Christianity during the Middle Ages. Using the same nine-note scale and instrumental and vocal combination, with the three sopranos alternating with the four-part male chorus, Rodrigo strives for a unified composition. However, for unexplained reasons, he gives greater importance to the male chorus in the third hymn. The dramatism of the third hymn is the greatest of all three, as the speaker here sets forth the battle between good and evil at the end of days. The chorus declaims the lyrics in a reverent, prayer-like recitative. The theme, we have seen, is more earthly, excluding the angelic soprano voices.

What interests us here are the precise musical means by which Rodrigo conveyed not just the meaning of the words that Kamhi provided him but the ambience of this religious gathering, its rituals and beliefs. He would have to resort to a musical language as distant from the *Concierto de Aranjuez* as the caves of Qumran were from his Paris apartment. This music would go well beyond being merely "exotic," replete with local color. It would have to be wholly "other." Even a cursory look at the score reveals salient characteristics of this alien soundscape. And the essence of this "otherness" is duality. The conflict between the opposing forces of Light and Dark suggests the binary nature of our world, which will manifest in ways both subtle and obvious in the music.

The composer himself posited a nine-note "scale" as the numerically symbolic basis for the work: B–F–A–C♯–D–E–F–G–C♮. Despite the two F's, it is more properly described as a pitch collection rather than a scale, insofar as the first four notes constitute an augmented triad on F resting on a tritone formed by B below the F. This highly dissonant chord is the one on which the male choir will chant its portions of text, and the symbolic implications of this sonority will become clear further on. The final four notes, D–E–F–G, and concluding with a perfect-fourth leap to C, provide the substance of a sequence of seven notes played on the celeste, with which the work begins (musical ex. 9.1). It is a sort of leitmotif that is stated three times, each rotation separated from the next by a measure of silence, and all of it in 4/4 meter, marked "Lento." This opening threefold statement is a framing device that is mimicked at the end of the first hymn with three intonations of "Amen."[28]

Rodrigo refers to this as the generative motive of the entire work.[29] The brief motive starts on D_5 and rises to Db_6 before descending to E_5 and then leaping up to C_6, which then vibrates through the ensuing measure rest. Regardless of their register, however, the pitches are laid out in a conspicuously symmetrical fashion: D–F–G–Db–F–E–C. That is, the last three notes constitute a retrograde reiteration of the first three, though one step lower and with a major rather than a minor third. The climactic Db forms a tritone with the preceding G, highlighting again that dissonant interval and creating a sensation of harmonic instability—and perhaps anticipation of what is about to unfold.

Musical ex. 9.1: *Himnos de los neófitos de Qumrán I*, m. 1

One might conclude that the basic modality here is centered on D, with the insertion of an enharmonically spelled leading tone (Db = C#). Yet, the real significance of C# becomes clear at the end of each of the three *Himnos*, which cadence on A major. Since modal determination hinges on the concluding note or harmony of a composition, we would be justified in viewing A as the "tonal center" of a work that exhibits in every other respect considerable tonal ambiguity and dissonance. This generative seven-note motive in the celeste serves an important structural function, insofar as it recurs not only throughout the first of the *Himnos* but also the second, thus providing thematic unity and continuity of affect. It even makes a cameo appearance in the third *Himno* at mm. 29–30, transposed up a whole step, and is then sounded one final time in its original form at mm. 56–57. Indeed, Rodrigo's concern for unity is apparent in the restatement of melodic and rhythmic motifs throughout the *Himnos*.

Though the score indicates that the final note of this opening gambit should be allowed to vibrate through the measure of rest, the contrast between sound and silence is a conspicuous instance of a very expressive kind of dualism. Another is the cross-relation between D♮ on which the motive begins and the Db at its peak. The significance of Db is its enharmonic relation with C#. It is curious that Rodrigo's nine-note "scale" repeats D but excludes Db, using only C#, whose key role as the Picardy third of the final A-major sonority of each *Himno* we have already noted. Finally, the sound of the celeste may suggest to some the ceremonial function of bells in the Christian liturgy, to summon worshippers to prayer, though bells and other instruments now play no role in Jewish worship. Nonetheless, there is a unifying consistency between the celeste's timbre and the other metallic percussion here, especially the gong and vibraphone. Regardless of all this, these isolated sounds of the celeste and the tonally ambiguous statement it utters create a sort of "alien" ambience that is both strange and alluring. Although Rodrigo eschews monophony in his vocal writing, the celeste solo is precisely that: monophonic.

The texture of the *Himnos* is sparse, and *tutti* passages are rare. Thus, though this is not a neoclassical work *per se*, the neoclassical aversion to late-Romantic orchestral opulence is clear. Also consistent with his neoclassical moorings is the use of bitonal harmonies and acerbic dissonances within an otherwise tonal/modal context, for instance in the harp toward the beginning of *Himno III*. The harp, traditionally associated with King David, is more prominent here than in the preceding *Himnos*, and its pungent bitonal juxtapositions consist of B–F♯–B in the left hand and C–E–A in the right.

What most intrigues is the handling of the voices, which are after all delivering the actual texts of the *Himnos*. The radically different textures assigned to the sopranos on the one hand and the male chorus on the other suggest to the listener a dualism directly related to the overarching theme of the conflict between Light and Dark, between heaven and earth, a dualism reinforced by the high notes of the sopranos and the low notes of the tenors and basses. Moreover, the texts sung by the male chorus are consistently presented in a homorhythmic fashion, marked "Quasi recitativo," that resembles a sort of mumbled chant. The emphasis is on the regimented rhythms in which they recite the text, generally in animated sixteenth notes that accord with the poetic meter. This effect is heightened by the dissonant chord on which they sing, the B–F–A–C♯ sonority, which creates the sensation of chanting that is purely rhythmic in character, devoid of melodic interest.

This no doubt simulates the vocal practice of the Qumran worshippers, but it also bears a passing resemblance to the homophonic *falsobordone*, a type of improvised choral singing with which Rodrigo was certainly familiar. In fact, when he refers to the "salmodia del coro" (psalmody of the chorus),[30] he is referring to one of three types of declamation associated with the monastic singing of Psalms: direct, in which all voices sing together, as opposed to antiphonal (half choirs in alternation) or responsorial (soloist alternating with choir). We are clearly intended to see the four low voices of the chanting tenors and basses as somehow associated with "darkness," especially insofar as the verses they intone exhibit just that sort of imagery. Up above, in the sopranos, textual and musical matters are different.

Their verses convey a sense of the heavenly rewards that await the faithful. And here the texture is often imitative polyphony, which probably does not correlate with the kind of vocalizing of actual Qumran devotees but does perhaps owe a debt to the motet or the madrigal of the late Renaissance, again a type of music very familiar to Rodrigo. This sort of melodious singing was considered far more elevated and thus suitable for the celestial sphere (musical ex. 9.2).

The outlier here is the third movement, which was composed several years after the first. It opens with a sort of *sotto voce* fanfare in the winds, with annunciatory triplet rhythms and an

Musical ex. 9.2: *Himnos de los neófitos de Qumrán II*, mm. 10–13 upward-vaulting melodic contour. These triplet sixteenths represent a new motive, one that will recur throughout and unify this movement. However, at m. 54, the "Lento" pace that has prevailed throughout the *Himnos* to this point is disrupted by an "Allegro moderato," marked *fortissimo*, in which the fanfare becomes quite strident and its significance clear, as the choir declaims in its insistent recitative the following text describing the cosmic struggle between the forces of Light and Dark:

> Warriors are besieging me
> and surround me with their deadly weapons,
> hurtling arrows upon me ceaselessly;
> their lances shine like a forest in flames,
> the din of their shouting roars like a torrent,
> like a storm, bringing destruction.

The Lento tranquility returns, and like the previous two movements, the third concludes on A major, though preceded by B major, in a sort of II–I cadence. This is further evidence, if any were required, that Rodrigo has avoided at every turn any suggestion of traditional harmony and textbook chord progressions, instead striving to create the atmosphere of a world and a worldview very distant in time and space. In light of this, we can readily agree with the assessment of Antonio Gallego, who declared this "one of the most important works by Rodrigo. It demonstrated yet again his capacity for innovative originality."[31]

A Second Youth

In late October of 1965, the United Nations Children's Fund received a Nobel Peace Prize. Victoria Kamhi attended a board meeting of the Friends of UNICEF and from that time on she became "a zealous supporter of that magnificent project, attending all the weekly meetings and participating in all campaigns to support its services."[32] This activity tells us something about her energy and capacity for hard work, as well as her high humanitarian ideals and commitment to larger causes. But she drew the line at disruptive demonstrations.

She reports that there were sit-ins and demonstrations by political science and law students at the Complutense University where Rodrigo taught. "They broke the glass in the doors and windows, shouting, 'Unite, Unite! We want freedom of the press!'"[33] Interestingly, they got their wish with the Ley de Prensa e Imprenta in 1966, a law that granted greater freedom to newspapers and publishers, but they wanted more. The protests were threatening at times, and one day in May 1966, when the music history course Rodrigo was teaching at the university would soon wrap up, there were few students in the classroom or the hallways. A violent protest was taking place, and the Rodrigos were advised to leave the campus right away. They exited the building and got into their car, but, according to Kamhi, they "couldn't go very far because just a few yards from the campus a gang of enraged students blocked the way, shouting, 'Freedom! Freedom!' At the same time they threatened us with stones, one of which struck the car, making a dent in a door. I have seldom been so frightened!" During the spring semester of 1967, "it was impossible for Joaquín to present his classes in the School. Strikes and sit-ins were the order of the day. Not until mid-May did tranquility return."[34] Though she deftly avoids expressing political opinions in her memoirs, one senses her indignation. Then again, there was plenty of good news to counterbalance the bad.

In April 1966, as he did every day, Joaquín turned on the radio at breakfast time. There it was announced that he was on the list of those to be decorated with the Grand Cross of Civil Merit. "That can't be me, there are many others with the same name!" he exclaimed in astonishment. But it was indeed him, and the ceremony of investiture occurred on 21 April 1966. In his acceptance remarks he offered the Cross to his wife for helping him to accomplish his work. And the awards kept coming. That summer the radio again announced an award, this time the Gold Medal for Merit in his Work. When an interviewer asked him the reason for this prize, he answered: "I don't know. Perhaps because this year has been the most productive of my career. I don't know. Perhaps I don't deserve it, but I am happy. The past spring was one of my best, the kind I need to compose, warm and happy. This is my best period. Once clearing the bar of one's sixties, one returns to his youth."[35] He also added that he was composing the "magnum opus" of his career. We do not know which work he was referring to, but in the meanwhile he had added two very original compositions to his catalogue: the *Sonata pimpante* and *Adagio para instrumentos de viento*.

The *Sonata pimpante* for violin and piano is a piece of extraordinary brilliance in its exploitation of the instrument's resources. It is a work conceived as the high point of a violin recital, with an accompaniment that is just as challenging as the solo part. It was composed in early 1966 and was dedicated to his son-in-law, Agustín León Ara, who premiered it at the Cercle Royal Gaulois of Brussels on February 25, with Albert Jiménez Atenelle at the keyboard.[36] In the composer's words, the sonata opens "like a colorful fan" with an *Allegro con brio* first movement in traditional sonata form, featuring a principal theme group in the tonic of A major and a secondary group in the dominant, E major. The *Adagio* movement is interrupted by a humorous melody in the style of the *sevillana*, after which there is a return to the initial theme, resulting in a ternary (ABA) form. The ensuing *tempo lento* has much in common with a theme that will appear in the last movement of the *Concierto andaluz* (1967) for four guitars and orchestra and the orchestral work *A la busca del más allá* (1976). This is an interesting case of self-quotation, which can often be found in his works. The third and final movement is a rondo—"terrible and yet full of boundless joy," according to the composer—in the style of a *zapateado*, a type of flamenco dance characterized by fancy footwork, based on a famous melody by Paganini, "La Campanella." One might wonder what the adjective "pimpante" refers to, other than the high spirits of this music. It can mean well-pleased, even smug and self-satisfied, smart (as in clever), showy—as indeed this clever and self-assured music is.[37]

The *Adagio para instrumentos de viento* (Adagio for Wind Instruments) is one of several works for wind ensemble that Rodrigo composed or arranged, and it is the most distinctive. It was commissioned by and dedicated to the American Wind Symphony Orchestra, under the direction of Robert Boudreau, who had gone to Spain to solicit a work by Rodrigo for a Festival of Spanish Music in Pittsburgh.[38] It premiered in June 1966.

The *Adagio* is scored for piccolo, two flutes, three oboes, three clarinets, two bassoons, four horns, three trumpets, three trombones, tuba, timpani, cymbals, tam-tam, and snare drum. The music is quite virtuosic, especially in the woodwinds, and the dramatic contrasts in dynamics and shifting meters demand a tight ensemble. In the composer's own words, it is laid out in sonata form, but without a development section.[39] Thus, there is an exposition, in which there are two starkly contrasting theme groups in different tonalities, and then a recapitulation in which the themes are restated but under the same tonal "roof," so to speak. A recurrence of the principal theme constitutes a sort of coda, and the work ends *pianissimo*. The six basic sections are marked *Adagio, Allegro moderato, Poco più moderato, Adagio* (Tempo I), *Allegro moderato,* and *Adagio* (Tempo I). The *Poco più moderato* functions as a sort of retransition leading from the *Adagio-Allegro* exposition to the *Adagio-Allegro* recapitulation, concluding with an *Adagio* coda.

Rodrigo states what knowledgeable listeners at once perceive, and that is "an unmistakable Spanish character" to the music in both sections. This is established by the florid, "melismatic" runs in the woodwinds in the A section, reminiscent of flamenco singing, as well as the indispensable harmonic device of the descending minor tetrachord, a standard progression in Andalusian flamenco. The mood of this section is melancholic. The *Allegro* offers a stark contrast in its "stormy character," and its emotional agitation is conveyed in driving rhythmic figurations throughout the winds and brass, augmented by outbursts in the percussion, especially timpani. The overall harmonic language is diatonic, but the use of cuartal and quintal harmonies occasionally makes the tonal center ambiguous.

There is scant secondary literature on this work, and nowhere is there any mention, even by the composer, of something that might seem even to the casual observer as immediately obvious:

Musical ex. 9.3a: *Concierto de Aranjuez*, Adagio movement, principal theme, mm. 7–11

Musical ex. 9.3b: *Adagio para instrumentos de viento*, principal theme, mm. 1–4

the similarity of the A theme, initially present in the solo flute, to the famous Adagio melody of the *Aranjuez* concerto (musical ex. 9.3). Rodrigo was never hesitant to quote himself, and though this is not a direct quotation, it seems at least to be a deliberate allusion. Perhaps he thought it so obvious that it did not have to be pointed out.

By this time, the *Aranjuez* concerto had achieved global popularity, in its original form and in numerous arrangements. He may well have felt that this allusion would ensure some measure of success for a work that might otherwise be difficult for American audiences to approach with much understanding upon first hearing. But this is all speculation, and we may never know for sure.

A Popular Colossus

Victoria Kamhi deemed Miles Davis's appropriation of the Adagio theme "an act of piracy," and it was one soon imitated by other jazz and pop musicians. In fact, on 24 February 1967, there was a hearing of a suit against the Sociedad General de Autores y Editores (SGAE), which had authorized the transcription of the *Concierto de Aranjuez* for trumpet and jazz, recorded by Davis, a decision that the Rodrigos and their lawyers were contesting. They lost the case, and the various popularizations, starting with Davis, in fact "served as promotion," through which Rodrigo became known to many without any other connection to classical music. Kamhi related many such anecdotes. In New York, for instance, the taxi driver, "a Sevillian, [. . .] recognized Joaquín and, full of admiration, asked for his autograph." In Tokyo, "the waiter, a fan of guitar music, requested an autograph." And in Istanbul, "the Italian pianist at the Park Hotel played the *Adagio*, without suspecting that the author was in the room, applauding him. [. . .] When we went to congratulate him he almost wept with emotion [. . .] exclaiming, 'You are a genius.'"[40]

In light of all this attention, it comes as no surprise that in mid-December of 1967, the periodical *Pueblo* chose him as "Most Popular Musician of the Year," in particular for the song *Aranjuez, mon amour*, a vocal setting of the popular *Adagio* movement. Kamhi reported that he was mobbed by "an entire group of young people, boys and girls, [. . .] applauding enthusiastically and asking for autographs. What popularity he had attained! [. . .] We often had telephone calls from newsmen who wanted interviews for new agencies or for the radio."[41]

The year 1967 was also momentous for witnessing the beginning of an important collaboration between Rodrigo and an expatriate family of talented guitarists, the Romeros, who had settled in southern California and formed a guitar quartet, a concert novelty at the time. The Romero guitar quartet originally consisted of father Celedonio and his three sons, Celín, Pepe, and Ángel. Celín's son, Celino, replaced Ángel after his departure from the quartet in 1990, while Ángel's son, Lito, replaced Celedonio after his demise in 1996. Three generations of Romeros thus had long had a close and productive relationship with Rodrigo. Originally from Málaga, the family moved to southern California in 1957, where they have remained ever since, making it their home base for a global career spanning more than six decades.[42] Ángel Romero gave the *Concierto de Aranjuez* its West Coast premiere at the Hollywood Bowl with the Los Angeles Philharmonic in 1964, when he was just 18 years old. Both he and his brother Pepe have since championed it in several classic recordings and in innumerable performances. This fact, in tandem with the novelty of a guitar quartet and a growing friendship with the Romeros, persuaded Rodrigo to compose works for them.

On 30 June 1966, Celedonio wrote to Rodrigo asking him to compose a concerto for the quartet, an invitation Rodrigo fortunately accepted. Celedonio introduced himself by reminding the composer that they had met many years earlier, at an event sponsored by the Ateneo de Sevilla in which Rodrigo spoke and Celedonio played. Rodrigo immediately saw the potential of a collaboration with the Romeros and set about writing music for them. He wrote the following to the Romeros' Columbia Artists manager, Herb Fox, on 29 October 1966: "As I said in my former letters, I have decided to start immediately with the composition of the four-guitar Concerto for the Romeros, postponing the composition of all the other works I was commissioned with."[43]

This work was the *Concierto andaluz*, for four guitars and orchestra, which they premiered on 18 November 1967 with the San Antonio Symphony under the baton of family friend Victor Alessandro (Ángel played the *Concierto de Aranjuez* on this same program). The title of this major work was actually Celedonio's idea, as he wanted a musical homage to his native Andalusia that would include characteristic songs and dances, as a sort of musical portrait of the region. In that same year of 1967, the Romeros recorded the *Concierto andaluz* and *Concierto de Aranjuez* on the Mercury label (SR90488), and this album remains one of their best and most iconic recordings.[44]

The concerto sounds very Spanish from the first note to the last, but it is not based on preexisting melodies; rather, Rodrigo has freely composed themes that nonetheless evoke the *bolero, sevillana, zapateado,* and *fandango.* Rodrigo adheres to the traditional concerto structure of three movements, fast, slow, fast. Those familiar with the *Concierto de Aranjuez* immediately note, however, that this middle movement is not nearly as dramatic; it does not climax in a sort of *cri de coeur* laden with tragic desperation followed by muted resignation. Nonetheless, it produces a lyrically tranquil mood that contrasts effectively with the very dancelike outer movements, brimming as they are with the sort of effects one expects in an "Andalusian concerto."

Given the fact that Celedonio's brothers had fought on the Republican side during the Civil War, it is more than a little ironic that a fan of the *Concierto andaluz* was none other than Francisco Franco. Victoria Kamhi wrote to the Romeros on 4 August 1972, concerning a ballet choreography of this concerto by Antonio and his dance company for a performance at the Palacio de la Granja the previous July 18, the anniversary of the 1936 military uprising. The occasion was an annual reception that Franco held there for members of the government and diplomatic corps. The production, using recorded music, proved to be a hit. Kamhi notes that the dictator, who almost never attended concerts and took little interest in music, actually congratulated Antonio and said he would like to see it again sometime. Rodrigo was very pleased with the results of his collaboration with the Romeros, and his wife reported on his plans to write another concerto for them, whom he "love[d] and admire[d] so much."[45] This would eventually become the *Concierto para una fiesta,* to which we shall return.

In the meantime, in September 1969 they traveled to Portugal, where Rodrigo gave classes in musical analysis.[46] Then it was on to Seville, where he participated in a seminar on music in the university and gave a lecture on "Musical Creation," a subject on which he had considerable expertise. In 1970 he resumed teaching at the Universidad Complutense de Madrid, and his classes were very popular, attracting ever-larger numbers of students. But during these years they did not remain in any one place for

very long, and were soon jetting off to Los Angeles for the Hollywood Bowl premiere of the *Concierto madrigal.* Unfortunately, the
sound system malfunctioned at one point; a swift kick restored
it to working order, and the premiere was a glowing success.[47]

As we have noted, the *Concierto madrigal* for two guitars
and orchestra was originally composed for the duo of Presti and
Lagoya, but it was the duo of Pepe and Ángel Romero that finally
premiered and recorded it. This piece draws inspiration from
both the Spanish musical heritage and the Franco-Netherlands
Renaissance, in the context of a neoclassical language that is dis-
tinctively Rodrigo's. It also features some of the most breathtak-
ingly difficult guitar music written up to that time. John Duarte
was moved to say of this recording that "as a display of guitar
playing it is staggering."[48]

Unlike the traditional fast-slow-fast organization of the concerto, this work features ten movements, all of them elaborations on the madrigal *O felici occhi miei* (Oh My Happy Eyes)
from the *First Book of Madrigals* (1539) by Renaissance composer
Jacques Arcadelt (musical ex. 9.4), though Rodrigo's source is not
Arcadelt's madrigal but the variations on it published in by Diego
Ortiz in his *Tratado de Glosas* (1553).

1. Fanfare
2. Madrigal
3. Entrada
4. Pastorcico, tú que vienes. Pastorcico, tú que vas.
5. Girardilla
6. Pastoral
7. Fandango
8. Arietta
9. Zapateado
10. Caccia a la Española

After this triumph, they flew to Houston, where local friends
arranged for them to visit NASA headquarters as guests of
honor. There they met with astronauts, including Walter Cun-
ningham, hero of Apollo 7, whom Victoria Kamhi found to be "a

most congenial man." In fact, he was more than congenial—he was himself a guitarist and a great admirer of the *Concierto de Aranjuez*. In addition, "Joaquín had permission to touch all the objects on exhibit there: the modules, various instruments, the moon rocks."[49]

Once back in Madrid, they prepared to move from their apartment on Villalar, which seemed "increasingly small," to a much larger apartment on Calle San Germán. It was a new building, and they needed to find carpenters, plumbers, electricians, cabinet makers, and decorators—"an overwhelming task."[50] In March of that same year, the city council of Valencia invited them to celebrate St. Joseph's feast day. Rodrigo had been named "Colossus" of the year 1970, along with five other Valencians, and he was to receive a trophy there, a reproduction of the Colossus of Rhodes.

Musical ex. 9.4: Jacques Arcadelt, *O felici occhi miei*, mm. 1–5

One of Rodrigo's most satisfying vocal works is a set of ten songs he wrote on texts by the poet Antonio Machado. Rodrigo composed this work in 1971 at the request of the III Decena Musical de Sevilla, which solicited from him a set of songs utilizing texts by a Sevillan poet, and it premiered there on October 4 of that same year. The Catalan composer Federico Mompou was also invited to compose a similar work for this occasion, but he selected poems by Adolfo Bécquer. Though Rodrigo never met Antonio Machado, he did know his brother Manuel, with whom he became friends during the *tertulias* they frequented after the Civil War. The work, entitled *Con Antonio Machado*, is dedicated to Victoria Kamhi.

Rodrigo's attraction to Machado's poetry is not hard to comprehend. Merely on the basis of that poet's reputation as one of Spain's leading literary lights of the twentieth century, he would have been a logical choice. But the composer made clear his belief that

> Machado was the singer of Castile and of his own heart.
> He sang with a love of the blue mountains and the snows
> of Soria, of the green pines, the brownish-grey holm
> oaks, and the upper Duero River. He sang repeatedly of
> roses and the sweet April afternoons, of his lover with
> a childlike voice who was taken from him by death so
> [swiftly and so silently]. The poems of Antonio Machado
> are short and concentrated, and as they leave many things
> in the shadow of his feelings, they are suited to music.[51]

Machado is associated with the Generation of 1898, a group of writers active in the late nineteenth and early twentieth centuries who concerned themselves with Spain's cultural legacy and role in the world in the wake of its disastrous war with the United States and the loss of the final remnants of its once-vast overseas empire. His poetry is rooted in the late-Romantic period but also reveals the influence of Symbolism, mediated through the example of the Nicaraguan poet Rubén Darío (1867–1916), who clearly exerted a strong influence on the evolution of Machado's poetic craft.

Machado's detailed descriptions of the natural world—sunsets, rivers, parks, gardens, fountains—have symbolic resonance as they reflect his inner state of being, which was often distinguished by a pervasive mood of nostalgia, melancholy, solitude, and grief. In his later work there is an increasing concern with social inequality, placing him in the progressive camp.[52] Once again, Rodrigo's catholicity in terms of texts and philosophies reveals an impressive largeness of mind. And his familiarity with the poet's works was equally impressive, as the ten poems are taken from a variety of collections from different periods in his output.

Machado's verses inspired Rodrigo to observe of his own vocal works that "I continue to believe in melody, in the complete, measured phrase when it's a question of a song, and therefore this collection responds in this fashion of creating the way from which I have never deviated."[53] Rodrigo's lyricism, expressive tonal harmonies, and rhythmic flair are on display in these songs, with their various moods. There is little here that is musically experimental, and the style is as far removed from the postwar avant-garde as anything he wrote. In fact, it in no way resembles more adventurous essays from this same epoch in his output, such as the *Himnos de los neófitos de Qumrán*. As was always the case, Rodrigo's music is fashioned to meet the requirements of the text, to convey its meaning, not to impose a preconceived musical agenda on it, as if he were hanging a coat of notes on the nearest convenient hanger of words. Although we do not delve into analytical depth here, we summarize the observations of María Dolores Moreno Guil and Carolina Plata Ballesteros in regard to structure and sources before addressing the question of whether or not this can be called a "song cycle."

As Rodrigo himself observed, Machado rarely gave his poems titles, preferring instead to number them within a particular collection. Only three of the titles here are therefore original, and they appear in bold (table 9.1). In every other case, Rodrigo has simply taken a line from the poem to serve as the song's title, a time-honored practice in such cases.[54]

Rodrigo himself discountenanced the notion that this was a song cycle in the tradition of Schubert's *Die schöne Müllerin* or

TABLE 9.1 **Songs of *Con Antonio Machado***

Title	Literary source	Formal design	Tonality
Preludio	*Soledades*, XX. Del camino, 1	Intro. AA'A"	D♭ (cadencing on V)
Mi corazón te aguarda	*Soledades*, XII	ABCD	f
Tu voz y tu mano	*Campos de Castilla*, CXXII	AA'A"	A
Mañana de abril	*Soledades.* Canciones, XLIII	Intro. ABCA'	D♭
Los sueños	*Soledades.* Galerías, LXXXII	Intro. AB	A♭
Cantaban los niños	*Soledades*, VIII	Intro. AAA'A"A'''	f♯
¿Recuerdas?	*Soledades. Del camino*, XXXIII	Ritornello A Ritornello A' Ritornello A"	B Dorian
Fiesta en el prado	*Nuevas canciones*, CLIX. Canciones XIII	Intro. ABA'	F♯ Mixolydian
Abril galán	*Nuevas canciones*, CLIX. Canciones XV	Intro. AA'A	D
Canción del Duero	Canciones del alto Duero I, II, IV, VI from *Nuevas canciones*, CLX	Intro. AA'A–coda	f♯

Tempo	Meter	Mood; themes/symbols
Larghetto	4/4	Melancholic
Adagio	4/4	Melancholic; times of day and human mortality
Andante	4/4	Melancholic; times of day and with death
Andante moderato	4/4	Melancholic; times of day
Andante	4/4	Peaceful, pleasant; dreams
Allegro moderato	3/4	Melancholic; fountain, dancing, singing; children, youth
Andante	3/4	Melancholic; fountain
Allegro vivace	3/8	Festive; fountain dancing, singing; children, youth
Allegretto	6/8	Festive; river; dancing, singing; children, youth
Allegro vivace	3/4	Festive; river; dancing, singing; children, youth

Schumann's *Dichterliebe* because the composer did not find in Machado "a group of poems that allude to a person or continuous sentiment."[55] But Plata Ballesteros finds various elements in this collection that challenge the composer's assertion. Much depends, then, on how one defines a "song cycle"—what the necessary parameters are for classification in that genre.

There are actually several traits that give this collection a cyclic character. Plata's conclusion is that "there are three large-scale structuring factors: a large-scale harmonic plan, a unified 'lyric I' present in the poetry, and a coherent 'flux of mental/ emotional states.'"[56] In the first instance, she perceives that the ten songs can be divided into two basic groups, with the fifth song serving as a sort of transition. The work starts out in D♭ major and, over the course of ten songs, it finally cadences in F♯ major. The overarching harmonic scheme may not seem immediately obvious, but if we respell D♭ as C♯ (or F♯ as G♭), then there is indeed a large-scale movement from dominant to tonic. In the second instance, there is a consistent sense of the poet's perspective, that the "constant reflection on the flow of time, the fusion between soul and landscape [. . .] contribute to the feeling that a particular person is addressing us in these lyrics." Finally, there is a "coherent 'flux of mental/emotional states' created by Rodrigo's choice and ordering of the poems. *Con Antonio Machado* is an emotional journey largely dominated by melancholy and introspection," most notably in songs one through seven (with the exception of five, about dreams). But there is a sort of teleology at work, as songs eight through ten "mutate into festiveness and greater interaction with the outside world."[57]

An overarching tonal scheme, the avoidance of strongly conclusive cadences (until the last two songs), and the recurrence of motivic-gestural melodic ideas are the means of unifying this multi-movement work, techniques that Rodrigo had utilized numerous times before. The choice and ordering of the poems, however, are very distinctive here, perhaps unique among his vocal works. Thus, though this may not be a song cycle in the Schubertian sense, neither is it merely a collection of songs. There is an internal logic to its organization that belies any possibility that the songs were loosely assembled, and we are justified in referring to it as a song cycle. One might sing the songs individually, but the entire cycle must be rendered in the order specified by the composer. The progression of moods, transient cadences, and harmonic design require it.

Enjoying Life and Fame

Rodrigo was now at the apex of his career, and he was reaping the monetary rewards of his celebrity. Certainly, the royalties from the *Concierto de Aranjuez* and its various popularized arrangements were welcome. So, when the couple decided that they needed a summer house in Madrid, money was no problem, and they built a chalet near the reservoir of San Juan. They traveled to Turkey in April and May 1972, where Alirio Díaz gave concerts in Istanbul and Ankara. His performances of the *Concierto de Aranjuez* got standing ovations. Later that year, in October, they moved into their new flat on San Germán.

In November, they were off to Japan, where they were treated to a performance of some of Rodrigo's works interpreted on a traditional Japanese instrument called a koto, a horizontal zither plucked with the fingers of the right hand while the left depresses the strings to change their pitch. Considering the general similarity of the koto to the guitar, these transcriptions were apparently quite convincing. Subsequent concerts of his music took place in Tokyo, Nagoya, Osaka, and Kyoto, where the couple marveled at the city's historic charm and enchantment. They were interviewed on the radio several times and toured an institute for the blind, where the children enjoyed a concert the Spanish visitors gave. They also met Prince Akihito and Princess Michiko. Rodrigo played his works at the keyboard, followed by the *Gran marcha de los subsecretarios*, memorably rendered by the two of them.[58] Events like these cemented their status as cultural diplomats, promoting not just Spanish music but Spain itself.

However, prosperity and globe-trotting celebrity were increasingly accompanied by mental and physical hardships. In April 1973 "Joaquín had a mild nervous depression with great loss of weight, which weakened him considerably."[59] Now in his seventies, his health was declining, though he still had twenty-six years of life left in him.

In January 1974 he was able to resume his teaching at the university, and August found the couple in Sagunto for a revival of the drama La destrucción de Sagunto, in the historic Roman amphitheater. In October they ventured to Mexico, where performances of Rodrigo's music were planned in Acapulco. Kamhi's memoirs offer us a rather cryptic but nonetheless meaningful aside about this trip: "We talked to the people, the common people, who told us their joys and sorrows."[60] Despite their celebrity, they never forgot the "common" circumstances from which that celebrity had emerged. This interest in ordinary people finds a parallel in the composer's willingness to write music that was at once well crafted and yet accessible to the public, an aesthetic stance rejected by the postwar avant-garde. This was a stance that guaranteed him both recognition and remuneration, though his artistic motives were genuine.

Unfortunately, Rodrigo caught a bad cold and had to convalesce, so on October 31, they returned to Madrid. Over time, his health continued to deteriorate. In March 1977 after a lunch in Sagunto restaurant, "Joaquín gave us a dreadful fright when he collapsed in a faint, probably from sheer exhaustion."[61] Nonetheless, by May Rodrigo had recovered sufficiently to make a trip to Rome, where he gave a talk on Falla at the Spanish Institute of Language and Literature. But he was increasingly dependent on his wife for emotional and physical support, something of which the world was quite well aware. So, in recognition of that reality, on 25 June 1977 she was awarded the Ribbon of Alfonso X, "The Wise," which was "proof that my work at Joaquín's side was recognized and appreciated."[62]

In November 1977 they ventured to London as guests of the British Council and to attend a performance of Fantasía para un gentilhombre (1954), with the renowned Australian virtuoso John Williams as soloist and the Birmingham Orchestra at Royal Festival Hall. But this trip was also a major step forward in the creation of a new concerto, for flute. Rodrigo's Concierto pastoral (1978) was commissioned by the celebrated flute virtuoso James Galway, who had requested this work in a letter to the composer dated 16 December 1976. Rodrigo now finalized arrangements for premiering the new concerto in 1978. He showed Galway some of the completed score, which the Irishman read at sight, causing Victoria Kamhi to exclaim, "What tone! What technique! What musicality! He left us amazed." During this visit, the BBC filmed Galway along with the composer and his wife for a documentary they were making about the new concerto. But before the *Concierto pastoral's* premiere, another work would be christened across the Atlantic in March 1978, and that is where our story takes us next.

A la busca del más allá (1976) was commissioned by the Houston Symphony Orchestra to celebrate the Bicentennial of U.S. independence, but the seeds of its inspiration were planted several years before, during the visit to NASA headquarters in Houston in 1970.[63] It premiered on 27 March 1978 at the Jesse H. Jones Hall for the Performing Arts.

As the composer observed, "It could be classified as a symphonic poem, but of a markedly abstract character." For, despite the evocative title, the "music contains no concretely descriptive content."[64] The work begins and ends with a rolling rhythm on the suspended cymbal to suggest the vast distances of space, the "beyond." Two themes are repeated frequently throughout the work, occasionally interrupted by "brief and rapid segments." These "gusts" complicate the harmonic language with "allusions to atonality." Although Rodrigo deploys a full symphony orchestra, certain timbres are highlighted more than others, especially the flute, harp, xylophone, and celeste, instruments whose colors suggest the mysteries of outer space. The work ends *pianissimo*, "as a vanishing point in space, in the 'beyond.'" The premiere was a success, and the Spaniards were treated as visiting dignitaries. The mayor of Houston gave them the key to the city, and Rodrigo was invited to give a lecture on his compositions at the University of Houston.[65]

And yet more honors were heaped on the composer. In June 1978 "he was enrolled in the Royal Academy of Sciences, Letters and Fine Arts of Belgium, as a corresponding member, in the

vacancy left by Benjamin Britten."⁶⁶ Back in Madrid they were
invited to a reception at the Aranjuez palace given by Giscard
d'Estaing for the king and queen of Spain. It was then off to
London in October for the highly anticipated premiere of the
Concierto pastoral. As a warm-up to this concert, Galway performed his arrangement of the *Fantasía para un gentilhombre*
for flute, at Wimbledon. He and the Rodrigos attended a private
preview of the BBC film about the composer and Galway that
was shot the previous year.

Rodrigo's *Concierto pastoral* premiered on 17 October 1978,
with the Philharmonia Orchestra conducted by David Mata at
the Royal Festival Hall. The "happiness and clarity" typical of
the composer are apparent from the outset. In the traditional
manner, there are three movements, the first in textbook sonata
form, eschewing the double exposition of the classical concerto.
The technical challenges here are notable, especially in the "rapid
figurations" of the first theme (as characterized by Gallego). The
contrasting second theme is more "pastoral" and evocative of
Rodrigo's native province of Valencia. The second movement is,
perhaps predictably at this point in his career, marked *Adagio,*
though it is interrupted by a brief scherzo. The third movement is
a rondo "with an air of a pastoral dance" and in which the ritornello, happy and vivacious, alternates with more lyrical ideas.⁶⁷

In June 1978, during an excursion to the Aranjuez palace and
gardens, "A group of Japanese tourists was walking toward us,
and one of them, catching sight of Joaquín, exclaimed, 'Look,
there's the one who was such a hit in Japan!'" They asked for
his autograph. Such incidents were becoming increasingly common. A program about Rodrigo was filmed and broadcast all over
Spain, and

> We were the 'couple of the hour!' [. . .] Wherever we went
> we heard, 'There goes Maestro Rodrigo!' I was much
> amused by a group of workers unloading sacks at the
> door of the restaurant where we had just had dinner
> with some friends. They stood watching us for a few
> minutes, and then one of them nudged his companion,

saying, 'Yes, it is Maestro Rodrigo!' At which point they all stood up straight to give us a proper salute. The same sort of thing happened [. . .] in Sagunto, where men, women and children would come up to us in the street to shake hands and tell us the *Concierto de Aranjuez* was their favorite work.[68]

In 1979 they were invited to the home of the Soviet ambassador, Yuri Dubinin, where they learned of a proposal for the creation of a Spanish-Russian Association, to promote cultural exchange. Rodrigo's *Concierto de Aranjuez* was already a big hit in the Soviet Union, and there were plans for a Rodrigo Festival in Moscow. In 1980, Rodrigo received Spain's Gold Medal of Fine Arts, news of which was broadcast on the radio even before they were notified. The ceremony took place on May 29 in the Prado Museum, with the king and queen in attendance. In November, the composer was honored yet again, this time with a commemorative plaque in recognition of his work for the Red Cross. Philanthropy was a serious avocation for both Victoria and Joaquín Rodrigo.

The Final Outbursts

On 14 April 1979, English cellist Julian Lloyd Webber came from London to meet Rodrigo and commission a concerto from him. He was the brother of Andrew Lloyd Webber, the famous composer of such hit musicals as *Jesus Christ Superstar* (1970), *Cats* (1981), and *Phantom of the Opera* (1986). The cellist had become familiar with Rodrigo's music as a result of its performances in London, and he specifically requested a work with a Spanish flavor. The London premiere was slated for April 1982; however, in late 1981, "Joaquín was depressed and gloomy, and nothing could distract him. His creative work had stagnated during the last months. This depression was perhaps due to the hair-raising news coming from abroad as well as from Spain. Italy had been devastated by an earthquake."[69] Exactly what news this might have been, Kamhi does not specify, perhaps seeking to avoid political controversy. On 23 February 1981, right-wing members of the Guardia Civil, commanded by Lieutenant-Colonel Antonio Tejero, had attempted a coup, briefly seizing control of the Cortes Generales. In a further show of force, the army sent tanks into the streets of Valencia.[70] King Juan Carlos, confirmed as a constitutional monarch by the Constitution of 1978, went on national television to defend that constitution by denouncing the coup, reminding the soldiers of their loyalty oath, and compelling the conspirators to back down. The siege ended only a day after it had begun. And that was also the year in which there was an attempted assassination of Ronald Reagan, on 30 March. Some good news from that troublesome year of 1981 was the organization and presentation of a Rodrigo Festival in Mexico, on 17 March 1981.

The following year was less troubling on the political front and saw yet more triumphs for the composer, who was to receive the National Award for Music as well as an honorary doctorate to be conferred on him by the University of Southern California in Los Angeles, where Pepe Romero was on the faculty.[71]

The *Concierto como un divertimento* (1981) was to be Rodrigo's penultimate concerto and his second for cello and orchestra. Rodrigo composed the work during the first half of 1981, before his bout with depression and gloom. It premiered on 15 April 1982 at the Royal Festival Hall in London, with the Philharmonia Orchestra conducted by Jesús López Cobos, but it would not premiere in Madrid until February of 1985. Webber's manager had arranged for a promotional film to be shot about the new concerto for London Weekend Television.

Rodrigo wanted to signal to the public that his was an accessible work, and thus entitled it as a "Divertimento-like Concerto." This served to distinguish it from its neoclassical predecessor, the *Concerto en modo galante*. However, it is scored for an orchestra that could have come straight from the eighteenth century, with two apiece of flutes, oboes, clarinets, horns, and trumpets, as well as the usual complement of strings. The first movement, Allegretto, features a toe-tapping alternation of 3/4 and 2/4 while evoking several Spanish song-and-dance genres. It commences with an ear-catching presentation of the quasi-*bolero* rhythm in the cello pizzicato. The second movement, marked *Adagio nostalgico*, is inspired by a sixteenth-century Castilian *romance*, "Ya se asienta el rey Ramiro," which the composer interrupts with more animated material and a cadenza that harkens to the *Allegretto* first movement, before a return to the *Adagio*.[72] The final movement, *Allegro scherzando*, is in sonata form, with a *scherzando* principal theme and a contrasting second theme that is more *cantabile* and passionate in character. This very diverting work was well received at its premiere and more than satisfied the requirements of the soloist who commissioned it.

Another manifestation of the creative fecundity that marked the year 1982 was a work for his son-in-law, the violinist Agustín León Ara, to whom it is dedicated. Almost seventy years after the Valencian evocation *Dos esbozos* (1923), Rodrigo concluded his catalogue of works for violin and piano by writing seven pieces—the iconic number of Falla's *Siete canciones populares españolas*—under the Valencian title of *Set cançons valencianes*. They were composed in 1982 and premiered in May of that same year, with the dedicatee playing violin and José Tordesillas at the keyboard.[73]

The seven songs bear no titles other than their number in the collection and their respective tempo markings. In the view of Gallego, the opening *Allegretto* exhibits a melancholy mood reminiscent of the "Enamorada junto al pequeño surtidor" of decades earlier, though here with greater harmonic subtlety. The *Andante moderato* appeared to Raymond Calcraft like a Jewish lament, recalling Victoria Kamhi's Sephardic ancestry. The succeeding *Allegro* "has the simplicity of a children's song," something that also harkens back to a much earlier work, the *Cinco piezas infantiles*. Next is an *Andante moderato e molto cantabile* that exudes the "languid serenity of memories." The *Andantino* commences with a nod toward J. S. Bach but quickly transforms into a popular melody with surprising harmonic twists. The *Andante religioso* features parallel fourths (a no-no in traditional voice leading, as the composer well knew) "that open the space to remote environments." The final movement is marked *Tempo di bolero* and reminds us that the bolero is a dance by no means confined to Andalusia or Castile, as its Valencian cousin makes clear.[74] These comments were made before the popular sources of these songs were found. Though Rodrigo conspicuously made no mention of it, the whole set was based on Valencian popular · tunes from the *Cancionero musical de la provincia de Valencia*, compiled and edited by Salvador Seguí in 1980.

Later in 1982 the Rodrigos were invited by the University of Jerusalem to attend a weeklong Rodrigo Festival, which would include concerts, recitals, lectures, a master class with Rodrigo, excursions, press interviews, a reception, and four days on a kibbutz. But "Joaquín, who at that time was feeling very tired and nervous, seemed to me in no condition to undertake a professional tour." They postponed the invitation. One morning not long thereafter, "Joaquín became dizzy and collapsed, pulling me down with him. Those were dreadful days which I would like to forget."[75] And yet, even in the midst of a mental and physical collapse, Rodrigo remained capable of creating a masterpiece, in this case the *Cántico de San Francisco de Asís* (1982).

The word "canticle" derives from the Latin *canticum*, or song. It may refer to an actual song or just the poetic lyrics of the song for which there is no longer (or perhaps never was) any music. The most famous example of this genre is the so-called Canticle of Mary, from the Gospel of Luke 1:46–55, which begins with the famous words "Magnificat anima mea dominum" (My soul doth magnify the Lord). The Magnificat has been set countless times both monophonically and polyphonically from the Middle Ages to the present day. Settings of the Canticle of Saint Francis of Assisi are far less numerous, though such luminaries as Franz Liszt, Amy Beach, William Walton, and Roy Harris devoted themselves to the task. Rodrigo's is an exemplary contribution to this tradition by virtue not only of its relative rarity but also its sophistication and affective impact.

This poem is often referred to as the Canticle of the Sun or the Canticle of the Creatures, as it is a paean to the creator of the natural world and all the wonders it contains, both animate and inanimate. Tradition holds that it was composed by the gentle saint of Assisi in 1224, after a serious illness, and that he did not write it out himself but rather dictated it to his followers because he had by then lost his eyesight as a result of disease. Rodrigo's setting was intended to commemorate the 800th anniversary of the saint's birth in 1183; he would give new life to these hallowed verses without the benefit of sight himself.

To our twenty-first-century sensibilities, the Canticle may inspire some misgivings, insofar as it is addressed to a God who appears to be at once immensely powerful and horribly insecure. Thus, his cosmic ego needs to be slathered with the most obsequious flattery, meekly offered up by mere humans who are barely fit to utter his name. What is more, St. Francis's love of nature seems to verge on pantheism at times, so strong is the identification of his God with Brother Sun, Sister Moon, Brother Wind, Sister Water, Brother Fire, Sister Mother Earth—and, yes, Sister Bodily Death, which must come to all but is a blessing for those who do not perish in mortal sin.

The most detailed study ever undertaken of this work is the recent dissertation by Terrance Pitt-Brooke, previously cited in connection with the *Música para un Códice Salmantino*, a composition of some thirty years earlier.[76] His discoveries inform much of the ensuing analysis.

Like that earlier work, this begins with a lengthy instrumental introduction that sets out the motives to be taken up later by the voices. The *Cántico* commences with a hauntingly evocative flute solo, whose solitary presence symbolizes this most revered of medieval hermits. The melody's modality also suggests something of the exotic and the mystical insofar as it is does not fit into any standard taxonomy. It bears some resemblance to the Andalusian mode on A, but its pitch materials stray from the model, especially in the use of F$\sharp$. This opening theme will recur eight times throughout the work and may thus be considered a ritornello.[77] It is followed by a celeste playing arpeggiations in fourths and fifths, but in which the tonality of the left hand, D, is separated by a semitone from that in the right hand, E$\flat$. We are once again confronting a bitonal device harkening back to the *Suite para piano* of some sixty years earlier and one strongly associated with Les Six and neoclassicism, though there is little else here to suggest the 1920s and '30s. Indeed, in Pitt-Brooke's view, "the resulting sensation can be characterized as a feeling of suspension or 'shimmer' [. . .] bitonality suspends our temporal frame."[78] It can also suggest distance in space as well as time, as if the "choir is come from afar, singing 'Loado,' the first word of the Antiphon, 'Praised be you, my Lord.'"[79] Bimodality is on display at various points as well. Subsequent to the celeste is a brief hummed interjection in the chorus, with two whole-note chords moving from G minor to A major. Rodrigo reveals a predilection for root-movement chord progressions, prohibitions against parallel perfect fifths be damned. Added-note sonorities are also prominent, with a preference for nonfunctional seventh chords and chords with a sixth or ninth above the root. To anchor progressions that would otherwise obscure any tonal sense, he resorts to pedal notes, especially in the French horns.

The work can be broken down into four basic sections: the "Concerto" instrumental opening, or ritornello; an Invocation; the Litany of Thanks; and a solemn and restful Conclusion. Rodrigo was a master of rhetorical devices, and these verses give him plenty of opportunities for painting the text with musical tones. In particular, his choice of keys reveals the symbolic value they had in this context.[80] For example, Brother Sun is in confident F major, while Brother Fire is portrayed in strident D major. A major and Mixolydian express "unworthiness of humanity before God" as well as praise and "those who suffer in peace." F Dorian prevails in the Invocation, while F minor is reserved for corporeal death. Rodrigo saves a completely new key, B major, for the Conclusion. "After death comes a new beginning and a new life, and this calls for a new and fresh key."[81] "The immediate impression is of a similarity to the 'Amen' of a Handel chorus in texture and in function."[82]

In short, the variety of textures, monophonic, homophonic, and polyphonic; expressive harmonies verging at times on atonality but always reaffirming tonality; colorful sonorities in the orchestra, which is rarely deployed *tutti* but instead in evocative bits and pieces; the assorted types of declamation, from syllabic to melismatic, with an effective use of *falsobordone*-type declamation in the choir; and the skillfully organic utilizing of melodic materials to provide both unity and variety throughout the score—all of this serves to heighten not only the meaning of the words but our respect for the ingenuity of the composer, whose sheer skill never overpowers his genuine inspiration.

The Rodrigos returned to Mexico on 10 March 1983 to attend another Rodrigo Festival, on March 19, in the Nezahualcoyotl Hall in Mexico City. They were received "with great cordiality" by ex-president José López Portillo, who was a devotee of Rodrigo's music, especially the *Concierto de Aranjuez*.[83] But the composer was suffering an attack of gout, with a swollen foot and much pain. One evening at about 8:30 p.m., as they lay in bed, Victoria Kamhi heard a crackling sound. It turns out that a fire had broken out in their high-rise hotel, resulting in a real-life towering inferno. The quick-thinking spouse got her husband out of bed and dressed. They had to get out of the hotel as soon as possible: "Now I felt real panic, but I didn't lose control."[84] With just some treasured jewelry and their passports, they managed to take a freight elevator to safety. After the Rodrigo Festival concert on the 19th, there was "clamorous applause" and "I was praised for my 'courage and calmness worthy of an Amazon, in the face of danger,' and was awarded the Gold Medal of the City of Mexico."[85] This trip to Mexico could have had a tragic ending, but for the heroism and quick thinking of Victoria Kamhi. Her memoirs thus conclude not with Rodrigo's fiery demise but rather with his second and final solo concerto for the guitar, the *Concierto para una fiesta* (1982), which premiered in 1983.

Victoria Kamhi remarked on the special relationship that existed between her husband and Pepe Romero. The *Concierto para una fiesta* was composed for him but commissioned by William and Carol McKay of Fort Worth, Texas, on the occasion of their two daughters' debutante ball, in 1983 (the "fiesta" to which the title refers). The McKays were a prosperous ranching family who clearly thought this would be a very distinctive way to introduce their daughters to polite society. It remains only the second solo-guitar concerto Rodrigo ever composed, after the *Aranjuez* of over four decades earlier. Pepe Romero gave the premiere on

5 March 1983, with the Fort Worth Chamber Orchestra in the ballroom of Redglea Country Club.[86]

During this period, there was a very popular American prime-time television soap opera called *Dallas*, popular in Europe as well, that presented viewers with a weekly glimpse into the supposedly sordid and selfish world of well-to-do Texans. The genesis of this concerto provides a refreshing rebuttal to that tawdry narrative. In fact, one journalistic commentator at the time remarked, "The composition already is going a long way toward changing the image of Texas." The *Dallas* TV series was a huge hit in Spain and in Germany too, so not surprisingly an article in *Stern* magazine commented that

> *Dallas* fans have to change their views. Those who
> were pretty sure all the time that Texas's high society
> is satisfying its cultural needs only with cocktails,
> intrigues, and country music are set right by a
> colleague from the same branch as J.R. The reason is: oil
> millionaire William McKay has two charming daughters,
> Alden Elizabeth and Lauri Ann, who were allowed a
> small wish from Papá on the occasion of their debutante
> ball. They had no Porsche, no diamonds from Tiffany on
> their wish list, but a guitar concerto for them by Joaquín
> Rodrigo.[87]

To be sure, Rodrigo received $20,000 for his composition, and the entire event cost the McKays upward of five times that much. Concerning the music itself, Pepe declared that Rodrigo's *Concierto para una fiesta* is "by far the most difficult piece ever written for the guitar."[88] The guitarist once confided to John Duarte something of the work's genesis,

> [Rodrigo and I] always had a ritual of smoking cigars
> together. [The composer said,] "You know I am going
> to die soon, but, you will die soon too because everyone
> dies. And then think how much fun we are going to
> have smoking our cigars and saying—'Look at those

poor bastards down there trying to play our piece.'
[. . .] Though standards rise from year to year, it may
be near the truth for some time. After some 35 years of
reviewing I am left without an adequate superlative to
describe Pepe Romero's performance.[89]

Pepe Romero further informs us that "I take the music he sends
me and I play it for him. In some places, I come up with alternate
ways to play certain passages, closer to what I think he wants to
say—maybe some re-voicing of chords or perhaps a little different technique to use on the guitar."[90]

According to the composer himself, this is a largely "happy"
work and the "impression of optimism" is dominant.[91] The first
movement features two themes of a Valencian character, the second of which "evokes the spirit of El Cid and the Moorish past
of Valencia."[92] The restlessly introspective second movement
provides more rhythmic than lyric interest and is animated by
the alternation of 6/8 and 5/8, as well as complex groupings
of beats within each measure. The result is a "continuous and
agitated wave of disquiet throughout the movement."[93] Though
the English horn is prominent here, the composer warns against
trying to find some parallel with the Adagio movement of the
Aranjuez. The final movement is a spirited rondo that bursts
forth with *sevillanas*-inspired rhythms and tunes, providing the
musical "fiesta" we have awaited.[94]

Two additional concerto collaborations merit mention here.
As it turned out, Pepe Romero would go on to arrange *Sones
en la Giralda* ("Fantasía Sevillana") for guitar and orchestra in
1993. Originally composed in 1963 for harp and orchestra, it is
an enchanting evocation of sounds in the historic bell tower
of Seville Cathedral. Ángel Romero requested a concerto from
the maestro about this time, but the aging composer respect-
fully refused, citing his declining energies. However, he provided
Ángel with some harmonized melodies based on folkloric prototypes, which he encouraged the guitarist to fashion into a concerto of his own. In 1990, Ángel composed *Rincones de España*
(Corners of Spain).

Finales

From here, we depend on Carlos Laredo Verdejo for the concluding events of this amazing life.[95] There was no real treatment for Rodrigo's malady, and his episodes of depression were accompanied by fluctuations in his energy. These could last for months. He became more closed in on himself, not responding to anyone whose voice he did not recognize. And he suffered panic attacks, even as he had when he was very young. He suffered like a "lost and abandoned child amidst a catastrophe." At other times, he even questioned his own identity: "Who am I?" All of these are classic symptoms of senility. Only music could calm him down, and one effective therapy was to seat him at the piano and let him play. And composing was the "best treatment for his depression."[96] But as a result of all this, long stretches went by without composition. One bright spot was a Rodrigo Festival in London in 1986, from March 3 to 15, organized by Raymond Calcraft, one of the leading interpreters of his choral and orchestral works, and supported by the Institute of Spain and Citicorp. Laredo considers this the most important of all the Rodrigo festivals.[97]

In 1987, Agustín León Ara and Cecilia Rodrigo moved from Brussels to Madrid with their daughters to help with an increasingly difficult domestic situation. As Laredo reports, the papers and manuscripts were in complete disarray: letters, diplomas, press clippings, photographs, hundreds of writings, lectures, courses, manuscripts, honorary degrees, and documentation of memberships in numerous professional and academic societies around the world. There were a large number of contracts with publishers in North America and Europe, and with 200 works being played around the world, publishers were easily cheating Rodrigo out of royalties. Everything was stashed in dust-covered boxes all mixed up and disorganized. There was no secretary or administrator to assist with accounting and legal matters. Basically, a lot of their transactions were verbal agreements, which Victoria Kamhi kept in her head. And the couple had become very isolated, spending Christmas of 1986 alone. Rodrigo could still get up, wash and dress himself, prepare breakfast, turn on

The Rodrigos in 1987

the radio, figure out what time it was, light a cigarette, even go for a walk. But everything else required assistance. Victoria Kamhi had stuck with him through thick and thin, and she was not going to relent until the end. Though they were now wealthy and famous, they had started out living from one scholarship or award to the next. She fiercely protected her husband, and to get to him, you had to go through her.

Meanwhile, Cecilia Rodrigo brought order out of chaos. In 1989 she created Ediciones Joaquín Rodrigo with the eventual aim of publishing and controlling the rights to all his works, an aim finally achieved. She began setting up a serviceable archive, organizing the mountain of paper into a fully catalogued collection that would benefit not only the family but also musicians and music scholars. Of course, there was one thing she could not do, and that was delay her father's aging.

However, once he reached his nineties, his emotional state actually improved over what it had been in the late 1980s, and despite the progress of senility, he was happier. As Laredo points out, he had achieved everything that a composer of classical music could hope for—international recognition, fame, and money.[98] He led a peaceful and comfortable life with his wife and enjoyed the company of his extended family. His ninetieth birthday brought forth a plenitude of events in his honor, in Madrid, Puerto Rico, Berlin, Mexico, Barcelona, Moscow, Munich, London, Vienna, New York City, Cincinnati, Buenos Aires, Seville, and Tokyo. He was interviewed by newspapers and magazines national and international and was the subject of radio and television programs.

And to cap it all off, on 27 December 1991 he received an especially important phone call. The maid answered the phone and thought that when the caller identified himself as the king, it must be a mistake or prank. She was afraid that if she told Victoria Kamhi that King Juan Carlos was on the line, she would think her stupid or gullible. On the phone with the king, she was incredulous, temporized, and the king, understanding the reaction, said he would call back later. She reported the incident instead to Cecilia Rodrigo, who made her way to the apartment, arriving just as the king called again. This time, Cecilia took the bull by the horns, so to speak, and answered in the affirmative. The king informed her that he had decided to make Rodrigo the marquis of Aranjuez, which would also make Victoria Kamhi the marquise. Well, not quite. The next day the royal palace called to clarify that Rodrigo could not be the marquis of Aranjuez because only members of the royal family were permitted to hold that title. However, he would instead be the Marquis of the Gardens of Aranjuez! He was now a member of the nobility, in fact

Standing in front of the Aranjuez Palace in 1981

as well as deed. A final major distinction was awarded him in 1996: the Prince of Asturias Award for the Arts (Premio Príncipe de Asturias de las Artes), the highest such honor given by Spain. The selection committee singled out his "definitive contribution to the dignification and internationalization of the guitar as a concert instrument."[99]

But the party could not go on indefinitely. On 21 July 1997, at six in the morning, Victoria Kamhi passed away peacefully. She had returned from her daily walk the previous day feeling fatigued and in need of rest. Her heart simply gave out, after having given so much. The family decided not to tell Rodrigo, because they were afraid that he would not be able to stand the shock and grief over losing his wife. When he would ask for her, they just answered in vague and evasive ways, saying that she was sleeping or that she would come later. It is impossible to say if he ever figured out what was going on. More and more he lived inside his own mind, where no one else could venture. Finally, on 6 July 1999, Rodrigo was not able to get out of bed, and a few hours later, he was gone.

They are both buried in the Cementerio de Santa Isabel in Aranjuez, about a fifteen-minute walk from the palace. Their tomb is adorned with a modernistic sculpture by Pablo Serrano bearing, of course, the *Adagio* melody that helped to make him so famous. "My glass is small, but I drink from my glass" is the humble epitaph adorning his final resting place.

Legacy of Rodrigo

Over the past three decades, after the celebration of his nine-tieth birthday, there has been a steady profusion of recordings, books, journal articles, and newspaper pieces assaying his life and music, and years ending in either a 1 or a 9 seem to bring forth another raft of commemorations, concerts, exhibitions, and festivals. Our composer's legacy is thus assured, as the enduring popularity of his music proves.

However, the overwhelming popularity of the *Concierto de Aranjuez*, particularly the middle movement, has had the unfortunate tendency of putting the rest of his vast and varied output in the shadows. It has been arranged for instrumental ensemble by numerous jazz and pop artists, beginning with Miles Davis's 1960 *Sketches of Spain* album previously mentioned and continuing with Chick Corea,[100] the Modern Jazz Quartet,[101] and Brian May.[102] The Adagio has been texted and used as the basis for popular songs, for instance *Aranjuez mon amour* (1967) by Richard Anthony and *En Aranjuez, con tu amor* (1968), with a Spanish text by Alfredo García Segura. Even the composer and his wife got into the act, with his musical arrangement of and her lyrics for *Aranjuez, ma pensée* (1988).

The Adagio has been employed numerous times in film scores, from horror flicks to comedies and from serious dramas to animated features about penguins (see table 9.2). It has also been in demand as the musical backdrop for car commercials on television. Though he never intended it to be used in this context, it is by far and away his most successful and widely disseminated film score.

Rodrigo has thus gained a secure niche in the pantheon of modern popular culture, the unintended consequence of a supremely inspired and inspiring work, one that speaks to us of both joy and sorrow in a life-affirming way that makes its appeal universal, cutting across cultural, historical, and linguistic boundaries. As he himself said, "La música nos une en la distancia" (Music unites us from afar). Perhaps not all music, but his music, to be sure.

But despite the ineluctable reality of the *Aranjuez*'s shadow-casting stature, anyone who takes the time to become acquainted

TABLE 9.2 **Use of the Adagio movement from the *Concierto de Aranjuez* in films and on television**

Title	Year	Genre	Type of reference
Don Juan Tenorio	1952	Dramatic film	Direct quotation
El jardín de las delicias	1970	Dramatic film	Direct quotation
Lisa and the Devil	1974	Horror movie	Arrangement
Chrysler Cordoba	1975	Car commercial	Arrangement (with Angel Romero, soloist, and Ricardo Montalban, pitchman)
Honda Rafaga	1993	Car commercial	Arrangement
Brassed Off!	1996	Dramatic comedy	Arrangement
The School of Rock	2003	Comedy	Direct quotation
Ghost in the Shell: Innocence	2004	Animated feature	Arrangement
Happy Feet	2006	Animated feature	Arrangement
Suicide Squad 2	2021	Action Adventure	Direct quotation (with Pepe Romero, soloist)

with his oeuvre will come away with genuine admiration for his technique and range as a creative artist, one who composed for the stage as well as the silver screen, for chamber ensemble, orchestra, solo voice, choir, keyboard, and of course for guitar, the instrument with which his legacy is inextricably connected. And his sources of inspiration were impressively varied, including folklore, history, poetry, drama, and the natural world, especially cuckoos and other birds. Ultimately, a wider exposure of his lesser-known works is not a matter of fairness to Rodrigo but rather to ourselves, that we may derive satisfaction from musical experiences that are at once delightful and deeply moving. Music was a light that illumined the darkness of his world, and it will do the same for us.

The work of the Fundación Victoria y Joaquín Rodrigo, headed by his daughter as president and granddaughter Cecilia León as director, has been invaluable in advancing the cause.[103] The foundation now controls the publication, rights, and royalties of all of his music, and its staff maintains a well-organized archive of many thousands of documents, making this priceless resource available to music scholars. It also preserves the Rodrigos' apartment as a museum, with its various instruments, memorabilia, awards, and library. This herculean task is a truly impressive accomplishment, and it will safeguard his legacy from the erosion that time and neglect would otherwise inflict upon it.

Another enduring aspect of Rodrigo's legacy was his heroic persistence in the face of his blindness. His life and career serve as a beacon of hope to those who persist on their chosen path despite a crippling disability. Rodrigo was one of several noted musicians in history who lost their sight, including the fourteenth-century Italian composer Francesco Landini and the sixteenth-century Spanish organist Antonio de Cabezón. Both Bach and Handel lost their vision toward the end of their lives, as did Frederick Delius. In the world of popular music, names like José Feliciano, Stevie Wonder, and Ray Charles come to mind. Every such person experiences their disability differently, but we know that in Rodrigo's case, he was able to turn it to his advantage. He believed that the lack of eyesight intensified his sense of hearing, which was already acute and grew more so with time.

We also marvel at his sheer will power, as the force of his creative inspiration repeatedly overcame the tedious process of composition that being blind compelled him to adopt. And his legacy as a blind person was not confined to composing music but also includes a prolific output as an author of reviews, essays, and analyses of his own works as well as those of other composers, in addition to being a professional music historian who lectured internationally on a wide variety of topics.

Perhaps the most telling aspect of his legacy however is this: in a very real sense, Rodrigo summed up 800 years of Spanish music and culture, from medieval *cantigas* to Renaissance vihuela music, from the seventeenth-century Baroque to evocations of the Classical style in his use of sonata form, and from a Romantic nationalism indebted to the example of Albéniz to his own *neocasticista* manner. Of course, he drew richly and repeatedly from the vast heritage of regional music and dance in Spain. And his literary interests also ranged widely, from the mysticism of Saint John of the Cross to the *Quijote* of Cervantes, and from the poetry of the Siglo de Oro to that of Unamuno and Machado. Though he was not a proponent of the postwar avant-garde, of atonality, aleatory, and electronic music, even in his twilight years he remained capable of bold experimentation, of venturing beyond the aesthetic boundaries to which he was accustomed. This is evident in such works as the *Himnos de los neófitos de Qumrán* and *A la busca del más allá*, which broke the Rodrigo "mold," such as it was, and affirmed his willingness to utilize any and all resources to convey the message, mood, or image he had in mind, divorced as these particular works were from any reference to the traditional music of his native land.

It is not our purpose to make invidious comparisons of Rodrigo with any other Spanish composer, but his embrace of nearly a millennium of Spanish music sets him apart from both his contemporaries and predecessors. Historicism of some kind infuses nearly every measure he wrote, without any loss of relevance and appeal to performers, listeners, and scholars. He is in every respect a singular figure in the long and illustrious history of Spanish music and musicians, and his place in the pantheon of Iberian composers is assured. He drank from his cup, small though full, and we ourselves continue to find refreshment in it as well.

ACKNOWLEDGMENTS

EXAMINING IN DEPTH the life and work of Joaquín Rodrigo is a daunting task. He lived to the ripe old age of 97, and for over seven decades he was active as a performer, composer, writer, cultural diplomat, and even something of a media celebrity. And he accomplished all of this in the midst of some of the most tumultuous decades in human history, including civil, world, and "cold" wars. Thus, a herculean labor such as this biography would never have been conceivable without the assistance and encouragement of a small army of both individuals and organizations. First and foremost is Cecilia Rodrigo, daughter of the composer and president of the Fundación Victoria y Joaquín Rodrigo in Madrid, which is the Mecca for all researchers in this area. She is assisted by her daughter Cecilia, director of the Foundation, and its superlative staff—Yolanda Domínguez Torreadrado, Mili Fernández, Paula Lorenzo, Carmen Santás, and Santiago de Rábago León. A heartfelt *mil gracias* to them all.

Professor Nelson Orringer (emeritus University of Connecticut, Storrs) is an eminent scholar of Spanish, one at home in the realms of both literature and music, and he was responsible for translating Javier's portions of the text from Spanish into English. He also provided crucial insights into historical and literary aspects of the narrative, as well as invaluable editorial suggestions. We thank him for his contribution to making this book a reality.

Javier is grateful to his former students Carmen Noheda and Javier Pino for their editorial support in proofreading the manuscript, to the composers Santiago Lanchares and David del Puerto for assistance in the analysis of various scores, and particularly to guitar teacher and scholar Julio Gimeno for his analytical insights into the all-important *Concierto de Aranjuez*. Walter is indebted to present and former students Pedro López de la Osa, Jorge Calaf, and Dr. Bernard Gordillo for their research support. Naturally, both of us are grateful to our respective spouses, Belén (Javier) and Nancy (Walter), for their patience with us during the past few years of frequent distraction.

Last but by no means least, we are especially thankful to Julian Lloyd Webber, cello virtuoso, for contributing so eloquent a foreword to this biography; and to Norton editor Christopher Freitag, himself an accomplished guitarist and Rodrigo enthusiast without whose unstinting support and sage counsel this book would not have been possible. Finally, we are enormously grateful to Jodi Beder for her meticulous and expert copyediting of the manuscript.

As the maestro beautifully stated, "Music unites us from afar." The process of researching and writing this biography has brought together a wide variety of people and organizations, united by their love of Rodrigo's music and admiration for his remarkable genius and humanity. May the example of his life and music continue to unite us during these difficult times.

Javier Suárez-Pajares
Universidad Complutense de Madrid

Walter Aaron Clark
University of California, Riverside
2022

APPENDIX 1

Manuscripts of Rodrigo's Early Works

This list includes both works that were published (shaded rows) and those that were not. The letters A, B, and C stand for distinct but unidentified copyists. Most of the manuscripts bear dates or are datable.

Date	Title	Copyist
May, 1921	*Vals*	A?
20 April 1922	*Melodía* "Ensayo para voz de soprano y piano sobre la poesía *Soliloquio* de Carrasquilla Mallarino"	A (two copies)
14 August 1922	[Without title]	B
22 August 1922	*Fuga a cuatro partes para piano*	Francisco Antich
26 September 1922	*Dos esbozos para violín y piano* (Dedicated to Antonio Calabuig) [I] Lento	B
22 September 1922	[II] Andante	
November–December, 1922	*Homenaje a un viejo clavicordio* Fragmentos de una suite ("Sarabanda"—"Pavana"— "Giga")	Francisco Antich B
23 November 1922	"Sarabanda"	
Without date	*Danza* (orquestación de "Sarabanda")	A
1922	*Fuga de cuatro partes*	B
February, 1923	*Sonata*	B
5 March 1923	*Lied para piano*	B (one copy); "Sanchís" (one copy)
31 March 1923	*La enamorada junto al pequeño surtidor* [First of *Dos esbozos* violin and piano]	A

Manuscripts of Rodrigo's Early Works (continued)

This list includes both works that were published (shaded rows) and those that
were not. The letters A, B, and C stand for distinct but unidentified copyists.
Most of the manuscripts bear dates or are datable.

Date	Title	Copyist
11 April 1923	[Without title] Piece for violin and piano	B
20 April 1923	Ave María voice and group of woodwind instruments	A
1923?	Juglares. Impresiones de una farándula que pasó (piano solo version)	"Sanchís"
21 May 1923	Preludio No. 1	B (several copies); "Sanchís" (one copy)
9 July 1923	Pequeña ronda alborotada (violin y piano) [Second of Dos esbozos violin y piano] Sketch written in 2/4 (different ending) Draft copy written in 4/4	A B
18 August 1923	Canción en la noche violin and piano	A
July–October 1923	Suite para piano	C
1923	Berceuse d'automne	A
April, 1924?	Juglares (Ensayo sinfónico)	A
8 September 1925	Cantiga "Muy graciosa es la doncella" (soprano and piano)	A
January 1926	Balada de añoranza	López-Chavarri
15 September 1926	Preludio al atardecer (guitar)	Querol
December 1926	Gran marcha politónica del Año Nuevo (piano four hands)	Querol
1926	Preludio al gallo mañanero	López-Chavarri
[ca. 1926]	Rondoletto (piano)	Querol
[ca. 1926]	Pavana para la infanta del romance (piano)	López-Chavarri
May 1927	Jardin après la pluie (piano)	A

APPENDIX 2

Rodrigo's Concert Attendance in His First Weeks in Paris, November–December 1927

(from reports in Le Figaro, Le Gaulois, Comoedia, Le Ménestrel, and other newspapers)

Date	Authors / Works	Observations
12 Nov.	Dukas / Ariane and Bluebeard	Opéra-Comique. Repeated several times in the 1927–28 season with great success. Directed by Albert Wolff.
16 Nov.	Rimsky-Korsakov / The Golden Cockerel Dukas / The Peri	Théâtre National de l'Opéra.
19 Nov.	Wagner / Die Walküre	Théâtre National de l'Opéra. He might also have seen this opera 11 Dec.
26 Nov.	Honegger / King David Ibert / Song of Madness Roussel / Suite in F	Théâtre Mogador. Orchestre Pasdeloup.
27 Nov.	Franck / Les béatitudes	Palais du Trocadero. Lamoureux Orchestra and choirs Lamoureux (200 musicians) with the Singers of Saint-Gervais (directed by Paul Le Flem), all directed by Paul Paray.
30 Nov.	Ravel / The Spanish Hour and Daphnis and Chloé	Théâtre National de l'Opéra. He might also have gone to the performances of these works that took place 11 and 14 Nov. and 5 Dec.
1 Dec.	Bach / B-Minor Mass	Church of the Madeleine. Orchestre du Conservatoire and Choeur Mixte de Paris (200 musicians directed by Philippe Gaubert).

Rodrigo's Concert Attendance in His First Weeks in Paris, November–December 1927 (continued)

(from reports in *Le Figaro*, *Le Gaulois*, *Comoedia*, *Le Ménestrel*, and other newspapers)

Date	Authors / Works	Observations
7 Dec.	Mozart / *The Magic Flute*	Théâtre National de l'Opéra.
8 Dec.	Schoenberg / *Pierrot lunaire*, *Pelleas and Melisande* and "Cooing Doves!" of the *Gurre-Lieder*	Salle Pleyel. Schoenberg Festival. Orchestre Colonne directed by Schoenberg with Marya Freund as soloist.
9 Dec.	Debussy / *Pelléas et Melisande*	Théâtre National de l'Opéra.
16 Dec.	Beethoven / Ninth Symphony	Church of the Trinity. Centennial of Beethoven's birth. Orchestre du Conservatoire and a mixed choir of 200 voices, directed by Philippe Gaubert.
25 Dec.	Berlioz / *The Childhood of Christ* (fragments)	Christmas concert. Concerts Pasdeloup.
27 Dec.	Prokofiev / *The Steel Dance* Sauguet / *The Cat* Stravinsky / *The Firebird*	Théâtre National de l'Opéra. Ballets Russes of Diaghilev.
28 Dec.	Wagner / *Das Rheingold*	Théâtre National de l'Opéra.
29 Dec.	Rimsky-Korsakov / *Sadko*	Orquesta Lamoureux. Directed by Dimitri Slavianski d'Agreneff.
30 Dec.	Strauss / *Der Rosenkavalier*	Théâtre National de l'Opéra. Done in French translation as *Le chevalier à la rose*. Directed by Philippe Gaubert.

APPENDIX 3

Performances of Joaquín Rodrigo's music between 1928 and 1931 (premieres indicated with asterisk)

Date	Work	Place	Interpreters
14 March 1928	Preludio al gallo mañanero* Zarabanda lejana* Cantiga*	Paris, Hôtel de la Fondation Salomon de Rothschild	Alicia Felici and Joaquín Rodrigo
21 April 1928	Berceuse d'automne*	Paris, Salle Erard	Ricardo Viñes
6 May 1928	Zarabanda lejana (orchestra)*	Paris, École Normale de Musique	Interpreted by a double quartet
31 May 1928	Bagatela	Paris, Salle Chopin	Leopoldo Querol
9 June 1928	Zarabanda lejana (orchestra)*	Paris, Grand Palais Société internationale pour la musique contemporaine	?
18 Nov. 1928	Dos esbozos*	Paris, Salle Gaveau	Abelardo Mus and Encarnación Mus
2 Dec. 1928	Cantiga	Valencia, Conservatory of Music and Oratory	Carmen Andújar and Daniel de Nueda
16 March 1929	Dos esbozos	Castellón, Teatro Principal	Abelardo Mus and Encarnación Mus
28 March 1929	Cinco piezas infantiles	Paris, Théâtre des Champs-Élysées	Straram's Orchestra, Walther Straram
3 April 1929	Dos esbozos	Barcelona, Palau (Associació d'Amics de la Música)	Abelardo Mus and Encarnación Mus
20 April 1929	"Siciliana"* and "Minué"* from Suite para piano	Paris, Salle Gaveau (Société Nationale de Musique)	Ricardo Viñes

Performances of Joaquín Rodrigo's music between 1928 and 1931 (premieres indicated with asterisk) (continued)

Date	Work	Place	Interpreters
25 Sept. 1929	Zarabanda lejana (guitar)*	Buenos Aires, Sala de la Asociación Wagneriana	Regino Sainz de la Maza
10 Jan. 1930	Zarabanda lejana (orchestra)	Madrid, Teatro de la Comedia	Orquesta Clásica, Arturo Saco del Valle
15 Jan. 1930	Zarabanda lejana (guitar)*	Santander	Regino Sainz de la Maza
24 Jan. 1930	Tres viejos aires de danza*	Valencia, Teatro Principal	Valencia Orquesta Sinfónica, José Manuel Izquierdo
31 Jan. 1930	Dos esbozos	Paris, Salle Gaveau	Andrée Fascholin and Marius-François Gaillard
4 Feb. 1930	Zarabanda lejana (guitar)	Madrid, Teatro de la Comedia (Asociación de Cultura Musical)	Regino Sainz de la Maza
8 Feb. 1930	Preludio al gallo mañanero Suite para piano*	Paris, Salle Chopin (Société National de Musique)	Ricardo Viñes
21 Feb. 1930	Dos esbozos	Paris, École Normale de Musique	José Figueroa and Joaquín Rodrigo
25 Feb. 1930	Deux berceuses*	Paris (La Musique des Quatre Saisons)	Ricardo Viñes
5 March 1930	Tres canciones (Cantiga, Romance de la infantina de Francia* and Serranilla*)	Paris, École Normale de Musique (Société Musicale Indépendante)	María Josefa Regnard and Joaquín Rodrigo
9 March 1930	Siciliana*	Paris, École Normale de Musique	Diran Alexanian and Joaquín Rodrigo
9 March 1930	Suite para piano	Paris, École Normale de Musique	Ricardo Viñes
27 March 1930	Petite marche où vous voudrez, mais pas trop loin (Gran marcha politónica?)	Paris, École Normale de Musique (Fête de la Mi-Carême)	Mihail and Isaacs (piano four-hands)
2 April 1930	Cinco piezas infantiles	Madrid, Teatro de la Zarzuela	Orquesta Sinfónica, Madrid, Enrique Fernández Arbós
4 April 1930	Serranilla	Loches, Salle du Groupe Jeanne d'Arc	Bernardette Delprat and Luis Esteban

Date	Work	Place	Interpreters
6 April 1930	"Preludio," "Siciliana,"* and "Minué"* from *Suite para piano*	Châtellerault, Salle des Variétés-Cinèma	Luis Esteban
9 March 1930	*Suite para piano*	Paris, École Normale de Musique	Ricardo Viñes
1 May 1930	*Preludio para un poema a La Alhambra* (orchestra)*	Paris, Théâtre des Champs Élysées	Straram's Orchestra, Eugène Bigot
6 May 1930	*Zarabanda lejana* (guitar)	Madrid, Teatro de la Comedia (Asociación de Cultura Musical)	Regino Sainz de la Maza
May 1930	*Zarabanda lejana* (orchestra)	Palma de Mallorca	Chamber Orchestra, José Juan
5 June 1930	*Cinco piezas infantiles*	Barcelona, Palacio Nacional	Orquestra Pau Casals, Ricardo Lamote de Grignon
13 June 1930	*Juglares*	Madrid, Teatro de la Comedia	Orquesta Filarmónica, Madrid, Bartolomé Pérez Casas
9 July 1930	*Tres viejos aires de danza*	Valencia, Jardines del Real	Valencia Orquesta Sinfónica, José Manuel Izquierdo
8 Nov. 1930	*Juglares*	Valencia, Teatro Principal	Orquesta Filarmónica, Bartolomé Pérez Casas
20 Dec. 1930	*Zarabanda lejana* (piano)	Paris, Théâtre du Vieux-Colombier	María del Pilar Cruz (piano)
1 Feb. 1931	*Serranilla*	Paris, Salle Gaveau	Conchita Supervía and Alejandro Vilalta
17 Feb. 1931	*Serranilla*	Paris, Salle Gaveau	Conchita Supervía and Alejandro Vilalta
22 Feb. 1931	*Serranilla*	Barcelona, Palau de la Música Catalana	Conchita Supervía and Alejandro Vilalta
6 March 1931	*Bagatela*	Mexico, Anfiteatro "Bolívar"	Concepción Díaz Santana
9 March 1931	*Zarabanda lejana y villancico**	Paris, École Normale de Musique	Orchestre Féminin, dir. Jane Evrard
19 March 1931	*Tres canciones* (*Cantiga, Romance de la infantina de Francia* and *Serranilla*)	Paris, Salle Chopin	Madame Da Rosa and Joaquín Rodrigo

Performances of Joaquín Rodrigo's music between 1928 and 1931 (premieres indicated with asterisk) *(continued)*

Date	Work	Place	Interpreters
29 March 1931	Zarabanda lejana (guitar)	Mexico, Anfiteatro "Bolívar"	Regino Sainz de la Maza
16 May 1931	Tres canciones (Cantiga, Romance de la infantina de Francia and Serranilla)	Paris, Conservatorio antiguo (Société National de Musique)	María Josefa Regnard and Joaquín Rodrigo
19 June 1931	Cantiga Romance de la infantina de Francia Serranilla	Paris, Salle Chopin	Lissie von Rosen and Joaquín Rodrigo
14 Sept. 1931	"Siciliana" and "Bourrée" from Suite para piano Serranilla	Saint-Jean-de-Luz, Casimo de la Pérgola	María Josefa Regnard and Joaquín Rodrigo

APPENDIX 4

Joaquín Rodrigo: Prizes and Honors

1934   First prize from the Circle of Fine Arts in Valencia for his symphonic poem *Per la flor del lliri blau*.

1940   Prize of the National Union for the Performing Arts for his *Concierto de Aranjuez*.

1942   National Music Prize for *Concierto heroico*, for piano and orchestra.

1945   Encomienda de Alfonso X el Sabio.

1948   First prize for *Ausencias de Dulcinea*, for voice and orchestra, in the Cervantes Competition.

1950   Elected full member of the Royal Academy of Fine Arts of San Fernando, Madrid.

1952   First prize in the National Competition for *Retablo de Navidad*, for voice and orchestra.

1953   Great Cross of Alfonso X el Sabio.

1954   Vice president of the Spanish section of the International Society of Contemporary Music (ISCM).

1960   Officier des Arts et des Lettres (France).

1961   First prize, ORTF Coupe de la Guitare, for *Invocación y Danza*.

1963   Legion of Honor (France).

1964   Honorary doctorate, University of Salamanca.

1966   Great Cross of Civil Merit.
            Gold Medal, Mérito en el Trabajo, awarded by the Spanish government.

1967   Member of the Société Européenne de Culture.

1968   Member of the Académie du Monde Latin, Paris.

1969   Member of Honor of the San Carlos Academy of Fine Arts, Valencia.

1976   Honorary member of the Madrid Athenaeum.
            President of the Spanish National Committee of the International Council of Music, UNESCO.

1978   Member of the Royal Academy of Sciences, Letters and Fine Arts of Belgium.

1980   Gold medal, merit in Fine Arts from the Spanish government.
1982   National Music Prize of Spain.
        Honorary Doctorate, University of Southern California.
1985   Elected a Corresponding Member of the Hispanic Society of
        America.
1987   Gold medal and member of honor of the Valencian Generalitat.
1988   Honorary doctorate, Polytechnical University of Valencia.
        Director of the Royal Academy of Fine Arts of San Fernando,
        Madrid.
1989   Gold medal, Complutense University of Madrid.
        Honorary doctorate, University of Alicante.
        Honorary doctorate, Complutense University of Madrid.
        Honorary board member of the Sociedad General de Autores de
        España, SGAE.
1990   Honorary doctorate, University of Exeter (UK).
        Gold medal of Madrid.
1991   Awarded hereditary title of nobility Marqués de los Jardines de
        Aranjuez (Marquis of the Gardens of Aranjuez) by King Juan Car-
        los I.
        Official naming of the Conservatorio Superior de Música Joaquín
        Rodrigo in Valencia.
        Knight of the Royal Order of Santa María del Puig, Valencia.
        Silver seal of the city of Valencia.
        Guerrero Foundation Prize for Spanish Music.
1992   Awarded the Order of Félix Varela, First Degree (Cuba).
        Academician of Honor, Royal Academy of Valencian Culture.
1994   Gold medal from the Circle of Fine Arts, Valencia.
1995   Gold medal, Royal Conservatory of Music of Madrid.
        Radio Ondas Prize for classical music.
        Distinction for Cultural Merit, Generalitat of Valencia.
1996   Príncipe de Asturias Prize for the Arts.
        Gold Medal of Sagunto.
        Great Cross of the Order of Social Solidarity.
        Gold star, Autonomous Community of Madrid.
1997   Gerion for the Arts Prize.
1998   Commandeur des Arts et des Lettres (France).
        Prize for Best Composer of Classical Music, SGAE and AIE.
        Medal of honor of UIMP, International University Menéndez
        Pelayo, Santander (Spain).
1999   Gold medal, Festival of Granada.

NOTES

Chapter 1: Ah, la maledizione!

1. For a full account of these events, see Francesc A. Martínez Gallego, Manuel Chust Calero, and Eugenio Hernández Gascón, *Valencia 1900: Movimientos sociales y conflictos políticos durante la guerra de Marruecos, 1906–1914* (Castellón de la Plana: Publicaciones de la Universitat Jaume I, 2001), 137–44.
2. See *La Correspondencia de Valencia*, 25 June 1908.
3. "What happened in the community was a show of protest against the insults hurled by said gentleman at the Saguntans during last Monday's demonstration at the very door to his home," *ABC* (Madrid), 2 January 1907.
4. Sinforiano García Mansilla, *Tratado elemental de oftalmología* (Madrid, 1905), 382.
5. Florentina del Mar (pseud. Carmen Conde), "En busca de infancias: La del compositor Joaquín Rodrigo" (radio interview), Radio Nacional de España, 1949. A transcript of this interview is located in the Archivo de la Fundación Victoria y Joaquín Rodrigo in Madrid, henceforth referred to as AFVJR.
6. Louis de Wecker, *Tratado teórico y práctico de las enfermedades de los ojos*, 2nd ed., trans. and rev. by Francisco Delgado Jugo (Madrid, 1870), 66.
7. Acorde (pseud. Víctor Ruiz Albéniz), "Joaquín Rodrigo. El laureado músico" (interview), *Informaciones* (Madrid), 24 April 1946.
8. Félix Azzati, "El hombre-Idea," *El Pueblo* (Valencia), 21 February 1909.
9. See Nelson R. Orringer, "El krauso-institucionismo," in M. Garrido, N. Orringer, L. Valdés, and Margarita Valdés, *El legado filosófico español e hispanoamericano del siglo XX* (Madrid: Tecnos, 2009), 74–77.
10. For more information on Brígida Alonso, see her obituary in *Diario de Valencia*, 30 November 1922, 1–2, and *Las Provincias* (Valencia), 30 November 1922, 5.
11. *Colegio de sordo-mudos y ciegos de Valencia dirigido por las Religiosas Terceras de San Francisco de Asís* (Valencia, 1893), 5–6.
12. Ibid., 7.
13. For example, Agustín García won a composition prize for a large orchestral work at the Valencian Regional Exhibition of 1909. See *La Correspondencia de Valencia*, 23 December 1909.
14. *Las Provincias* (Valencia), 29 June 1911, in which Rodrigo's reading is mentioned, and *La Correspondencia de Valencia*, 30 June 1911, where other details of the show are indicated.
15. *La Correspondencia de Valencia*, *Diario de Valencia*, and *Las Provincias* (Valencia), 23 June 1917.
16. *Diario de Valencia*, 27 April 1920.
17. Escolástico Medina García [Tico Medina], "El maestro Rodrigo, el músico ciego,

triunfó súbitamente a los veintidós años" (interview), *Careta* (Madrid), 17 March 1955. Perhaps *Princesita?* In *La Correspondencia de Valencia* we have found a brief mention of Rodrigo's first compositions, which must have existed because they were actually registered: "In the Register of Intellectual Property of the Library of this University [Valencia] the following works have been inscribed: Don Alberto Vicent Mengual, Álbum Vight, Princesita, Soy propietario rumbista a la fuerza, music by Don Joaquín Rodrigo." See *La Correspondencia de Valencia*, 23 August 1920, and *Las Provincias* (Valencia), 24 August 1920.

18. Eduardo López-Chavarri, "[Chronicle of musical activity in Valencia]," *Revista Musical Hispano-Americana* (March 1915), 13.

19. Raymond Calcraft, "Voces y visiones de España: Joaquín Rodrigo y Joaquín Sorrolla," in Alberto González Lapuente, ed., *90 Aniversario Joaquín Rodrigo* (Madrid: Sociedad General de Autores y Editores, 1991), 51–59.

20. Cecilia Rodrigo, Agustín León Ara, and Carlos Laredo Verdejo, eds., *Joaquín Rodrigo a través de sus escritos* (Madrid: Ediciones Joaquín Rodrigo, 2019), 223. A recent English translation of these and other writings is now available. See *Joaquín Rodrigo: Writings on Music*, trans. Raymond Calcraft and Elizabeth Matthews (Abingdon: Routledge, 2021).

21. "Círculo de Bellas Artes. Concierto Iturbi," *Las Provincias* (Valencia), 3 January 1915.

22. Francisco Cuesta, "Desde que nací hasta ahora," *Los Ciegos. Revista Mensual Tyflófila Hispano-Americana* (June 1921), 5–6.

23. Gloria Abanda Cendoya, "[Interview with Joaquín Rodrigo]," *El Diario Vasco* (San Sebastián), 10 September 1986.

24. Pamphlet of the Philharmonic Society of Valencia of February 1922, with the names of members and dates of their entrance. Cited in Sergio Sapena Martínez, "La Sociedad Filarmónica de Valencia (1911–1945): Origen y consolidación" (PhD diss., Universitat Politècnica de València, 2007), i, 105.

25. He presumably used the Spanish translation: François-Auguste Gevaert, *Tratado general de instrumentación*, trans. José Parada Barreto (Madrid, 1873).

26. Eduardo López-Chavarri, "Joaquín Rodrigo antes de marcharse a París," *Música: Revista Quincenal* (Barcelona), no. 16 (1 September 1945).

27. *Las Provincias* (Valencia), 18 January 1911.

28. According to the *Diario de Valencia*, 6 May 1912.

29. See "Wanda Landowska, la sutil," *La Correspondencia de Valencia*, 20 January 1920.

30. Reported in *La Correspondencia de Valencia*, 15 December 1920.

Chapter 2: "Music! . . . Music!"

1. Vicente Blasco Ibáñez, *Arroz y tartana* (Valencia: Prometeo, 1919), 130.

2. Pasqual Hernández Farinós, "Francesc Antich Carbonell. Músic de Silla," *Algudor*, no. 3 (January 2004), 85.

3. Marino Gómez-Santos, "Pequeña historia de grandes personajes. Joaquín Rodrigo cuenta su vida" (interview), *Pueblo* (Madrid), 30 June 1959, 13.

4. *Joaquín Rodrigo a través de sus escritos*, 223.

5. Eduardo López-Chavarri, "Francisco Cuesta," *Las Provincias* (Valencia), 24 May 1921.

6. Ibid.

7. Enrique González Gomá, "El compositor Francisco Cuesta," *Diario de Valencia*, 24 May 1921, 1.

8. Cited in Raymond Calcraft's liner notes for *Joaquín Rodrigo, Music for Violin*, Agustín León Ara (violin), Eugène de Canck (piano), cpo 999 186–2, 1993.

9. Ibid.

10. Antonio Gallego, *El arte de Joaquín Rodrigo* (Madrid: SGAE, 2003), 29.

11. *Gaceta de Madrid*, 23 May 1923, 790. The deadline for entries was 31 January 1924. Rodrigo's *Suite para piano* arrived late and was not admitted to the contest,

whose prize was ultimately not awarded. See *Gaceta de Madrid*, 29 March 1924, 1648.

12. Antonio Iglesias, *Joaquín Rodrigo (su obra para piano): Piano a cuatro manos, dos pianos y piano y orquesta*, 2nd ed. (Madrid: Alpuerto, 1996), 56.
13. Ibid., 429.
14. Gallego, *El arte de Joaquín Rodrigo*, 25.
15. Graham Wade, *Joaquín Rodrigo: A Life in Music*, vol. 1: *Travelling to Aranjuez, 1901–1939* (Leeds: GRM, 2006), 11–12.
16. See Dena Kay Jones, "The Piano Works of Joaquin Rodrigo: An Evaluation of Social Influences and Compositional Style" (DMA diss., University of Arizona, Tucson, 2001), 74–75.
17. Ibid., 73.
18. Ibid., 80.
19. Ibid.
20. Ibid., 85.
21. Iglesias, *Joaquín Rodrigo (su obra para piano)*, 63.
22. Gallego, *El arte de Joaquín Rodrigo*, 34.
23. Jones, "Piano Works of Joaquin Rodrigo," 92.
24. Ibid., 97.
25. Ibid.
26. His dissertation, a study of the then titled *Cancionero de Upsala* (Songbook of Upsala) and more recently renamed the *Cancionero de los Duques de Calabria* (Songbook of the Duke of Calabria), received the Doctoral Prize in 1928. See "Leopoldo Querol vence en el doctorado de Filosofía y Letras," *Las Provincias* (Valencia), 31 January 1928, 3.
27. Eduardo López-Chavarri, "Joaquín Rodrigo, antes de marcharse a París," *Música. Revista Quincenal*, no. 16 (1 August 1945).
28. *Joaquín Rodrigo a través de sus escritos*, 223.
29. María Ángeles Arazo, "Hombres de Valencia. Joaquín Rodrigo" (interview), *Levante* (Valencia), undated article (13 October 1967). AFVJR, sig. B-1-116.
30. "Concierto por Leopoldo Querol," *Las Provincias* (Valencia), 9 January 1923, 5.
31. Program for Concert XXIV of the Season 1926–27, Sociedad Filarmónica de Valencia, 23 May 1927. AFVJR.
32. "Chavarri, an excellent writer, a man of high culture, also had *La Revue Musicale*. Joaquín devoured it, as this was the epoch of Les Six, the times of the anti-Impressionist fury." See Federico Sopeña, *Joaquín Rodrigo* (Madrid: Ediciones y Publicaciones Españolas, 1946), 20.
33. "Sociedad Filarmónica," *Diario de Valencia*, 15 February 1925, 2.
34. This list, preserved in the AFVJR, is reproduced in Javier Suárez Pajares, ed., *Centenario Joaquín Rodrigo: el hombre, el músico, el maestro* (Madrid: Sinsentido, 2001), 109.
35. Xavier Montsalvatge: "La vida y la obra. Joaquín Rodrigo" (interview), *Destino* (Barcelona), January, 1953, 19.
36. Sopeña, *Joaquín Rodrigo*, 49.
37. Consuelo Martín Colinet, "La música pianística de Joaquín Rodrigo" (PhD diss., Universidad Autónoma de Madrid, 2001), 355.
38. Jones, "The Piano Works of Joaquin Rodrigo," 113.
39. Martin Colinet, "La música pianística de Joaquín Rodrigo," 363.
40. Jones, "Piano Works of Joaquin Rodrigo," 107.
41. Ibid., 110.
42. Joaquín Rodrigo, "La música para piano comentada e interpretada por su autor," *Anales de la Academia Médico-Quirúrgica Española*, May 1964.
43. Jones, "Piano Works of Joaquin Rodrigo," 106.
44. Ibid., 113.
45. Martín Colinet, "La música pianística de Joaquín Rodrigo," 368.
46. *El Pueblo* (Valencia), 29 June 1924, 6.

47. G. [Enrique González Gomá], "Crónica musical. Viveros municipales. Orquesta Valenciana," *Diario de Valencia*, 22 July 1924, 2.
48. Ibid.
49. "En los Viveros la Orquesta Valenciana," *El Pueblo* (Valencia), 23 July 1924, 2.
50. [Eduardo López-Chavarri], "De música. Rodrigo, compositor valenciano," *Las Provincias* (Valencia), 24 July 1924, 4.
51. Eduardo López-Chavarri, "A Joaquín Rodrigo le editan las obras en París," *Las Provincias* (Valencia), 23 August 1928, 1.
52. Álvaro de Albornoz, "Las ideas y el carácter: El juglar, el bufón y el hombre de ingenio," *El Pueblo* (Valencia), 22 March 1924, 1.
53. "En los Viveros. La Orquesta Valenciana," *El Pueblo* (Valencia) 21 July 1925.
54. "En los Viveros. Los conciertos de la Orquesta Valenciana," *Diario de Valencia*, 19 July 1925, 3.
55. Manuel Palau, "Orquesta Sinfónica Valenciana," *La Correspondencia de Valencia*, 20 July 1926, 3.
56. As we may gather from the various news articles on the awarding of the prize. See *El Sol* (Madrid), 13 May 1925, or *El Liberal* (Madrid), 13 May 1925.
57. *Gaceta de Madrid*, 5 November 1925, 682.
58. Adolfo Salazar, "La vida musical. La joven generación musical. Un músico ciego valenciano: J. Rodrigo," *El Sol* (Madrid), 4 September 1925, 4.
59. Ibid.
60. Eduardus [Eduardo López-Chavarri], "De arte. Se habla de un joven músico valenciano," *Las Provincias* (Valencia), 9 September 1925, 1–2. Salazar was gay and did not hestiate to make that clear. So when "Eduardus" refers to him as feminine and a seamstress, he fully expects the savvy reader to read between his lines. We are grateful to Nelson Orringer for this keen insight.
61. Ibid., 1.
62. Salazar, "La joven generación musical," 4.
63. Program for Concert XIV of the Season 1926–27, Sociedad Filarmónica de Valencia, 16 February 1927. AFVJR.
64. Wade, *Joaquín Rodrigo*, 15.
65. Iglesias, *Joaquín Rodrigo (su obra para piano)*, 360.
66. Wade, *Joaquín Rodrigo*, 16.
67. Fidelio [Bernardo Morales Sanmartín], "Concierto XIV por la Orquesta Sinfónica," *El Mercantil Valenciano*, 17 February 1927, 4.
68. S. [Salvador Ariño], "En la Filarmónica. La Orquesta Sinfónica de Valencia," *El Pueblo* (Valencia), 17 February 1927, 2.
69. Manuel Palau, "Musicales. La Orquesta Sinfónica de Valencia," *La Correspondencia de Valencia*, 17 February 1927, 6.
70. [Eduardo López-Chavarri], "En la Filarmónica. El concierto de ayer," *Las Provincias*, (Valencia), 17 February 1927, 1–2.
71. "Sociedad Filarmónica," *La Correspondencia de Valencia*, 31 January 1925, 1.
72. *Joaquín Rodrigo a través de sus escritos*, 239.
73. Enrique González Gomá, "Crónica musical. Segunda conferencia de M. Prunières," *Diario de Valencia*, 18 April 1923, 2. See also footnote 39 in this chapter.
74. Joaquín Rodrigo, "Recuerdos y consideraciones sobre Manuel de Falla," speech given upon his induction into the Académie Royale des Beaux-Arts, Brussels, 1978.
75. See Suzanne Rhodes Draayer, *A Singer's Guide to the Songs of Joaquin Rodrigo* (Lanham: Scarecrow Press, 1999), 92.
76. For this and other useful observations, see María Dolores Moreno Guil, "La canción con piano de Joaquín Rodrigo. Un estudio poético musical y psicoeducativo" (PhD diss., Universidad de Córdoba, 2014), 158.
77. For more on Longfellow's interest in Vicente's poetry, see Jack Horace Parker, *Gil Vicente* (New York: Twayne Publishers, 1967), 129–31.
78. Gallego, *El arte de Joaquín Rodrigo*, 4.
79. See Moreno Guil, "La canción con piano de Joaquín Rodrigo," 162.

80. Sopeña, *Joaquín Rodrigo*, 77–78.
81. Gallego, *El arte de Joaquín Rodrigo*, 23.
82. Javier Suárez-Pajares, "En torno a Miguel Llobet y la interpretación del *Homenaje a Debussy* de Manuel de Falla," en Javier Riba, ed., *Nombres propios de la guitarra. Miguel Llobet* (Córdoba: IMAE Gran Teatro, 2016), 169–205.
83. Segovia's concert activity can be traced in a detailed study by Julio Gimeno, "Los conciertos de Andrés Segovia," guitarra.artepulsado.com/foros/showthread. php?21031 (accessed 30 October 2018).
84. Letter from Andrés Segovia to Eduardo López-Chavarri, Stettin, n.d. (though most likely written in the autumn of 1924). See Rafael Díaz Gómez and Vicente Galbis López, eds., *Eduardo López-Chavarri Marco. Correspondencia* (Valencia: Generaltitat Valenciana, Biblioteca de Música Valenciana, 1996), ii, 271.
85. Miquel Llàcer, "Retrat de Josefina Robledo," *Butlletí d'Informació Municipal de Godella*, 2/9 (fall 2009), 42.
86. "Una concertista notable," *El Pueblo* (Valencia), 19 November 1907.
87. See the entry on "Sarabande" in *Grove Music Online* by Richard Hudson and Meredith Ellis Little.
88. Leopoldo Neri, "La edición musical española para guitarra en la primera mitad del siglo XX," in Begoña Lolo and José Carlos Gosálvez, eds., *Imprenta y edición musical en España (ss. XVIII–XX)* (Madrid: Universidad Autónoma, 2012), 723–41.
89. See Walter Aaron Clark and William C. Krause, *Federico Moreno Torroba: A Musical Life in Three Acts* (New York: Oxford University Press, 2013/16), 70–71, 111–14, for a history and analysis of this seminal work.
90. Michael Christoforidis, *Manuel de Falla and Visions of Spanish Music* (New York: Routledge, 2018), 105–6.
91. See Graham Wade, *Distant Sarabandes: The Solo Guitar Music of Joaquín Rodrigo* (Leeds: GRM Publications, 1996), 8–11.
92. See Colinet, "La música pianística de Joaquín Rodrigo," 284–86, for a detailed examination of various possible readings of the formal scheme in this piece.
93. Wade, *Distant Sarabandes*, 10.
94. Joaquín Rodrigo, "El vuelo actual de la guitarra," *Ya* (Madrid), 19 July 1961.
95. Alfredo Romea, "Joaquín Rodrigo: *Zarabanda lejana*, per a guitarra," *Revista Musical Catalana*, no. 291 (March 1928), 108–9.
96. Iglesias, *Joaquín Rodrigo (su obra para piano)*, 430.
97. Rodrigo, "Aspectos de la vida musical contemporánea," 27 July 1949, mechanographic notes for a summer course in Segovia. AFJVR.

Chapter 3: "Long Live Paris!"

1. Vicente Rodrigo Polo died in Ambers, Belgium, on 4 March 1926. See the obituary on the first page of *Las Provincias* (Valencia), 6 March 1926.
2. The French franc had risen a minimal amount in relation to the Spanish peseta in October 1927, when 100 francs cost an average of 22.8 pesetas. See Pedro Martínez Méndez, *Nuevos datos sobre la evolución de la peseta entre 1900 y 1936. Información complementaria* (Madrid: Banco de España, 1990), 28.
3. Carlos Bosch, "Del Levante español. Conversando con Leopoldo Querol," *El Imparcial* (Madrid), 5 July 1927, 3–4.
4. Letter from Leopoldo Querol to Eduardo López-Chavarri, dated Madrid, 6 April 1927. See Díaz Gómez and Galbis López, eds., *Eduardo López-Chavarri*, ii, no. 614.
5. *Gaceta de Madrid*, 13 September 1927, 1480.
6. Letter from Leopoldo Querol to Eduardo López-Chavarri, dated Paris, 9 October 1927. Biblioteca Valenciana "Nicolau Primitiu," Department of Personal and Institutional Archives. This letter is not found in the two volumes published by Díaz Gómez and Galbis López.
7. *Gaceta de Madrid*, 19 January 1928, 512.
8. "La exposición Povo en París," *La Esfera* (Madrid), 26 June 1926, 28.

9. Letter from Joaquín Rodrigo to Eduardo López-Chavarri, dated Paris, 30 November 1927. See Díaz Gómez and Galbis López, eds., *Eduardo López-Chavarri*, ii, no. 664.

10. Joaquín Rodrigo, "Los músicos que conocí a través de mis recuerdos: Paul Dukas," typescript, AFVJR.

11. Ibid.

12. Letter from Joaquin Rodrigo to Eduardo López-Chavarri, dated Paris, 30 November 1927.

13. Active students paid 2000 francs for three trimesters of class (complete school term), 1400 for two trimesters, or 750 for one trimester; auditors paid half and could attend a single class at 25 francs per class. Advertisement published in *Le Monde Musical* (Paris), no. 1 (January 1926), 37. See Pilar Serrano Betored, "Paul Dukas: la influencia silenciada de la escuela musical española. De la Generación de los Maestros a la Generación del 27" (PhD diss., Madrid, Universidad Complutense, 2019), 253.

14. The information about the concerts he attended from his arrival in Paris to the beginning of December appears in the letter of Joaquín Rodrigo to Eduardo López-Chavarri dated Paris, 5 January 1928. See Díaz Gómez and Galbis López, eds., *Eduardo López-Chavarri*, ii, no. 665.

15. Schoenberg gave a lecture entitled "Conviction and Knowledge" at the École Normale de Musique. This was reported on by Arthur Hoérée, "A Lecture by M. Arnold Schoenberg," *Le Ménestrel* (Paris), 30 December 1927, 546–47.

16. Letter from Joaquín Rodrigo to Eduardo López-Chavarri, dated Paris, 5 January 1928. See Díaz Gómez and Galbis López, eds., *Eduardo López-Chavarri*, ii, no. 665.

17. Ibid.

18. Ibid.

19. Manuel M. Ponce, "Paul Dukas," in *Gaceta Musical* (Paris), no. 2 (February 1928), 30–31.

20. Joaquín Rodrigo, "Los músicos que conocí a través de mis recuerdos: Paul Dukas," typescript, AFVJR.

21. Bernardino Gálvez Bellido, "A modo de entrevista. Joaquín Rodrigo," *Ritmo* (Madrid), nos. 30–31 (15 and 30 April 1931), 6.

22. Manuel M. Ponce, "Paul Dukas," *La Correspondencia de Valencia*, 27 January 1928, 4.

23. Ricardo Miranda-Perez, "José Rolón: A Study of His Life and Music" (PhD diss., City University London, 1992), 85.

24. Ibid., 83.

25. Yolanda Acker, "Ernesto Halffter: a Study of the Years 1905–1946," *Revista de Musicología* (Madrid) 17/1–2 (January–December 1994), 121, 167.

26. Carpentier attributes that post to himself in his article "El concierto mexicano," *El Nacional* (Caracas), 15 December 1954.

27. Henri Collet, "El porvenir de la música española," *Gaceta Musical* (Paris), no. 5 (May 1928), 19.

28. Letter from Joaquín Rodrigo to Eduardo López-Chavarri, dated Paris, 5 February 1928. See Díaz Gómez and Galbis López, eds., *Eduardo López-Chavarri*, ii, no. 666.

29. Gálvez Bellido, "A modo de entrevista," 6.

30. Xavier Montsalvatge, "La vida y la obra. Joaquín Rodrigo," *Destino* (Barcelona) (January 1953), 11–12.

31. José Ruiz Medrano, "La influencia italiana en nuestra canción," *Bandera de Provincias* (Guadalajara, Mexico), no. 1 (1 May 1929). See Ricardo Miranda, *La voz de lo propio. José Rolón y su música* (Mexico: Dirección General de Publicaciones, 2007), 93.

32. Manuel M. Ponce, "Paul Dukas," *La Correspondencia de Valencia*, 27 January 1928, 4.

33. Letter from Robert Brussel to Manuel de Falla, 29 February 1928. Granada, Fundación Archivo Manuel de Falla, sig. 6804-008.

34. Letter from Joaquín Rodrigo to Eduardo López-Chavarri, dated Paris, 19 March 1928. See Díaz Gómez and Galbis López, eds., *Eduardo López-Chavarri*, ii, no. 667.

35. Joaquín Rodrigo, "Los músicos que conocí a través de mis recuerdos: Manuel de Falla," typescript, AFVJR.
36. Letter from Joaquín Rodrigo to Eduardo López-Chavarri, dated Paris, 19 March 1928. See Díaz Gómez and Galbis López, eds., *Eduardo López-Chavarri*, ii, no. 667.
37. Ibid.
38. Robert Brussel, "Cinq pieces enfantines de Joaquín Rodrigo," *Le Figaro* (Paris), 4 April 1929, 3.
39. "Album musical," *Le Monde Musical* (Paris), 31 July 1928.
40. *Le Gaulois* (Paris), 17 March 1928, 2; *L'Intransigeant* (Paris), 20 March 1928, 5.
41. Adolfo Salazar, "Paisaje de la actual música española," *Gaceta Musical* (Paris), no. 5 (May 1928), 9–10.
42. Letter from Adolfo Salazar to Manuel de Falla, dated Madrid, 27 November 1928. Fundación Archivo Manuel de Falla, sig. 7571-030.
43. Letter from Joaquín Rodrigo to Eduardo López-Chavarri, dated Paris, 19 March 1928. See Díaz Gómez and Galbis López, eds., *Eduardo López-Chavarri*, ii, no. 667.
44. The general rehearsal took place on March 6. *Comoedia* (Paris), 6 March 1923, 3.
45. *Comoedia* (Paris), 15 March 1928, 3, and 6 April 1928, 3.
46. Letter from Joaquín Rodrigo to Eduardo López-Chavarri, dated Paris, 19 March 1928. See Díaz Gómez and Galbis López, eds., *Eduardo López-Chavarri*, ii, no. 667.
47. Rodrigo, "Los músicos que conocí a través de mis recuerdos: Manuel de Falla," AFVJR.
48. Eduardo López-Chavarri, "De cómo Joaquín Rodrigo es más que un aprendiz de brujo," *Las Provincias* (Valencia), 9 May 1928, 1.
49. Ibid.
50. Letter from Joaquín Rodrigo to Eduardo López-Chavarri, dated Paris, 9 May 1928. See Díaz Gómez and Galbis López, eds., *Eduardo López-Chavarri*, ii, no. 668.
51. Paul Le Flem, "Le Récital de M. Ricardo Viñes," *Comoedia* (Paris), 29 April 1928, 3.
52. Paris, Bibliothèque Nationale de France, call number M-19732.
53. *Joaquín Rodrigo a través de sus escritos*, 125.
54. Marialuisa Rolón, *Testimonio sobre José Rolón* (Mexico: UNAM, 1969), 20.
55. Concert program, AFVJR, sig. P-00-05(v).
56. Advertisements in *Excelsior* (Paris), 8 June 1928, 2, and *Le Gaulois* (Paris), 9 June 1928, 4.
57. Eduardo López-Chavarri, "Nuevos éxitos de un valenciano y de un balear," *Las Provincias* (Valencia), 3 July 1928, 5.
58. *La Semaine à Paris*, 25 May 1928, 76; "Leopoldo Querol triunfa Paris," *Las Provincias* (Valencia), 3 June 1928, 6.
59. Henri Collet, "Concert Leopoldo Querol." *Le Ménestrel* (Paris), 8 June 1928, 259.
60. Eduardo López-Chavarri, "Leopoldo Querol, hombre de ciencia y artista," *Las Provincias* (Valencia), 6 June 1928, 1.
61. Henri Collet, "Le Mouvement Musical à l'Étranger," *Le Ménestrel* (Paris), 25 May 1928, 237.
62. "Viveros Municipales. Grandes conciertos por la Orquesta Sinfónica," *El Pueblo* (Valencia), 21 June 1928, 5; "Los tres últimos conciertos de la temporada," *Las Provincias* (Valencia), 26 June 1928, 3.
63. For more about Ravel's trip to Valencia, see Nelson R. Orringer, "La estancia de Maurice Ravel en la comunidad musical de Valencia," *Diagonal: An Ibero-American Music Review* 4/2 (2019), 76–89.
64. Eduardo Ranch, "Jelly d'Arányi," *La Correspondencia de Valencia*, 6 April 1927, 3.
65. Eduardo Ranch, "Mauricio Ravel, gran músico de Francia," *La Correspondencia de Valencia*, 16 November 1928, 3; Eduardo Ranch, "Festival Ravel en la Filarmónica," *La Correspondencia de Valencia*, 20 November 1928, 7.
66. "La estancia en Valencia de Mauricio Ravel," *La Correspondencia de Valencia*, 21 November 1928, 4.
67. Letter from Joaquín Rodrigo to Eduardo López-Chavarri, dated Paris, 9 December 1931. Biblioteca Valenciana "Nicolau Primitiu," Departament d'Arxius Personals

i Institucionals. This letter is not found in the two volumes published by Díaz Gómez and Galbis López.

68. Fidelio [Bernardo Morales Sanmartín], "Sociedad Filarmónica," *El Mercantil Valenciano*, 18 November 1928, 3.

69. Enrique González Gomá, "Valencia," *Revista Musical Catalana* (Barcelona) 26/301 (January 1929), 32.

70. Letter from Claude Lévy to Robert Brussel dated Valencia, 18 November 1928. Bibliothèque Nationale de France, département Musique, call number LA-LEVY CLAUDE-8.

71. *La Semaine à Paris*, 16 November 1928, 73.

72. Joaquín Rodrigo, "Los músicos que conocí a través de mis recuerdos: Maurice Ravel," typescript, AFVJR.

73. "El mestre Joaquim Rodrigo a Barcelona," *La Veu de Catalunya* (Barcelona), 22 November 1928, 2.

74. Letter from Joaquín Rodrigo to Eduardo López-Chavarri dated, Paris, 10 December 1928. See Díaz Gómez and Galbis López, eds., *Eduardo López-Chavarri*, ii, no. 670.

75. Eduardo López-Chavarri, "A Joaquín Rodrigo le editan las obras en París," *Las Provincias* (Valencia), 23 August 1928, 1.

76. "Nuevo triunfo de Joaquín Rodrigo Paris," *Las Provincias* (Valencia), 23 April 1929, 5.

77. Letter from Joaquín Rodrigo to Eduardo López-Chavarri, dated Paris, 4 April 1929. See Díaz Gómez and Galbis López, eds., *Eduardo López-Chavarri*, ii, no. 671.

78. Ibid.

79. Letter from Joaquín Rodrigo to Eduardo López-Chavarri, dated Paris, 21 May 1929. See Díaz Gómez and Galbis López, eds., *Eduardo López-Chavarri*, ii, no. 673.

80. "Échos et nouvelles," *Le Ménestrel* (Paris), 30 November 1928, 512.

81. Victoria Kamhi, *Hand in Hand with Joaquín Rodrigo: My Life at the Maestro's Side*, trans. Ellen Wilkerson (Pittsburgh: Latin American Literary Review Press, 1992), 61–62.

82. Ibid., 63.

83. Joaquín Rodrigo, "París," *Revista Musical Catalana* 26/307 (July 1929), 292.

84. Auguste Mangeot, "Le 1er Salon International de la Symphonie," *Le Monde Musical* (Paris), 30 June 1929, 207–8; Paul Le Flem, "Une ideé intéressante. Un salon de la symphonie," *Le Monde Musical* (Paris), 31 July 1929, 253. Manuel Palau, "Primer salón internacional de sinfonía," *La Correspondencia de Valencia*, 25 June 1929.

85. Henri Collet, "Le mouvement musical à l'étranger. Espagne," *Le Ménestrel*, Paris, 27 September 1929, 415. Titles of works presented by Rodrigo can be seen in "Le salon international de la symphonie," *Le Monde Musical* (Paris), 31 May 1929, 192–93; the others in "Le salon international de la symphonie," *Le Monde Musical* (Paris), 30 April 1929, 154.

86. Postcard from Joaquín Rodrigo to Victoria Kamhi, dated Paris, 4 June 1929. AFVJR (private collection).

87. Letter from Joaquín Rodrigo to Victoria Kamhi, dated Paris, 25 May 1929. AFVJR (private collection).

88. Letter from Joaquín Rodrigo to Victoria Kamhi, dated Valencia, 4 August 1929. AFVJR (private collection).

89. Letter from Joaquín Rodrigo to Victoria Kamhi, dated Valencia, 29 September 1929. AFVJR (private collection).

90. Letter from Joaquín Rodrigo to Victoria Kamhi, dated Estivella, 15 September 1929. AFVJR (private collection).

91. Concert program of the debut. Concert X of Philharmonic Society of Valencia, 20 January 1930 (the initial date was cancelled and the concert took place January 24). AFVJR, sig. P-01-05.

92. N. [Eduardo Ranch?], "Orquesta Sinfónica," *La Correspondencia de Valencia*, 25 January 1939, 3.

93. [Eduardo López-Chavarri], "En la Filarmónica," *Las Provincias* (Valencia), 25 January 1930, 5.
94. "Feria de julio. El concierto de mañana," *La Correspondencia de Valencia*, 1 August 1930, 1.
95. Letter from Joaquín Rodrigo to Victoria Kamhi, dated Valencia, 28 July 1930, AFVJR (private collection).
96. Letter from Joaquín Rodrigo to Victoria Kamhi, dated Valencia, 5 August 1930. AFVJR (private collection).
97. Letter from Joaquín Rodrigo to Victoria Kamhi, dated Valencia, 17 July 1930. AFVJR (private collection).
98. Letter from Joaquín Rodrigo to Victoria Kamhi, dated Valencia, 9 November 1930. AFVJR (private collection).
99. Letter from Joaquín Rodrigo to Victoria Kamhi, dated Valencia, 5 November 1929. AFVJR (private collection).
100. Ibid.
101. Concert program in the AFVJR, sig. P-00-08.
102. "Pablo Casals dirige une orchestre de plus de cinquante violoncellistes," *Excelsior* (Paris), 19 March 1930, 1.
103. *Joaquín Rodrigo a través de sus escritos*, 233.
104. *Joaquín Rodrigo a través de sus escritos*, 151.
105. For a fascinating and insightful comparison of Rodrigo and Vaughan Williams, see the essay by Raymond Calcraft, "Tradition and Faith: Ralph Vaughan Williams and Joaquín Rodrigo," *Ralph Vaughan Williams Society Journal*, no. 68 (February 2017), 7–10.
106. Eric Sams, "Cryptography, musical," *Grove Music Online* (accessed 10 May 2019).
107. Letter from Joaquín Rodrigo to Victoria Kamhi, dated Valencia, 24 December 1930. AFVJR (private collection).
108. Letter from Joaquín Rodrigo to Victoria Kamhi, dated Valencia, 11 June 1930. AFVJR (private collection).
109. Joaquín Nin-Culmell, "Los compositores españoles de mi generación," Joaquín Nin-Culmell and José Joaquín Nin y Castellanos family papers. Special Collections and Archives. University of California, Riverside, MS 076B15F16.t31.
110. Leopoldo Neri de Caso, *De ideales y melancolías: Regino Sainz de la Maza y la guitarra en el siglo XX en España*, 100.
111. Paul Le Flem, "Débuts de Printemps," *Comœdia* (París), 5 May 1930, 7.
112. Letter from Joaquín Rodrigo to Victoria Kamhi, dated Valencia, June 1930. AFVJR (private collection).
113. Pierre-Octave Ferroud, "La musique," *Paris-soir*, 8 May 1930, 5.
114. Florent Schmitt, "Les Concerts," *Le Temps* (Paris), 17 May 1930, 3, and 14 March 1931, 3.
115. Letter from Joaquín Rodrigo to Victoria Kamhi, dated Valencia, 1 July 1930. AFVJR (private collection).
116. Ángel María Castell, "Los conciertos de la Orquesta Sinfónica," *ABC* (Madrid), 3 April 1930, 39.
117. Adolfo Salazar, "Orquesta Sinfónica," *El Sol* (Madrid), 4 April 1930, 2.
118. Letter from Paul Dukas to Joaquín Rodrigo, dated Tours, 24 June 1928. AFVJR.
119. Joaquín Rodrigo, "París," *Revista Musical Catalana* 27/313 (January 1930), 32.
120. Joaquín Rodrigo, "París," *Revista Musical Catalana* 27/314 (February 1930), 71.
121. Joaquín Rodrigo, "París," *Revista Musical Catalana* 27/316 (April 1930), 178.
122. Joaquín Rodrigo, "París," *Revista Musical Catalana* 27/318 (June 1930), 282.
123. Ibid.
124. Letter from Leopoldo Querol to Eduardo López-Chavarri, dated Madrid, 1 February 1930. See Díaz Gómez and Galbis López, eds., *Eduardo López-Chavarri*, ii, no. 675.
125. Joaquín Rodrigo, "París," *Revista Musical Catalana* 27/319 (July 1930), 326.
126. Joaquín Rodrigo, "En la Filarmónica. Orquesta Sinfónica de Madrid," *Las Provincias* (Valencia), 28 June 1930, 2.

127. Joaquín Rodrigo, "La música Paris. La *Sinfonía de los salmos* de Igor Stravinski," *Las Provincias* (Valencia), 20 March 1931, 4.
128. Joaquín Rodrigo, "París," *Revista Musical Catalana* 28/319 (31 May 1931), 167.
129. Letter from Joaquín Rodrigo to Eduardo López-Chavarri, dated Paris, 31 March 1931. See Díaz Gómez and Galbis López, eds., *Eduardo López-Chavarri*, ii, no. 682.
130. Joaquín Rodrigo, "París," *Revista Musical Catalana* 28/336 (December 1931), 502.
131. Letter from Joaquín Rodrigo to Victoria Kamhi, dated Valencia, 5 July 1930. AFVJR (private collection).
132. Acker, "Ernesto Halffter," 166.
133. Joaquín Rodrigo, "París," *Revista Musical Catalana* 26/307 (July 1929), 291.
134. Gálvez Bellido, "A modo de entrevista," 7.
135. Acker, "Ernesto Halffter," 126.
136. Letter from Joaquín Rodrigo to Victoria Kamhi, dated Valencia, 11 October 1930. AFVJR (private collection).
137. Letter from Joaquín Rodrigo to Victoria Kamhi dated Valencia 5 August 1930. AFVJR (private collection).
138. Gálvez Bellido, "A modo de entrevista," 7.
139. Ibid., 7.
140. Letter from Joaquín Rodrigo to Victoria Kamhi, dated Valencia, 19 July 1931. AFVJR (private collection).
141. Letter from Joaquín Rodrigo to Victoria Kamhi, dated Valencia, 28 October 1931. AFVJR (private collection).
142. Letter from Joaquín Rodrigo to Victoria Kamhi, dated Valencia, 6 October 1931. AFVJR (private collection).
143. Letter from Joaquín Rodrigo to Victoria Kamhi, dated Valencia, 9 November 1931. AFVJR (private collection).

Chapter 4: Dark Times

1. Kamhi, *Hand in Hand with Joaquín Rodrigo*, 53.
2. Letter from Joaquín Rodrigo to Victoria Kamhi dated Valencia, 7 March 1932. AFVJR (private collection).
3. Joaquín Rodrigo, Joaquín Nin-Culmell, Yves Lenoir, "Recordando a Enrique Jordá," *Musiker*, no. 9 (1997): 8.
4. Letter from Enrique Jordá to Joaquín Rodrigo dated in Brussels, 7 October 1995. AFVJR.
5. L.S. [Luis Sánchez], "Música de cámara," *La Correspondencia de Valencia*, 14 December 1932, 2.
6. "Orquesta de Cambra," *Las Provincias* (Valencia), 14 December 1932, 3.
7. Letter from Joaquín Rodrigo to Victoria Kamhi dated Valencia, 22 March 1932. AFVJR (private collection).
8. Letter from Victoria Kamhi to Joaquín Rodrigo dated Paris, 15 October 1932. AFVJR (private collection).
9. "La Orquesta de Cámara en el Ateneo," *El Luchador* (Alicante), 9 December 1932.
10. Letter from Paul Dukas to Joaquín Rodrigo dated Paris, 25 November 1932. AFVJR.
11. Letter from Jacques Larolle to Joaquín Rodrigo. AFVJR.
12. Kamhi, *Hand in Hand with Joaquín Rodrigo*, 77.
13. *Gaceta de Madrid*, 3 July 1932, 60.
14. Letter from Victoria Kamhi to Joaquín Rodrigo dated Paris, 2 November 1932. AFVJR (private collection).
15. *Las Provincias* (Valencia), 21 March 1933, 3.
16. Juan del Brezo (pseudonym of Juan José Mantecón), "Orquesta Femenina Francesa en el Institut Français en Espagne," *La Voz* (Madrid), 4 February 1933.
17. Eduardo López-Chavarri, "En la Filarmónica," *Las Provincias* (Valencia), 5 February 1933, 5.
18. Z. [Joaquín Zamacois?], "La Orquesta Femenina de París," *La Vanguardia* (Barcelona), 9 February 1933, 29.

19. M. H. Barroso, "Música y músicos. Orquesta Filarmónica de Madrid," *La Libertad*, (Madrid), 31 January 1933, 2.
20. Letter from Manuel de Falla to Joaquín Rodrigo dated Granada, 6 February 1933. AFVJR.
21. "Los intelectuales de España por la victoria total del pueblo," *La Vanguardia* (Barcelona), 1 March 1938, 2.
22. *Gaceta de Madrid*, 19 July 1933, 1955.
23. "Reglamento del Colegio Nacional de Ciegos," *Gaceta de Madrid*, 13 September 1933, 1680.
24. "Homenaje a Leopoldo Querol," *Luz* (Madrid), 3 March 1933, 6.
25. "El banquete a Leopoldo Querol," *El Sol* (Madrid), 7 March 1933, 10.
26. [Juan José Mantecón], "Información musical. Los últimos conciertos," *La Voz* (Madrid), 28 March 1933, 4; Gerardo Diego, "Crónica musical. Orquesta Filarmónica. Orquesta de Cámara," *El Imparcial* (Madrid), 29 March 1933.
27. A.M.C. [Ángel María Castell], "Informaciones musicales. Crónica de música. Cinco conciertos en dos días," *ABC* (Madrid), 28 March 1933, 43–44.
28. Kamhi, *Hand in Hand with Joaquín Rodrigo*, 79–80.
29. The original is in the Fundación Victoria y Joaquín Rodrigo, dated, "August 14, Estivella 1933." A clean copy is in the private collection of Gonzalo Sainz de la Maza dated "Estivella, August 1933."
30. Letter from Joaquín Rodrigo to Regino Sainz de la Maza dated Paris, 22 May 1936. Madrid, Biblioteca Nacional de España.
31. For a distillation of his important findings regarding the *Tocata*, see Leopoldo Neri de Caso, "Joaquin Rodrigo e la *Tocata para guitarra*," *Il Fronimo*, 34/133 (January–March 2006), 1, 5–24.
32. Kamhi, *Hand in Hand with Joaquín Rodrigo*, 94.
33. Ibid., 81. In the AFVJR is the receipt for the redemption of the piano dated 4 November 1933. This cost them 800 out of the 3,500 pesetas of prize money
34. S. [Adolfo Salazar]: "La vida musical. Orquesta Sinfónica," *El Sol* (Madrid), 16 November 1933.
35. Ad. S. [Adolfo Salazar]: "La vida musical. Una nueva visita de Stravinsky," *El Sol* (Madrid), 23 November 1933; Regino Sainz de la Maza, "La música. Stravinsky, en Madrid," *La Libertad* (Madrid), 24 November 1933, 4.
36. Urbano Fernández Zanni, "Asociación de Música de Cámara. Festival Stravinsky," *La Vanguardia* (Barcelona), 17 November 1933, 15.
37. "Joaquín Rodrigo," *Le Monde Musical* (Paris), September–October 1933. Cf. Allan Clives, "Regino Sainz de la Maza," *Classical Guitar* 19/1 (September 2000), 54.
38. [Eduardo López-Chavarri], "Orfeó Valenciá," *Las Provincias* (Valencia), 31 January 1934, 3.
39. Letter from Victoria Kamhi to Joaquín Rodrigo, dated Paris, 7 February 1934. AFVJR (private collection).
40. Letter from Victoria Kamhi to Joaquín Rodrigo, dated Paris, 15 February 1934. AFVJR (private collection).
41. *Gaceta de Madrid*, 15 February 1934, 1267–68.
42. Letter from Conchita Supervía to Joaquín Rodrigo dated Sussex, 7 September 1934. AFVJR.
43. Letter from Victoria Kamhi to Joaquín Rodrigo, dated Paris, 22 March 1934. AFVJR (private collection).
44. *Gaceta de Madrid*, 26 April 1934, 626.
45. *Gaceta de Madrid*, 28 July 1934, 968–69.
46. "Los Concursos Musicales del Estado" [Editorial], *Musicografía* (Monóvar, Alicante), no. 14 (June 1934), 124–25.
47. Letter from Joaquín Rodrigo to Frank Marshall, dated Valencia, 14 November 1934.
48. Letter from Joaquín Rodrigo to Manuel de Falla, dated Valencia, 15 November 1934. Granada, Archivo Manuel de Falla, call number 7503-011. The correspondence between Falla and Rodrigo was published in the program for "Homenaje a

Joaquín Rodrigo," Fundación Juan March (Madrid), 9 December 1981. It is available online at digital.march.es/clamor/es/fedora/repository/atm%3A1493.

49. "Radiotelefonía," Las Provincias (Valencia), 4 April 1934, 5.
50. "At least it has two qualities: freshness and a youthful naïvetè." Letter from Victoria Kamhi to Joaquín Rodrigo, dated Paris, 3 May 1934. AFVJR (private collection).
51. Letter from Victoria Kamhi to Joaquín Rodrigo, dated Paris, 3 May 1934. AFVJR (private collection).
52. "Círculo de Bellas Artes. Concurso de Obras Musicales. Bases," Las Provincias (Valencia), 16 May 1934, 13.
53. Letter of Manuel Palau to Joaquín Rodrigo, dated Valencia, 15 May 1934.
54. Letter of Victoria Kamhi to Joaquín Rodrigo dated Paris, 16 June 1934. AFVJR (private collection).
55. Letter of Victoria Kamhi to Joaquín Rodrigo, dated Paris, 22 June 1934. AFVJR (private collection).
56. Letter of Victoria Kamhi to Joaquín Rodrigo, dated Paris, 25 June 1934. AFVJR (private collection).
57. Letter from Joaquín Rodrigo to Gilbert Chase, dated Freiburg, 31 October 1936. Located in the New York Public Library, Gilbert Chase Papers, call number JPB 04-32, Series I: Correspondence, b. 1 f. 9.
58. "Círculo de Bellas Artes. Sección de Música," Las Provincias (Valencia), 5 July 1934, 5.
59. "Círculo de Bellas Artes. Sección de Música," Las Provincias (Valencia), 11 July 1934, 3.
60. Letter from Victoria Kamhi to Joaquín Rodrigo, dated Paris, 13 July 1934. AFVJR (private collection).
61. Letter from Victoria Kamhi to Joaquín Rodrigo, dated Paris, 11 July 1934. AFVJR (private collection).
62. Eduardo López-Chavarri, "Conciertos en los Viveros. Estreno de un poema sinfónico de Joaquín Rodrigo," Las Provincias (Valencia), 1 August 1934, 13.
63. Ibid.
64. Letter from Victoria Kamhi to Joaquín Rodrigo, dated Paris, 30 June 1934. AFVJR (private collection).
65. [Eduardo López-Chavarri?], "Conciertos en los Viveros," Las Provincias (Valencia), 1 August 1934, 13.
66. "En la Filarmónica," Las Provincias (Valencia), 21 December 1934, 2.
67. Ondas (Madrid), 17 November 1934, 14–15.
68. Rodolfo Halffter Escriche, "Información Musical. Varios conciertos," La Voz (Madrid), 24 November 1934, 6.
69. Jesús A. Ribó [José Subirá], "Vida musical. España. Madrid," Musicografía (Monóvar, Alicante), no. 20 (December 1934), 273–74.
70. S. [Adolfo Salazar], "La vida musical. Las orquestas. J. Rodrigo. P. Sanjuán," El Sol (Madrid), 27 November 1934, 3.
71. Letter from Joaquín Rodrigo to Manuel de Falla, dated Valencia, 15 November 1934. Granada, Archivo Manuel de Falla, call number 7503-011.
72. Copy made by Victoria Kamhi of a letter from Paul Dukas, dated 25 October 1934. AFVJR (private collection).
73. Letter from Joaquín Rodrigo to Gilbert Chase, dated Freiburg, 31 October 1936. The New York Public Library, Gilbert Chase Papers, Call number JPB 04-32, Series I, Correspondence, b. 1 f. 9. Rodrigo's commentary quoted in the analysis of this work are fragments from this source.
74. The program cited is the one appearing printed in the score itself.
75. "En el Monumental Cinema. Cuarto concierto matinal de la Orquesta Sinfónica," Hoja Oficial del Lunes (Madrid), 19 November 1934, 3.
76. Henri Collet, "Le mouvement musical en Province. Espagne," Le Ménestrel (Paris), 7 December 1934, 415.
77. Ondas (Madrid), 1 December 1934, 27.

78. S. [Adolfo Salazar]: "La vida musical. D. Haralambis y la música griega contemporánea," *El Sol* (Madrid), 7 January 1934, 4.
79. P. Rives, "Un recital de piano," *La Voz de Aragón*, 28 October 1934, 11.
80. Letter from Joaquín Rodrigo to Frank Marshall, dated Valencia, 14 November 1934.
81. Letter from Victoria Kamhi to Joaquín Rodrigo, dated Paris, 21 March 1934. AFVJR (private collection).
82. Letter from Victoria Kamhi to Joaquín Rodrigo, dated Paris, 16 March 1934. AFVJR (private collection).
83. Letter from Victoria Kamhi to Joaquín Rodrigo without a date, but written in Paris in 1934. AFVJR (private collection).
84. Letter from Victoria Kamhi to Joaquín Rodrigo, dated Paris, 17 February 1934. AFVJR (private collection).
85. *Gaceta de Madrid*, 27 November 1934, 1635.
86. *Gaceta de Madrid*, 26 December 1934, 2451.
87. *Gaceta de Madrid*, 16 November 1934, 1335.
88. Letter from Victoria Kamhi to Joaquín Rodrigo, dated Paris, 19 April 1934. AFVJR (private collection).
89. Letter from Joaquín Rodrigo to Manuel de Falla, dated Valencia November 15, 1934. Granada, Archivo Manuel de Falla, call number 7503-011.
90. Draft of Manuel de Falla's letter to Álvaro Figueroa y Torres, Count of Romanones, dated Granada, 21 November 1934. Granada, Archivo Manuel de Falla, call number 7524-008.
91. Letter from Joaquín Rodrigo to Manuel de Falla, dated Madrid, 29 November 1934. Granada, Archivo Manuel de Falla, call number 7503-012. See note 48.
92. Letter from Joaquín Turina to Joaquín Rodrigo (in support of his request for the "Count of Cartagena" Scholarship), dated Madrid, 7 December 1934. AFVJR.
93. "In the Academy of Fine Arts. The Scholarships of the Count of Cartagena Foundation," *ABC* (Madrid), 18 December 1934, 36.
94. "En la Academia de Bellas Artes. Las becas de la Fundación del conde de Cartagena," *ABC* (Madrid), 2 January 1935, 38.
95. Kamhi, *Hand in Hand with Joaquín Rodrigo*, 88, 91.
96. Consuelo Carredano, "Devociones ejemplares: algunas pautas en la relación de Manuel de Falla y Ernesto Halffter," *Cuadernos de Música Iberoamericana* 11 (2006), 40–41.
97. Salvador de Madariaga, "La música española. El Casals de la guitarra," *El Sol* (Madrid), 5 November 1925, 1.
98. "El concierto de la Sinfónica de Bilbao en el Nuevo Teatro," *Pensamiento Alavés* (Vitoria), 29 March 1935, 5.
99. Kamhi, *Hand in Hand with Joaquín Rodrigo*, 87.
100. Joaquín Nin-Culmell, "Los compositores españoles de mi generación," Joaquín Nin-Culmell and José Joaquín Nin y Castellanos Family Papers. Special Collections and Archives. University of California, Riverside, call number MS 076B1516.t31.
101. Letter from Joaquín Rodrigo to Eduardo López-Chavarri dated Paris, 23 May 1935. See Díaz Gómez and Galbis López, *Eduardo López-Chavarri*, ii, no. 685.
102. Kamhi, *Hand in Hand with Joaquín Rodrigo*, 88.
103. Letter from Joaquín Rodrigo to Manuel de Falla, dated Paris, 30 December 1935. Granada, Archivo Manuel de Falla, call number 7503-017.
104. Draft of Manuel de Falla's letter to Joaquín Rodrigo, dated Granada, 2 March 1936. Granada, Fundación Archivo Manuel de Falla, call number 7503-032.
105. Paul Le Flem, "La vie musicale. *Le Tombeau de Paul Dukas*," *Comœdia* (Paris), 27 April 1936, 1–2.
106. Peter Hill and Nigel Simeone, *Messiaen* (New Haven and London: Yale University Press, 2005), 57, 69.
107. The publication date is the one appearing in the copyright, but the contract with Max Eschig is nonetheless signed 17 January 1967.

108. *Joaquín Rodrigo a través de sus escritos*, 146.
109. Wade, *Distant Sarabandes*, 250. In his discussion of this piece, Iglesias (*Joaquín Rodrigo [su obra para piano]*, 137) detects an allusion to Dukas's opera *Ariane et Barbe-Bleue*, in a motive that materializes in the third rotation of the A theme but which he believes is "the true seed of the whole composition [. . .] and axis of the entire work." It is an ascending six-note idea associated with the imprisoned wives in the drama.
110. Maurice Emmanuel, "La musique de piano de Paul Dukas," *Revue Musicale* (Paris) (May–June 1936), 69–78.
111. Letter from Maurice Emmanuel to Joaquín Rodrigo, dated Montaure (Eure), 22 August 1936. AFVJR.
112. Joaquín Rodrigo, "Moviment musical. París," *Revista Musical Catalana*, 32/379 (July 1935), 307–9.
113. Adolfo Salazar, "La vida musical. *El pintor Matías* de Hindemith, en la Orquesta Sinfónica," *El Sol* (Madrid), 4 April 1935, 4.
114. Kamhi, *Hand in Hand with Joaquín Rodrigo*, 90–91.
115. *La Semaine à Paris*, 17 May 1935, 40; Mariano Daranas, "Presentation of Maestro Rodrigo," *ABC* (Madrid), 24 May 1935, 48.
116. *L'Art Musical* (Paris), 3 April 1936, 563–64.
117. *L'Art Musical* (Paris), 13 March 1936, 479.
118. Letter from Joaquín Rodrigo to Eduardo López-Chavarri, dated Paris, 23 May 1935. See Díaz Gómez and Galbis López (eds.), *Eduardo López-Chavarri*, ii, no. 685.
119. Kamhi, *Hand in Hand with Joaquín Rodrigo*, 87.
120. Joaquín Rodrigo, "Moviment musicale. Paris," *Revista Musical Catalana* 33/388 (April 1936), 171, 173–309.
121. Joaquín Rodrigo, "Vida musical en París," *Ritmo* (Madrid), 15 April 1935, 4.
122. Joan Llongueres, "Els programes del XIV Festival de la Societat Internacional per la Música Contemporània," *Revista Musical Catalana* 33/389 (May 1936), 180–84.
123. "De música. La Orquesta Sinfónica de Bilbao," *El Nervión* (Bilbao), 7 April 1936, 6.
124. José Subirá, *Musicografía* (Monóvar, Alicante), no. 38 (June 1936), 83–87.
125. Letter from Jesús Arámbarri to Joaquín Rodrigo, dated Bilbao, 3 June 1936. AFVJR.
126. *Le Jour* (Paris), 23 April 1936, 6.
127. [Mariano] Daranas, "Conferencia en París sobre música española del siglo XVI," *ABC* (Madrid), 8 May 1936, 6.
128. Joël Dugot, "La vihuela del Musée Jacquemart-André," *Studies on the Vihuela* (Madrid: Sociedad de la Vihuela, 2007), 85–95.
129. Letter from Joaquín Rodrigo to Regino Sainz de la Maza, dated Paris, 12 May 1936 (Biblioteca Nacional de España).
130. *Gaceta de Madrid*, 12 September 1936.
131. Letter from Joaquín Rodrigo to unknown addressee, dated Freiburg, 8 October 1936. AFVJR (private collection).
132. The invitation to this lecture is preserved in the AFVJR, sig. P-01-24bis.
133. Kamhi, *Hand in Hand with Joaquín Rodrigo*, 93.
134. Letter from José Rolón to Joaquín Rodrigo, dated Mexico, 8 December 1936. AFVJR.
135. Much later, when fortune smiled on them and Germany began its descent into the Second World War, the Rodrigos payed back the hospitality of their hosts with a donation that Otto Vanoli gratefully acknowledged in a letter dated Freiburg, 10 March 1944. AFVJR.
136. Letter from Joaquín Nin-Culmell to Joaquín Rodrigo, dated 19 September 1937. AFVJR.
137. A detailed and insightful analysis of this work is available in María Dolores Moreno Guil, "La canción con piano de Joaquín Rodrigo. Un estudio poético musical y psicoeducativo" (PhD diss., Universidad de Córdoba, 2014), 239–44.
138. Kamhi, *Hand in Hand with Joaquín Rodrigo*, 96–97.
139. "Gran concierto del pianista Cubiles," *El Adelanto* (Salamanca), 8 December 1937.

140. Letter from Antonio Magaz to Joaquín Rodrigo, dated Berlin, 3 December 1937. AFVJR.
141. Letter from Jacques Lerolle to Joaquín Rodrigo dated Haute-Savoie, 15 September 1937. AFVJR.
142. Kamhi, *Hand in Hand with Joaquín Rodrigo*, 98.
143. Letter from Joaquín Nin-Culmell to Joaquín Rodrigo, dated Paris, 16 April 1937. AFVJR.
144. Manuel de Falla, "La alta esperanza," *Orientación española* (Buenos Aires), 15 February 1938.
145. "Estafeta de Frente Popular. Delegación de Agricultura," *Heraldo de Castellón*, 3 September 1936.

Chapter 5: All about the *Concierto de Aranjuez*

1. These are mentioned in a letter from the publisher Jacques Lerolle to Joaquín Rodrigo, dated in Haute-Savoie, 15 September 1937. AFVJR.
2. "Par T. S.," *L'Express de Mulhouse*, 5 October 1937.
3. AFVJR, Archive of Programs, P-00-32(v).
4. Letter from Nemesio Otaño to Valentín Ruiz-Aznar, dated 6 September 1938, quoted by José López-Calo, *Nemesio Otaño: Half a Century of Spanish Music* (Madrid: ICCMU, 2010), 219.
5. Official Bulletin of the State, 2 January 1938, no. 438, 5074.
6. Letter from Manuel de Falla to Joaquín Rodrigo, dated Granada, 18 August 1938. AFVJR.
7. Letter from Joaquín Rodrigo to Manuel de Falla, dated Bilbao, 8 September 1938. Granada, Fundación Archivo Manuel de Falla, sig. 7503-019.
8. Letter from Manuel de Falla to Eugenio d'Ors, dated Granada, 30 September 1938. Barcelona: Arxiu Nacional de Catalunya, sig. ANCI-255/T-3318.
9. Draft of letter from Manuel de Falla to Pedro Sainz Rodríguez, dated Granada, 4 October 1938. Granada, Fundación Archivo Manuel de Falla, sig. 7562-009.
10. A professor's normal yearly salary was almost twice as much. Letter from Pedro Sainz Rodríguez to Manuel de Falla, dated Vitoria, 6 October 1938. Granada, Fundación Archivo Manuel de Falla, sig. 7562-003.
11. Kamhi, *Hand in Hand with Joaquín Rodrigo*, 105.
12. Joaquín Rodrigo, "El porqué y cómo se hizo el *Concierto de Aranjuez* (recuerdos y vagas apostillas a la obra)," dated Madrid 11 October 1943. See *Joaquín Rodrigo a través de sus escritos*, 110.
13. Letter from Joaquín Rodrigo to Regino Sainz de la Maza, dated Paris, 22 May 1936. Biblioteca Nacional de España.
14. Kamhi, *Hand in Hand with Joaquín Rodrigo*, 333.
15. Ibid., 105.
16. Alejandro L. Madrid, "Rafael Adame: il primo concerto per chitarra e orchestre del XX secolo," *Guitart*, no. 12 (October 1998), 12–15.
17. Ismael Ramos Giménez, "Ángel Barrios: el compositor en su época" (PhD diss., Universidad de Granada, 2016), 213–17.
18. Javier Suárez-Pajares, "Quintín Esquembre (1885–1965). Vida y obra de un maestro independiente," *Roseta. Revista de Sociedad Española de la Guitarra*, no. 2 (2009), 91–92.
19. Mario Castelnuovo-Tedesco, *Una vita di musica: Un libro di recordi* (Fiesole, Florence: Cadmo, 2005), i, 263.
20. Joaquín Rodrigo, "Autocrítica. El Concierto de Aranjuez," *Radio Nacional* (Madrid), no. 111, 21 November 1940.
21. Regino Sainz de la Maza, "El Concierto de Aranjuez," *Leonardo: Revista de las ideas y las formas* (Barcelona), vol. I (April 1945), 145.
22. Letter from Joaquín Rodrigo to Manuel de Falla, dated 21 December 1938, Granada, Fundación Archivo Manuel de Falla, sig. 7503-021.

23. Claude Altomont, "Passion selon Saint-Matthieu, de Bach," *Le Ménestrel* (Paris), 4 November 1938, 248.
24. Rodrigo, "El porqué y cómo . . . " in *Joaquín Rodrigo a través de sus escritos*, 110.
25. Joaquín Rodrigo, "Concierto de Aranjuez (II)," in *Joaquín Rodrigo a través de sus escritos*, 113.
26. Paul Dukas, "Le nouveau lyrisme," *Minerva: revue des lettres et des arts* (Paris), 15 February 1903, 567–78.
27. Kamhi, *Hand in Hand with Joaquín Rodrigo*, 109.
28. Ibid., 107.
29. *Joaquín Rodrigo a través de sus escritos*, 110.
30. Letter from Regino Sainz de la Maza to Joaquín Rodrigo, dated Luzmela (Santander), 11 March 1939. AFVJR.
31. Joaquín Rodrigo, "El porqué y cómo se hizo el *Concierto de Aranjuez*," *Joaquín Rodrigo a través de sus escritos*, 110–11.
32. Kamhi, *Hand in Hand with Joaquín Rodrigo*, 111.
33. Joaquín Rodrigo, "Concierto de Aranjuez (II)," *Joaquín Rodrigo a través de sus escritos*, 112.
34. Leopoldo Neri studies the variants shown in this source in his article "El *Concierto de Aranjuez* a través de los escritos de Regino Sainz de la Maza," in Javier Suárez-Pajares (ed.), *Joaquín Rodrigo. Nombres propios de la guitarra* (Córdoba: Guitar Festival/Ediciones La Posada, 2010), 82–87.
35. *Joaquín Rodrigo a través de sus escritos*, 114.
36. Kamhi, *Hand in Hand with Joaquín Rodrigo*, 108.
37. Gallego, *El arte de Joaquín Rodrigo*, 120.
38. AFVJR, Archive of Programs, P-00-34.
39. Kamhi, *Hand in Hand with Joaquín Rodrigo*, 106.
40. "Concursos musicales del Frente de Juventudes," *El Adelanto* (Salamanca), 12 May 1942, 5.
41. "Poste national Radio Paris," *L'Ouest-Éclair* (Rennes), 27 March 1939, 12.
42. *Joaquín Rodrigo a través de sus escritos*, 136–37.
43. A. [Víctor Ruiz Albéniz], "Calderón: música y bailes rusos," *Hoja Oficial del Lunes* (Madrid), 20 November 1939, 3.
44. *Joaquín Rodrigo a través de sus escritos*, 136.
45. Letter from Regino Sainz de la Maza to Joaquín Rodrigo, Luzmela (Santander), 10 August 1939. AFVJR.
46. Rodrigo, "El porqué y cómo . . . ," in *Joaquín Rodrigo a través de sus escritos*, 111.
47. *Joaquín Rodrigo a través de sus escritos*, 112–13.
48. [Joaquín Rodrigo], "Concierto de Aranjuez." Program notes, Barcelona, Palau de la Música, 9 November 1940.
49. *Joaquín Rodrigo a través de sus escritos*, 115.
50. Peter Manuel, "The Guajira between Cuba and Spain. A Study in Continuity and Change," *Latin American Music Review* 25/2 (Fall–Winter 2004), 137–62.
51. We gratefully acknowledge Julio Giménez's thorough revision of our analysis of the *Concierto de Aranjuez*, and particularly his observation on the use of the Andalusian mode.
52. *Joaquín Rodrigo a través de sus escritos*, 110.
53. Juan Riera, *Emilio Pujol* (Lérida: Instituto de Estudios Ilerdenses, 1974), 42.
54. Fabián Edmundo Hernández Ramírez, "La obra compositiva de Emilio Pujol (*1886–†1980): estudio comparativo, catálogo y edición crítica" (PhD diss., Barcelona, Universitat Autònoma, 2010), i, 56–67.
55. Aldo Rodríguez, *Isaac Nicola, maestro de maestros* (Havana: Letras Cubanas, 1997), 42.
56. Javier Suárez-Pajares, "Manuel de Falla: entre la política, el exilio, la confabulación y la muerte," in Consuelo Carredano and Olga Picún, eds., *Huellas y rostros. Exilios y migraciones en la construcción de la memoria musical de Latinoamérica* (Universidad Autónoma de México, 2007), 285.
57. *Radio Nacional* (Madrid), no. 51, 29 September 1939.

58. *Boletín Oficial del Estado* (Madrid), no. 307 (3 November 1939), 6187–88.
59. Letter from Joaquín Rodrigo to Eduardo López-Chavarri, dated Madrid, 18 November 1939. See Díaz Gómez and Galbis López, eds., *Eduardo López-Chavarri*, ii, no. 689.
60. Letter from Joaquín Rodrigo to Eduardo López-Chavarri, dated Madrid, 23 November 1939. See Díaz Gómez and Galbis López, eds., *Eduardo López-Chavarri*, ii, no. 690.
61. "Primer Congreso de la Organización Nacional de Ciegos," *ABC* (Seville), 7 December 1939, 9.
62. Kamhi, *Hand in Hand with Joaquín Rodrigo*, 111–12.
63. Federico Sopeña, *Joaquín Rodrigo* (Madrid: EPESA, 1946), 13–14.
64. Regino Sainz de la Maza, "Español: homenaje a Antonia Mercé," *ABC* (Madrid), 21 October 1939, 17.
65. Conrado del Campo, "Leopoldo Querol en la Asociación de Cultura Musical," *El Alcázar* (Madrid), 25 October 1939.
66. Regino Sainz de la Maza, "Orquesta Sinfónica. Joaquín Rodrigo," *ABC* (Madrid), 19 March 1940, 15.
67. Joaquín Rodrigo, "Concierto de gala organizado por el Departamento de Radiodifusión," *Radio Nacional* (Madrid), no. 74, 7 April 1940.
68. Letter from César de Mendoza Lassalle to Joaquín Rodrigo, dated San Sebastián, 15 September 1939. AFVJR.
69. Letter from the Count of Superunda [Ignacio de Gortázar] to Joaquín Rodrigo, dated Bilbao, 21 March 1942. AFVJR.
70. Neri de Caso, "El *Concierto de Aranjuez* a través de los escritos de Regino Sainz de la Maza," 68.
71. Neri de Caso, *De ideales y melancolías: Regino Sainz de la Maza y la guitarra en el siglo XX en España*, 194.
72. Letter from César de Mendoza Lassalle to Regino Sainz de la Maza, dated San Sebastián, 31 July 1940. Private collection of Jean Alexandre de Mendoza. The letters between Mendoza Lassalle and Sainz de la Maza were published by Neri de Caso in his article "El *Concierto de Aranjuez* a través de los escritos de Regino Sainz de la Maza," 100–102.
73. Letter from Regino Sainz de la Maza to César de Mendoza Lassalle, dated Madrid, 5 August 1940. Private collection Jean Alexander de Mendoza. Neri de Caso, "El *Concierto de Aranjuez*," 101–2.
74. Letter from Josefina de la Maza to Joaquín Rodrigo, dated Mazcuerras (Santander), August 1940. AFVJR.
75. Letter from César de Mendoza Lassalle to Regino Sainz de la Maza, dated San Sebastián, 17 September 1940. Private collection Jean Alexandre de Mendoza. Neri de Caso, "El *Concierto de Aranjuez*," 101–2.
76. Letter from Regino Sainz de la Maza to César de Mendoza Lassalle, dated Madrid, 19 [September 1940]. Private collection Jean Alexandre de Mendoza. Neri de Caso, "El *Concierto de Aranjuez*," 102.
77. "Concierto de hoy de la Filarmónica," *La Vanguardia Española* (Barcelona), 9 November 1940, 3.
78. Joaquín Rodrigo, "Mi vieja y fraternal amistad con Regino Sainz de la Maza," *Ritmo* (Madrid), January 1982, 12.
79. [Joaquín Rodrigo], "Concierto de Aranjuez." Program notes for the premiere, Barcelona, Palacio de la Música, 9 November 1940.
80. Xavier Montsalvatge, "Primera audición de una obra de Joaquín Rodrigo," *Destino* (Barcelona), 16 November 1940, 12.
81. *El Noticiero Universal*, 11 November 1940, 6–7.
82. "La cultura por la música. Sainz de la Maza y la Orquesta Filarmónica, dirigida por el maestro Mendoza Lassalle en el Palacio de la Música," *La Vanguardia Española* (Barcelona), 10 November 1940, 3.
83. G. D. [Gerardo Diego], "El *Concierto de Aranjuez*," *ABC* (Madrid), 12 December 1940, 10.
84. A [Víctor Ruiz Albéniz], "Novedades de la semana. Español. Estreno del concierto *Aranjuez*," *Hoja Oficial del Lunes* (Madrid), 16 December 1940, 3.

85. José María Franco, "La Orquesta Nacional estrena el *Concierto de Aranjuez* de J. Rodrigo," Ya (Madrid), 10 November 1940.
86. [Joaquín Rodrigo], "Concierto de Aranjuez," program notes, Barcelona, Palacio de la Música, 9 November 1940.
87. An indispensable source of information about Andrés Segovia's travels and concerts is Julio Gimeno, "Andrés Segovia en la prensa" (Andres Segovia in the Press), https://guitarra.artepulsado.com/foros/showthread.php?9939-Andr%E9s-Segovia-en-la-prensa (consulted November 2023).
88. "Por el éxito del *Concierto de Aranjuez*," *Hoja Oficial del Lunes* (Madrid), 23 December 1940.
89. José Antonio Gutiérrez, "La labor crítica de Rodrigo en el diario *Pueblo* (1940–1946)," in Javier Suárez-Pajares, ed., *Joaquín Rodrigo y la música española de los años cuarenta* (Universidad de Valladolid, 2005), 403–30.

Chapter 6: The Postwar Years

1. Sopeña, *Joaquín Rodrigo*, 25.
2. Kamhi, *Hand in Hand with Joaquín Rodrigo*, 17.
3. *Boletín Oficial del Estado*, 1 May 1940, no. 122, 3005, and 8 April 1941, no. 98, 2358–59.
4. "Sobre la música pianística de Joaquín Turina," in *Joaquín Rodrigo a través de sus escritos*, 253.
5. *Boletín Oficial del Estado*, 1 May 1940, no. 122, 3005, and 8 April 1941, no. 98, 2358–59.
6. *Boletín Oficial del Estado*, 20 January 1949, no. 20, 323.
7. Federico Sopeña, *Memorias de músicos* (Madrid: EPESA, 1971), 61.
8. *Boletín Oficial del Estado*, 18 May 1941, no. 138, 3545.
9. Foreword by Francisco Umbral to Antonio Díaz-Cañabate, *Historia de una tertulia* (Madrid: Espasa-Calpe, 1978).
10. Acorde [Víctor Ruiz Albéniz], "En Escorial. Homenaje a Viñes," *Hoja del Lunes* (Madrid), 17 March 1941, 2.
11. A review of this edition indicating its rarity given the painful lack of paper in Spain at the time can be seen in Federico Sopeña, "La edición musical," *Arriba* (Madrid), 22 June 1941.
12. Federico Sopeña, "Inauguración de la Exposición Zuloaga en la revista Escorial," *Arriba* (Madrid), 25 June 1941, 10.
13. Joaquín Turina, [Untitled], *Dígame* (Madrid), 8 July 1941; "Canciones de Joaquín Rodrigo en Escorial," *Pueblo*, 2 July 1941.
14. Javier Suárez-Pajares, "Festivals and Orchestras. Nazi Musical Propaganda in Spain during the Early 1940s," in Gemma Pérez Zalduondo and Germán Gan Quesada, eds., *Music and Francoism* (Thurnhout, Belgium: Brepols, 2013), 25–59.
15. Letter from Regino Sainz de la Maza to Joaquín Rodrigo, undated. AFVJR.
16. Joaquín Rodrigo, "El CL Aniversario de la muerte Mozart. Crónica de Viena," *Radio Nacional*, 4 January 1942, 14.
17. "Entrega de los premios de 1940 del Teatro, la Cinematografía y la Música," *ABC* (Madrid), 6 June 1941, 7.
18. "Concurso de himnos del Frente de Juventudes," *Imperio, Diario de Zamora de Falange*, 27 February 1942, 6.
19. "Concurso de canciones," *Ritmo* (Madrid), May 1942, 18.
20. *Cancionero juvenil* (Madrid: Frente de Juventudes, 1947), 128. The lyrics are also attributed to Joaquín Rodrigo in José de Arraca, *Canciones de Juventudes* (Madrid: Doncel, 1967), 194.
21. Federico Sopeña, "El año musical," *Arriba* (Madrid), 1 January 1942, 11.
22. Kamhi, *Hand in Hand with Joaquín Rodrigo*, 124.
23. AFVJR, Programs, P-02-10(v).
24. "El ciclo de conferencias sobre la música española contemporánea," *ABC* (Madrid), 16 December 1942, 17.

25. Letter from Leopoldo Querol to Joaquín Rodrigo, dated Benicasim, 30 August 1941. AFVJR.
26. Letter from Federico Sopeña to Lola Rodríguez Aragón, dated 22 April 1942. Santander, Fundación Marcelino Botín, call number 17855.
27. *Boletín Oficial del Estado*, 30 June 1942, no. 181, 4678.
28. *Boletín Oficial del Estado*, 15 July 1942, no. 196, 5170.
29. Marino Gómez-Santos, "Joaquín Rodrigo cuenta su vida," *Pueblo* (Madrid), 4 July 1959, 3.
30. Joaquín Rodrigo, "Concierto de la Orquesta Nacional," *Pueblo* (Madrid), 5 August 1943.
31. Ángel Sagardía, "Con motivo del estreno de un concierto," *Imperio* (Zamora), 27 May 1943, 3.
32. *Boletín Oficial del Estado*, 4 March 1943, no. 63, 2067.
33. Marta Rodríguez Cuervo, "El Concierto heroico de Joaquín Rodrigo: Un estudio analítico," in Javier Suárez-Pajares, ed., *Joaquín Rodrigo y la música española de los años cuarenta* (Valladolid: Universidad de Valladolid, 2005), 107.
34. Joaquín Rodrigo, "El Concierto heroico," *Pueblo* (Madrid), 8 May 1944, 6. Cited and translated in Eva Moreda-Rodríguez, "Musical Commemorations in Post-Civil War Spain: Joaquín Rodrigo's *Concierto Heroico*," in Pauline Fairclough, ed., *Twentieth-century Music and Politics: Essays in Memory of Neil Edmunds* (Abingdon: Routledge, 2016), 184.
35. Antonio Iglesias, Óscar Esplá, *Joaquín Rodrigo, Rodolfo Halffter, Manuel de Falla, Isaac Albéniz-Cristóbal Halffter, Isaac Albéniz, Joaquín Turina (Sus obras para piano y orquesta)* (Madrid: Alpuerto, 1994), 419.
36. Translation from the bilingual study by Paula Coronas, *El universo pianístico en la obra de Joaquín Rodrigo/The Piano in the Works of Joaquín Rodrigo* (Málaga: Ediciones Maestro, 2006), 116.
37. Moreda-Rodríguez, "Musical Commemorations in Post-Civil War Spain," 185.
38. Víctor Ruiz Albéniz, "El Concierto heroic de Joaquin Rodrigo," *Hoja Oficial del Lunes* (Madrid), 10 May 1943. Ruiz Albéniz was related to the famous composer, the son of Albéniz's sister Clementia. This translation is taken from Eva Moreda-Rodríguez, "Musical Commemorations in Post-Civil War Spain," 185.
39. Ibid., 186.
40. Ibid., 185.
41. Ibid., 189.
42. See Igor Contreras and Manuel Deniz Silva, "Obligados a convivir pared con pared. Los intercambios musicales entre España y Portugal durante los primeros años del franquismo (1939–1944)," in Pérez Zalduondo and Gan Quesadas, eds., *Music and Francoism*, 25–57.
43. Letter from Joaquín Rodrigo to Federico Sopeña, dated Madrid, 30 April 1944. Santander, Fundación Marcelino Botín, call number 17716.
44. Letter from Joaquín Rodrigo to Federico Sopeña, dated Madrid, 31 October 1943. Santander, Fundación Marcelino Botín, call number 17710.
45. This complete correspondence, comprising 193 letters, is found transcribed in Javier Suárez-Pajares, "El epistolario entre Joaquín Rodrigo y Federico Sopeña. Una historia entre líneas," in Suárez-Pajares, ed., *Joaquín Rodrigo y Federico Sopeña en la música española de los años cincuenta*, 258–468.
46. Letter from Joaquín Rodrigo to Federico Sopeña, dated Madrid, 14 February 1944. Santander, Fundación Marcelino Botín, call number 17701.
47. L. M., "Homenaje a Joaquín Rodrigo," *Destino* (Barcelona), 26 February 1944.
48. Letter from Joaquín Rodrigo to Federico Sopeña, dated Madrid, 13 March 1944. Santander, Fundación Marcelino Botín, call number 17702.
49. Eva León, "A Performer's Guide to Joaquín Rodrigo's *Concierto de Estío* (1943) in the Context of the Twentieth-Century Spanish Violin Concerto" (DMA diss., City University of New York, 2017), 22–23.
50. Ibid., 84.
51. Ibid., 86.

52. Ibid., 118.
53. Letter from Joaquín Rodrigo to Pilar Bayona, dated Madrid, 17 September 1943. Santander, Fundación Marcelino Botín, call number 15898.
54. "Diálogos en contrapunto. Joaquín Rodrigo, su *Concierto de estío* y el bombo del sorteo de los iguales," *Buenas Noches* (supplement of the Madrid daily *Pueblo*), 23 March 1944.
55. Fernando Lopes-Graça, "Círculo de Cultura Musical: A Orquesta Nacional de Madrid," *Seara Nova* (Lisbon), no. 871, 22 April 1944, 245.
56. Santiago Kastner, "A Orquestra Nacional Española e o Maestro Pérez Casas," *Jornal do Comercio* (Lisboa), 16 April 1944.
57. Salvador Campos Zaldiernas, "El incidente 'Concierto de estío'. Avatares de su estreno en Barcelona a través del epistolario Toldrá-Rodrigo (1944–1945)," *Revista de Musicología* 40/1 (2017), 177–94.
58. Xavier Montsalvatge, "Al final de la temporada," *Destino* (Barcelona), 9 June 1945, 12.
59. Kamhi, *Hand in Hand with Joaquín Rodrigo*, 125.
60. Letter from Federico Sopeña to Joaquín Rodrigo, undated (November 1943?). AFVJR.
61. AFVJR, Archivo de Programas, call number P-4-2.
62. Juan Alós Tormo (1914–82) in March 1949. Joaquín Rodrigo, "La semana musical," *Marca* (Madrid), 25 March 1949.
63. *Boletín Oficial del Estado*, 6 December 1944, no. 351, 9450.
64. Letter from Joaquín Rodrigo to Federico Sopeña, dated Madrid, 5 December 1944. Santander, Fundación Marcelino Botín, call number 17709. Sopeña had been head of the Department of Music of the Vice Secretariat of Popular Education until he left for the seminary in 1943.
65. "Joaquín Rodrigo, primer premio de música sinfónica y de cámara," *Pueblo* (Madrid), 3 January 1945.
66. Joaquín Rodrigo, "Ha fallecido en Barcelona el ilustre pianista español Ricardo Viñes," *Pueblo* (Madrid), 29 April 1943.
67. In the program notes of a concert at the Liceu in Barcelona commemorating the centenary of Albéniz's birth. This program is located in the Albéniz collection of the Museu de la Música in Barcelona, carpeta 1.
68. Douglas Riva, "The Piano Works of Joaquín Rodrigo," in *From Spain to the United States: Joaquín Rodrigo's Transatlantic Legacy. Observatorio Studies/Estudios del Observatorio* (Cambridge, MA: Instituto Cervantes at the Faculty of Arts and Sciences of Harvard University, 2019), 53.
69. Ibid., 53.
70. "À l'ombre de Torre Bermeja: Homenaje al pianista Ricardo Viñes," *Joaquín Rodrigo a través de sus escritos*, 89–90.
71. Iglesias, *Obra para piano*, 2nd ed., 199.
72. All quotes of this paragraph stem from Joaquín Rodrigo, "Autocrítica de la última obra de Joaquín Rodrigo *A l'ombre de Torre Bermeja*, que estrenará José Cubiles el próximo lunes," *Pueblo* (Madrid), 15 December 1945.
73. *Boletín Oficial del Estado*, 25 December 1944, no. 360, 9660.
74. *Boletín Oficial del Estado*, 3 February 1945, no. 34, 1007.
75. Letter from Joaquín Rodrigo to Federico Sopeña, dated Madrid, 20 February 1945. Santander, Fundación Marcelino Botín, call number 17712.
76. *Boletín Oficial del Estado*, 6 April 1945, no. 96, 2712.
77. José Antonio Gutiérrez, "The labor of Joaquín Rodrigo as critic in the daily *Pueblo* (1940–1946), in Javier Suárez-Pajares, ed., *Joaquín Rodrigo y la música española de los años cuarenta* (Valladolid: Universidad de Valladolid, 2005), 403–30.
78. Letter from Federico Sopeña to Joaquín Rodrigo, dated 2 May 1946. AFVJR.
79. Letter from Joaquín Rodrigo to Federico Sopeña, dated Madrid, 31 October 1943. Santander, Fundación Marcelino Botín, call number 17710.
80. Federico Moreno Torroba y Joaquín Rodrigo, "Autocríticas," *ABC* (Madrid), 22 May 1946, 21.

81. Letter from Joaquín Rodrigo to Rafael Rodríguez Albert, dated Madrid, 10 June 1946. The correspondence between Rodrigo and Rodríguez Albert, consisting of forty-five letters, was published by María Palacios Nieto, "Una amistad en tiempos difíciles: análisis de la correspondencia entre Joaquín Rodrigo y Rafael Rodríguez Albert en los años 40," in Javier Suárez-Pajares, ed., *Joaquín Rodrigo y la música española de los años cuarenta* (Valladolid: Universidad de Valladolid, 2005), 211–73.

82. Javier Suárez-Pajares, "Una cuestión de Estado: la repatriación de Manuel de Falla vivo o muerto," in *Creación musical, cultura popular y construcción nacional en la España contemporánea* (Madrid: ICCMU, 2010), 169–86.

83. Letter from Joaquín Rodrigo to Federico Mompou, dated Madrid, 23 January 1947. Biblioteca de Catalunya, Fons Frederic Mompou, call number M 5022-4.

84. Letter from Joaquín Rodrigo to Pablo Bilbao, dated Madrid, 26 November 1946. Santander, Fundación Marcelino Botín, call number 15901.

85. M. L., "Primer concierto de la Asociación de Cultura Musical," *Destino* (Barcelona), 26 October 1946, 11.

86. *Boletín Oficial del Estado*, 11 January 1946, no. 11, 346.

87. *Boletín Oficial del Estado*, 19 April 1945, no. 109, 3125–26. On the history of this orchestra, see Álvaro García Estefanía, "Pioneros musicales de Radio Nacional de España: Ataúlfo Argenta y la Orquesta de Cámara de Radio Nacional," *Cuadernos de Música Iberoamericana*, no. 7 (1999), 215–33.

88. "La inauguración. Detalle del programa radiado," *ABC* (Madrid), 21 June 1945, 16.

89. On Argenta, see Juan González-Castelao, *Ataúlfo Argenta. Claves de un mito de la dirección de orquesta* (Madrid: ICCMU, 2008), and Ana Arámbarri, *Ataúlfo Argenta, música interrumpida* (Barcelona: Galaxia Gutenberg, 2017).

90. Ana Higueras, *Lola Rodríguez Aragón. Crónica de una vida, 1910-1984* (Madrid: Higueras Arte, 2004).

91. *Boletín Oficial del Estado*, 13 July 1947, no. 194, 3935–36.

92. Miguel de Cervantes, *El ingenioso hidalgo don Quijote de la Mancha* (Madrid, 1605), primera parte, capítulo 26.

93. Kamhi, *Hand in Hand with Joaquín Rodrigo*, 140.

94. Letter from Joaquín Rodrigo to Federico Sopeña, undated. We deduce, though, that it was written in Madrid in January 1948. Santander, Fundación Marcelino Botín, call number 17696. See Javier Suárez-Pajares, "El epistolario entre Joaquín Rodrigo y Federico Sopeña. Una historia entre líneas," in Suárez-Pajares, ed., *Joaquín Rodrigo y Federico Sopeña en la música española de los años cincuenta*, 396.

95. This translation is taken from chapter 6, "The Absent Dulcinea: Joaquín Rodrigo's Song to Music Itself," in Nelson Orringer, *Uniting Music and Poetry in Twentieth-Century Spain* (Lanham, MD: Lexington Books, 2021), 127–28. This is a revision of an earlier article with that same title that appeared in *Hispanic Journal of Research* 21/2 (April 2020): 115–26. Unless otherwise indicated, all subsequent citations refer to the chapter, not the article.

96. See Héctor Fernández Bahillo, "Circunstancia y cervantismo en las *Ausencias de Dulcinea* de Joaquín Rodrigo," in Suárez Pajares, ed., *Joaquín Rodrigo y Federico Sopeña en la música española de los años cincuenta*, 95–112.

97. Ibid., 105.

98. Orringer, *Uniting Music and Poetry in Twentieth-Century Spain*, 115.

99. Ibid., 129. The famous four-note motive also makes a fleeting appearance in Falla's ballet *El sombrero de tres picos*.

100. Fernández Bahillo, "Circunstancia y cervantismo en las *Ausencias de Dulcinea*," 101.

101. Ibid., 105.

102. Orringer, *Uniting Music and Poetry in Twentieth-Century Spain*, 129.

103. In an email message of 12 August 2021, Prof. Orringer confirmed that the cuckoo's appearnace at this point might well have been a musical symbol of insanity, though in Spanish the word is not synonymous with craziness as it is in English: "The placement of the 'cucú,' in my opinion, signals off-balance, crazy. Vicky

[Victoria Kamhi] was fluent in English, [and] I think we can safely assume that in this particular case, *cucú* means nuts."

104. Nelson Orringer, "The Absent Dulcinea: Joaquín Rodrigo's Song to Music Itself," *Hispanic Journal of Research*, 21/2 (April 2020), 115.

105. Letter from Federico Sopeña to Joaquín Rodrigo, dated 24 May 1946. AFVJR.

106. Joaquín Rodrigo, "Gaspar Cassadó en la Asociación de Cultura Musical," *Pueblo* (Madrid), 10 May 1946.

107. Joaquín Rodrigo, "Componer música," *Buenos Aires Musical*, 15 August 1954, 4.

108. Kamhi, *Hand in Hand with Joaquín Rodrigo*, 143.

109. Letter from Gaspar Cassadó to Joaquín Rodrigo, dated Siena 11 August 1949. AFVJR.

110. Ana Llorens, "El dieciochismo de Rodrigo: Su *Concierto in modo galante*," in *Scherzo*, 34/356 (November 2019), 84.

111. After the 1949 premiere, Rodrigo revised the work, whose final version dates from 1952.

112. Raanan Rein, *La salvación de una dictadura. Alianza Franco-Perón, 1946–1955* (Madrid: Consejo Superior de Investigaciones Científicas, 1995).

113. Miguel Moya Huertas, "Un recital de Joaquín Rodrigo," *ABC* (Madrid), 11 May 1947, 27.

114. Letter from Federico Sopeña to Joaquín Rodrigo, dated 11 May 1949. AFVJR.

115. Andrés Guilmáin: "Lo que cuenta Joaquín Rodrigo," Madrid, 5 January 1950. Newspaper clipping in AFVJR.

116. There were four stowaways on the ship to Buenos Aires, fleeing hardships in Spain. "Llegó el 'Monte Udala': Trajo un músico ciego y cuatro polizones," *La Espera* (Buenos Aires), 12 November 1949.

117. Joaquín Rodrigo, Gerardo Diego, and Federico Sopeña, *Diez años de música en España* (Madrid: Espasa-Calpe, 1949), 178–90.

118. Neri de Caso, *De ideales y melancolías: Regino Sainz de la Maza y la guitarra en el siglo XX en España*, 261.

119. Letter from Andrés Segovia to Joaquín Rodrigo, dated Amsterdam, 16 October 1948. AFVJR.

120. Julio Gimeno, "Un viaje sin destino: Andrés Segovia hacia el *Concierto de Aranjuez*," in Javier Suárez-Pajares, ed., *Jornadas de Estudio Joaquín Rodrigo* (Córdoba: IMAE Gran Teatro, 2010), 119–86.

121. The concert program is to be found in the AFVJR, sig. P-05-22.

122. Joaquín Rodrigo, "La semana musical," *Marca* (Madrid), 22 December 1947, 15.

123. Javier Suárez-Pajares, "Apuntes para una historia crítica de la discografía guitarrística de Joaquín Rodrigo," in Suárez-Pajares, ed., *Jornadas de Estudio Joaquín Rodrigo*, 183.

124. "¿Qué desea usted para la música y los músicos españoles en el año 1946?" *Ritmo* (Madrid), December 1945, no. 192, 23.

125. Federico Sopeña, "Hoy, en Buenos Aires, el *Concierto de Aranjuez*," *Arriba* (Madrid), 28 July 1947, 3.

126. Lugano, Fonoteca nazionale svizzera (Swiss National Sound Archives), call number DAT1503. Studio recording of four disks of shellac over aluminum, duration 25'28".

127. Gonzalo Anes and Antonio Gómez Mendoza, *Cultura sin libertad. La Sociedaden Estudios y Publicaciones (1947-1980)* (Valencia: Pre-Textos, 2009), 71–72.

Chapter 7: Between Creation and Depression

1. Manuel de Falla, "Prólogo," in Joaquín Turina, *Enciclopedia abreviada de música* (Madrid: Renacimiento, 1917), i, 9.

2. Joaquín Rodrigo, *Técnica enseñada e inspiración no aprendida* (Madrid: Academia de Bellas Artes, 1951), 19.

3. Falla, "Prólogo," in Turina, *Enciclopedia abreviada de música*, i, 9.

4. All the quotations in this paragraph come from Rodrigo, *Técnica enseñada e inspiración no aprendida*, 19–20.

5. Letter from Joaquín Rodrigo to Federico Mompou, undated. Biblioteca de Catalunya, Fons Frederic Mompou, call number M 5022/4.
6. Letter from Federico Sopeña to Joaquín Rodrigo, dated 11 August 1943. AFVJR.
7. Letter from Joaquín Rodrigo to Federico Sopeña, dated 20 February 1945. Santander, Fundación Marcelino Botín, call number 17712.
8. Letter from Joaquín Rodrigo to Pablo Bilbao Arístegui, dated Madrid, 19 March 1947. Santander, Fundación Marcelino Botín, call number 15902.
9. Kamhi, *Hand in Hand with Joaquín Rodrigo*, 150.
10. "Text of the State Department's Views on Relations with Spain," *The New York Times*, 20 January 1950, 2.
11. Foreign Relations of the United States, 1948, vol. III. Memorandum of Conversation by the Secretary of State, París, 4 October 1948, 1053–54. Quoted in Arturo Jarque Íñiguez, "The United States Facing the Spanish Case in the UN, 1945–1950," *REDEN. Revista Española de Estudios Norteamericanos*, no. 7 (1994), 169.
12. Mark S. Byrnes, "*Overruled and Worn Down*: Truman sends an Ambassador to Spain," *Presidential Studies Quarterly* 29/2 (June 1999), 263–79.
13. "Urges Spain to Aid Music," *The Bristol News Bulletin* (Tennessee), 14 October 1948, 12 (the first time we find this news item, which was repeated countless times thereafter in the U.S. press during the final three months of 1948).
14. "Music Notes," *Chicago Tribune*, 17 October 1948, 120.
15. "Composers in Spotlight at Louisville," *Dayton Daily News* (Ohio), 17 October 1948, 57.
16. "Louisville Philharmonic Orchestra to Give Third of Concert Series Feb. 26," *Messenger-Inquirer* (Kentucky), 13 February 1949, 9.
17. Norman Shavin, "Louisville Commissions Policy," *Music Journal*, September 1953, 21.
18. Javier Suárez-Pajares, "The Reception of Joaquín Rodrigo's Works in the United States," in *From Spain to the United States: Joaquín Rodrigo's Transatlantic Legacy* (Cambridge, MA: Observatorio Studies, Instituto Cervantes, Faculty of Arts and Sciences, Harvard University, 2019), 40–41.
19. "*Pop* concert will honor Sun Court," *The El Paso Times* (Texas), 9 December 1948, 1.
20. Letter from Joaquín Rodrigo to Andrés Segovia, dated Madrid, 17 February 1950. Archivo de la Fundación Casa-Museo Andrés Segovia, Linares (Jaén).
21. Jesús Ferrer Cayón, "Del Hollywood Bowl a los Festivales de España: José Iturbi o *Bienvenido, Mister Marshall*," in Enrique Bengochea Tirado *et al.*: *Relaciones en conflicto. Nuevas perspectivas sobre relaciones internacionales desde la historia* (Valencia: Universitàt de València-Asociación de Historia Contemporánea, 2015), 97–98.
22. "Los Coros y Danzas, de nuevo en América," *La Vanguardia* (Barcelona), 10 August 1950, 3.
23. Letter from Federico Sopeña to Joaquín Rodrigo, undated [August 1950]. AFVJR.
24. Letter from Federico Sopeña to Joaquín Rodrigo from Rome, undated [around September 1, 1950]. AFVJR.
25. Ibid.
26. Federico García Sanchiz: "El Centenario de los Reyes Católicos. Misión en América y peregrinación en España," *Madrid*, 16 October 1950.
27. Letter from Gaspar Cassadó to Joaquín Rodrigo, dated Duisburgo, 26 November 1950. AFVJR.
28. Letter from Gaspar Cassadó to Joaquín Rodrigo, dated Montecatini-Terme, 30 September 1950. AFVJR.
29. Letter from Gaspar Cassadó to Joaquín Rodrigo, dated Siena, 31 July 1950. AFVJR.
30. Kamhi, *Hand in Hand with Joaquín Rodrigo*, 144.
31. Letter from Gaspar Cassadó to Joaquín Rodrigo, dated Uddevalla, 30 May 1950. AFVJR.
32. Letter from Walter Starkie to Joaquín Rodrigo, dated 14 December 1950. AFVJR.
33. *Arriba* (Madrid), 1 April 1951, 16–17.
34. Letter from Jesús Rubio to Joaquín Rodrigo, dated Madrid, 12 May 1951. AFVJR.

35. Letter from Joaquín Ruiz-Giménez a Joaquín Rodrigo, dated in Cattolica, 29 August 1951. AFVJR.
36. *Boletín Oficial del Estado*, 16 Feburary 1952, no. 47, 732.
37. *Boletín Oficial del Estado*, 22 April 1952, no. 113, 1838.
38. Letter from Joaquín Rodrigo to Eduardo López-Chavarri, dated 30 December 1950. See Díaz Gómez and Galbis López, *Eduardo López-Chavarri Marco*, ii, no. 703.
39. Private archive of the family of Luis Morondo, cit. in Marcos Andrés Vierge: *Fernando Remacha. El compositor y su obra* (Madrid: ICCMU, 1998), 151.
40. "Chair of Music in Philosophy and Letters," *ABC* (Madrid), 11 May 1952, 50.
41. Letter from Miguel Querol to Joaquín Rodrigo, dated 27 February 1951. Barcelona, Departamento de Musicología, Consejo Superior de Investigaciones Científicas.
42. Letter from Joaquín Rodrigo to Miguel Querol dated 30 December 1951. Barcelona, Departamento de Musicología, Consejo Superior de Investigaciones Científicas.
43. Joaquín Rodrigo, "Dos canciones sefardíes armonizadas," *Sefarad* 14/2 (1954), 353–54. Translated by Calcraft and Matthews, *Joaquín Rodrigo: Writings on Music*, 143.
44. The most detailed study of the music itself is available in a dissertation by Terrance Pitt-Brooke, "Tonality and Expression in Two Choral-Orchestral Works by Joaquín Rodrigo" (DMA diss., University of Arizona, 2019). The ensuing discussion owes much to his insights.
45. Iglesias, ed., *Escritos de Joaquín Rodrigo*, 54.
46. Emilio Salcedo, "Con Joaquín Rodrigo en la Universidad," *La Gaceta Regional*, 30 May 1954.
47. For a detailed study of this work, consult Orringer's chapter "Creative Landscapes of Salamanca in Unamuno and Joaquín Rodrigo," in *Uniting Music and Poetry in Twentieth-Century Spain* (Lanham, MD: Lexington Books, 2021), 139–64.
48. Orringer, "Creative Landscapes," 148.
49. Ibid., 139.
50. "Introducción a la obra por el autor," in Joaquín Rodrigo, *Música para un códice salmantino* (Madrid: Ediciones Joaquín Rodrigo, 1996).
51. Pitt-Brooke, "Tonality and Expression in Two Choral-Orchestral Works by Joaquín Rodrigo," 30.
52. Ibid., 33.
53. "Introducción a la obra por el autor."
54. *Joaquín Rodrigo a través de sus escritos*, 121.
55. Letter from Nicanor Zabaleta to Joaquín Rodrigo, dated San Sebastián, 30 September 1953. AFVJR.
56. Joaquín Rodrigo, "Concierto serenata," typescript. AFVJR, call number E-02/21(v).
57. Letter from Nicanor Zabaleta to Joaquín Rodrigo, dated San Sebastián, 15 October 1956. AFVJR.
58. Letter from Nicanor Zabaleta to Joaquín Rodrigo, dated San Sebastián, 17 October 1959. AFVJR.
59. "El I Festival de Música y Danza, arranque de una empresa española de universal resonancia," *Hoja Oficial del Lunes* (Madrid), 16 June 1952, 6.
60. Miguel Moral Guerrero, "In Granada. Festival of Music and Dance," *Ritmo* (Madrid), July–August 1952, 9.
61. Lettre from Joaquín Rodrigo to Andrés Segovia, dated Madrid, 24 March 1949. Archive of Fundación Casa-Museo Andrés Segovia, Linares (Jaén).
62. Letter from Andrés Segovia to Joaquín Rodrigo, dated Dallas (Texas), 9 April 1950. AFVJR.
63. Letter from Andrés Segovia to Joaquín Rodrigo, dated Oviedo, 30 December 1952. AFVJR.
64. Letter from Joaquín Rodrigo to Andrés Segovia, dated Madrid, 7 January 1953. Archive of Fundación Casa-Museo Andrés Segovia, Linares (Jaén).
65. Letter from Andrés Segovia to Joaquín Rodrigo, dated Denver (Colorado), 15 January 1954. AFVJR.

66. Letter from Andrés Segovia to Joaquín Rodrigo, dated New York, 14 May 1954. AFVJR.
67. Letter from Andrés Segovia to Joaquín Rodrigo, dated New York, 20 May 1954. AFVJR.
68. Letter from Andrés Segovia a Joaquín Rodrigo, dated Geneva, 6 August 1954. AFVJR.
69. Letter from Andrés Segovia to Joaquín Rodrigo, dated Buenos Aires, 10 July 1957. AFVJR.
70. Jacinto Miquelarena, "Andrés Segovia triumphs again in London," *ABC* (Seville), 30 October 1957, 35.
71. Claudia Cassidy, "On the aisle: Andrés Segovia, his guitar, and his climate take over Orchestra Hall," *Chicago Daily Tribune*, 13 January 1958, B11.
72. Letter from Andrés Segovia to Joaquín Rodrigo, dated Geneva, 24 September 1954. AFVJR.
73. Letter from Joaquín Rodrigo to Andrés Segovia, dated Madrid, 14 October 1954. Archive of Fundación Casa-Museo Andrés Segovia, Linares (Jaén).
74. *Instrucción de música sobre la guitarra española*, reproduction in fascimile. Prologue and notes of Luis García-Abrines (Zaragoza: Institución "Fernando el Católico," 1952).
75. Marino Gómez-Santos, "Joaquín Rodrigo narrates his life (3)," *Pueblo* (Madrid), 2 July 1959, 13.
76. Ángel Mingote, *Cancionero popular de la provincia de Zaragoza* (Zaragoza: Institución "Fernando el Católico," 1950), 370–96.
77. Letter from Joaquín Rodrigo to Andrés Segovia, dated Madrid, 14 October 1954. Archive of Fundación Casa-Museo Andrés Segovia, Linares (Jaén).
78. Letter from Andrés Segovia to Joaquín Rodrigo, dated Chicago, 7 November 1954. AFVJR.
79. Letter from Joaquín Rodrigo to Andrés Segovia, dated Madrid, 14 October 1954. Archive of Fundación Casa-Museo Andrés Segovia, Linares (Jaén).
80. Letter from Joaquín Rodrigo to Andrés Segovia, dated Madrid, 11 November 1954. Archive of Fundación Casa-Museo Andrés Segovia, Linares (Jaén).
81. Marino Gómez-Santos, "Joaquín Rodrigo relates his life (3)," *Pueblo* (Madrid), 2 July 1959, 13.
82. "Segovia and Jordá Combine Talents in Symphony Concert," *Oakland Tribune*, 22 November 1954, 10; Clifford Gessler, "Segovia Scores in Symphony Concert," *Oakland Tribune*, 27 November 1954, 4.
83. Letter from Andrés Segovia to Joaquín Rodrigo, dated San Francisco, 24 November 1954. AFVJR.
84. Larry Rothe, *Music for a City, Music for the World. 100 Years with the San Francisco Symphony* (San Francisco: Chronicle Books, 2011), 117.
85. Letter from Enrique Jordá to Joaquín Rodrigo, dated France, 8 September 1955. AFVJR.
86. Howard Taubman, "Composers from Americas exchange views while meeting at Caracas," *The New York Times*, 31 March 1957, 129.
87. Kamhi, *Hand in Hand with Joaquín Rodrigo*, 168–69.
88. Letter from Enrique Jordá to Joaquín Rodrigo, dated Sydney, 14 June 1957. AFVJR.
89. Letter from Joaquín Rodrigo to Andrés Segovia, dated 26 October 1958. Archive of Fundación Casa-Museo Andrés Segovia, Linares (Jaén).
90. Antonio Fernández-Cid, "Segovia, Jordá y la Nacional, iniciaron el ciclo del Palacio de la Música," *ABC* (Madrid), 25 October 1958, 59.
91. Javier Suárez-Pajares, "Joaquín Rodrigo y Julian Bream," in Julio Gimeno, ed., *Nombres propios de la guitarra. Julian Bream* (Córdoba: Ediciones La Posada, 2009), 111–41.
92. Letter from Julian Bream to Victoria Kamhi, dated London, 5 January 1958. AFVJR.
93. Letter from Julian Bream to Joaquín Rodrigo, dated London, 31 May 1959. AFVJR.
94. Statements of Bream transcribed in Tony Palmer, *Julian Bream. A Life on the Road* (London: Macdonald & Co, 1982), 53.

95. Letter from Ida Presti to Alexandre Lagoya, dated in Sena and Oise, 28 April 1959. AFVJR.
96. Letter from Joaquín Rodrigo to Ida Presti, dated Madrid, 6 May 1959. AFVJR.
97. Letter from Ida Presti to Joaquín Rodrigo, dated La Couronne, 25 July 1959. AFVJR.
98. Letter from Victoria Kamhi to Ida Presti, dated in Villajoyosa (Alicante), 18 August 1959. AFVJR.
99. Letter from Alexandre Lagoya to Joaquín Rodrigo, dated en Deuil-la-barre, 3 September 1959, but probably corresponding to October 3. AFVJR.
100. Letter from Ida Presti to Joaquín Rodrigo, dated 21 October 1959. AFVJR.
101. Telegram from Presti/Lagoya to Joaquín Rodrigo, dated 4 November 1959. AFVJR.
102. Letter from Ida Presti a Joaquín Rodrigo, dated 11 November 1959. AFVJR.
103. Letter from Victoria Kamhi to Andrés Segovia, dated 23 November 1958. Archive of Fundación Casa-Museo Andrés Segovia, Linares (Jaén).
104. Letter from Victoria Kamhi to Andrés Segovia, dated 28 December 1958. Archive of Fundación Casa-Museo Andrés Segovia, Linares (Jaén).
105. Letter from Joaquín Rodrigo to Andrés Segovia, dated Madrid, 17 March 1949. Fundación Casa-Museo Andrés Segovia, Linares (Jaén).
106. Stuart W. Button, *Julian Bream. The Foundations of a Musical Career* (Hants, U.K.: Scholar Press, 1997), 116.
107. Terry Usher, "The Guitar," *B.M.G.* 48/554 (June 1951), 192.
108. Letter from Adolfo Salazar, Jesús Bal y Gay and Rodolfo Halffter to Carlos Chávez, dated Mexico, 27 November 1951. See Consuelo Carredano, ed., *Adolfo Salazar: Epistolario, 1912–1958* (Madrid: Residencia de Estudiantes, 2008), 801–2.
109. Hans Sachs [Gerónimo Baqueiro Foster], "Fondos musicales," *El Universal* (Mexico), 28 August 1952, 4.
110. Letter from Andrés Segovia a Joaquín Rodrigo, dated San Antonio (Texas), 24 February 1949. AFVJR.
111. "Spanish Dancing," *The Times*, 3 September 1953, 9.
112. "Pilar Lopez's Spanish Ballet," *The Times*, 1 October 1953, 9.
113. Antoni Pizà, "The Fusions and Confusions of the *Concierto de Aranjuez* in Jazz: A listener's Musings," in *From Spain to the United States: Joaquín Rodrigo's Transatlantic Legacy* (Cambridge, MA: Observatorio Studies, Instituto Cervantes, Faculty of Arts and Sciences, Harvard University, 2019), 63–76.

Chapter 8: Theatrical Adventures and Misadventures

1. "Concursos de acuarelas y villancicos," *ABC* (Madrid), 2 December 1952, 28.
2. "Informaciones musicales, de teatro y cinematográficas," *ABC* (Madrid), 28 December 1952, 53.
3. Letter from Gerardo Diego to Joaquín Rodrigo, dated 3 March 1953. Copy preserved in the Archive of the Madrid Atheneum, call number 42/2, RE-195.
4. Letter from Gerardo Diego to Joaquín Rodrigo, dated 24 April 1953. Copy preserved in the Archive of the Madrid Atheneum, call number 42/2, RE-195.
5. Gallego, *El arte de Joaquín Rodrigo*, 248.
6. José Forns, *Historia de la música* (Madrid: Talleres Gráficos Marisal, 1951), vol. 3, 297.
7. Joaquín López González, "La magia de la sala oscura: Joaquín Rodrigo y el cine," in Javier Suárez-Pajares, ed., *Joaquín Rodrigo y Federico Sopeña en la música española de los años cincuenta* (Valladolid, Universidad de Valladolid, 2008), 143–69.
8. Marino Gómez-Santos, "Joaquín Rodrigo cuenta su vida (3)," *Pueblo* (Madrid), 2 July 1959, 5.
9. Fernando Castán Palomar, "Deducciones que hace el maestro Joaquín Rodrigo cuando ha terminado la partitura para *La guerra de Dios* [interview]," undated newspaper clipping (April 1953?). AFVJR, Newspaper Archive, folder 2-II, no. 356.
10. Ibid.
11. Kamhi, *Hand in Hand with Joaquín Rodrigo*, 154.
12. Gallego, *El arte de Joaquín Rodrigo*, 248.

13. Letter from Albert Blancafort to Manuel Blancafort, dated 3 July 1957, Biblioteca de Catalunya, Fons Manuel Blancafort, sig. M 4896/3.

14. J. Ma. C., "Joaquín Rodrigo escribirá la música de *Platero y yo*," newspaper clipping dated February 1959. AFVJR, Newspaper Archive, folder 3-I, no. 103.

15. María Paz Cornejo, "Joaquín Rodrigo y el teatro de los años cincuenta," in Suárez-Pajares, ed., *Joaquín Rodrigo y Federico Sopeña en la música española de los años cincuenta*, 127–41.

16. Luis Calvo, "En el teatro María Guerrero se representó anoche, con carácter de estreno, *El desdén con el desdén*," *ABC* (Madrid), 17 November 1951, 25.

17. [Minutes of the contest decision], dated Madrid, 25 February 1961. Salamanca, Library of the Pontifical University, Archive of the Spanish Catholic Action (ACE).

18. Letter from José María Pemán to Santiago Corral dated Cádiz, 17 March 1961. Salamanca, Library of the Pontifical University, Archive of the Spanish Catholic Action (ACE).

19. Kamhi, *Hand in Hand with Joaquín Rodrigo*, 157.

20. Joaquín Nin, ed., *Classiques espagnols du piano. Seize sonates anciennes d'auteurs espagnols* (Paris: Max Eschig, 1925).

21. Dolores Segarra Muñoz, "La danza española en los años 50 a través de la obra de Joaquín Rodrigo," in Suárez-Pajares, ed., *Joaquín Rodrigo y Federico Sopeña en la música española de los años cincuenta*, 171–91.

22. Antonio Fernández-Cid, "Tríptico filarmónico de un domingo en el Festival de Música y Danzas de Granada," *ABC* (Madrid), 23 June 1953, 48.

23. F. de C. Arduengo, "El pianista del bailarín Antonio 'calca' una obra de Joaquín Rodrigo," *Pueblo*, undated newspaper clipping. AFVJR, Newspaper Archive, folder 2-II, no. 409.

24. Xavier Montsalvatge, "Dos estrenos en el Liceo," *Destino* (Barcelona), 24 December 1955, 39.

25. Kamhi, *Hand in Hand with Joaquín Rodrigo*, 159.

26. Letter from Joaquín Rodrigo to Antonio Iglesias, dated Vienna, 14 July(?) 1956, reproduced in Iglesias, ed., *Escritos de Joaquín Rodrigo*, 247.

27. Javier Suárez-Pajares and Yolanda F. Acker, "Los compositores españoles y el ballet en el siglo XX," in the catalogue of the exhibit *Ritmo para el espacio* (Madrid: Centro de Documentación de Música y Danza, 1998), 31–33.

28. *Boletín Oficial del Estado*, 9 May 1954, no. 129, 3106.

29. *Boletín Oficial del Estado*, 1 January 1955, no. 12, 251.

30. Acorde [Víctor Ruiz Albéniz], "Joaquín Rodrigo [Interview]," *Informaciones* (Madrid), 24 April 1948, 3.

31. R. Díaz-Alejo, "Joaquín Rodrigo, el músico de los secretos maravillosos," *Estampa* (Buenos Aires), 24 November 1949.

32. Ramón Sobrino, "Hacia un neocasticismo lírico en la obra de Joaquín Rodrigo: *El hijo fingido*," in *El hijo fingido*, program of the theater production of the Teatro de la Zarzuela (Madrid: Teatro de la Zarzuela, 2001), 23–41.

33. "Ante el estreno de la comedia musical *El hijo fingido* de Joaquín Rodrigo," Madrid, 2 December 1964, 15.

34. Kamhi, *Hand in Hand with Joaquín Rodrigo*, 215–16.

35. Antonio Ramírez-Ángel, "Ante una nueva obra de Joaquín Rodrigo," *Teresa* (Madrid), no. 132, December 1964, 37. Also see Joaquín Rodrigo, "Autocrítica de *El hijo fingido*," *ABC* (Madrid), 5 December 1964, 109.

36. Enrique Franco, "Estreno en el Teatro de La Zarzuela de *El hijo fingido* de Arozamena, Kamhi y Rodrigo," *Arriba* (Madrid), 6 December 1964, 34.

37. Fernando Ruiz Coca, "Estreno de *El hijo fingido* de Rodrigo Arozamena y Kamhi en el Teatro de La Zarzuela," *El Alcázar* (Madrid), 8 December 1964, 28.

38. Federico Sopeña, "*El hijo fingido* en La Zarzuela," *ABC* (Madrid), 12 December 1964, 121; José María Franco, "Estreno de *El hijo fingido* en el Teatro de La Zarzuela," *Ya* (Madrid), 6 December 1964, 33.

39. Ibid., 284–86.

Chapter 9: The Final Years

1. Kamhi, *Hand in Hand with Joaquín Rodrigo*, 208.
2. Ibid., 211.
3. Ibid., 212.
4. Mary Vincent and R. A. Stradling, *Cultural Atlas of Spain and Portugal* (New York: Facts on File, 1995), 163.
5. "Between 1964 and 1974 Spain experienced about 5,000 strikes; 1975, the last year of Franco's rule, saw a further 3,156 stoppages. Furthermore, 45 percent of strikes staged after 1967 were political in nature, as against a mere 4 percent of those called from 1963–67." Ibid., 166.
6. Jorge Luis Marzo, *Art modern i franquisme. Els origens conservadors de l'avant-guarda i de la política artística a l'estat Espanyol* (Girona: Fundació Espais d'Art Contemporani, 2007), 12.
7. Santos Juliá, "History, Politics, Culture, 1975–1996," in *The Cambridge Companion to Modern Spanish Culture*, ed. David T. Gies (Cambridge: Cambridge University Press, 1999), 106.
8. Kamhi, *Hand in Hand with Joaquín Rodrigo*, 249.
9. Jorge Luis Marzo, "The Spectacle of Spain's Amnesia: Spanish Cultural Policy from the Dictatorship to Expo'92," trans. Ian Kennedy, *Alphabet City*, 4–5 (1995), 93.
10. Ángel Medina, "Primeras oleadas vanguardistas en el área de Madrid," in *España en la música de Occidente: Actas del Congreso Internacional celebrado en Salamanca 29 de octubre – 5 de noviembre de 1985*, 2 vols., ed. Emilio Casares, Ismael Fernández de la Cuesta, and José López-Calo (Madrid: Ministerio de Cultura, 1987), ii, 386–87.
11. Joaquín Rodrigo, "Por una música de vanguardia," *Ya* (Madrid), 13 January 1971.
12. Kamhi, *Hand in Hand with Joaquín Rodrigo*, 251.
13. Ibid., 206.
14. See Gallego, *El Arte de Joaquín Rodrigo*, 311–13. See also Suzanne Rhodes Draayer, *A Singer's Guide to the Songs of Joaquín Rodrigo* (Lanham: Scarecrow Press, 1999), 157–62.
15. Gallego, *El Arte de Joaquín Rodrigo*, 311.
16. Ibid.
17. For a detailed study of these songs, see Moreno Guil, "La canción con piano de Joaquín Rodrigo. Un estudio poético musical y psicoeducativo," 337–48.
18. A valuable source of information about this work is Suzanne R. Draayer, "Joaquín Rodrigo and His *Doce canciones españolas* and *Cantos de amor y de guerra*," *NATS Journal* 51/4 (March–April 1995): 14–17.
19. *Joaquín Rodrigo a través de sus escritos*, 99.
20. Quoted in Gallego, *El arte de Joaquín Rodrigo*, 314.
21. However, Shemaryahu Talmon rejects this association with the Essene and further has argued that to designate Qumran as a "community" is somewhat misleading, insofar as the 200–250 male members resident there were "but the spearhead of a much wider movement, the Community of the renewed Covenant, which could boast a much larger membership." See his seminal article "Qumran Studies: Past, Present, and Future," *The Jewish Quarterly Review* 85/1–2 (July–October 1994): 6.
22. Kamhi, *Hand in Hand with Joaquín Rodrigo*, 220.
23. Ibid., 219.
24. Much of the following discussion of the literary aspects of the *Himnos* is indebted to Orringer and appears in an essay he has co-authored with Walter Aaron Clark, entitled "Conviviendo con los ángeles en los *Himnos de los neófitos de Qumrán* de Joaquín Rodrigo," slated for publication in a future volume edited by Germán Gan, *Música y danza en los procesos socioculturales, identitarios y políticos del Segundo franquismo y la transición (1959–1978)*.
25. John Marco Allegro, *The Dead Sea Scrolls*, 6th ed. (London: Pelican, 1961), 110–11.
26. *Joaquín Rodrigo a través de sus escritos*, 135.

27. Rodrigo alludes to the "nueva liturgia" on page 135 of *Joaquín Rodrigo a través de sus escritos* to mean that he subordinates music to the text of the *Himnos*. Hence his humble admission that the music cannot capture the fullness of the psalm-like text.
28. The utterance of "amen" for the end of a prayer or musical rendition thereof is a Christian practice, not Jewish. Jewish invocations may include interjections of "amen" anywhere within the text, as well as at the end.
29. *Joaquín Rodrigo a través de sus escritos*, 136.
30. Ibid.
31. Gallego, *El Arte de Joaquín Rodrigo*, 346.
32. Kamhi, *Hand in Hand with Joaquín Rodrigo*, 221.
33. Ibid., 222.
34. Ibid., 228.
35. Santy Arriazu, "Joaquin Rodrigo prepara la obra magna de su gran carrera" [interview], *Diario de Burgos*, 6 October 1966, 3.
36. *Joaquín Rodrigo a través de sus escritos*, 147–48.
37. See Gallego, *El Arte de Joaquín Rodrigo*, 317–18.
38. See Lawrence Newcomb, "Joaquín Rodrigo's Works for Wind Instruments," *NACWPI* [National Association of College Wind and Percussion Instructors] *Journal*, 45/3 (Spring 1997): 15.
39. See Rodrigo's brief commentary on this work in *Joaquín Rodrigo a través de sus escritos*, 91.
40. Kamhi, *Hand in Hand with Joaquín Rodrigo*, 225–26.
41. Ibid., 229.
42. See Walter Aaron Clark, *Los Romeros: Royal Family of the Spanish Guitar* (Urbana: University of Illinois Press, 2018).
43. This letter is in the Romero Archive, now located in Special Collections at the University of California, Riverside.
44. In an interview by Laurel Ornish ("Guitar's First Family Visits: Romeros, Symphony Made History Together," *San Antonio Express-News*, 9 May 1995), Celedonio proudly declares that they have played it hundreds of times around the world, in every city with a major symphony orchestra.
45. See Clark, *Los Romeros*, 220–21.
46. Kamhi, *Hand in Hand with Joaquín Rodrigo*, 231.
47. Ibid., 232–33.
48. John Duarte, review, *Records and Recording* (December 1975), 48–49.
49. Kamhi, *Hand in Hand with Joaquín Rodrigo*, 234.
50. Ibid., 235–56.
51. The Spanish original is in *Joaquín Rodrigo a través de sus escritos*, 101. This translation is taken from Carolina Plata Ballesteros, "Joaquín Rodrigo's *Con Antonio Machado*: A Performer's Guide to the Work, Focusing on the Analysis of Song-cyclic Features" (DMA diss., University of British Columbia, 2009), 3. This is the most detailed study ever undertaken of the work, though another excellent source of analytical insight is María Dolores Moreno Guil, "Joaquín Rodrigo en la III decena musical de Sevilla (1971): El estreno mundial de *Con Antonio Machado*," in *Música en Sevilla en el siglo XX*, ed. Miguel López Fernández, 345–66 (Granada: Libargo, 2018). For another translation of this passage, see Calcraft and Matthews, *Joaquín Rodrigo: Writings on Music*, 124.
52. An excellent biography of the great poet is by Ian Gibson, *Ligero de equipaje* (Madrid: Prisa Ediciones, 2006).
53. In *Joaquín Rodrigo a través de sus escritos*, 101.
54. This chart is a compilation of information found in Moreno Guil, "La canción con piano," 353–81, and Plata Ballesteros, "Joaquín Rodrigo's *Con Antonio Machado . . .*" 107.
55. *Joaquín Rodrigo a través de sus escritos*, 101.
56. Plata Ballesteros "Joaquín Rodrigo's *Con Antonio Machado . . .*" 103.
57. Ibid., 104.

58. Kamhi, *Hand in Hand with Joaquín Rodrigo*, 241.
59. Ibid., 239.
60. Ibid., 245.
61. Ibid., 252.
62. Ibid., 253.
63. Gallego, *El Arte de Joaquín Rodrigo*, 351–52.
64. *Joaquín Rodrigo a través de sus escritos*, 90.
65. Kamhi, *Hand in Hand with Joaquín Rodrigo*, 256–57.
66. Ibid., 257.
67. Gallego, *El Arte de Joaquín Rodrigo*, 358.
68. Kamhi, *Hand in Hand with Joaquín Rodrigo*, 263.
69. Ibid., 272.
70. See Vincent and Stradling, *Cultural Atlas of Spain and Portugal*, 167.
71. Kamhi, *Hand in Hand with Joaquín Rodrigo*, 283.
72. Gallego, *El Arte de Joaquín Rodrigo*, 367, points out that this romance appears in the collection *El Delfín de música* by the sixteenth-century vihuelist and composer Luys de Narváez, though Rodrigo may well have taken it from Felipe Pedrell's *Cancionero musical popular español* of 1922.
73. They were later arranged for viola and piano by Emilio Mateu and premiered on 9 December 1993 in Barcelona. See Gallego, *El Arte de Joaquín Rodrigo*, 374.
74. Ibid.
75. Kamhi, *Hand in Hand with Joaquín Rodrigo*, 289.
76. "Tonality and Expression in Two Choral-Orchestral Works by Joaquín Rodrigo" (DMA diss., University of Arizona, 2019).
77. Ibid., 43.
78. Ibid., 54.
79. Ibid., 55.
80. Pitt-Brooke, "Tonality and Expression in Two Choral-Orchestral Works by Joaquín Rodrigo," provides a complete list of associations on p. 52.
81. Ibid., 53.
82. Ibid., 50.
83. Kamhi, *Hand in Hand with Joaquín Rodrigo*, 275.
84. Ibid., 278.
85. Ibid., 279.
86. For additional insights concerning Pepe's relationship with Rodrigo and this work, see Walter Aaron Clark, "Rodrigo's *Concierto para una fiesta*—Its Genesis and Interpretation: An Interview with Pepe Romero," *Soundboard* 47/4 (December 2021): 15–20.
87. Lloyd Stewart, "A Magical Evening Planned for Jewel City Charity Ball," from a Texas newspaper at the time of the premiere (name and date of the paper not included in the clipping from the Romero Archive at UC Riverside), translated by the reviewer from the original German.
88. "Unique Festival of Spanish Guitar Music," *Ambassador International Cultural Foundation: News of the Performing Arts and Ambassador Auditorium Calendar of Events*, December 1983–February 1984), 1–2.
89. John Duarte, "Record Reviews," *Gramophone* (1984), 36.
90. "Rodrigo, Torroba and the Romeros: An Important Triangle," *Virtuoso* 3/3 (March–May 1992): 7.
91. *Joaquín Rodrigo a través de sus escritos*, 119.
92. Ibid., 120. He states that scales in the strings are reminiscent of *Scheherezade*.
93. Ibid.
94. Ibid. Rodrigo further reveals that the deployment of themes resembles Stravinsky's *Fiesta Carnaval*.
95. Carlos Laredo Verdejo, *Joaquín Rodrigo: Biografía* (Valencia: Institució Alfons el Magnánim, 2011).
96. Ibid., 381.
97. Ibid.

98. Ibid., 386.
99. Ibid., 389.
100. In a number called "Spain" on the 1973 *Light as a Feather* album with the group Return to Forever.
101. The first movement of the *Aranjuez* was later arranged by Jim Hall and recorded by Laurindo Almeida with the Modern Jazz Quartet, in addition to the second movement on that same recording.
102. With the group Queen. See https://www.youtube.com/watch?v=ehYOf5fTBOs.
103. See Walter Aaron Clark, *Joaquín Rodrigo: A Research and Information Guide* (New York: Routledge, 2021), 26–31, for a detailed listing of the archive's contents.

BIBLIOGRAPHY

Primary Sources

The indispensable stop for any Rodrigo scholar is the Fundación Victoria y Joaquín Rodrigo in Madrid. The Archive is located at:

San Germán, 11, 4J

28020 Madrid

www.joaquin-rodrigo.com

This contains the composer's writings, manuscripts, correspondence, press clippings, audiovisual materials, sound recordings, and an extensive database.

Secondary Sources

Benavides, Ana. "El piano de Joaquín Rodrigo." In *El paisaje acústico de Joaquín Rodrigo*. Ed. Ana Benavides and Walter Aaron Clark, 17–37. Madrid: Biblioteca Nacional de España, 2019.

———, and Walter Aaron Clark, eds. *El paisaje acústico de Joaquín Rodrigo*. Madrid: Biblioteca Nacional de España, 2019.

Calcraft, Raymond. *Catalogue*. Madrid: Ediciones Joaquín Rodrigo, 2013.

———. "Tradition and Faith: Ralph Vaughan Williams and Joaquín Rodrigo." *Ralph Vaughan Williams Society Journal* 68 (February 2017): 7–10.

———. "Voces y visiones de España: Rodrigo y Sorolla." *Scherzo*, 34/356 (November 2019): 85–87.

Calcraft, Raymond, and Elizabeth Matthews, trans. *Joaquín Rodrigo: Writings on Music*. Abingdon: Routledge, 2021.

Campos Zaldiernas, Salvador. "El incidente *Concierto de estío*. Avatares de su estreno en Barcelona a través del epistolario Toldrá-Rodrigo (1944–1945)." *Revista de Musicología* 40/1 (January 2017): 177–94.

Christoforidis, Michael. *Manuel de Falla and Visions of Spanish Music*. New York: Routledge, 2018.

Clark, Walter Aaron. *Isaac Albéniz: Portrait of a Romantic*. Oxford: Oxford University Press, 1999/2002; *Isaac Albéniz: Retrato de un romántico*. Trans. Paul Silles. Madrid: Turner Ediciones, 2002.

———. *Joaquín Rodrigo: A Research and Information Guide*. New York: Routledge, 2021.

———. *Los Romeros: Royal Family of the Spanish Guitar*. Urbana: University of Illinois Press, 2018.

———. "Más allá de Aranjuez. El legado musical de Joaquín Rodrigo." In *El paisaje acústico de Joaquín Rodrigo*. Ed. Ana Benavides and Walter Aaron Clark, 39–61. Madrid: Biblioteca Nacional de España, 2019.

———. "Rodrigo and Los Romeros in the Land of Rock 'n' Roll: A Brief History of a Historic Relationship." *From Spain to the United States: Joaquín Rodrigo's Transatlantic Legacy. Observatorio Studies*, 055-11/2019EN & 055-11/2019SP, 19–32. Cambridge, MA: Instituto Cervantes at the Faculty of Arts and Sciences of Harvard University, 2019.

———. "Rodrigo's *Concierto para una fiesta*. Its Genesis and Interpretation: An Interview with Pepe Romero." *Soundboard: The Journal of the Guitar Foundation of America* 47/4 (December 2021): 15–20.

Díaz Gómez, Rafael, and Vicente Galbis, eds. *Eduardo López-Chavarri Marco. Correspondencia*. Valencia: Generaltitat Valenciana, Biblioteca de Música Valenciana, 1996.

Draayer, Suzanne Rhodes. "Joaquín Rodrigo and his *Doce canciones españolas* and *Cantos de amor y de guerra*." *The NATS Journal* 51/4 (March–April 1995): 5–17.

———. *A Singer's Guide to the Songs of Joaquín Rodrigo*. Lanham, MD: Scarecrow Press, 1999.

Fernández Bahillo, Héctor. "Circunstancia y cervantismo en la *Ausencias de Dulcinea* de Joaquín Rodrigo." In *Joaquín Rodrigo y Federico Sopeña en la música española de los años cincuenta*. Ed. Javier Suárez-Pajares, 95–112. Valladolid: Universidad de Valladolid, 2008.

Gallego, Antonio. *El Arte de Joaquín Rodrigo*. Madrid: Sociedad General de Autores y Editores, 2003.

Gimeno, Julio. "Un viaje sin destino: Andrés Segovia hacia el Concierto de Aranjuez." In *Jornadas de Estudio Joaquín Rodrigo*. Ed. Javier Suárez-Pajares, 119–86. Córdoba: IMAE Gran Teatro, 2010.

Gutiérrez Álvarez, José Antonio. "La labor crítica de Joaquín Rodrigo en el diario *Pueblo* (1940–1946)." In *Joaquín Rodrigo y la música española de los años cuarenta*. Ed. Javier Suárez-Pajares, 403–30. Valladolid: Universidad de Valladolid, 2005.

Hess, Carol Ann. *Sacred Passions: The Life and Music of Manuel de Falla*. New York: Oxford University Press, 2005.

Iglesias, Antonio. *Escritos de Joaquín Rodrigo: Recopilación y comentarios.* Madrid: Alpuerto, 1999.

———. *Joaquín Rodrigo (su obra para piano): Piano a cuatro manos, dos pianos y piano y orquesta.* 2nd ed. Madrid: Alpuerto, 1996.

Joaquín Rodrigo: 90 Aniversario. Ed. Enrique Rubio. Trans. Raymond Calcraft and Elizabeth Matthews. Madrid: Sociedad General de Autores de España, 1992.

Jones, Dena Kay. "The Piano Works of Joaquín Rodrigo: An Evaluation of Social Influences and Compositional Style." DMA diss., University of Arizona, Tucson, 2001.

Kamhi de Rodrigo, Victoria. *De la mano de Joaquín Rodrigo: Historia de nuestra vida.* Madrid: Ediciones Joaquín Rodrigo, 1995.

———. *Hand in Hand with Joaquín Rodrigo: My Life at the Maestro's Side.* Trans. Ellen Wilkerson. Prologue by Pedro Rocamora. Pittsburgh: Latin American Literary Review Press, 1992.

Laredo Verdejo, Carlos. *Joaquín Rodrigo: Biografía.* Valencia: Institució Alfons el Magnánim, 2011.

León, Eva. "A Performer's Guide to Joaquín Rodrigo's *Concierto de Estío* (1943) in the Context of the Twentieth-Century Spanish Violin Concerto." DMA diss., City University of New York, 2017.

León Tello, Francisco José: "La estética de la música vocal de Joaquín Rodrigo: Catorce canciones para canto y piano." *Cuadernos Hispanoamericanos* 355 (January 1980): 70–106.

Llorens, Ana. "El dieciochismo de Rodrigo: Su *Concierto in modo galante.*" *Scherzo* 34/356 (November 2019): 82–84.

López González, Joaquín. "La magia de la sala oscura: Joaquín Rodrigo y el cine." In *Joaquín Rodrigo y Federico Sopeña en la música española de los años cincuenta.* Ed. Javier Suárez-Pajares, 143–69. Valladolid: Universidad de Valladolid, 2008.

Manuel, Peter. "The Guajira between Cuba and Spain: A Study in Continuity and Change." *Latin American Music Review* 25/2 (Fall–Winter 2004): 137–62.

Martín Colinet, María Consuelo. "La música pianística de Joaquín Rodrigo." PhD diss., Universidad Autónoma de Madrid, 2001. 3 vols.

Martínez Gallego, Francesc A., Manuel Chust Calero, and Eugenio Hernández Gascón. *Valencia 1900: Movimientos sociales y conflictos políticos durante la guerra de Marruecos, 1906–1914.* Castellón de la Plana: Publicacions de la Universitat Jaume I, 2001.

Marzo, Jorge Luis. *Art modern i franquisme: Els origens conservadors de l'avantguarda i de la política artística a l'estat Espanyol.* Girona: Fundació Espais d'Art Contemporani, 2007.

Moreda-Rodríguez, Eva. "Musical Commemorations in Post–Civil War Spain: Joaquín Rodrigo's *Concierto Heroico.*" In *Twentieth-century*

Music and Politics: Essays in Memory of Neil Edmunds. Ed. Pauline Fairclough, 177–89. Abingdon: Routledge, 2016.

Moreno Guil, María Dolores. "Joaquín Rodrigo en la III decena musical de Sevilla (1971): El estreno mundial de *Con Antonio Machado*." In *Música en Sevilla en el siglo XX.* Ed. Miguel López Fernández, 345–66. Granada: Libargo, 2018.

———. "La canción con piano de Joaquín Rodrigo: Un estudio poético musical psicoeducativo." PhD diss., Universidad de Córdoba, 2014.

Neri de Caso, José Leopoldo. *De ideales y melancolías: Regino Sainz de la Maza y la guitarra en el siglo XX en España.* Valencia: Piles Editorial de Musica, Madrid: Sociedad Española de la Guitarra, 2023.

———. "El *Concierto de Aranjuez* a través de los escritos de Regino Sainz de la Maza." In *Jornadas de Estudio Joaquín Rodrigo.* Collection: Nombres propios de la guitarra. Ed. Javier Suárez-Pajares, 61–118. Córdoba: IMAE Gran Teatro, 2010.

———. "Joaquín Rodrigo e la *Tocata para guitarra*." *Il Fronimo: Rivista di Chitarra* 34/133 (January–March 2006): 15–24.

———. "La edición musical española para guitarra en la primera mitad del siglo XX: El caso de la *Biblioteca de Música para Guitarra* (UME) de Regino Sainz de la Maza." In *Imprenta y edición musical en España (ss. XVIII–XX).* Ed. Begoña Lolo and José Carlos Gosálvez, 723–41. Madrid: Universidad Autónoma de Madrid, 2012.

———. "Regino Sainz de la Maza y el renacimiento español de la guitarra en el siglo XX." PhD thesis, Universidad de Valladolid, 2013.

Orringer, Nelson. "The Absent Dulcinea: Joaquín Rodrigo's Song to Music Itself." *Hispanic Journal of Research* 21/2 (2020): 115–26.

———. "La estancia de Maurice Ravel en la comunidad musical de Valencia." *Diagonal: An Ibero-American Music Review* 4/2 (2019): 76–89.

———. *Uniting Music and Poetry in Twentieth-Century Spain.* Lanham, MD: Lexington Books, 2021.

Palacios Nieto, María. "Una amistad en tiempos difíciles: Análisis de la correspondencia entre Joaquín Rodrigo y Rafael Rodríguez Albert en los años cuarenta." In *Joaquín Rodrigo y la música española de los años cuarenta.* Ed. Javier Suárez-Pajares, 211–73. Valladolid: Universidad de Valladolid, 2005.

Payne, Alyson. "The 1964 Festival of Music of the Americas and Spain: A Critical Examination of Ibero-American Musical Relations in the Context of Cold War Politics." PhD diss., University of California, Riverside, 2012.

Pitt-Brooke, Terrance. "Tonality and Expression in Two Choral-Orchestral Works by Joaquín Rodrigo." DMA diss., University of Arizona, 2019.

Pizà, Antoni. "The Fusions and Confusion of the *Concierto de Aranjuez* in Jazz: A Listener's Musings." *From Spain to the United States: Joaquín Rodrigo's Transatlantic Legacy. Observatorio Studies,* 055-11/2019EN

& 055-11/2019SP, 63–76. Cambridge, MA: Instituto Cervantes at the Faculty of Arts and Sciences of Harvard University, 2019.

Plata Ballesteros, Carolina. "Joaquín Rodrigo's *Con Antonio Machado*: A Performer's Guide to the Work, Focusing on the Analysis of Song-cyclic Features." DMA diss., University of British Columbia, 2009.

Riva, Douglas. "The Piano Works of Joaquín Rodrigo." *From Spain to the United States: Joaquín Rodrigo's Transatlantic Legacy. Observatorio Studies*, 055-11/2019EN & 055-11/2019SP, 49–62. Cambridge, MA: Instituto Cervantes at the Faculty of Arts and Sciences of Harvard University, 2019.

Rodrigo, Cecilia, Agustín León Ara, and Carlos Laredo Verdejo, eds. *Joaquín Rodrigo a través de sus escritos*. Madrid: Ediciones Joaquín Rodrigo, 2019.

Rodrigo, Joaquín. *Catálogo*. Introduction by Raymond Calcraft. Madrid: Ediciones Joaquín Rodrigo, 2017.

———. *Técnica enseñada e inspiración no aprendida*. Madrid: Academia de Bellas Artes, 1951.

Rodrigo, Joaquín, Gerardo Diego, and Federico Sopeña. *Diez años de música en España*. Madrid: Espasa-Calpe, 1949.

Rodríguez Cuervo, Marta. "El *Concierto heroico* de Joaquín Rodrigo: Un estudio analítico." In *Joaquín Rodrigo y la música española de los años cuarenta*. Ed. Javier Suárez-Pajares, 97–116. Valladolid: Universidad de Valladolid, 2005.

Segarra, Dolores. "Correspondencia entre Joaquín Rodrigo y Federico Mompou (1944–1978)." In *Joaquín Rodrigo y la música española de los años cuarenta*. Ed. Javier Suárez-Pajares, 275–315. Valladolid: Universidad de Valladolid, 2005.

———. "La danza española en los años cincuenta a través de la obra de J. Rodrigo." In *Joaquín Rodrigo y Federico Sopeña en la música española de los años cincuenta*. Ed. Javier Suárez-Pajares, 171–91. Valladolid: Universidad de Valladolid, 2008.

Sobrino, Ramón. "Hacia un neocasticismo Lírico en la obra de Joaquín Rodrigo: *El hijo fingido*." Program notes for production of *El hijo fingido* (Madrid: Teatro de la Zarzuela, 2000–2001), 23–42.

Sopeña Ibáñez, Federico. *Joaquín Rodrigo*. Madrid: Ediciones y Publicaciones Españolas, S.A., 1946.

———. *Joaquín Rodrigo*. Series: Artistas españoles contemporáneos. Madrid: Ministerio de Educación y Ciencia, 1970.

Suárez-Pajares, Javier. "Apuntes para una historia crítica de la discografía guitarrística de Joaquín Rodrigo." In *Jornadas de Estudio Joaquín Rodrigo*. Collection: Nombres propios de la guitarra. Ed. Javier Suárez-Pajares, 187–205. Córdoba: IMAE Gran Teatro, 2010.

———, ed. *Centenario Joaquín Rodrigo: El hombre, el músico, el maestro*. Madrid: Ediciones Sinsentido, 2001.

———. "Circunstancias de la composición, estreno y difusión del *Concierto de Aranjuez.*" *Scherzo* 34/356 (November 2019): 72–77.

———. *De Madrid, a Joaquín Rodrigo: Una vida por la música.* Madrid: Ediciones Joaquín Rodrigo, 2001.

———. "El epistolario entre J. Rodrigo y F. Sopeña. Una historia entre líneas." In *Joaquín Rodrigo y Federico Sopeña en la música española de los años cincuenta.* Ed. Javier Suárez-Pajares, 259–468. Valladolid: Universidad de Valladolid, 2008.

———. "El músico de estos años: Joaquín Rodrigo, 1949–1954." In *Joaquín Rodrigo y Federico Sopeña en la música española de los años cincuenta.* Ed. Javier Suárez-Pajares, 3–24. Valladolid: Universidad de Valladolid, 2008.

———. "Festivals and Orchestras. Nazi Musical Propaganda in Spain during the Early 1940s." In *Music and Francoism.* Ed. Gemma Pérez Zalduondo and Germán Gan Quesada, 25–59. Thurnhout, Belgium: Brepols, 2013.

———. *Iconografía: Joaquín Rodrigo: Imágenes de una vida plena: 1901–1999. Iconography: Joaquín Rodrigo: Images of a Life Fulfilled: 1901–1999.* Madrid: Sociedad General de Autores y Editores, 2001.

———. "Joaquín Rodrigo: del sinfonismo a la escena." Program notes for production of *El hijo fingido* (Madrid: Teatro de la Zarzuela, 2000–01), 11–22.

———. "Joaquín Rodrigo en la cultura de su tiempo." *El Mono-Gráfico. Revista Literaria* (2004): 17–28.

———. "Joaquín Rodrigo en la vida musical y la cultura española de los años 40. Ficciones, realidades, verdades y mentiras de un tiempo extraño." In *Joaquín Rodrigo y la música española de los años cuarenta.* Ed Javier Suárez-Pajares, 15–56. Valladolid: Universidad de Valladolid, 2005.

———, ed. *Joaquín Rodrigo y Federico Sopeña en la música española de los años cincuenta.* Valladolid: Universidad de Valladolid, 2008.

———. "Joaquín Rodrigo y Julian Bream: Aspectos de una relación." In *Julian Bream: Nombres propios de la guitarra,* 111–41. Córdoba: Ediciones La Posada, 2009.

———. "Joaquín Rodrigo y la guitarra." In *El paisaje acústico de Joaquín Rodrigo.* Ed. Ana Benavides and Walter Aaron Clark, 137–58. Madrid: Biblioteca Nacional de España, 2019.

———, ed. *Joaquín Rodrigo y la música española de los años cuarenta.* Valladolid: Universidad de Valladolid, 2005.

———, ed. *Jornadas de Estudio Joaquín Rodrigo.* Collection: Nombres propios de la guitarra. Córdoba: IMAE Gran Teatro, 2010.

———. "Los virtuosismos de la guitarra española: del alhambrismo de Tárrega al neocasticismo de Rodrigo." In *La musique entre France et*

Espagne. Interactions stylistiques 1870–1939. Ed. Louis L. Jambou, 231–52. Paris: Presses de l'Université de Paris Sorbonne, 2003.

―――. "Manuel de Falla: entre la política, el exilio, la confabulación y la muerte." In *Huellas y rostros. Exilios y migraciones en la construcción de la memoria musical de Latinoamérica*. Ed. Consuelo Carredano y Olga Picún, 279–310. Mexico City: Universidad Autónoma de México, 2007.

―――. "The Reception of Joaquín Rodrigo's Works in the United States." *From Spain to the United States: Joaquín Rodrigo's Transatlantic Legacy. Observatorio Studies*, 055-11/2019EN & 055-11/2019SP, 33–48. Cambridge, MA: Instituto Cervantes at the Faculty of Arts and Sciences of Harvard University, 2019.

―――. "Una cuestión de Estado: la repatriación de Manuel de Falla vivo o muerto." In *Creación musical, cultura popular y construcción nacional en la España contemporánea*. Ed. Celsa Alonso González, 169–86. Madrid: Instituto Complutense de Ciencias Musicales, 2010.

Vincent, Mary, and R. A. Stradling. *Cultural Atlas of Spain and Portugal*. New York: Facts on File, 1995.

INDEX

Note: Page numbers in *italics* indicate figures.

Berlin Philharmonic Orchestra, 132–33, 252, 350
Berlin Radio Symphony Orchestra, 323
Biblioteca Valenciana "Nicolau Primitiu," 78
Bibliothèque de Musique Ancienne et Moderne pour Guitare, 78
Bicentennial of U.S. Independence, 393
Bigot, Eugène, 129
Bilbao, Spain, 143–44, 149, 199, 235, 235, 245, 293
Bilbao Orquesta Sinfónica, 143–44, 175, 183
bimodality, 278, 400
bird songs, 40–43, 119–20, 154, 188, 304, 315
Birmingham Orchestra, 392–93
Bizet, Georges, 14
Black Forest, 188
Blancafort, Albert, 344
Blancafort, Manuel, 95, 116, 344
Blancafort family, 128
Blasco Ibáñez, Vicente, 5–6, 7–8, 14, 82, 146
 Arroz y tartana, 17
"Blasquism," 5, 7
Blindenheim, 187–90
blues scale, 34
Boccherini, Luigi, 241, 288, 290, 334
Böhm, Karl, 252, 253
Bohr, Cecilia, 162–63
bolero, 383, 397–98
Borja Meno, Francisco, El hereje, 340, 343–44
Borski, Alex, 86
bossism, 2–3
Boudreau, Robert, 379
Boulanger, Nadia, 88, 89, 103, 104
Bourbon monarchy, 2, 216. See also specific monarchs
bourrée, 33
Brahms, Johannes, 258
Braille, composition in, 10, 22, 81, 145, 209, 215, 255
Braithwaite, Henry Warwick, 307
Bream, Julian, 332–33, 336
Briceño, Luis, 217
British Council, 309

Britten, Benjamin, 332, 394
Brown, Hine Arthur, 306–7
Browning, Robert, 76
Bruckner, Anton, 259
Brussel, Robert, 94–95, 113
Buenos Aires, Argentina, 129, 292, 293, 301, 309, 311, 326, 352, 406
bulería, 217–18
Burgos, Emilio, 346
Burmann, Sigfrido, 346

Caballero, Fernán, 162–63
Cabanilles, Juan Bautista, 6
Cabezón, Antonio de, 196, 410
Cádiz, Spain, 273, 277, 331
Cage, John, 362
Calcraft, Raymond, 397, 404
Calderón de la Barca, Pedro, La vida es sueño, 197, 340, 345, 346
California, 381–82
Calvo, Luis, 345
Camp, Jean, 213
 La chanson de ma vie, 212
Campo, Conrado del, 116, 160, 203, 239
Canary Islands, 277
Cancionero del Duque de Calabria, 6
cancioneros, 367
Canetti, Elias, 146
Canon of the Community of Qumrân, 370
canticles, 398–99
cantigas, 319
Cantigas de Santa María, 61, 319, 320
Caracas, Venezuela, 330
Carrasquilla Mallarino, Eduardo, 21–22
Cárdenas, Lázaro, 186
Carnegie Hall, 349
Carner, Josep, 175
Carpenter, John Alden, 133–34
Carpentier, Alejo, 90
Carrasco, Amalia, 205, 207–8
Carrillo, Julián, 203
Carthaginians, 263
Carulli, Ferdinando, 203
Casals, Pablo, 123, 124, 127, 132, 267, 288
Cassadó, Gaspar, 288, 292, 308–9, 324